The Democracy Amendments

The Democracy Amendments

Constitutional Reforms to Save the United States

John J. Davenport
Fordham University

ANTHEM PRESS

Anthem Press
An imprint of Wimbledon Publishing Company
www.anthempress.com

This edition first published in UK and USA 2023
by ANTHEM PRESS
75–76 Blackfriars Road, London SE1 8HA, UK
or PO Box 9779, London SW19 7ZG, UK
and
244 Madison Ave #116, New York, NY 10016, USA

British Library Cataloguing-in-Publication Data
A catalogue record for this book is available from the British Library.

Library of Congress Cataloging-in-Publication Data
A catalog record for this book has been requested.
2022949975

ISBN-13: 978-1-83998-661-1 (Hbk)
ISBN-10: 1-83998-661-1 (Hbk)

ISBN-13: 978-1-83998-662-8 (Pbk)
ISBN-10: 1-83998-662-X (Pbk)

Cover Credits
1. "Washington as Statesman at the National Convention," courtesy of the Virginia Museum of Fine Arts.
2. "Young Americans in Convention," photo by Carlos Serra, taken in Caldwell NJ, December 2022.

This title is also available as an e-book.

This work is dedicated to my incredible wife, Robin, and to all of our children, nieces, nephews, and grandchildren to come, who will grow and lead their lives under the institutions that our older generations leave to them.

In this sacred trust, we must not fail.

CONTENTS

LIST OF FIGURES AND TABLES

Figures

Tables

ACKNOWLEDGMENTS

The ideas in this book are indebted not only to the works cited, including especially Samuel Levinson's and Larry Sabato's pathbreaking scholarship, but also to many insightful students in my classes at Fordham University over the years. I'm highly indebted to two referees who each made great suggestions for revisions and additions, and also to Greg Blonder, who furnished countless valuable thoughts and suggestions. Several other friends, relatives, and acquaintances including Jim Peloquin and Gene Ginsberg, looked at parts of the manuscript and also made penetrating observations that helped temper my expressions and approach at several points. My graduate assistant in 2022–2023, Yanai Sened, was extremely helpful with the notes, bibliography, and figures. The whole team at Anthem, especially Ms. Nathiya Thirumurugan in Editorial and Mr. Mathew Rohit in Production, have been supportive throughout the long process of synthesizing so much material. But of course, I bear sole responsibility for the 25 proposals and for any errors or omissions that may come to light. Criticisms and suggestions may be sent my way through the website extension of this work at *TheDemocracyAmendments.org*, on which readers can also download spreadsheets from which several of the charts in this book were derived.

For kind permission to reprint charts, graphs, maps, and other figures, I would like to thank first and foremost the invaluable Pew Research Center, and Vox Media; the National Oceanic and Atmospheric Administration (NOAA) National Centers for Environmental Information; the Washington Office on Latin America (WOLA); the Peter G. Peterson Foundation; Dr. John Holbein; the Associated Press and National Center for Public Affairs Research; Dr. Jeffrey B. Lewis of UCLA; Dr. Sam Wang, Dr. Richard Ober, and their team at the Princeton Gerrymandering Project; Ms. Teresa Hudock; Rob Richie and Jeremy Seitz-Brown of FairVote.org; the Annenberg Center for Public Policy; OpenSecrets and Gallup for use of their statistics; Mr. Neil Freeman for his creative artwork; UCLA's *Daily Bruin* newspaper; the *Baltimore Capital Gazette*; National Public Radio; the Center on Budget Policy and Priorities; the Council on Foreign Relations; the Congressional Budget Office; and the Congressional Research Service.

Concerning the cover illustrations, I thank the Virginia Museum of Fine Arts for permission to reprint Junius Brutus Stearns' painting, "Washington as Statesman at the National Convention," a Gift of Edgar William and Bernice Chrysler Garbisch. For the second cover image, a photograph taken on December 5, 2022 at Caldwell University in New Jersey, I thank the photographer Carlos Serra, and the Mount St. Dominic Academy for permission to use their Bishop's Common Room as a substitute for Independence Hall. The volunteers for the imagined "new convention"—all college students at Caldwell University—include Samuel Annan, Raul Gonzalez, Juan Armas, Logan Schaefer, Danna Manzano, Blessing Odoemena, Tatyana Rodriguez, Kasandra Gonzalez, Benjamin Fernandez, Madison Arizmendi, Aniyah Williams, Adam Lasek, Carolynn Hadalgo, and Sarah Rankin. I would also like to thank several faculty members and staff at Caldwell University who helped me prepare for this photo shoot. The people, institutions, and sources who made the images in this book possible do not thereby endorse any of my political recommendations. But some day, Americans of many different backgrounds and ages may gather once again in convention to help us restore liberty and justice for all.

PREFACE

It has become a truism that Americans are more politically divided now than at any time in living memory, including the 1960s. In the December 2022 issue of *The New Republic*, several analysts even predicted a breakup of the union, which would weaken all free nations across the world. While they agree on little else, Americans of all backgrounds recognize that the nation and its institutions are in serious trouble and need an overhaul. In many respects, they disagree about what the exact problems are, let alone how to fix them. But these, fortunately, are topics that careful analysis can illuminate.

The Democracy Amendments is based on the sense that national discussion needs to refocus explicitly on the constitutional roots of the legislative paralysis and rising extremism we see around us. As divisive religious and economic problems dominate our headlines, the deeper origins of our political woes remain largely hidden from public attention. This book aims to clarify them and explain a balanced set of concrete reforms that can stop the mutually self-destructive cycles into which our elections have descended.

More than anything, Americans across the political spectrum need to remember that constitutional change is possible and has brought us through political crises in the past into better days. The same holds today: a tangible prospect of new constitutional compromises to get our government working again can lift us out of the dark hole into which we have been digging ourselves.

Maybe then we can remember that elections are ultimately a *cooperative* endeavor in which even candidates we do not like and their current supporters are actually doing us a favor by making the competitive part of the process possible. To the extent that these candidates actually support and defend a fair process overall, we should be thanking rather than vilifying them.

Restoring hope for more effective and civil political debate aimed at progress is the way to reengage Americans who currently fail to register, to vote, or participate much in political discussions, despite their high stakes. More people will take an interest if we show them a way for their participation to make a big difference. For this to happen, people have to see tangible legislative consequences flowing from electoral majorities. They also need to see that their concerns really matter to lawmakers, even when they do not immediately win key votes in Congress. That is the core of democratic *responsiveness.*

There are many good ideas out there to make federal politics more responsive in these ways. Not all of them come from lawyers and political scientists; people from different backgrounds and all manner of professions have made valuable suggestions. In fact, one point in this work comes from my professional arborist. This should encourage faith in the power of democracy when it can work through sound institutions.[1] Yet very few of the needed ideas get mass media coverage or make their way into mainstream political news and everyday conversations. They are found and in textbooks, scholarly essays, and monographs for researchers and advanced students, and a few important articles in venues such as *Atlantic Monthly*, the *Democracy Journal*, or the National Constitution Center site. Thus dispersed, the great potential in these ideas is going largely unused.

There are also excellent books that focus on a single constitutional issue, such as the Electoral College, filibuster maneuvers that lock up the Senate, gerrymandering of election districts, stealth campaign donations and the influence of big money lobbies, and the role of the Supreme Court. But in two decades of teaching American political philosophy and constitutional debates, I have found no single accessible volume with a moderate reform agenda that addresses (almost) all the most important procedural problems in the federal system.

This book is written to fill that lacuna by gathering together a subset of constitutional reform proposals that are especially urgent, and that should also have wide appeal when explained and connected together. This approach is inspired by the famous "Virginia Plan" and "Connecticut Plan:" it helped the original convention in 1787 to start off with two partial but robust drafts. Because my list includes a full 25 constitutional problems and fixes, the treatment of each topic is inevitably briefer than it warrants. I have tried to keep scholarly apparatus to a minimum, but the endnotes and online bibliography indicate where interested readers can look for more thorough analyses of each issue. I also emphasize connections between the proposed amendments with cross-references, because the proposals are meant to form a coherent package.

Constitutional proposals in a large and diverse democratic society ought to be guided by such universal goals as basic fairness and effectiveness in government provision of public goods that (by definition) markets cannot efficiently provide. Serious proposals should not be based on dogmatic or highly controversial conceptions of justice. For example, I ignore far-left demands that emphasize group identities so much that individual uniqueness and responsibility vanish from view. I also set aside far-right libertarian outlooks that fail to grasp the coordinative power needed to secure national public goods. Their proposals are nonstarters because they would dramatically reduce the ability of federal law to secure national goods by regressing the nation into a loose conglomerate of independent states. Go too far down this road and you will find yourself having to convert your money into a new currency at every state border.

Instead, *The Democracy Amendments* offers a sane, practical, middle way—a largely centrist set of solutions that are guided by a few simple desiderata, which are explained in Chapter One §V. The 25 proposals are guided by a civic republican interpretation of democratic values, which supports free and fair media, basic civic literacy, and substantively equal opportunities to participate and influence collective political decisions. This is not an egoistic vision. While ordinary voters and experts have distinct roles to play, we all have obligations to offer reasons for our favored policies that appeal to more than to mere individual interests (see #23). For other people may have to live under laws that we vote for. These reasons, as argued in the *Federalist Papers*, should be based on national goods that only government at the national level can secure.[2]

As a result, all competent citizens need to be educated and informed enough to participate in basic social and political reflection (see #10). Our duty to preserve and improve the institutions of democracy is not compatible with giving in to wishful thinking that flatters our preexisting biases. Across the board, people need to be *more honest with themselves*, have the courage to face hard facts, and be willing to sacrifice a little when that is needed make the nation better for our children.

I believe that most Americans are up for this, as long as they see that enough others will reciprocate. But that assurance of reciprocation is lost when the game appears to be rigged. Thus unrigging it, and making it clear that everyone is doing their share, is essential for progress.

This vision of democracy is nonpartisan and consistent with central themes defended by American leaders involved in the Revolutionary era from the 1760s through the early 1800s (whom I refer to as "the founders" for short).[3] In particular, it builds on James Wilson's, Alexander Hamilton's, and James Madison's civic republican ideals. As conservative constitutional scholars still say today, a "sound constitution will serve justice and the common good."[4] But in this book, I only rarely need to refer to my underlying conception of democratic norms and theories of public goods, because the most urgent constitutional problems are now evident to anyone willing to take an honest look at recent events. We do not need any grand theory to recognize them, or to imagine moderate and feasible solutions to them.

Most of the commonsensical fixes I propose can also be supported on the basis of a wide range of different interpretations of democratic ideals or social justice as a whole. There are a few exceptions where I draw on deeper normative considerations. For example, the discussion of "primary constituent power"—a concept in democratic theory—addresses some issues that arise with a possible constitutional convention. And I occasionally mention "collective action problems," such as "prisoner's dilemmas" and "chicken" games, in which people, legislators, or states may interact in mutually self-defeating ways unless they cooperate by making rules to avoid self-defeat. But for the most part, no special training is needed to read this book or to understand and evaluate each proposed reform on its merits.

Finally, I'm far from imagining myself to have a monopoly on good ideas to fix our Constitution. I've tried to devise the 25 amendments based on the best ideas available in political scholarship and journalism across the ideological spectrum. My main goal is to draw ideas from many experts together into a viable and unified program. At each step, there are interesting alternatives that I can only briefly note, or not mention at all, given space constraints. But see this book's online extension, *TheDemocracyAmendents.org*, for more discussion of such alternatives and other possible amendments briefly mentioned in this book's Interlude.

A national process devoted to debating constitutional reform will surely produce other valuable suggestions that I cannot predict in advance. A robust agenda for constitutional reform may galvanize Americans from all walks of life to contribute to a "crowdsourcing" process that yields a richer and more widely shared awareness of feasible solutions to our constitutional obstacles.

Such a process has worked well in other democratic nations that have recently revised their constitutions. Some of them have called together "citizen juries"—small groups of ordinary people reflecting the demographic and political diversity of the nation who come together for guided discussion—to study proposals on each salient issue and come up with recommendations for their nation as a whole to consider.[5] In the US case, a group that has started to look for consensus amendments via citizen juries showcases its results on *WeAmend.us*.

Political leaders who hardly ever bring up constitutional amendments also need to get moving and educate their constituents about options for improving key provisions of our Constitution. The same goes for law schools and political science programs: as Sandy Levinson notes in a recent essay, the training that new lawyers receive typically treats horribly flawed features of our constitutional institutions as simply fixed, thus ignoring the possibility of changing them.[6] With this mindset, no wonder that the public has largely forgotten the vital role that constitutional improvements play in keeping democracy alive and healthy.

The amendments that are now so indispensable for saving our democracy will never happen unless more people in politics and our leading professions start mainstreaming these vital topics, as they have with global warming. Constitutional reform is ultimately *far* more important and powerful than any current legislative initiative, and we need to start giving it the priority it deserves.

A Note on Style and Abbreviations. To avoid confusion, I capitalize the "Constitution" only when referring to current American constitutional law as a whole, including amendments and long-settled points of interpretation. I capitalize "Congress" throughout to refer to the federal legislature. But I refer to the "president" in lower-case unless naming a specific president with his title, or offering suggested language for an amendment (which demands a more formal style). To avoid confusion in referring to both "houses" of Congress in the plural, I refer to the two "chambers" instead. "House" is capitalized only when referring to the House of Representatives, and "Court" is short for the federal Supreme Court (as opposed to state supreme courts). Usually "senator," "elector," "judge," or "justice" are not capitalized unless referring to individuals.

Likewise, "Amendment" is capitalized only when referring to an amendment, usually known by its number, that has been ratified by $3/4^{th}$ of states and thus is part of the Constitution. Formal "amendment proposals" are those passed by Congress (or a new convention) and sent to states for possible ratification. Also note that Anthem Press policy requires capitalization of terms for racial groups such as "Black," "Brown," and "White" to be uniform; so I elected to omit capitalization.

Cross-references use a numeral preceded by the "#" sign to refer to one of the 25 amendment ideas in this book. Because a lot of other numbers are needed in this text, I use numerals 1–10 in most cases for brevity, rather than "three" or "six," etc. The same goes for fractions like $2/3^{rds}$. At points, I also use various abbreviations for states, institutions such as the Electoral College (EC), and much-discussed laws like the Voting Rights Act of 1965 (VRA).

Chapter One

THE PROBLEMS: WHY THE FEDERAL GOVERNMENT BARELY FUNCTIONS AND POLARIZATION IS RISING

I. Crises and the Crumbling Pillars of American Democracy

In the US today, political malaise looms like a dark cloud over daily life. Already by 2018, 69% of Americans reported feeling stressed by worries about the nation's future. By March 2021, 87% were somewhat or "very" worried that US political leaders are not capable of addressing the nation's biggest problems.[1] In January 2023, the new Republican majority in the House took a week just to elect a Speaker and get business going.

The stability of our national government is being eroded by problems in a constitutional design that has not received a deep structural makeover in over 100 years since the amendments for women's suffrage, the income tax, and direct election of senators became law. It is not surprising that our Constitution is showing its age: our founders could not foresee everything to come, and later constitutional reformers could only do so much. It has been far too long since we updated their work. Left untreated, these growing constitutional ills have become a cancer rotting out the heart of our federal union and spreading to every part of government and civil society.

So what *is* the Constitution really, other than words on a large old parchment paper that you can see in the National Archives building? Many people instead think of it as a set of technicalities debated by lawyers before the Supreme Court. But these popular notions are reductive and misleading. Constitutional law is like an invisible container within which we live our daily lives and run our political processes: we do not usually see it, because the constitutional order lies in the background behind the familiar institutions we interact with every day—banks, employers, schools, communication networks, airports, post offices, etc.

In legal terms, the Constitution is a set of higher-order laws and related customs (as interpreted by our courts) that determine how ordinary laws (statutes) and legal policies are made, enforced, challenged, adjudicated, and revised. Its provisions are like rules of a game in which the "moves" are not about advancing a ball or puck, but instead about making, altering, and applying rules for *other* types of interaction among people—in business and commerce, in medicine and education, in media and childcare, in religious practices and foreign relations, and so on. President Abraham Lincoln called the Constitution a "frame" within which the picture of equal basic liberties is situated.[2]

In sum, the Constitution is a *matrix* of basic laws, kept alive by interpretation and application, that profoundly conditions almost everything that we do and everything that is legally possible in the US. It is just as real and important as the mathematics used in designing our bridges and buildings. We cannot afford to take it for granted.

But the living Constitution's procedures and guardrails have proven inadequate to control forces now at work in our politics that block advancement toward a higher quality of life. Moderate policy proposals aimed at consensus and rebuilding a strong middle class can make little headway because key legislative processes are frozen and our elections are nearing breakdown. With assistance from federal judges who have little interest in democratic norms and ideals, our political parties have found ways to twist our constitutional system to their own advantage at the expense of the national good. In this legal "game," they now routinely move goalposts, deflate balls, buy umpires, and whip up their fans to attack the other team in the parking lot.

People commonly perceive the results of these manipulations without understanding the constitutional flaws that cause them.[3] Americans of virtually all political persuasions perceive that the institutional fabric of our nation is being torn apart by the politics of division and trickery. As of September 2022, trust in Congress hovered around 20%, and a tsunami of misinformation that played to fears and biases was fueling conspiracy theories and hatred of people who appear to have different values and priorities than ours. As Joel Hirschhorn put it, "When Americans love their country but hate their government, we have a problem."[4] The rising distrust leads to events like the January 6, 2021 invasion and resulting assaults on Capitol police. It is a safe bet that the 2024 presidential election will not go smoothly.

While the nation has seen sharp polarization and violence between bitterly opposed factions before—most recently, during the Vietnam War and the civil rights movement—things do feel different this time. According to recent polls, over 19% of Americans say that political disputes have hurt relations with family and former friends. The sense that we are verging on dangerous instability is palpable. As a recent analysis concluded, the US is by far the most "perniciously polarized" among developed democratic societies; historically this level of polarization often leads democratic processes to collapse into autocracy.[5]

This dire situation has developed through an unprecedented series of crises since the turn of the century, beginning with the vote counting problems in Florida after the presidential election of November 2000, followed by the September 11 attacks just ten months later. With each new crisis, the federal government is having a harder and harder time responding effectively. And the longer-term threats, such as budgetary meltdown, are barely addressed at all.

Consider just five examples. (i) From 2000 through 2021, four massive hurricanes devastated New Orleans, parts of Florida, Puerto Rico, and the east coast, exceeding the rescue capacities of our Federal Emergency Management Agency (FEMA). There were 25 weather disasters costing over $1 billion *each* in 2021 alone (see Figure 1.1). Hurricane Charlie cost roughly $24.6 billion. According to Climate.gov, the annual cost of weather disasters has increased steeply in recent decades to $148 billion a year.

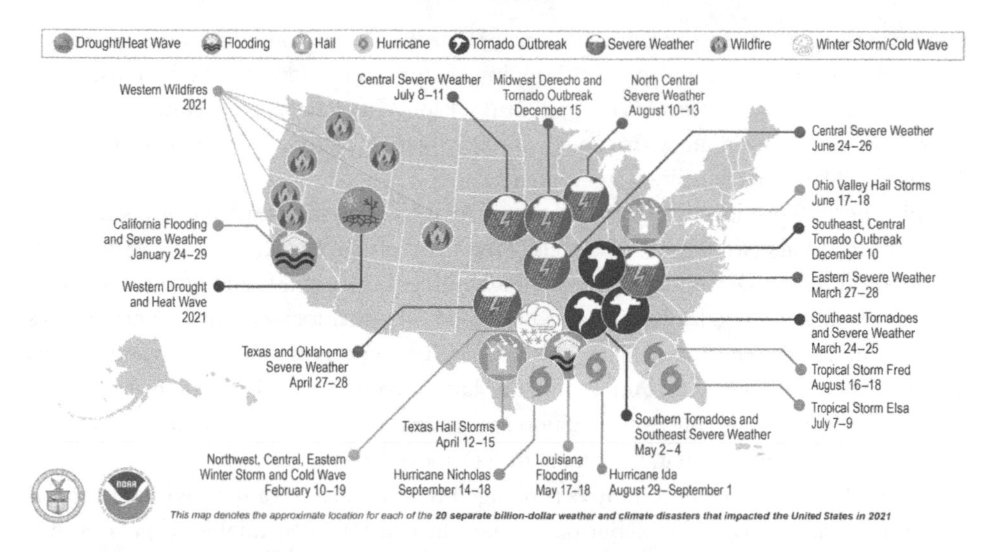

Figure 1.1 US 2021 Billion Dollar Weather and Climate Disasters

Two-thirds of that figure would cover the cost of continuing the expanded child tax credit provided during the Covid pandemic, which lifted millions of children out of poverty. Or, cutting our annual losses from storm damage in half could free up over $1,400 per student in K-12 education—a lot of books, lab equipment, field trips, tutorials for struggling students, and more.

Then came September 2022. In one month, Hurricane Fiona did at least $500 million of damage in Puerto Rico, destroying large parts of its power grid, and Hurricane Ian killed over 100 Floridians and wrecked Fort Myers and nearby communities. Weather reporters said that three Hurricane Charlies could have fit *inside the eye* of Ian. Yet less than 30% of homes in Florida have flood insurance, and many have no disaster insurance at all, leaving a lot of people broke, with perhaps $80 billion in rebuilding costs. At least half of this may be paid by federal taxpayers—enough to foot the entire annual gasoline bill of 25 million Americans. This continues because our leaders will not make hard choices to *require* homeowner's insurance with hurricane and flood coverage in all vulnerable areas.[6]

What of the hotter climate problem behind these increasing storms? Efforts to reduce US greenhouse emissions and collaborate with other large emission nations were stalled for three decades until the very modest steps in the Inflation Reduction Act of August, 2022.[7] In the interim, we have poured hundreds of billions into temporary measures to build up beaches and storm surge barriers—subsidizing quite a few millionaires with beachfront homes in the process.

(ii) The 2008–2009 financial crisis did long-term damage to many families. Some blame government regulations that encouraged subprime loans; others laud subsequent efforts to control ultra-speculative banking. But either way, the power of big financial firms to extract wealth at the expense of the rest of the economy has only increased. They make $138 billion each year just from "swipe" fees in a largely cashless purchase system, taking $900 a year from an average family. When combined with enormous oligopolies in new tech and online shopping sectors, these forces have increased our wealth gap to the highest level in over a century. Elon Musk may soon become the world's first *trillionaire*—one man with enough money to fund a $50,000 down payment on homes for 20 million families if he wanted to.

(iii) The 2016 presidential elections featured direct foreign manipulation on a scale that, before the cyber age, would have been considered an act of war. Russian agents stole messages and plans from the Democratic National Committee (DNC) and from Clinton campaign staff to use against one leading candidate. Public attention focused on the personalities involved and evidence of backchannel connections between Trump associates and various Russian operatives close to Putin.[8] But the basic challenge to democratic institutions is ultimately far more important: if foreign governments can manipulate American elections and get away with it, no campaign—Democrat or Republican—is safe.

(iv) In May 2020, George Floyd's prolonged death on camera sparked broad social movements for police reform. But our Senate has so far been unable to pass even a chokehold ban aimed at reducing avoidable deaths during arrests and police custody. Following the mass protests, some cities have also seen big spikes in violent crime, which has significantly magnified partisan tensions. Yet there is no national plan to improve educational outcomes in ways that could significantly reduce the cycles of poverty and crime in the poorest parts of the US.

(v) In the last two decades, many millions of people have crossed the southern US border illegally or to claim asylum, driven primarily by lethal poverty and gang warfare in parts of Central America. Over 2 million have crossed in 2022 alone. It is difficult even for beefed-up border patrol units to handle the influx of unaccompanied minors, in particular (see Figure 1.2); and the courts are many years behind in deciding on

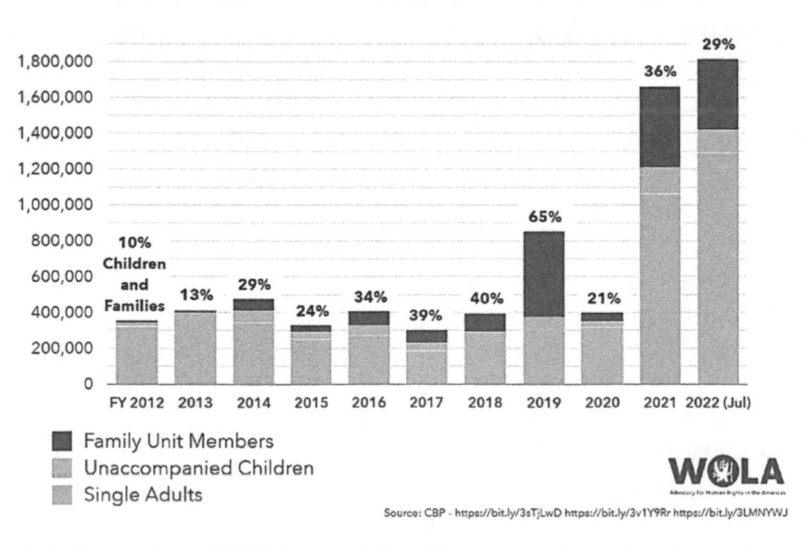

Figure 1.2 Proportion of Children and Families among Apprehended or Encountered Migrants

applications for asylum. The flows of hard drugs to the north and guns to the south are also difficult to control, even though every administration has raised the budget for border patrol from $263 million in 1990 to over $6,160 million in 2022—a *23-fold* increase in three decades. More than 10 million undocumented residents who entered or were brought into the US illegally[9] live in legal limbo—a twilight zone where they are at risk of crime or abuse by employers because they cannot go to authorities for help. Those who come via people smugglers are also at high risk of injury, disease, rape, and death during the journey.

To address such problems effectively, we probably need a complete overhaul of immigration laws and a bold international plan to stabilize Guatemala, Honduras, El Salvador, Haiti, and Venezuela. But in 2007, the Republican majority in Congress failed to pass the Comprehensive Immigration Reform Act—a compromise bill supported by President George W. Bush to secure boarders and normalize the status of undocumented people in the US. Then came the "Gang of Eight" immigration bill that took a year to negotiate via rare bipartisan cooperation. It was killed by the Speaker of the House in 2013, who refused to bring it up for a vote.[10] So the border crisis has expanded for another decade, inflaming xenophobic hatreds in the process.

These are only five of several crises that have brought turmoil, bitter culture wars, and violence to our society since the century began. Additional examples include a lackluster federal response to the Covid crisis, rapid inflation triggered by Russia's invasion of Ukraine and Covid lockdowns across the world, and mistakes in Iraq and Afghanistan that failed to build sound governments and impacted military families. Like the symptoms of a disease, these crises are the surface phenomena, the indicators of something amiss deeper within our system. To fully diagnose what is going wrong, we must distinguish at least *four different kinds of problems*.

1. At the first level, while the crises listed above were each precipitated by distinct events, they were also manifestations of larger social and economic difficulties with multiple causes outside of our government—like pathogens that attack a body.

2. But now these challenges fester unsolved for decades in American society due to institutional dysfunctions of the federal system that impair its ability to respond effectively. These reduced capacities for action are the immediate reason why we make little progress as a nation on addressing the first set of problems. In the medical analogy, federal institutional malfunctions are like a weakened immune system that fails to respond adequately to pathogens.

3. Then there are further distortions in our political parties, our election processes, and the attitudes of citizens, which are all prompted by rising public frustration with problems in the first two categories. Like secondary infections, they further weaken the body politic, making it even harder for federal institutions to do their jobs well. As Daniel Immerwahr puts it, the "hardening of … political arteries" in our system is dangerous, because "when passion can't flow easily into policymaking, it congeals as angry protest, growing wilder and more paranoid."[11] When people cannot channel their discontents into collective political action, they turn on each other instead.

4. Finally, there are omissions, flaws, and inequities in our Constitution itself that allow all of these other kinds of problems to arise. Like a cancer or HIV virus that damages the immune system itself, these structural flaws are the ultimate causes of the nation's declining condition.

This book will explain these deficiencies in our constitutional law and offer realistic cures for them through a series of constitutional amendments. In unison, these amendments would restore all the main organs of American government and civil society to fully functioning vigor. To understand the true scale of this challenge, let's consider the four kinds of problems just outlined in a bit more detail.

II. Analysis: Institutional Obstacles

The Republican governor of Maryland, Larry Hogan, recently said that "a large majority of Americans … are completely convinced that our system [of government] is fundamentally broken" and want to understand how to fix it.[12] After living through our last few big election cycles, it is hard *not* to see that something is deeply amiss in our federal system. Hogan is correct: even when they loath people in the rival party, most Americans want institutional change. But few understand that the deficiencies they see have constitutional roots in our processes for making, enforcing, and applying laws, and assessing their legitimacy in the courts.

Let's begin with a wider inventory of problems in the first of the four categories, namely major social and economic issues out in the world that reduce opportunities and negatively impact quality of life for most Americans. These "real-world problems" and lackluster responses to them include the five crises mentioned above and much more:

- lack of trust in election results among Republicans but also among many Democrats;
- illegal immigration and vulnerabilities of undocumented residents;
- health care costs rising at twice the rate of average inflation;
- college costs rising at nearly twice the rate of average inflation over two decades;
- growing inequalities in income and household wealth;
- growing monopolies and anticompetitive practices, outdated antitrust laws;
- tax loopholes for the wealthiest and strategies to avoid paying corporate taxes;
- deficiencies and inequities in police responses to suspects and disturbances;
- mass shootings, and accidental and intentional death by firearm more generally;
- an annual budget deficit that is driving federal debt higher by leaps and bounds;
- badly outdated requirements in secondary education, culture wars over curricula;
- failing schools, drug addiction, and high dropout rates in some districts;
- high rates of violent crime and high recidivism in some of our poorest areas;
- a banking system that sucks $370 million a day out of an economy now run on what is effectively privatized currency;
- private equity and financial firms that profit from big risks but demand bailouts when a financial crash occurs;
- crumbling infrastructure and big gaps in social services needed for productivity;

- population shifts from rural areas into cities with spiraling housing costs;
- rising threats to democratic nations from Chinese and Russian dictators, ranging from military invasion to massive intellectual property theft, cyberattacks, ransomware, and pressures on businesses to keep silent about tyranny and mass atrocities;
- fragile or nonsecure supply chains for vital medical equipment and medicines, oil and natural gas, computer chips, baby formula, and other important consumer goods.

These are not one-party complaints; they affect people across the country and among all walks of life. Our 50 states cannot solve these ongoing problems by themselves, because they all involve *national public goods* (NPGs) that cannot be secured without coordination among many states. Sometimes, as with climate issues, refugee crises, and totalitarian regimes threatening democratic ideals, workable solutions require coordination with other nations as well.[13]

The federal government was created precisely to tackle such national and international issues. But now, as Ezekiel Kweku wrote, it seems "creaky and hidebound," like a once fast machine that is almost seized up with rust.[14] We have dithered over health care for three decades without full resolution. Few big decisions are made, whether to implement smart *or* mistaken legal strategies. Experiment, failure, and progress through federal action are becoming things of the past.

In fact, the situation is worse than mere inertia. The annual federal budget has not been balanced for over 22 years since Bill Clinton's tax increases ultimately balanced it by 2000. Instead, we have been borrowing hundreds of billions every year (the annual deficit).[15] After three massive rounds of tax cuts since the early 1980s, two long wars since 2001, financial crises, over $6 trillion spent on stimulus to keep families and businesses going during the Covid pandemic, our national debt is over $31.2 trillion (= $31,200 billion or $31.2 million million). It has grown by $2 trillion just since I started to write this book in September 2021.

This collective debt equals over $90,000 is red ink for every single American. Imagine that even a third of this vast amount had instead been available as a $30,000 voucher for every 18-year-old to use for college, or for a down payment on a home, or to invest in a new business. How much productivity could have been gained? Instead, we owe it all to federal bondholders, including many in China.

As the late 2022 financial crisis in Britain illustrates, this much debt makes us vulnerable in future economic crashes or a new war forced on us by foreign adversaries. It also diverts massive amounts of federal money away from urgent needs. The *interest alone* that we collectively paid on the federal debt in the 2021 fiscal year was over $562 billion. For perspective, this annual interest payment is roughly 10 times all federal spending on K-12 public education in the last pre-Covid year. It is also 20 times the spending on Federal Pell Grants for low-income college students, and almost twice the amount of all federal subsidies for employer-based health insurance under Obamacare (compare the shocking 10-year numbers in Figure 1.3).

Our huge annual deficits are driven partly by tax cuts and partly by 370% increase in (inflation-adjusted) federal spending since 1970. This is not due to increases

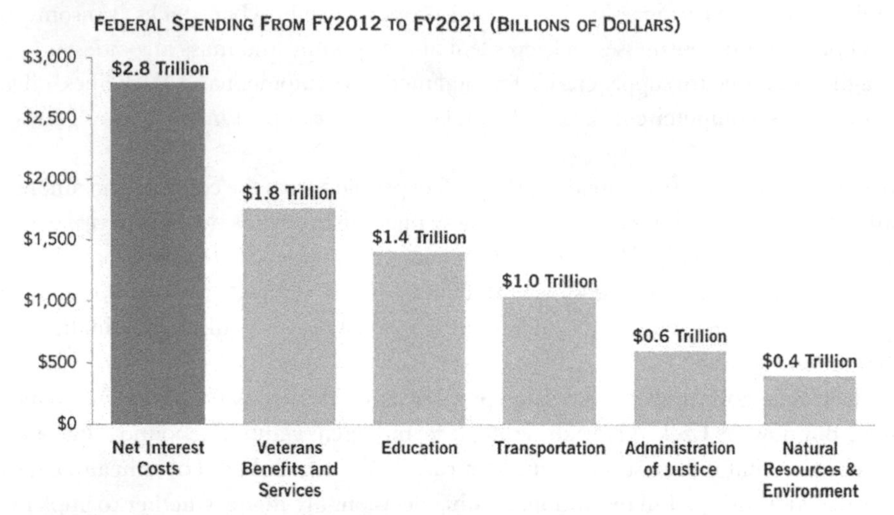

Figure 1.3 Interest on the US Federal Debt vs. Other Priorities

in the federal headcount. Actually, the number of full-time federal employees has declined slightly since 1970 as our population rose by over 50% (although contractors have increased). And many federal positions are so underpaid that people from wealthier families dominate their applicant pool.[16] Rather, federal spending is mostly driven by big entitlement programs like Medicare.

In the last decade, despite our big military spending, the US and our allies have also been attacked by wave after wave of cyber propaganda, hacking, and ransomware coming primarily from Russia, China, and their vassals. Autocracy is on the rise around the world after nine different democratic reform movements have been crushed by dictators in Egypt, Syria, Hong Kong, Myanmar, Venezuela, Belarus, Sudan, Russia, and Iran. Actual and potential dictators across the world are emboldened by US weakness. Our government seems unable to even to take basic steps in response, such as outlawing the cryptocurrencies that enable fraud, ransomware, money laundering, trafficking in people and arms, tax evasion, and kleptocratic military regimes.

But if these problems are so damaging and serious policy solutions would improve our children's prospects so much, why does the federal government not do enough to address them? To answer this, we have to turn to the second type of problem, namely *institutional breakdowns* in the federal system—both the ones people recognize and others that happen largely below the public radar, like unseen corrosion inside a machine.

The most apparent symptom is gridlock in Congress: while the federal system was designed so that no small national majority of voters could ram through radical changes without compromising to protect the interests of dissenting groups, these original protections against "majority tyranny" are now being abused to the point of halting legislative processes that used to be routine. In political science speak, there are too many "veto-gates" that legislation must pass through. To take a single example, by the end of October 2021, the Senate had confirmed only 6 of President Joe Biden's 69 appointed ambassadors due to obstruction by one single senator. With every new president in the last two decades, it takes longer and longer to confirm presidential nominees to all of the roughly 1,200 positions that require Senate confirmation.[17]

In fact, gridlock is a major risk in "presidential" democracies with a strong chief executive who is not selected by a majority coalition in the legislature, as they are in parliamentary democracies. If the will to compromise disappears in any part of a system like ours, Yoni Appelbaum argues, that system can become partly paralyzed, leading to inferior workarounds that stretch the capacities of other parts. "Filibusters, shutdowns, and executive orders multiply."[18]

Good will among Americans and loyalty to our shared system are also eroded by the outsized power of certain minority blocs. In 1992, 2000, and 2016, Clinton, Bush, and Trump were each, respectively, elected with less than half of the popular vote. The presidential veto—threatened and actual—is used far more now than in the past. Important treaties cannot get ratified, and full budgets rarely get completed in Congress. As we saw again in 2021, even default on the ballooning federal debt, which was once unthinkable because it would destabilize the entire global financial order, is now on the table in high-stakes games of "chicken" between rival party leaders. In recent years, many presidential appointments to important executive and judicial offices, including to the Supreme Court, have been blocked indefinitely in the Senate, which is itself becoming less representative of the American public year by year.

Basic standards for good governance are also increasingly violated within the federal government. Because we do not require financial disclosures from all candidates for federal office or sufficiently limit movement between federal positions and industries that they regulate, opportunities for conflicts of interest abound. Call it the "swamp effect." The potentials for clandestine foreign influence, use of stolen data by our political campaigns, and potentially even blackmail of US officials are all rising. When legislation to resolve key national issues cannot get passed, people turn to administrative bureaus and federal courts to decide controversies instead. This increasingly politicizes unelected officials who should be impartially implementing laws, thus eroding public confidence in them and turning appointments to the Supreme Court into nasty fights.

Then there are oversight functions. The pardon power is abused and standards for impeachment are far too vague to provide sufficient guidance, as we have seen three times in the last 30 years. Congress can undertake to investigate abuses, but its subpoena powers are also unclear, as are the limits of "executive privilege." And given the sheer size of the federal bureaucracy today and the vastness of its various budgets, abuse of office in the executive branch cannot now be adequately checked unless the Federal Bureau of Investigation (FBI) and Department of Justice remain impartial and distant from everyday political battles.

Finally, there are many flaws in the way we fund political campaigns, structure primary elections, manage voter registration, and run elections for federal offices. Ballot distribution and counting is so underfunded that private gifts to pay for staff and equipment in 2020 (including $350 million from Mark Zuckerberg) exceeded federal aid to county voter services and election boards.[19] The rest of the election process is tainted by large donations to candidates and issue groups from wealthy individuals, corporations, and other lobbies. Candidates who cannot raise enough money from wealthy donors to compete in the primaries are filtered out. Without limits on third-party advertising, an arms race has set in that massively inflates the costs, length, and hostility of campaigns, because much of the donor class benefits from electing more extreme candidates.[20] People are also disgusted that they cannot vote for third party candidates without helping a dominant party candidate to win instead. We call ourselves a democracy, but in this system, it is even possible for a minority of those voting to control the House, Senate, and presidency.

People's trust in election processes has been eroded by shortsighted and ignoble tactics aimed at near-term political gain, including election fraud conspiracies; state laws aimed at making it harder for people to vote (dressed up as anti-fraud measures); wanton accusations against honest, hardworking, and underpaid officials who manage vote counting; and stunts like Democratic donors giving large sums to far-right Republican candidates in primary races, in hopes of making it easier for a Democrat to win the general election.

Those engaged in such abuses are not trying to persuade voters on the merits of their policy proposals. They only want to tilt the playing field and whip up strong emotions to drive turnout. These grossly immoral tactics erode our shared loyalty to rules of fair play and badly damage vital social capital that took generations to build. Challenging election results and election officials for the sake of propagandizing is like trying to win a race by setting fire to the racetrack.

Simple national standards could assure people that election results are accurate and that everyone had roughly equal opportunities to vote in a secure process (see #6). But even modest bipartisan bills to restore voter confidence have repeatedly been blocked by Senate filibusters, which require 60% of senators to overcome.

The resulting peril is now enormous. In political theory, democracy can be defined in weaker or more demanding terms, but most conceptions include formal equality in voting rights, equality before the law, and a list of civil liberties including substantial freedoms of expression and political association. Some accounts add in substantially equal opportunities to serve in government and to participate in shaping collective political judgments. But on every definition, democracy *at least* requires

1. that multiple parties can compete for votes in free and competitive elections;
2. that their leaders and supporters all respect the outcomes of these elections when they lose;
3. and thus, with some frequency, incumbent officials are voted out of office, and parties lose their present majority, resulting in a peaceful transfer of power to the winners.

Without loyalty on all sides to these rules of the game, and common respect for our civil service "umpires," democracy collapses. When one team is willing to bar some of the opposing team's players (voters) from the field, challenges legitimate goals scored (election wins), and attacks the referees (vote counters), then the other team(s) will also stop playing by the rules. In that scenario, the only winners are the autocrats in Beijing and Moscow. With nudging from their hackers and online propagandists, the institutions that have sustained us for generations and inspired democratic reform movements across the world are weakening with each election cycle. Our own blindness to the scale of these threats is playing right into Putin's and Xi's blood-drenched hands.

III. The Public's Response: Populism, Polarization, and Impotent Elections

How do these breakdowns in the federal government and elections affect political attitudes, beliefs, and feelings across our society? People see that real-world problems are not being solved. While they mostly blame supporters of the other party, awareness of structural problems is slowly growing: despite cultural differences, Americans share concerns that the legislature is bought, that administrative arms of government have too much unaccountable power, that Supreme Court justices stay on the bench way too long, and that a lot of waste or inefficiency exists in federal spending. When members of Congress spend far more time with a few wealthy donors than meeting with their constituents, no wonder that public confidence in the US government is near all-time lows.

In sum, people across the political spectrum share a sense that the system is rigged against those working in ordinary jobs outside of Washington, D.C. and Wall Street. On the other hand, few Americans understand that *constitutional* flaws underlie the more visible dysfunctions in federal governance—from shutdowns that close national parks to rushed budgets loaded with "pork barrel" projects, and popular bills that remain stuck forever in the Senate. Journalists, political commentators, and the reading public tend to focus only on these *symptoms* of the underlying constitutional disease. Political and media leaders have not focused attention on the constitutional obstacles that are causing these problems, so most Americans are baffled about why our national government seems so useless on many urgent issues.

People respond to this confusion in two main ways.

First, in disgust, some simply ignore national politics. In a democracy, increasing disengagement is a bad sign, and turnout among eligible voters in our elections has been trending lower since 1970. While strong feelings about Donald Trump propelled higher turnout in 2020, even then, with wide use of mail-in ballots in many states, almost *a third of eligible voters did not cast a vote.* Of course, some people are so busy that they forget; and some are politically lazy (see #10). But many more are driven away for serious reasons:

- their work times conflict with poll hours, or they do not have the necessary transport;
- voter registration seems too hard or confusing;
- it is too difficult to get a mail or absentee ballot, or tricky to fill it out properly;
- they strongly dislike both main candidates;
- they feel their vote is useless when they do not live in a swing district;
- and/or they are turned off by the sheer divisiveness of campaigns, all the negative advertising, and the violent talk at campaign rallies.[21]

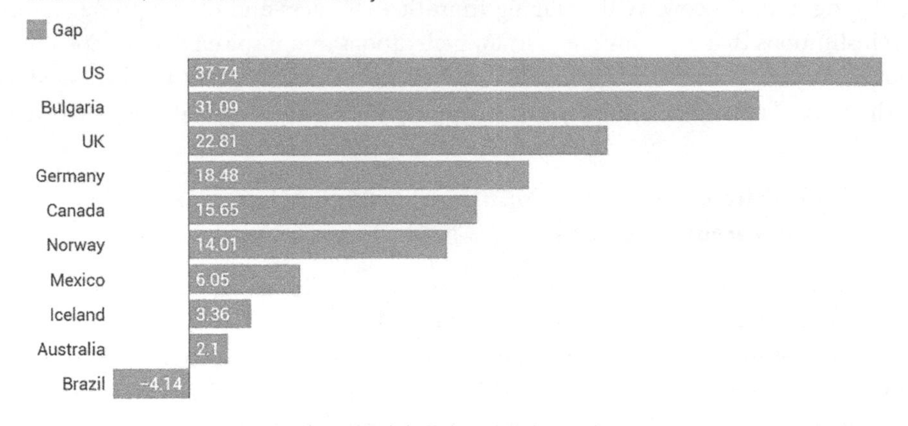

Figure 1.4 The Gap between Youngest and Oldest Voters

These problems especially affect Americans under 30 according to a recent study, which also found that the gap between youth and senior turnout is much higher in the US (see Figure 1.4).[22] Fewer than half of 18–29-year olds voted in the 2016 US general election, whereas 66% or more of young people regularly vote in several European nations.

Second, in anger, many other Americans turn to more "populist" presidential and congressional candidates who talk about corruption and promise to fix it. In 2016, for example, people flocked to Donald Trump and Bernie Sanders during the primary elections in part because Trump and Sanders portrayed themselves as men of the people who could challenge "the Washington establishment," Wall Street, and irritating cultural elites. These messages were combined with simplistic insinuations about immigrants, the richest 1 percent, global trade, Hollywood, or "mainstream media" being to blame for national problems.

This turn to populist radicals is entirely understandable: frustrated voters imagine that only a president who comes from outside the mainstream political class can right the ship of state. As Gerald Seib observed in mid-2016, a lot of support for Trump was "rooted in the simple and utterly non-ideological idea that he will get something done," even if it was hard to be sure what that something would be. That's the price of institutional dysfunction, especially in a democracy with highly partisan media: more radical and less-qualified candidates seem like the only hope.[23]

In fact, though, the system defeated most of Trump's priorities, just as it has with our last four presidents. Even with both chambers of Congress behind him for the usual two years, Trump's team scored only a couple major legislative changes, including big tax cuts on corporations and higher earners in a December 2017 bill (see #5). Eventually, Trump grew so frustrated at the filibuster roadblock in the Senate that he publicly called for it be abolished.[24]

More generally, populist candidates have been selling comforting illusions. According to them, we can have advanced space-age health care for all without paying anything for it, or withdraw from all foreign conflicts with no resulting dangers, or simply wall ourselves off from Central America, or pass tax cuts that miraculously "pay for themselves," or build endless "low-income housing" (actually high rises that are 10–20% low rent) in densely populated suburbs, or tax only the highest earners and still balance the national budget, and so on.

Worst of all, these radical candidates inflame cultural or group-identity "wedge" issues to increase their voter turnout. This tactic, like starting a war, distracts attention from the deep structural flaws that prevent the federal government from doing normal business and effectively tackling big issues. For example, far-left groups push "white supremacy" rhetoric,[25] suggest indiscriminate cuts in police forces, make college students with conservative opinions self-censor in class, and focus on confederate statues. In response, right-wing groups and media respond that "critical race theory" is being imposed on children without even knowing what it is. This once-postmodern term has become a catchall for anything they dislike, including even Toni Morrison novels. The result is what Rachel Kleinfeld calls "competitive victimhood," with each group trying to claim the more offended and aggrieved status.[26] Bread-and-butter policy issues are increasingly misconstrued in terms of racial or gender group rivalries.[27]

All of this has driven rapidly rising disrespect of people affiliated with the other main political party (see Figure 1.5).[28] But neither approach improves rates of home ownership, credit scores, household wealth, childhood nutrition, educational outcomes, family stability, or mental health. And somehow the disenfranchisement of over 3 million black and brown Americans who live in Washington D.C. and Puerto Rico gets far less attention than, say, transgender athletes.

Because of this focus on cultural clickbait topics, populist political movements produce wildly skewed priorities and do not help their followers understand the material challenges facing our nation. Voters learn nothing from party leaders about how to increase economic opportunity across the country, boost the labor participation rate, improve education in high tech areas where jobs are plentiful, clean up our most blighted slums, curb steep rises in health care and college costs, balance the federal budget, or achieve independence from Saudi oil.

Americans are upset that these big problems are not being solved, but their party leaders routinely lie about the causes. Inflation and high gasoline prices in 2022 are classic examples. Democrats correctly blamed Russia's invasion of Ukraine and backlogs in supply chains caused by Covid lockdowns in Asia, but they did not acknowledge that massive Covid stimulus payments were also big inflation drivers. For their part, Republicans on Fox News never mentioned the historic cutbacks in oil production and refining during the two Covid recession years that led to low gasoline inventories, nor the $190 million in new leases for oil drilling in the Gulf of Mexico included in the summer 2022 Biden–Manchin deal.

In sum, both parties work hard to dupe Americans on economic issues, which is easy in a nation that does not require basic economic education for all citizens. Party leaders sell the convenient illusion that everything squeezing family budgets is due to the other

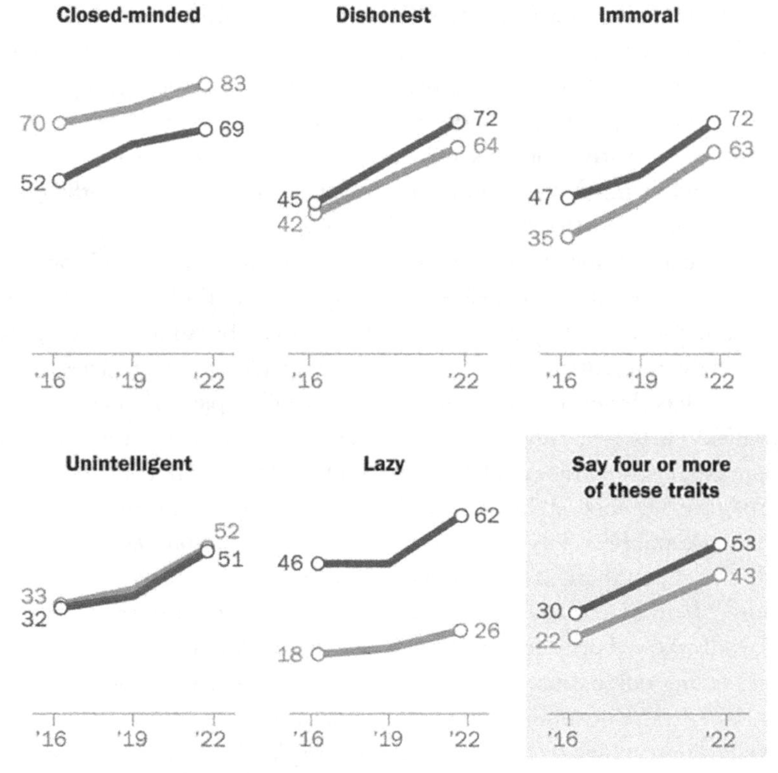

Figure 1.5 Rising Condemnation of People in the Opposing Political Party

party's great evils: Republicans only help the richest; Democrats give your tax money to layabouts who want everything for free. Neither party's leaders honestly explain that (a) real solutions require major economic restructuring, which (b) they cannot pass even when they have majorities in Congress, because of divisions within their party, incentives distorted by big lobbies, and the filibuster.

Due to this feedback loop between institutional dysfunction and public anger, both parties now believe that they gain better publicity from blocking the main initiatives attempted by their rivals than from enacting their own legislation.

Their hard-core base of most loyal voters are more motivated to spoil the other side's alleged agendas than to build something positive. So, when their party is in the minority in the House or Senate, party leaders work to prevent their members from compromising with the other party's top priority bills. They no longer expect that favor to be returned when they are back in the majority. The result is that many congresspersons in the current minority end up voting against bills they actually support or would support with negotiable changes. A recent example is Joe Manchin's moderate compromise proposal on voting rights, which not a single Republican senator was "allowed" to support.[29]

This dilemma has deeper social roots. As gerrymandering increased political polarization, more active supporters wanted their party to be maximally combative and unbending. Once enough legislators adopted this mode of politics, they appealed to even more extreme groups of potential voters who had previously seen no leaders "like them" in regular party politics. In an era of culture wars driven by mass medias' rage-promoting algorithms, literally demonizing the other side—branding them as Nazis, communists, terrorists, or even devil-worshippers and child rapists[30]—pays more dividends (see #15).

These factors, as Kleinfeld says, lead to a "vicious" downward spiral: "severe polarization is narrowing the available solution[s]."[31] As compromise on serious policy solutions declines, more people looking for answers shift their attention to demagogues who condemn the other tribe for their idiocy and malice, threaten to have their opponents arrested, attack prosecutors, judges, and election officials who are just doing their jobs, and demand election fraud inquisitions with no objective evidence. When politics is led by such demagogues, the heady campaign rally aspect of politics never ends, even immediately after elections.[32] In this emotional feeding frenzy, nothing can be accepted as mundane fact; even beliefs about election results that use to flow from routine trust in official reports are now hyped up into tests of faith: if you refuse to accept obviously dubious claims, you are a traitor.

It is natural for people to value belonging to worthwhile causes and productive joint efforts. But when they are centered on the charisma of individual demagogues who invite followers into a "constant blurring of fantasy and reality," the danger of autocracy becomes real.[33] Some people revel in feelings of solidarity that come from giving absolute loyalty to the cult-like social movement that has replaced the older form of their political party. For them, it feels great to vent pent-up angers, know who to hate, and never face hard truths that are not consistent with what they want to believe.

But when politics is lived in this all-consuming 'tribal' way, reasons for and against particular policies become irrelevant: they are only for show.[34] The charisma of particular personalities is the real focus. So responses to concrete national problems are reduced to slogans with little substantive meaning, such as "smaller government," "America first," or "reparations." For most people, these are just passcodes they must repeat to be accepted by peers. In this mode of politics, any compromise that could win strong majority support across the nation is misperceived as a personal betrayal.

Many other Americans recoil from this partisan fervor that replaces (or merges with) religion and tries to dominate domestic life. They find it absurd for ordinary political disagreements to become existential fights to the death even among family members. And they are absolutely correct, because the main purpose of democracy is precisely to offer a *more constructive alternative* to this take-no-prisoners war mentality. Elections, public debate, and compromise in Congress are supposed to let us manage disagreements constructively for our common benefit.

Yet, by checking out from the mindless fervor of mass rallies and tribal politics, political moderates cede the field to those who are intoxicated by their own ideologies. The result is a Congress in which virtually no member will object to abuses of power or false statements by a president or leader within their own party. More moderate congressmen and congresswomen are replaced by fanatics who see any underhanded tactic as justified by the mortal peril posed by their "enemies."[35]

Political historians have long recognized these phenomena as warning signs of a slide toward despotism.[36] In 2024, we are facing a presidential election in which some poll "watchers" and election workers may show up armed with guns, and massive numbers of election officials are quitting due to death threats. When voters and their representatives are willing to do nearly anything to win, however unjust, they can betray the basic principles on which democracy depends.[37]

These are all examples of the third type of problem noted above: they are the negative ways in which our political parties and individual attitudes are warped by the results of largely unrecognized deep institutional flaws. Reduced confidence in elections, kneejerk assumptions about others based on a couple remarks in a political discussion, bitter feelings toward the rival party, and more violent talk on social media and radio are all knock-on effects that, in turn, unfortunately worsen the existing institutional deficits. They make the hard work of crafting serious policy solutions even less likely to succeed. When people moved by hormonal camaraderie try to misappropriate the flag as a symbol for one political movement—thereby dishonoring Americans of all political persuasions who have died defending it—patriotic sentiment is clearly being perverted for ulterior ends.

In this situation, trying to make the best of the failing system we have is a nearly hopeless bet. Only a fool would keep replacing a car battery that dies every two weeks instead of replacing the broken alternator that is draining the battery. It's even worse in our political apparatus: multiple essential components are now failing, and courts are trying to hold it together with duct tape. We need to *alter the entire incentive structure* that is producing stagnation and mindless identity politics.

That begins by altering the narrative through a sustained focus on constitutional fixes that address the fundamental causes of government failure and the resulting steep decline in our democratic values. One thing is for certain: while there is plenty of blame to go around, our families are all in this predicament together. We need to bridge our divides in order to alter the self-destructive path that we are on, which threatens our children and grandchildren to come. The biggest problem is that not enough Americans are willing to see the true peril arising from our constitutional flaws. Bringing them around requires offering a more constructive national mission.

IV. A New Way Forward: Focus on the Root Causes of Our Political Troubles

Analysis of the American national situation has led us to a stark verdict: the US cannot make adequate progress on real-world problems that are threatening our collective future until we fix the main institutional flaws that hobble the federal government, allow distortions in our elections, and fuel the rise of collectively self-disabling political mindsets among otherwise good people (of whatever current political beliefs). Fundamental change is needed to restore belief that government—including the party (or parties) currently acting as a *loyal opposition* to the party in power—can work for the whole country.

Until we have deep reform, winning elections will not suffice to get much done: even a party holding the White House and a majority in both chambers of Congress may be lucky to pass a couple major bills in the first 12–14 months after a presidential election. In fact, experts were surprised that Biden's team could get a significant bill, including green energy incentives and an alternative minimum corporate tax, passed 19 months into his administration.[38] Steady reduction in the visible effects of winning elections, even with substantial majorities, has made our system less responsive to broad cross-sections of the nation, and made more potential voters cynical. No matter how many marches, social media campaigns, mass rallies, or citizen movements we try, it is nearly impossible to overcome the institutional obstacles that—like iron chains—trap most major legislative attempts to address national needs.

The only adequate solution is to break the chains themselves. We have to face the fact that paralysis and dysfunctions within our federal system ultimately flow from flaws in its basic design. As noted in section I, the Constitution as a whole defines a kind of political playing field and its ground rules. It is the framework within which our political debates and contests are played out—much as rules establish what is possible in a board game like chess or Monopoly.

Within these parameters, high-stakes struggles over federal law have motivated political parties and their sponsors to find every loophole that they might exploit—including illicit tactics contrary to the spirit of the system that our framers did not anticipate—and to promote judges who will help them do it. Like water that finds its way into seams in an aging structure, political strategists have sought out any possible way of sabotaging the processes of governing for partisan advantage. In the past, federal courts repaired or shored up some of these weak points by articulating conditions held to be implicit in constitutional language, such as the one-person-one-vote standard in elections. But in the last three decades, the Supreme Court has instead widened cracks in the edifice of our constitutional structure into gaping holes through which the parties can advance their own interests to the detriment of the American public.

This in turn leads to a "prisoner's dilemma"[39] between the main parties: each has to use unjust tactics to keep up with the other. The problem is *not* that most politicians are just spineless, greedy, or vain celebrity-seekers, let alone evil. While few may have the courage of a John McCain or Liz Cheney, most officials serving in federal offices set out with a sincere desire to help their constituents and make a valuable contribution to their country. Many federal legislators and cabinet members in both major parties are patriotic and honorable people. The tragedy is that, because the current rules *allow* strategically useful tactics that harm broad public interests, politicians *have* to use those tactics or lose to opponents who will.

This applies to every weapon in the new political arms races we have permitted to take hold: gerrymandered districts; changes to registration and voting requirements that are tailored to deter potential voters who (currently) favor the other party; turning television channels into heavily slanted propaganda machines; construing belief in hard science as a mere political stance; and drafting every kind of cultural group—temples and churches, veterans organizations, police unions, university faculty, gender-based and ethnic groups, business roundtables—into service as regiments in a total culture war. Once one party can do these destructive things, the other must do the same to survive.

As a result, there is no viable way to break our nation's downward spiral without updating the Constitution. As hard as it is to pass and ratify amendments in our present system of government (see #25), many root causes of federal dysfunction can be fixed in no other way. Some of the procedural flaws derive from bad Supreme Court rulings (see #4 and #5 below); but many other flaws trace to clauses within the original 1787 constitution that have never been improved by subsequent amendments. Precisely as Jefferson feared, the "dead hand of the past" is dragging American politics toward ruin.

This, I realize, is not a welcome conclusion. Many Americans revere the general idea of the Constitution, even imagining it to be sacrosanct and untouchable, as if thoughts of editing any part of it verge on treason or even heresy. But that is not what the founders thought. When they created our republic in 1787, they were forming one of the geographically largest nations in the world. The extent of US territory required states to retain a lot of power, because no affordable federal government could directly address problems across such a vast area, especially as it expanded west. Technology and life circumstances are very different today, even compared to conditions in the late 19th century. To think that the Constitution should remain as was written in 1787 or even 1887 is like saying that our rules of the road should remain as they were in horse and buggy times.

Over years of discussing this dilemma with different audiences, I have found that many people still fear that "now is just not the time." They worry that any talk about constitutional amendments will weaken what's left of people's loyalty to our rickety common framework. But this gets things exactly backward.

A calmer time that is ideal for a constitutional revamp will never come until major changes are made to the way our parties and election processes work. On the other hand, a broad movement for constitutional renewal could revive devotion to a national cause that transcends current party divisions, thereby inspiring solidarity and restoring belief that the government belongs to the people. For so many, it would feel like a breath of fresh air, an escape from the noxious fumes of our current poisonous politics into a cleansing sense of new hope.

The next two chapters offer a draft charter for such a movement. But before proceeding, we should consider three stumbling blocks for any such plan.

1. The first involves diametrically opposing views about our "founding fathers" in the Revolutionary period. They are sometimes enlarged into legendary heroes, and their work is depicted as nearly perfect, or even directed by God. On the other equally absurd extreme, they are reviled as evildoers bent only on perpetuating slavery, caste, domination, hatred of women, extraction of wealth, and structural injustice of every imaginable kind.

Neither of these popular images is even close to plausible; but fortunately for this book's purposes, it is enough that all the framers of the 1787 constitution intended it *to be amendable*: the delegates at Philadelphia understood their document as a replacement for the Articles of Confederation (ratified in 1781) and were certain that their new system of government would have to be adjusted later in light of experience and changing circumstance. That is why they added procedures for amendment in Article V, including approval by 2/3rds of Congress and 3/4ths of states (see #25 for more details).

We are lucky that the founders thought of this, because our constitutional system has survived this long only due to the 27 ratified amendments that we have. To reassure doubters, 12 amendments were proposed by the first Congress as a "Bill of Rights" just two years after the convention met. Ten of these were swiftly ratified within a few years of George Washington becoming President. But today, as Joseph Fishkin and William Forbath argue, refusing to consider new constitutional changes only "cedes power to courts."[40] That can prop up the system for a while, until justices refuse to do the hard work of constitutional repair for us, or one faction seizes control of the judiciary, whose power has expanded because we have lost the habit of constitutional reform.

Moreover, far from being sacrosanct, some of provisions in the 1787 constitution were manifestly nothing more than desperate compromises needed to refloat the national project after it had run aground in the 1780s. In other words, they were *temporary expediencies* to be reconsidered later, after the government was well-established. Some vital matters, such as how to end the curse of slavery, were largely left for future Americans to work out because they were political dynamite. Delegates at the convention realized that trying to solve them in their plan of government would destroy their slim chance of building a strong republic. Banning the importation of slaves after 1808 was as far as they could go.[41] The founders also overlooked some important issues, including the huge role that political parties would soon come to play.[42]

Mindful of such flaws, Thomas Jefferson famously held that a constitutional convention should meet at regular intervals to consider changes because "the Earth belongs to the living."[43] His point was that interpretations of justice and constitutional bargains between stakeholders made many generations ago cannot justly bind current citizens forever: that would be tyranny of the past, privileging the status quo even when much better options have been discovered (see Desideratum 8 below). Regarding any constitutional provision as unalterable would also be very dangerous: when we depend on a house for shelter, but termites are eating away its main beams, refusal to replace them out of reverence for the original builders would be madness.

This is one way to interpret what happened through the Civil War: the compromises that our founders had made with slavery, which tainted all their work[44]—as some slave-owners among them clearly recognized—were removed by the 13th, 14th, and 15th Amendments. In the mid-20th century, the corrupt expedient of segregation was also wholly rejected. These main beams of the national house were utterly rotten, and the whole structure would have collapsed if they were not replaced with legal and social equality. But today, we are fast approaching the same condition again: some of the essential pillars of our republic are crumbling around us.

In sum, seeking to amend our current Constitution is *not* a radical rejection of the founders' ideas for federalism, representative government, and protections against tyranny of the majority. On the contrary, republican government requires periodic renewal through constitutional reform, as our history richly illustrates.

2. However, it has been a long time since major constitutional change was seriously attempted. This prospect seems scary to many Americans now simply because the process is no longer familiar. As Ezekiel Kweku put it in a recent op-ed, we have to recapture the spirit of constitutional innovation and rebuild public confidence that we can tackle big challenges together.[45]

So let's briefly review the history. Our last phase of deep and pervasive constitutional improvement was in the Progressive Era over a century ago when women gained the vote, direct election of senators became universal, and the income tax was instituted (the 16th, 17th, and 19th Amendments). While other advanced democratic nations have made large constitutional reforms since World War II, we addressed big social problems through the Civil Rights Act of 1964 and the Voting Rights Act of 1965 (VRA), and via Supreme Court decisions like *Brown* v. *the Board of Education*, which desegregated schools. But despite their historic importance, these are statutes and precedents that can and have been weakened by later laws and court decisions. They also did nothing to give congressional representation to Puerto Rico or Washington, D.C.; nor can they, as now interpreted, block laws passed in many states to make voting harder.

The reformist spirit of the 1960s did produce the 24th Amendment, which increased access to the vote by banning poll taxes—a big step in expanding access to voting. That spirit also led to the 23rd Amendment, which gave Washington D.C. three electors—making it equal to the smallest states in the presidential election. But the Equal Rights Amendment (ERA) for women, passed by 2/3rds of the House and Senate in 1971–1972, was not ratified by enough states in the seven-year window that Congress initially set for its ratification. Likewise the "District of Columbia Voting Rights Amendment" was designed to give Washington D.C. full representation in the House and Senate. It passed Congress in 1978 but was not ratified by enough states in time (see #11). Another amendment for direct election of the president that originally had wide support in Congress and the broader public was eventually stalled to death in the Senate (see #12).

In the half-century since these three heroic but unsuccessful efforts, rather than renew and build on them, our political leaders have let them drop. So we have forgotten that constitutional reform can bring about badly needed fundamental changes. A mood of defeatism is the outcome: smart people everywhere scoff at the idea that any amendments could advance toward ratification. They forget that many previous amendments were dubbed "impossible" in their time, until less vocal Americans closer to the political middle realized that a deep constitutional improvement was within their grasp.

3. Still, even though the Constitution was *designed* to changeable, some Americans fear that this could be like opening Pandora's Box. Once Congress starts passing amendments,

could they impose draconian horrors on us?—controlling all medical decisions, ending free speech, installing tracking devices in us, instituting military dictatorship, restoring segregation—you name it. In an era rife with crazy conspiracy theories, all these worries and more have been seriously suggested in public forums. Because our curricula do not educate Americans sufficiently about the amendment process (see #10), some people even imagine that a sitting president might start decreeing whatever constitutional changes they like. At the selective private university where I teach, smart students have asked whether amendments to ban all abortions, to declare Christianity the official state religion, or to institute completely open borders might get adopted.

All such fears are unfounded. None of these ideas could come anywhere close to getting approval by 2/3^rds^ of both chambers of Congress or by a new convention. But even if some extreme amendment did clear that first hurdle, recall that Article V requires *3/4^ths^ of the states*—presently 38—to ratify any proposed amendment before it actually becomes constitutional law. That is an extremely high bar—in fact, probably harder in practice than the founders intended (see #25).

So there is literally a zero chance of extreme amendments pushed by one radical group or another hijacking our way of life. American history bears this out. In 235-some years since that original convention, *only one* out of 27 ratified amendments proved to be a harmful mistake. That was the 18th Amendment for prohibition of alcohol, which had to be repealed by the 21st Amendment to stop the street wars and underground markets that it spawned. Of course, other amendments might have fallen short of their intended purposes. But being insufficient is very different than being mostly harmful or counterproductive, as Prohibition was. Surely 26 good enough amendments out of 27 is an encouraging historical record! And as Prohibition illustrates, even if a harmful amendment did somehow slip through, the public can learn from experience and reverse such an error.

However, the relative unfamiliarity of amendments to most Americans now, and resulting widespread doubts, definitely show that constitutional reform will require a lot of work to explain. Without strong high school civics requirements, interest groups can try to demonize any constitutional proposal that might weaken their grip on power. Their scare tactics may work until people see that moderate amendments are really possible, and they learn from experience that constitutional change can bring big improvements. Building common ground around such constitutional fixes will be hard; yet there are three crucial factors that make it feasible:

A. As we have seen, Americans already recognize that the federal government is badly failing and that reforms so far attempted are not fixing the main dysfunctions.
B. While deep change can seem alarming, as the passion that goes into social movements attests, a majority of Democrats, Independents, and Republicans now favor fundamental reform. Even in early 2019, before the difficult aftermath of the 2020 election, roughly 2/3^rds^ of the nation wanted "major changes" or a completely new system (see Figure 1.6).[46]
C. Most Americans care not only about their material wealth but also about the future of their country: they want a better future for coming generations even more than they want their favorite party to prevail in elections.

Americans who are most critical of the government's performance on a range of issues are most likely to say the government system needs major changes.

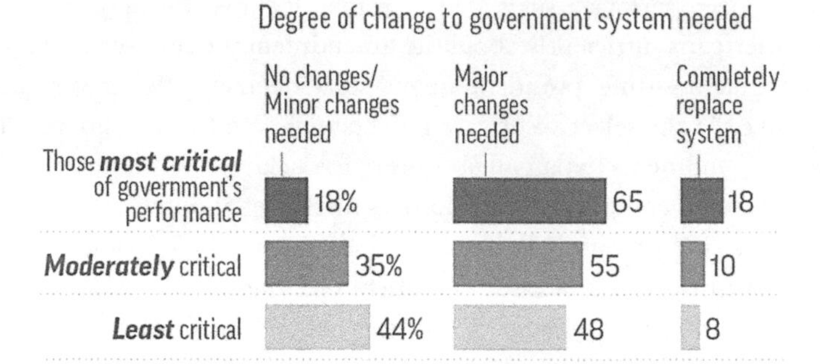

Results based on an index of views of government performance on 10 issues, among those who want government to be working on each issue. The UChicago/AP-NORC poll was conducted March 14-18 with 1,003 U.S. adults. The margin of error is ±4.2 percentage points for the full sample.

SOURCE: AP-NORC Center for Public Affairs Research AP

Figure 1.6 Critics of Government Want Big Changes

Precisely because so many Americans are sickened by the extreme wings of both parties, whose antics have destabilized the nation, constitutional compromise may now stand a chance. There is a very large audience waiting for a third way to open through more centrist proposals to fix our system.

As a result, a moderate and commonsense plan for constitutional reform could be just the inspiration needed at this moment in history. Recognizing that people can alter their form of government by building consensus from the local level on up is inherently empowering: it gives us a better alternative than remaining upset spectators who can do little more than occasionally vote to throw someone out of office. And once the idea of constitutional reform takes hold again, high school and college courses will use that occasion to focus students on related topics in American history and American government. Media coverage of constitutional reform will grow, aiding the virtuous cycle. This is a new kind of a movement waiting to take off, if only enough civic and political leaders will give it the initial push.

But for this approach to work, we need to think carefully about the best amendment ideas to emphasize in the initial stages. Leading with a whole new raft of proposed rights, for example, is not the way to build the sort of broad coalitions needed for constitutional change. The next section offers basic guidelines for deciding where the focus should be.

V. Eight Desiderata to Guide the Choice of Amendments

This book will review 25 distinct areas in which amendments are needed to end gridlock, corruption, and unresponsiveness in our federal government. Together, I call them a *Bill of Democracy* to parallel the 10 historic and profound constitutional amendments in our Bill of Rights. Probably no reader will agree with all of the agenda laid out in the next chapters. But virtually everyone will find some of the proposals initially attractive and be willing to entertain others after considering the problems that motivate them.

In fact, agreement on the problems is the most vital step in building a nationwide process to hammer out constitutional solutions. Even if you are not persuaded by my specific remedies, there are many intelligible variations on these proposals to resolve the 25 constitutional lacunas that I describe. More generally, we need open, sincere, and fact-based debate about the deficiencies in our Constitution—a democratic process that can overcome the negativity and shallowness in which American political discourse is now so mired.

For this reason, each section will mention one or two alternative solutions worth considering, in addition to my own suggested fix. In some cases, my proposals differ from solutions suggested by other scholars simply because I follow a few basic desiderata. These pragmatic pointers can guide deliberation about constitutional reforms that are feasible in our immediate future. These rules of thumb are not absolute, but they can help us sort through numerous options to identify amendments that are more likely to gain wide support and adequately (if not perfectly) repair our deepest constitutional deficits. When helpful, I will refer back to these eight desiderata to avoid common errors or pitfalls that can distort evaluation of options for constitutional reform.

1. *Only use constitutional provisions where regular law will not suffice.* Because it is much harder to pass and ratify a constitutional amendment, we should fix flaws in the operation of government and elections with ordinary statutes whenever possible. We will encounter several cases involving voting rights, new states, the functioning of the House and Senate, election financing, the Supreme Court, and more that might be addressed through normal federal law. But there are often two problems with this apparently easier alternative.

First, it involves trusting that once the change is made, it will be politically too controversial later on for a party holding a majority in Congress and the presidency to simply repeal the fix. That is a big risk. Those who fought for years to pass the VRA would be shocked to see state governments in 2022 reversing their efforts by enacting a whole array of state laws to make registration and voting more difficult (nb. I'm not rejecting ID requirements: see #6). In some areas, we can overcome partisan manipulation of the rules only by a constitutional provision that is not subject to change because of short-term political pressures.

Second, the Supreme Court may overrule systemic fixes made through ordinary law, as it has done repeatedly with campaign finance, election law, voting rights, gerrymandering of district lines, and more. For example, the Court may well gut another section of the VRA in its present 2023–2024 term. The politicization of the Court threatens statutory fixes to most of the problems addressed in this book.

There is a vicious feedback loop here, because using ordinary law to make deep procedural changes to the way our federal government operates actually increases incentives to try to hijack those reforms by placing radical judges on the Court. In short, even when current justices support statutory fixes to institutional breakdown, relying on the federal judiciary means that a more hostile Court in future can re-break patched-up lawmaking and election processes. Constitutional reform is more reliable.

2. *Where possible, focus on procedural amendments.* Procedural changes concern how elections and lawmakers operate, and the ways in which law is enacted and applied, rather than what substantive responses to "real-world" issues are enacted. For example, removing the filibuster in the Senate is a procedural fix, whereas altering the birthright citizenship clause in the 14th Amendment would be a substantive change. Because procedural changes do not decide substantive policy issues such as abortion rights, school curricula, appropriate sanctions in criminal justice, or ways reducing health care costs, they do not directly promote any party's priorities concerning the real-world problems. Thus it is easier for more Americans to recognize procedural amendments as impartial: they can be supported by reasons having nothing to do with party advantage. All political parties can attempt to use the changed procedures to promote their preferred ways of solving material, economic, and social challenges that the nation faces.

Of course, the procedural–substantive distinction is not absolute, and procedural amendments can also be controversial. Moreover, some substantive amendments may be needed. The civics education proposal that I offer (#10) is a substantive one. Many other substantive amendments have been suggested in recent works, such as the new constitution proposed by scholars in *Democracy Journal*.[47] I will mention a few possible substantive amendments in the Interlude, which are further discussed in the online extension at TheDemocracyAmendments.org.

3. *In assessing amendments, do not focus on how they would affect parties in their current flawed forms; focus instead on what the parties would become under the proposed new rules.* Critics are likely to assess each procedural fix only in terms of whether it might help or hurt their favored party. But there are three big reasons to reject that kind of tunnel-vision focus on immediate partisan advantage.

First, it is short-term thinking; political parties will change their strategies to succeed within a new set of rules. Our parties would be altered top to bottom by some of the constitutional reforms that I defend. So trying to predict whether *today*'s Democratic party or the Republican party in 2024 would be more likely to win after any given amendment is a mistake. It is like asking whether your favorite football team is more likely to win the tournament if all the teams start playing rugby instead. There is no answer, because the teams would have to be rebuilt to win rugby matches: they would not be *the same teams,* even if they retained the same names. Similarly, the constitutional reforms I propose will leave parties with vital roles to play in fair and effective democratic government, but reformed parties will work more constructively for the nation than today's parties do.

Here is an obvious example. Because Republican presidential candidates won the Electoral College (EC) while losing the popular vote in 2000 and 2016, many Republicans now imagine that the EC will always favor them (see #12). Yet this is incorrect. "Blue" states gain 10 to 16 more electors from noncitizen residents and would lose that advantage in a national popular election of the president.[48] Both main parties would also adopt positions and run presidential campaigns quite differently to win a majority of the national vote, because they would need to win as many votes as possible in every state. How many *more* Republicans in currently "blue" states and Democrats in "red" states would go to the polls when their presidential vote is no longer "wasted"? We do not know. So we really cannot say that "Trump would have lost in 2016 if we did not have the EC," because so much is different in that imaginary scenario. All we can predict is that the outcome without the EC would be much more representative of the whole nation.

Second, there is a moral reason to reject narrow partisan evaluation of amendment ideas. If a procedural amendment increases the fairness and/or effectiveness of the federal government overall, but you think it might reduce your party's chances of winning in the next few years, that amounts to saying that your party is getting an advantage from unfair or counterproductive features of the system. That is a *negative* relationship to our citizenry: a party and special interest groups it serves are gaining *at the expense* of everyone else, rather than improving their share by growing the whole social pie.

Third, that parasitic way of operating will eventually ruin such a party and cause parts of the system to break down. Cultivating unjust advantages distorts policy goals in any political party that pursues it, eventually twisting the ethos of the party beyond recognition. Like a Ponzi scheme, it requires more falsehoods, misrepresentations, and shady dealings to keep it going every year. In the long run, this devil's bargain destroys the party's viability.

A good example in American history is the Democratic party in the decades leading up to the Civil War. Jefferson's grand party, which once included a wide diversity of viewpoints on slavery, including some favoring compensated emancipation, had become a rabidly proslavery party that purged any member who was not fanatically committed to expanding slavery and spreading the myth that slavery was good for all involved. Deceit, lies, and pledging allegiance to a "naked emperor" became the price of acceptance by one's peers. This jaded party was determined to keep extracting wealth from unpaid labor by any means necessary, including mass self-deception and violent suppression of speech,[49] even if it meant destroying loyalty to a unified government. Thus the old Democratic party ultimately became a public enemy.

By contrast, as Akhil Amar argues, the 24th Amendment against poll taxes ratified in 1964 and the VRA deeply altered the political landscape in the old South, leading to a string of presidents elected from southern states, along with a lowering of barriers between racial and geographic groups in the US. The South emerged politically and socially stronger as a result.[50]

This does not mean that any American should give up her or his values or views on the pressing real-world issues that our national government needs to address. You are right to stick to your priorities unless or until you find good reasons to alter your policy judgments. But good ends do not justify immoral means. None of us should want to secure laws that agree with our values or priorities by cheating, rigging the system to be less democratic, or tilting the playing field toward minority domination. Coercion of that kind eventually stokes deep hostilities and puts many good people in compromised positions. Weakening our willingness to abide by a shared set of constitutional rules in this way invites a constitutional cataclysm.

Finally, let's remember why parties exist. Just as human beings created free markets for our benefit, rather than the reverse, we are not slaves to our political parties. They are meant to improve standards of living by informing citizens and organizing political action, not just to provide jobs for politicians and marketers. If today's major parties are making life worse rather than better on the whole, or serving their leaders' interest more than ours, then they should be redesigned. After all, parties are no more than tools that exist at our pleasure to promote the collective good of the nation.

For all these reasons, the procedural amendments that I defend in the next chapter rest on basic ideals in our tradition, rather than calculations of partisan advantage. Responsibly writing a rulebook or designing a playing field is a *very different task* than trying to win the game according to the rules. The constitutional task must be guided by different principles than the ones to which we usually appeal in arguing for this or that position on real-world policy issues.

In particular, a key criterion must be whether an amendment would make political parties serve public interests by reducing corruption and facilitating more consensus on policy priorities. The radical wings of both major parties might not be happy about such reforms, but the broad majority of Americans who would like to take back our government should be pleased. The result would be more political parties *that you can respect,* and whose main arguments for their policies you can seriously consider, even while you affiliate with a different party.

4. *Unless absolutely necessary, avoid proposals that would dramatically change large parts of our current system to something very unfamiliar.* I adopt this rule of thumb because amendments will not be accepted if many people cannot envision what they would entail. This does not mean that we can make do entirely with small tweaks to our current constitutional language. But it does counsel setting aside some alternatives that may be defensible, or even the best option in principle, when they are foreign to our national experience.

For example, William Hudson offers powerful arguments that the separation of powers instituted through our three branches of government was a mistake made during a period when a popular parliamentary system had not yet emerged to prove its worth. In a robust parliamentary system, voters are the main check, and the majority party is accountable because it *can and does* act: it is not blocked by multiple veto points or by individual members of Congress whose electability depends more on an individual personality cult than on their party's popularity.[51]

Hudson is right that our elections must produce tangible results if we are to re-engage citizens and restore confidence in our legislature. But in what follows, I assume that a complete shift to a parliamentary system is not feasible in the US; it would be too radical for most Americans. The same goes for electing the entire House of Representatives nationally, rather than district by district (or even electing half of it nationally, as the Germans do for their lower chamber[52]). Americans expect to have a member of Congress who is from their geographic location and could only get used to proportional representation if it were tried in state governments first (e.g. through a statewide election of the state assembly). Thus I seriously consider such a method only for a portion of the Senate (see #24).

Similarly, Hélène Landemore makes powerful arguments for selecting members of Congress by *lottery* from among qualified citizens, much as we do with juries, and frequently rotating these congressional "jurors."[53] Whatever downsides this system would have for institutional knowledge, enthusiasm of legislators, or maybe manipulation of congresspersons by long-term professional staff, it certainly would make for a highly representative legislature. Perhaps as with juries, a *voir dire* process could even be used to exclude a few people in the selected pool who are mentally unstable or extremely ignorant. This is an idea that some conservatives could support. A family friend reminds me of William F. Buckley's comment that he would trust the US government to "the first 400 people listed in the Boston telephone directory."

But despite its possible benefits over a system with elected representatives, a lottery system would have to be used and prove its worth in state governments before Americans generally would try it even for some portion of Congress. On the other hand, states could easily take up the recommendation of political scientists to start regularly convening small "citizens juries" to study different issues through expert-facilitated deliberation before making recommendations to their congressional delegations. This kind of "lottocracy" lite could really help counter the corrosive influence of polarized media bubbles.

I'm not saying that all more radical changes to elections or representation should first be tried at the state level. As we will see, several possible reforms would cause collective action problems if implemented this way. But in order to overcome deep fears of constitutional change fostered by influential fallacies, we need to be pragmatic. Those with vested interests in the status quo will use every imaginable scare tactic against any reform proposals, as we have seen with ranked choice voting in 2021–2022.

Overall, then, we should favor focusing on more modest procedural improvements to our current institutions, such as ending the filibuster in the Senate or establishing new checks on potential corruption. Many Americans could easily to envision our present system modified in these sorts of straightforward ways. With sufficient help and education through public outreach, civic journalism, and perhaps citizen juries, the public could predict sufficiently well what the results would be—much as with the narrative explanation that accompanies a ballot question.

By contrast, proposals that would completely remake one or more branches of the federal government are not viable. While the cancers of tribalism and corporate capture of executive and legislative offices are seriously weakening our body politic, and require strong constitutional tonics to cure them, the medicine cannot be so strong that the weakened patient refuses to take it. Only a much recovered patient could stand the most potent therapies and come out even healthier for it.

That said, I am not counseling timidity: a comprehensive constitutional agenda has to include amendments that some Americans will at first oppose for shortsighted partisan reasons. Our founders achieved much more in 1787 than almost anyone thought possible at the time. Like them, to bring desperately needed amendments to fruition, we will ultimately have to make deals giving different interest groups some of what they prefer. While certain amendments might be almost impossible to ratify on a stand-alone basis, they may become feasible as parts of a larger package, which leads to the next desideratum.

5. *Remember that many needed amendments are interdependent*: they make more sense when taken in combination with others. This is another crucial point that is easy to forget. Many features of our current system are mutually reinforcing. For example, having the president appoint cabinet officers is not undemocratic because the president is elected (albeit indirectly), and the Senate which approves these appointments is also elected. It is the same with several needed amendments: in fixing one procedural problem, an amendment might seem to cause a new problem, but not when it works in tandem with other proposals in the Bill of Democracy. A simple example: giving the president a line-item veto to control budget deficits is less worrying if Congress can override vetoes by a $3/5^{ths}$ margin, rather than needing a $2/3^{rds}$ majority.

In other cases, the beneficent effects of one amendment are much enhanced when combined with others on the list. This is especially true of needed reforms in campaign finance, districting, and electoral processes. As we will see, there are multiple changes that could increase voter impact and voter turnouts in different ways. Each of them tends to make political parties more responsive to a wider range of voters, which increases incentives for yet more citizens to get involved: a virtuous circle is created.

This is a central motive for the breadth of this book. For every amendment topic discussed herein, readers will find books that focus in depth on that topic, such as the filibuster, gerrymandering, or the EC. There is great value in many of these studies, and in recent public projects that have gathered ideas for amendments either via expert focus groups or guided citizen jury methods. However, students and general readers cannot fully appreciate the gravity of our situation without seeing a larger list of the constitutional flaws laid out together. This requires treating each constitutional flaw in less depth, but within a more wholistic frame.

Laying out a broad agenda to improve all parts of the US government has three related benefits. First, considering what a full constitutional overhaul might look like can reassure us that starting down this path is not a slippery slope into chaos. Instead, even a multipronged package of constitutional reforms can be limited, coherent, largely centrist, attentive to concerns with wide currency, and carefully tailored to build on good features that still remain in our federal institutions.[54]

Second, understanding the sheer range of constitutional problems needing attention may galvanize leaders to do something about it. Focusing on one constitutional problem at a time may seem simpler, but it can also give the wrong impression that we are talking about a few pet issues of particular interest groups. On the contrary, an impartial audit of the whole federal system clarifies the scale of the task before us.

Perhaps most importantly, this thorough inventory of constitutional deficits will explain why it makes sense to call a new constitutional convention. That might appear to be a crazy notion if we are only considering two, three, or four amendments, which Congress might by some stretch of the imagination take up one day. But with at least 25 urgent items to consider, the pathway through Congress is not adequate this time around.

As the book's last chapter argues, the point of a convention is not to propose a single amendment: its main benefit is to take a broad view, considering many constitutional problems in connection.

6. *Humility, openness, civility, and fairness.* A broad review of constitutional flaws in our federal government will make it abundantly clear that finding sufficient remedies requires more than the expertise of any one person, group, party, or social movement. The range of topics raised in the Bill of Democracy increases the probability that creative responses to my proposals will emerge, including ones that did not occur to me. The ideas in this book are all offered in that spirit.

This task will require enough humility to recognize that none of us has all the answers. To build momentum for constitutional change, name-calling will not suffice. For once we *really* need to listen to each other's concerns and accept possible insights from our rivals. This is what smart athletes would do—not when racing against one another, but rather if they were redesigning the Olympic Games. In the indispensable endeavor of constitutional renewal that could shape the prospects of American families (and allied nations) for generations to come, there is no time or room to indulge the petty grievances, suspicions, and juvenile displays of bravado that make up everyday politics. We need to transcend those small-minded excuses for dismissing other Americans with whom we disagree. Otherwise our heirs may reap the whirlwind.

Succeeding in this mission to save our nation also requires a sense of fair play. When aspects of our current system are grossly unfair to some parts of the nation, we need to fix them if we want public devotion to the connecting threads of history, tradition, and law to continue. There will be people ready to offer specious rationalizations to keep massively inequitable provisions in our constitutional order. But their scheme depends on keeping these injustices out of the limelight of public attention, which proposed amendments can shine on injustices.

7. *General and abstract constitutional provisions are not always better.* Our constitutional text, even with all ratified amendments added in, remains one of the shortest in the democratic world. There were few models to go on when the delegates wrote the original version in 1787. While they elaborated several points that were not in the prior Articles of Confederation (which were about 25% shorter still), our framers assumed that constitutional provisions should mostly be phrased in very terse and general terms, leaving plenty of room for the legislature to exercise discretion. They also left some things rather vague because they could not resolve every substantive disagreement within the convention—and when the "committee of detail" finally reported a full draft of the document in September, the delegates were exhausted and running out of time.

In 1787–1788, critics of the proposed constitution often complained about lack of sufficient detail in certain provisions, such as the absence of a full list of individual rights. However, when these were added, they were also stated in very general terms like "freedom of speech" and "the right to bear arms"—much as in the fledgling new state constitutions written after 1776.[55] Our Bill of Rights fits on two average-size book pages, while the Charter of the Fundamental Rights of the European Union, completed in 2000, is 12 pages long. Recent constitutions are much more detailed than ours because they draw on so much more experience of democratic government than our founders had available.

For example, as Steven Taylor and colleagues write, concerning how to run elections and structure representation, "most of the choices were simply unknown" in 1787. Thus the convention delegates largely left it to states to figure out election procedures (see #6).[56]

Many Americans think that the sparsity of our constitutional law is good, as evidenced by the brevity even of 20th-century amendments. So I have tried to keep my amendment proposals terse and general when this works well. As Sandy Levinson suggests, that approach facilitates ongoing "conversation" about the ideas in a constitutional clause and "a certain malleability of interpretation that makes it possible to adjust to circumstances." Short language leaves more discretion to Congress. By contrast, with constitutional text as difficult to amend as ours (see #25), "settled" specific details can make it almost impossible to fix past errors.[57]

However, lack of detail is definitely *not* always wise. A simple example: the ERA of 1972 would probably have been successfully ratified if it had retained an extra clause, which was in the 1970 Senate version, saying that the amendment did not require women to be drafted into the military.

One big effect of our brief and general constitutional language has been to vastly enhance the power of the federal judiciary, which may decide to allow laws and practices that depend on newer construals of general or vague constitutional terminology—or *not* to allow them. Thus over many decades, we came to rely more and more on the Courts of Appeal and the Supreme Court to use elasticity in constitutional meaning, or development to suit new needs, so that we did not have to alter the actual text of the Constitution.

This overreliance on federal courts could never be a permanent solution, and our founders did not expect it to be. With the thin notion of judicial review extant in their time, they never imagined how much constitutional jurisprudence would expand, to the point that practically every word in the official text became pregnant with hundreds of potential meanings when applied to concrete cases—manifold implications that require interpretative exercises running into thousands of pages to unfold. While these conversations and debates have yielded many good things, they have also misled the general public into assuming that the Constitution is a matter of arcane expertise rather than something that we all should have a hand in shaping.

This book argues that the people should take back control of the Constitution. The power of amendment is an essential check on the courts, which occasionally set damaging precedents, and on a Congress that cannot muster the will to fix its internal problems. The needed fixes sometimes require detailed provisions, which will be less risky if we make the amendment process itself somewhat easier (see #25). But even without that change, we cannot continue leaving big structural problems in our government to jurisprudential roulette in federal courts.[58]

8. *Civic republicanism and the original sovereignty of the people.* Constitutional reform depends on some working notion of rightful authority to make such changes and an interpretation of democratic principles that can support particular amendments. I briefly summarize such principles here. But as I said in the Preface, one can recognize glaring constitutional inadequacies and evaluate options to fix them without relying on a detailed philosophical theory. The deeper principles will be needed only at a few junctures.

I follow a civic republican ideal of democracy, which includes a deliberative principle: democracy should be the rule of collective reasoning about the goals and methods of government. Protecting individual rights and liberties is crucial in a legitimate republic, but this is not enough by itself to avoid majority or minority tyranny. We also need citizens to care about more than their own narrow material interests, so that elections are not mere aggregations of arbitrary or even manipulated desires; rather, they should express people's judgments about public goods. On this, classical liberalism and republicanism agree: citizens have some natural duties to one another. As John Kennedy said in his inaugural address, democracy is not only about what your country can do for you; it is even more important to ask "what you can do for your country." These ideas are nicely summarized in Teresa Hudock's flowchart (Figure 1.7).

This conception does not require that citizens become experts in politics. A great strength of democracy is that it can leverage all sorts of knowledge and understanding that are *distributed* throughout the population, rather than being unified only in expert minds. This crowdsourcing virtue has been recognized as long ago in western thought as Aristotle's *Politics*, although we now have a far better understanding of public goods, including defenses of human rights.

Living in a prosperous democracy remains a rare privilege in history, and ours was hard won through many brutal wars that cost so much suffering. As Abraham Lincoln said at Gettysburg, we have a solemn duty to make those sacrifices worth it. That means seeing our political life together as a serious cooperative venture, rather than as entertainment or war by tamer means. But for this to be possible, basic features of our economy, civil society, and government cannot add up to the wholesale

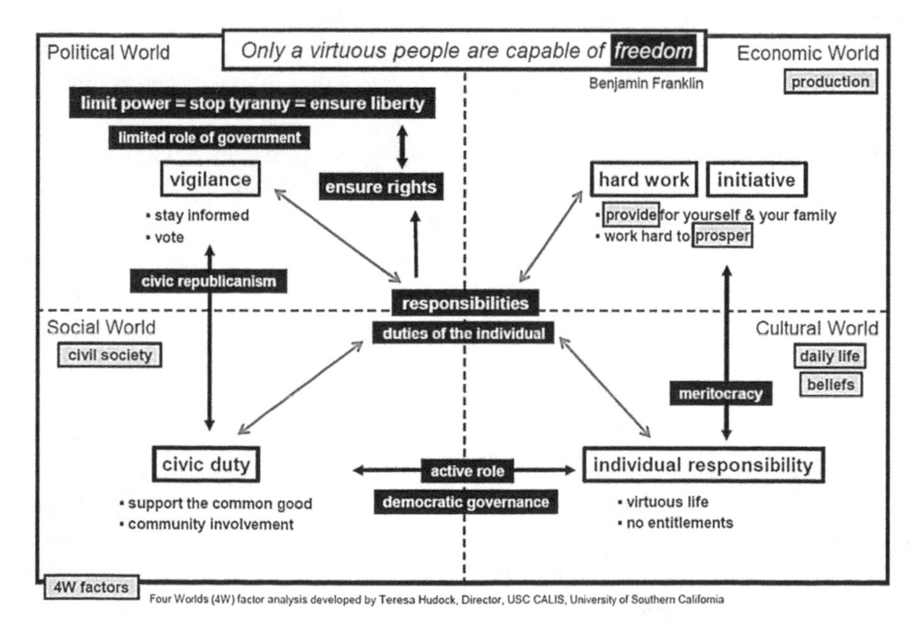

Figure 1.7 Classical Liberalism and Civic Republicanism

domination of some groups by others. Domination, which makes some people into mere means for others' convenience, corrodes the reciprocity that stable democracy demands. This is not a distinctively liberal view; it is held by many conservative jurists as well.[59]

The rule of law is also essential to any civic republican account, and a constitution is its foundation. That is why constitutional law should not be *too* easy to change: as we saw, it is a higher level of law that regulates all other law and policy, thereby forming a basis for the entire built environment in which we live. The constitutional framework shapes the invisible social ties of mutual expectations that knit us together.

Nonetheless, there is one kind of authority that transcends even constitutional law, although it always remains *conceptually linked* to the ideal of constitutional order as its proper goal or purpose. Political scientists call this source of political authority the "primary constituent power"—a dry name for what our founders and French revolutionaries in the 18th century called the people's original, inherent, and inalienable sovereignty. This includes the right to make an entirely new constitution outside prior legally defined pathways when that proves to be indispensable for the common good.

Most American founders recognized such a right. It was asserted not only in the Declaration of Independence but also in several state constitutions. For example, Pennsylvania's first constitution of 1776 said that whenever government fails to protect the community, "the people have a right, by common consent to change it, and take such measures as to them may appear necessary to promote their safety and happiness."[60] Madison even tried to add this statement to the 1787 constitution's preamble: "…that all [rightful] power is originally vested in, and consequently derived from, the people."[61]

That may sound radical, but the concept of originary sovereignty is unavoidable, because a constitution is an artifact: people have to make it, and they cannot always do that according to rules *previously* laid down in an existing constitution. In starting from anarchy, or after revolution, or in new-won independence from colonial rule, among other scenarios, families and groups have to come together to make "one people" who can draft and approve a new constitutional system.

Our people did this no less than three times in the Revolutionary period: when creating new state governments in 1776; when these states "in Congress assembled" adopted the Articles of Confederation as a semi-constitutional treaty; and again when the people adopted the 1787 constitution without following the unanimity condition in the Articles, thus altering state constitutions by implication as well.[62] Madison argued that this constitution proposed by the national convention should be ratified by state conventions rather than state legislatures because these special meetings were seen as embodiments of the people's originary sovereignty.[63]

Moreover, even when following a legal amendment process, the letter of existing constitutional law cannot tell you how to edit it. To decide on new language, we have use other criteria, such as the desiderata outlined here. Principles of collective reasoning (including universal canons of reason), fairness and distributive equity, the need stability and order, inclusiveness and/or equality, opportunity and solidarity, knowledge of public goods, and individual human rights are the kinds of stars by which we should navigate when revising our most fundamental positive law.

Primary constituent sovereignty is thus never perfectly contained, channeled, or limited by existing constitutional amendment procedures. Sometimes a convention that is convened to write a constitution can only rely on prior experience, moral principles, and norms of natural justice to determine how it should proceed. How else could Americans have written the initial constitutions of our 13 state governments after declaring separation from Great Britain?[64] Occasionally a people may decide through referenda, or actions by their representatives, to use methods of amendment that are not laid out in black letter law. State constitutions have often been altered in such "nonstandard" ways.

That does not mean that absolutely anything goes. The highest collective authority to adopt or alter a constitution is not unconditional: it rests on some moral presuppositions about people's capacities for autonomy, along with assumptions about the nature of law, and these groundings matter when writing or revising fundamental law. Thus the Supreme Court sometimes has to draw on what it calls the general underlying ideal of "ordered liberty." In that sense, proposed amendments could be illegitimate if they violate the organic preconditions of popular sovereignty (see #24)—even if the Court is not empowered to make that judgment.

Finally, original sovereignty is indispensable because justice is intergenerational. This is the point I attributed to Jefferson: later generations should not be stuck with badly outdated constitutional provisions for too long. "We the living" deserve the same chance as the authors of our 1787 constitution to decide for ourselves what the processes for making, executing, and adjudicating law and policy ought to be. And our grandchildren will inherit this basic moral-political right as well; we cannot legitimately deny it to them—for example, by adopting an amendment that says "no future amendments can be considered."

As a result, legal amendment processes are suspect whey they make it too difficult to improve existing constitutional provisions. Imagine a constitution written over a century ago that banned any use of electricity and required approval by 90% of citizens to change this, thus delaying modern technology by many decades. Surely our ancestors have no right to determine *that completely* how we must live centuries later.

Thus it is possible for certain clauses concerning amendment processes in a constitution to violate norms of natural justice, natural law, or moral principles for legal orders. The ideal of democracy says that in such cases, the people's inherent primary sovereignty entitles them, as a last resort if necessary, to ignore or summarily alter the Constitution's provisions, including those concerning amendment. To say otherwise is to accept a tyranny of generations long past.

But we may hope that in our case, this extraordinary resort to extra-legal means of amendment will not be necessary. A last resort cannot be used before we have made a serious attempt to use all the legal remedies available under our current system to fix the Constitution of the United States of America. The amendments outlined in the next two chapters are presented with exactly that hope in mind.

Chapter Two

SOLUTIONS I: THE TOP TEN AMENDMENTS TO REDUCE POLARIZATION AND MAKE OUR GOVERNMENT WORK

The American political landscape has changed dramatically in recent years. Many social conditions have improved during the last four decades. Child poverty rates have come down, and over 91% of Americans had some medical insurance during all of 2021 (up from 84% in 2010). Americans have collectively worked on reducing bullying in schools, domestic violence, harassment in workplaces, and denigration or exclusion on the basis of race and (more recently) sexual orientation. These are all examples of progress. But partly in response to these social changes, and goaded by media algorithms that profit from cultivating fear and loathing, political preferences have become ever more sharply polarized. Our major political parties have grown more uncompromising—two changes that feed into each other in a vicious cycle. People increasingly avoid political debate with anyone who is not likeminded because it has become too uncomfortable or stressful; this is driving political segregation as Americans increasingly seek to live and work where their political views are predominant.

In this situation, no president or political party can do much to help the US move forward simply by winning an election, even by a large margin. A decade ago, Thomas Mann (a moderately left-wing scholar) and Nicholas Ornstein (moderately right) partnered to diagnose the problems. They noted that highly polarized parties make it much harder to get results in a system with many checks and balances like ours. Thus in Obama's first term, hyper-partisanship resulted in unbending obstructionism, "the virtual disappearance of regular order from Congress" (which arguably began in 2007) and dramatic declines in "legislative productivity"[1]—trends that have continued ever since. Mann and Ornstein point to several factors driving the intense polarization: separate media bubbles, perverse incentives to reduce turnout, gerrymandering that reduces the number of competitive districts, closed primaries with generally low turnout, the lack of runoff mechanisms in winner-take-all elections, election funding that is held hostage by large donors and lobbies, and unlimited spending on political advertising.[2]

In this chapter. I offer proposals to fix these and other related institutional problems that are paralyzing our government. A single party usually holds the presidency and both chambers of Congress only for two years of any president's time in office. This was true for Clinton, Obama, Trump, and (so far) for Biden. Over the 54 years from 1969 through 2023, there were only 18 years in which the same party held the Oval Office, the House, and the Senate. It is sometimes said that this shows Americans *want* divided government. On contrary, we get divided government because our electoral systems naturally favor it, no matter what the people want.[3] We will review several examples of this (see #4, #8, and #24).

There is an extra obstacle to consider too. In the same 54 years, there was only one *three-month period* (during 2009) in which the same political party controlled the presidency, the House of Representatives, and 60 out of 100 senators—the threshold required for most legislation to overcome filibusters, bring debate to an end, and force a final vote in the Senate.[4] Even then, after his landslide mandate in the 2008 elections, Obama had great difficulty getting enough Democrats in Congress to agree on a single health care bill. Because his long efforts to negotiate led to no Republican votes, every Democratic senator was crucial. As a result, all could—and a few did—hold 'Obama-Care' hostage to extract unrelated benefits for their states.

Thus an eight-year presidency following a landslide initial victory almost came legislatively to nothing beyond an economic stimulus bill to reverse the steep recession of early 2009. To avoid the situation that Obama faced, a president would probably need at least 63 or 64 loyal senators, which is an unimaginably high hurdle today. We remain stuck in what one recent study called "the zone of legislative death" where neither party can ever win a functional filibuster-proof majority.[5]

Our government is often divided in part because we have close presidential races. That is not surprising by itself: game theory predicts that in a system with two dominant political parties, they will usually adjust what they stand for to bring them just above 51% of the vote; to gain more than this, they would have to sacrifice priorities that a majority of their voters favor.[6] This means that we have frequent changes in party control of government, which in itself is good for democracy. But without large margins, the filibuster becomes deadly, as Democrats discovered again in 2021–2022.

Divided government might still be workable if compromise was frequent, but the factors driving polarization now work against this. For example, despite offering many concessions, Biden was unable to win a single Republican vote for his "human infrastructure" bill in 2021. The polarization also reduces legislators' incentives to check overreach or even blatant corruption by a president of their own party: instead, party loyalty becomes everything.[7] This in turn feeds further extremism among the electorate, as I argued in the previous chapter.

To get out of the vicious cycle and overcome partisan gridlock, our highest priority must be to break the two-party stranglehold, which is the worst among all developed democracies,[8] and alter the present incentives not to compromise.[9] And our second highest priority must be to rid ourselves of excessive anti-majoritarian obstacles that have been *added over and above* the basic checks, balances, and divisions of powers in the original design of our government—to the point of making our legislature nearly useless. Unless we want to collapse into anarchy or become a parliamentary democracy without significant states' rights, we must make our federal system work.

∞

This chapter will review 10 changes to our Constitution that are essential to restoring effective government and preserving our democratic processes. They are all *procedural* changes affecting how law and policy are made, adjudicated, and understood by citizens, although #10 includes some substantive conditions. The first six proposals focus on making our political parties more representative and constraining them to govern in the interests of the nation as a whole rather than mainly serving special interest groups. After fixing our parties and elections, the most urgent reforms include two basic changes to Congress, staggered term limits for Supreme Court justices, and a straightforward way to insulate Americans from the tsunami of lies, misinformation, and knowledge deficits that are turning otherwise good people toward violence.

I say little immediately about how these amendments could actually be passed: that vital topic is mostly left for Chapter Four. But the need for fundamental reform in most of these 10 areas is already widely recognized, and several of these proposals could be relatively easy to pass if they are explained well to the public. Throughout, I will refer to such amendments as "low-hanging fruit." The three reforms concerning voting rights, the Senate filibuster, and the structure of the House might be somewhat more difficult to pass. But the hardest constitutional reforms, given entrenched partisan dogmas, are addressed in Chapter Three.

The present chapter is divided into sections on each proposed amendment, which are numbered sequentially throughout the book. Each section is also structured slightly differently, given the nature of its topic, but the basic format is similar: I offer background on the problem, including some historical context; an explanation of why the problem cannot be fully solved without a constitutional change; a proposed amendment; and a cross-section of other proposed fixes, with their strengths and weaknesses.

Usually the precise language of an amendment is not crucial; the basic idea or gist is enough. But when specific formulations are essential for clarity, I will indicate generally how they should go. Readers should remember that in virtually every case, my particular proposal has close cousins that would be almost as good or good enough. *What matters most is the spirit rather than the letter of each proposed amendment*—and that we recognize the problems to be solved. The main procedural goal is to make elections and political parties work for the common good.

1. Ranked Choice Voting: The End of Two-Party Domination

The presidential election of 2020 was certainly a wild ride. The massive increase in mail ballots during the pandemic delayed complete results and opened the door to many spurious charges of ballot theft and voter fraud. But the election of 2000 remains even more astonishing. On the evening of November 7, as George W. Bush's lead in Florida shrank to under a couple thousand votes, it became apparent that a recount would be necessary in the state. Although Al Gore had won over half a million more votes nationally, the outcome in Florida would determine who won the Electoral College (EC) and thus the White House.

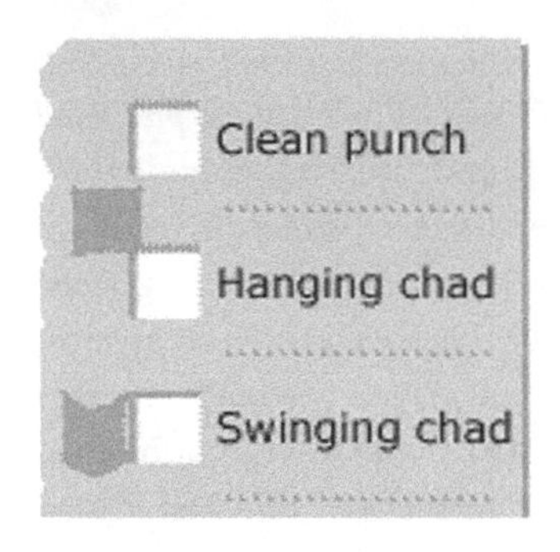

A long series of legal battles over that recount featured fierce debates about how to interpret poorly designed punchcard ballots that voters had only poked most of the way through—the so-called "hanging chads"—and ballots excluded for other errors caused by terrible ballot format. It ended when the Supreme Court stopped the recount in mid-process, with Bush a mere 537 ahead out of over 5.3 million votes cast by Florida residents. This shocking decision gave Bush all of Florida's electoral votes, which made him the next president.

RCV Illustrated. This divisive outcome in Florida is often held up as an example of the EC's basic injustice: it gives more weight to voters in small-population states, because they can have no fewer than three electors. Bush won more of the smallest states, which gave him the number needed to make Florida decisive (see #12).[10]

Yet the bigger problem on display in the Florida race is the way our system awards all the state's presidential electors to a candidate winning a *mere plurality* of votes, i.e. the largest share, even if that is less than 50%. The same thing has happened in many close House and Senate races in recent years. It can be easily fixed with a method commonly known as "ranked choice voting" (RCV) or "instant runoff" that is used for elections in Australia, and for some elections in Maine, Alaska, and a handful of US cities.

We can illustrate how this solution works by considering voters for smaller alternative parties in Florida's 2000 race.[11] When the recount was stopped on December 12, Ralph Nader had received 97,421 votes as the Green Party candidate in Florida. Pat Buchanan, the hard-right isolationist Reform Party candidate, received 17,484, while Harry Browne (Libertarian) received 16,415. Within this mix, roughly 24,000 people registered as Democrats in Florida voted for Nader. It is a very conservative bet that at least half of them would have ranked Al Gore as their second choice, if given that chance. We can safely stipulate the same for at least a quarter of Nader voters who were not registered Democrats. So let's assume that 31% of all Nader voters would have ranked Gore second. Let's also imagine that a full third of Buchanan and Brown voters would have ranked Bush as their second choice.

In this simplified scenario,[12] when neither Gore nor Bush won a majority of the (actually counted) Florida presidential ballots, which only recorded voters' first choices, the most common type of RCV—namely the instant runoff system—would eliminate the candidate with the *lowest number of first-choice votes* (in this case, Browne). It would transfer these ballots to second-choice candidates (if any) selected on them by Browne voters, thereby boosting Bush's numbers. Then Buchanan, with the next lowest vote tally, would be eliminated. Ballots cast by Buchanan voters would be transferred to

Table 2.1 Imaginary Ranked Choice Vote in Florida's 2000 Presidential Election

Florida 2000 Ballots	First-Choice Picks	Second-Choice Picks on Same Ballot	Votes Added in Later Rounds	Total
Gore	2,912,253		30,355	2,942,608
Bush	2,912,790		11,187	2,923,977
Nader	97,488	30,355 for Gore		
Buchanan	17,484	5,770 for Bush		
Browne	16,415	5,417 for Bush		
Total	5,956,430			

their stated second choices—most likely Bush. But these two transfers would still leave Bush with only 49% of the Florida vote.

So, finally, the system would reallocate Nader ballots to their casters' second choices. With 31% of them transferred to Gore, he would secure an absolute majority by a margin of 18,631 votes—over *thirty times* the margin by which Bush won the actual election. Of course, because I made up the numbers in the middle column to illustrate the ranked choice method, it is possible that in real life, more second-choice votes could have been cast for Bush (including by some Nader voters), thus increasing his lead. Either way though, the true wishes of third-party voters would have controlled the outcome in Florida, and thus the White House.

This system with a "single transferrable vote" is similar to holding an actual runoff election in which voters pick between the two candidates who finished highest on round 1. RCV ballots simply let voters say who they *would* choose in such a second or even a third round if their top-choice candidate came in last in the first round (or in the second round, if more than two candidates remained). This method thus combines multiple rounds into one ballot. It usually produces a majority winner, just as an actual runoff would, without the delay and costs. Even if an RCV election yields a plurality winner, it will usually increase the final margin of victory. This dramatically lowers the chance that a handful of late-arriving absentee votes or disputed ballots with problems could change the outcome in a high-stakes race.[13] So RCV *reduces controversy* and avoids court fights that make people question whether a reported outcome is reliable.

Most importantly of all, RCV allows third parties to grow without requiring a complete parliamentary system with proportional representation. Several states are now considering RCV for this reason. Democrats and Republicans have dominated almost every federal election for over a century because, without RCV or actual runoffs, to vote for third-party candidate probably means "wasting" your chance to impact the decision between the two frontrunners.

Consider the special election held in August 2022 for Alaska's one House seat, in which RCV was successfully used. Of 53,810 votes for Nick Begich (who came in third in round one), 27,053 were transferred to Sarah Palin, and 15,467 were transferred to Mary Peltola, leaving Peltola with a 51.5% margin. Thus a massive 79% of Begich voters took their new opportunity to name a second choice, and this determined the race. If Palin had convinced at least 2,621 of them who ranked Peltola second to favor her instead, then Palin would have won. These Begich voters really mattered, even though their first pick was eliminated in the first round.

Now consider Alaska's election for federal senator in November 2022. Three Republicans split much of the first-pick votes, leaving moderate Lisa Murkowski with 43.4%, just 2,015 votes ahead of hard-right Kelly Tshibaka. But many Alaskans who ranked the Democratic candidate first also put Murkowski second: she received 22,835 more votes to Tshibaka's 5,044 in the second round. Thus Murkowski finished with an absolute majority of 53.7% and a clear 18,806 vote margin of victory. There was no need for a recount, and Alaskans felt free to express their top choice, knowing they could still support Murkowski or Tshibaka as their fallback.[14] And less than 1,000 ballots suggested confusion about the RCV procedure.

By contrast, without RCV, Nader was the greatest third-party "spoiler" in recent American history. As we saw, if just 600 Nader voters had switched to Gore instead, he would have won. One chagrined Nader voter later wondered how things might have been different after the terrorist attacks on September 11, 2001, if Gore had been president. Perhaps, he thought, the US would still have gone to war in Afghanistan to stop Taliban support for al Qaeda. But we would not have invaded Iraq in 2003. Maybe, as so many Green Party voters wanted, we would even have seen an enforceable global compact on carbon and methane emissions to limit climate change by the end of Gore's presidency. And incidentally, without the massive tax cuts promoted and signed by Bush in spring 2001, the US federal debt might be half of its present size today.

This spoiler problem can hurt Republican candidates just as easily as Democratic ones. Democrats might not have won control of the Senate in 2006 if third parties in Virginia and Montana had not taken many votes from Republican candidates.[15] Similarly, the last time a third-party candidate gained a large share of the national vote in a presidential election was in 1992, when Ross Perot won almost 19%. Although this was not enough for him to win any single state (and its electors) outright, it may have helped Bill Clinton win pluralities in several states that gave him the EC—much as Nader did for Bush.[16]

This spoiler problem could impact other big elections in the near future. That is why, according to a Senate investigation, a few Republican operatives in 2016 worked to get Green Party candidates on the ballot in Wisconsin and in Pennsylvania "swing districts:" they believed the diversion of votes from Democrats to Greens could hand a plurality win to Republican candidates.[17] After all, during the 2016 presidential election, if even a third of the votes cast in Michigan for Green Party candidate Jill Stein had gone to Hillary Clinton instead, Clinton would have carried this swing state. The Russian regime clearly had the same idea; that is why it hired propagandists to post false narratives on social media sites in 2016 to support Jill Stein.[18] Similarly, a few Democratic groups tried to swing 2022 general elections in a handful of races by promoting minor party candidates who could siphon votes from official Republican nominees.[19]

Obviously, winning by tricking voters into wasting their votes is not what our framers intended. It is awful that our friends and neighbors can be manipulated in this way when they *should* be able to vote for third-party candidates without fear of helping a candidate they strongly detest (Nader was surely right about that much). A recent

Gallup poll shows that a striking 62% of Americans now say that viable third parties are needed, up sharply from 40% in 2003.[20] Over a third of Americans do not wish to register as either Republican or Democrat, even though most of them "lean" more to the left or right—and thus would probably put one of the major party candidates down as their second choice in RCV elections.

These voters are aware of the spoiler problem in current one-round plurality elections. This explains the huge gap between the number of Americans who say they would like to vote for third-party candidates and the number who actually do. Independent candidates have occasionally been elected to Congress, most recently in Maine, Vermont, and Alaska. But third parties cannot rise as national movements until the spoiler problem is fixed by instituting RCV voting processes.

If an amendment were adopted requiring RCV ballots in all federal and state elections, *at least three* dramatic improvements would rapidly be felt. First, turnout would jump because more independent-inclined voters would see participation as worthwhile. Their true preferences could now be recorded and publicized without risk, because they could also name one of the frontrunners as their second choice. Of course, some people would *only* vote for their alternative party candidate (call that candidate Smith), but many others would vote for Smith as their first choice and Jones as their second (plus possibly a third choice too). This would boost the reported first-round totals for Smith to a point that she might start getting wider attention.

Second, alternative parties would grow their strength in many districts to the point where they could actually start winning seats in Congress, thus breaking the two-party lock. Some studies have indicated that Americans actually coalesce around eight or nine distinct bundles of political views.[21] If so, this would be reflected in the range of competitive parties under RCV. More likely, 3–5 major parties would coalesce within a couple of decades according to varying positions on a small number of variables.[22] Either way, with their spoiler effect eliminated, smaller parties would quickly make many House and Senate races much more competitive and produce more "swing" states in the presidential races—even without the other reforms I recommend below.

Third, that shake-up would further increase voter registration and turnout, as election outcomes became less predictable and thus more interesting to all potential voters. A virtuous cycle would follow: rising registration and turnout among moderate voters who had given up on the old system would force Democrat and Republican candidates to court more moderate or centrist voters to win. Television channels that are currently catering to the activist wings of both major parties might even have to temper their extremism, as market incentives to address moderate party members increased. Once third-party candidates began to carry House and even Senate races, they might also become dealmakers who can broker compromise. Eventually, we might even see a grand coalition of center-left or center-right parties controlling Congress and the presidency—a complete reversal of our current trajectory.

All this would be achieved without cumbersome actual runoff elections that are held weeks after Election Day, which draw out the process, increase uncertainty, and—as Georgia voters know too well—drive a tsunami of advertising money into your phones and homes.[23]

Alternatives. I do not claim that the standard form of RCV described above is the only good alternative to our current one-round plurality elections. It has one technical problem that might rarely affect outcomes.[24] Eliminating the last-place finisher works well when it helps choose among two candidates who enter the general election as already frontrunners by large margins (as with Gore and Bush in 2000, or Murkowski and Tshibaka in 2022). But when three or four major candidates split the vote more evenly, the outcome turns on which of them happens to be the first choice of fewest number of voters, perhaps by a small margin.

The same issue has existed for centuries with actual runoffs. Consider the recent mayoral race in Boston, in which supporters of three black candidates among five total candidates split their vote widely: as a result, none of these black candidates placed among the top two in the actual runoff election that followed.[25] Similarly, standard RCV is not ideal in rare cases in which one candidate is the second favorite of a strong majority of voters but few voters' first choice. This candidate A may lose even though a majority prefers A over B in a two-way race, while a different majority prefers A over C if they went head to head. A would then beat B and C in a "round-robin" tournament by winning two contests between *pairs*. Such a round-robin winner is also called a "Condorcet winner," after the Marquis de Condorcet, who pioneered voting theory.[26]

This problem can be avoided by programming the computer that collects the voters' rank-ordered preferences to identify the candidate who would win a round-robin series. The machine does this in the first round by comparing the *two* candidates who get the least first-place votes and eliminating the one of these who was ranked lower by more voters over all. It then reassigns ballots for the eliminated candidate—and so on in the next automated rounds. For instance, in our initial example from 2000, this system would look at how Buchanan and Browne were ranked *relative to each other* before eliminating one of them, rather than just eliminating Brown for having the least first-place votes.[27]

However, this alternative itself needs a couple tweaks. First, in small electorates, occasionally a Condorcet winner does not exist because ties are possible: ballots could indicate that A, B, and C would *each win one* of the matchups between pairs. In that case, the system could revert to the standard-method RCV system that Alaska uses.[28] Second, an instant round-robin vote tabulation works well only if most voters rank-order all or most of the candidates. But many voters might not want to rank-order more than 2 (or have clear preferences beyond this). For example, a lot of voters in Florida 2000 would have only ranked Browne first and Bush second, or Buchanan first and Bush second; far less would have ranked Browne *and* Buchanan along with Bush. To deal with this, the system could eliminate candidates who are not ranked at all by over two-thirds (or three quarters) of voters, before figuring the round-robin winner.

Finally, such Condorcet methods are harder for voters to understand. Imagine, for example, a process in which every candidate but the Condorcet winner and runner-up are eliminated, and ballots ranking any of the eliminated candidates first are transferred to whichever Condorcet frontrunner (if either) their casters ranked higher on those ballots after their first choice. This may be a superior method, but it is tough to grasp.

"Cumulative" voting systems, in which each voter has more than one vote to allocate, offer another way to reduce the spoiler problem in single-member districts.[29] They can increase the number of legislators from minority backgrounds when voters from minority groups care very much about electing someone from the same demographic groups as themselves.[30] But they can also give voters strategic incentives to allocate votes in ways that hide their true preferences.

Overall, experts on voting systems find that there is no absolutely perfect method; each fulfill some, but not all, intuitive criteria for fairness in voting, including being easy to grasp.[31] But standard RCV is the simplest alternative to our current one-round plurality elections, as Alaska has shown. It should be the default, before states try out its superior but more complex variations down the road.

A Proposal and Objections. The main lesson is that our current plurality winner system is utterly out-of-date. This much is the consensus finding of virtually every expert on voting theory. If our founders had known everything that the social science of elections has taught us in the last century, they would not have allowed our current system in federal elections. We embrace ultra-hightech medicines and procedures for our physical health. Why then would we stick with an 18th-century balloting method that was adopted before its problems were understood? To do better, we have only to educate Americans about the alternatives that have been designed by election theorists.

The constitutional amendment should require states to move away from single-round plurality winner voting in both federal and state elections. States could choose between standard RCV and methods that improve on it with a round-robin (Condorcet) component. Voters must be allowed to rank at least three candidates. Otherwise the two dominant parties will collude to block the rise of third parties, as they have for decades by banning "fusion" candidates cross-nominated by two or more parties—and federal courts will let them do it.

Against this, critics argue that, once two parties cannot monopolize the political landscape, radical minor parties with destructive ideologies may gain visibility. And it is true that small radical parties can gain a foothold in parliamentary systems using proportional representation if there are no bottom thresholds (e.g. 8%–10%) to win *any* seats in parliament. However, my proposal is not to abandon single-member congressional or statehouse districts for multimember districts (see #4). But even if a state created districts with (say) three representatives elected by finishing first, second, and third out of a large pool, the law could eliminate candidates polling less than 10% by the end of the second automated round. Neither Communist nor Execute-all-Immigrants parties are going to grow to the point of winning outright in many races decided by any version of RCV.

As an added benefit, RCV elections would require many states to improve their voting machines and any paper ballots read by machines, so that the reassignment of ballots to second choices when needed can be done seamlessly. This alone would have prevented the design flaws that led to over 175,000 ballots not being counted in Florida's 2000 election—over 325 times the margin of victory! If we supplement the automatic runoff with uniform federal standards for voting (see #6), the results will become even more reliable and representative.

One might object that the federal government can mandate RCV by ordinary statute, just as it could create national standards for registration and ballot design by law. But unfortunately this will not work for two reasons. First, the two-party system is the basis of legislators' job security: while it makes them less responsive to a majority of constituents, it also makes their life easier. Second, even if by some miracle Congress passed a national RCV law, the Supreme Court could well overturn it. The Court has held that states control most aspects of their election processes and have a lot of discretion in how they format ballots and aggregate votes—as long as they do not violate the one-person-one-vote standard.[32]

The Court has also allowed states to keep small parties off the ballot or to prevent viable candidates—who received well beyond 10% or 15% of all primary votes cast for all candidates—from appearing in televised debates. It's as if the Court reads the Constitution as mandating or preferring a two-party system, even though it actually says nothing about political parties at all.

An amendment, then, is the only secure way to fix the spoiler problem and end two-party dominance. The amendment could specify that state governments will manage election processes: it would only mandate that all states adopt some version of RCV (the standard runoff by lowest elimination or its superior variants) and give candidates with some proven level of popular support equal treatment. An amendment is also far better than waiting for different states to adopt RCV one by one: that might weaken one of our two main parties in some states while leaving the other in total command in other states. The only fair solution is to ensure that all voters have *the same* opportunity everywhere to support third parties without helping a candidate they oppose by backing a spoiler like Nader, Perot, or Stein.

2. Rotate the Early Primary Elections between All States

We have primary elections so that voters, rather than political bosses and their cronies, can select their party's standard bearers for each office in the general election. Political parties are essential for democracy in a massive society like ours: when rightly structured, they provide many benefits. As Tarunabh Khaitan says, well-functioning parties act as bidirectional intermediaries between government and the general public, and thereby lower four key types of "information and transaction costs," including "political participation costs, voter' information costs, policy packaging costs, and ally prediction costs."[33]

In lay terms, parties vet potential candidates, think through policy options, and help citizens determine how they might best coordinate with other citizens for shared goals by organizing flexible coalitions. Parties thereby aggregate tons of information for voters who could not research even 1% of all this information on their own. This is why, as even Madison admitted in his later years, political parties arise naturally within democracies and are essential to its operation on a mass scale.

The problem is that our Constitution does not direct and constrain political parties: the founders did not anticipate their rise, and framers of later amendments were themselves party leaders. In this respect, a central feature of the Constitution was out-of-date within a decade after it was ratified. The result is that political parties operate according to 50 different states' laws, which in turn are limited by Supreme Court decisions on freedom of association and campaign spending (see #5). The great freedom parties enjoy makes it hard to prevent collective action problems that distort party functioning.

This constitutional lacuna underlies two big problems with our primary elections: the "front-loading" effect and the way that low turnout in primaries empowers the most zealous or militant Republican and Democratic "base" voters. The first problem especially impacts the presidential race, while the second pushes incumbents in Congress toward the extremes in order to avoid primary challengers who might get support from single-issue interest groups and fanatics. The first problem is relatively easy to fix, but the second is somewhat harder to correct (so I'll save that for the next section).

Front-loading is not a problem unique to elections. In his bestselling book *Who Gets What—and Why*, Nobel prize-winning economist Alvin Roth describes several cases in which market efficiency unravels and leads to suboptimal results because some participants "jump the gun" by trying to buy, trade, or seal a deal before competitors can enter the market. You may have seen this on "Shark Tank," but Roth's examples range from absurd to damaging and infuriating. Federal judges trying to hire clerks from top law schools ignore rules that establish a common calendar and make "exploding" offers that candidates have to accept or reject on the spot. The NCAA tries to prevent groups organizing popular bowl games from signing up college teams before late November; but teams kept signing contracts earlier anyway before their rankings are clear. Electronic traders spend millions on cables that are nanoseconds faster than their competition's wires.

Without a rule to restrict people from transacting before rivals can compete, everyone can end up worse off. Roth describes one polygamous tribe of aboriginal people in Australia who had to betroth their unborn grandchildren—future children of their infant children—to ensure them an adequate opportunity for a good match.[34]

Consider in this light our crazy calendar for primary elections during presidential years: states keep trying to move their primary date earlier to one-up other states, thereby elongating the campaigning season, which now starts more than year in advance for the presidency. As Caroline Tolbert describes, the national parties tried to control this "race to the front" by denying or reducing delegates for any state that held its primary election before February 5. But Iowa, New Hampshire, Florida, and South Carolina pushed their primaries earlier anyway.[35] Eventually, a temporary compromise took hold for the first seven races in 2020:

Table 2.2 Primary Election Dates in 2020

Feb. 3	Iowa (caucuses)
Feb. 11	New Hampshire
Feb. 22	Nevada caucus (Democrat only)
Feb. 29	South Carolina
March 1	Wyoming presidential primary caucus (Republican only)
March 3	Alabama, Arkansas, California, Colorado, Maine, Massachusetts, Minnesota, North Carolina, Oklahoma, Tennessee, Texas, Utah, Vermont, Virginia
March 10	Idaho, Michigan, Mississippi, Missouri, North Dakota, Washington

The pattern is clear: to be viable past early March, presidential candidates must win some of the first five states, and then seal the deal when 14 states (count them!) all vote on Super Tuesday. After that, even the next 6 states whose elections are held a week later are largely a formality: candidates without a lot of delegates after Super Tuesday cannot secure enough big donor funding and small contributions from ordinary citizens to advertise and tour in the next states.

Thus in recent presidential elections, the Democratic and Republican frontrunners have largely secured by the nomination once Super Tuesday voting is complete. Voters see this, and so turnout in primary elections after Super Tuesday drops precipitously, which affects down-ballot races for the House and Senate, and state elections as well.[36]

The result is that Iowa, New Hampshire, Nevada, South Carolina, and Wyoming have enormous advantages over all other states in presidential elections. In addition to bringing in millions of dollars in extra business, the primary calendar gives them far more influence over presidential elections. Although mass media coverage is also key, one study of the 2004 Democratic primaries found that early primary voters had five times (500%) more influence in deciding between John Kerry and Howard Dean.[37]

That all of us in the other 45 states have tolerated this outrage for so long is a good indicator of the institutional inertia that makes people assume that we just have to put up with big procedural injustices. We don't. As Larry Sabato says of IA and NH, "[t]hese two states seem to assume that the Constitution guarantees that they should go first," but actually it says nothing about primary elections. Why, he asks, "should two small, heavily white, disproportionately rural states have a hammerlock" on presidential nominations? As one irate commentator noted in 2020, the combined population of IA and NH is smaller than Kansas City, Missouri.[38] Even by March 10, a week after Super Tuesday, only *three* larger and more diverse coastal states had voted in 2020.

But the solution is not more competition among states. Already IA and NH look likely to move their primaries into January for 2024. MI, GA, and NY are trying to move their primaries into February, and more states aim to get into Super Tuesday as well.[39] By the 2028 election season, we might see IA and NH holding their primaries in December 2027. To end this absurdity and shorten the election period, we need a constitutional amendment guided by basic fairness (see Desideratum 6): "Every state and region ought to have essentially an equal chance, over time, to influence the outcome of parties' presidential nominations."[40]

Although it is tempting to write an amendment saying that IA and NH cannot hold their primaries before June 30 for the next century, the best solution is a rotation in which states are divided into four or five regions that take turns holding the earliest primaries. A single primary per region, with a couple weeks between regions, would give candidates, their teams, and journalists more opportunity to spend longer within each region, meeting more residents in smaller venues. How many regions? Three would make the regions too large for campaigns to interact with people at local levels. Still, the first two or three regional results are likely to have a nearly decisive influence on large party nominations, which is a reason not to make six or more.

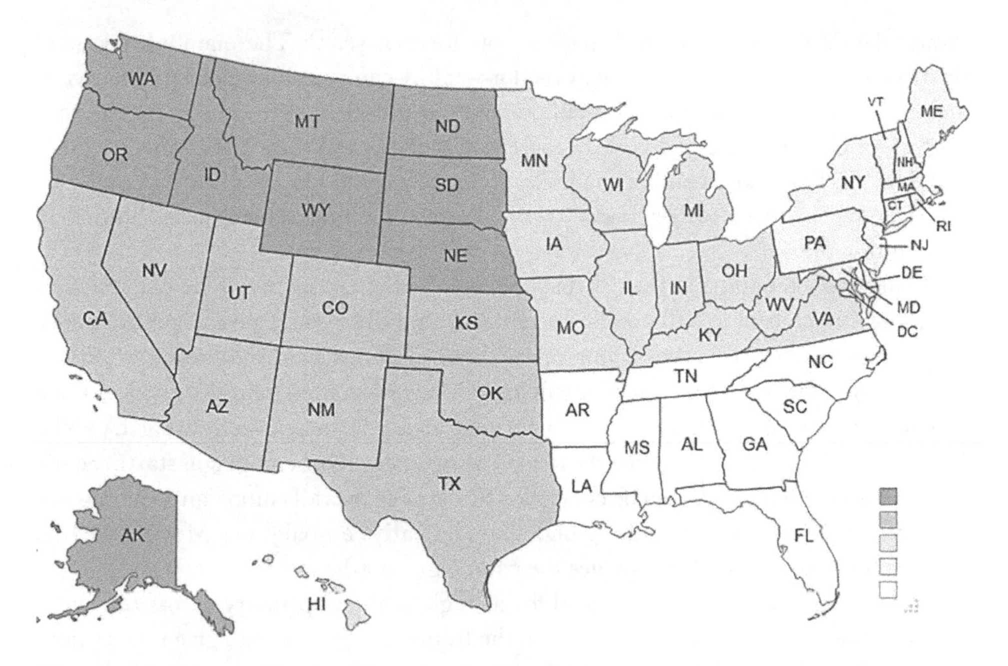

Figure 2.1 Primary Elections Rotating by Five Regions

I favor five regions of 9–11 states each: the Northwest (including Alaska), Southwest (including Hawaii), the Midwest, Southeast, and Northeast (see Figure 2.1). The amendment should list states in each region, with a provision for new states, to prevent any party that later controls Congress from altering the schedule for some imagined strategic advantage.

The first primary date could be set for the Saturday closest to April 2, reducing the time and expense of big campaigns. The subsequent dates could follow on three-week intervals ending around June 25. The party conventions could then occur in late July or August. Others have suggested even more compressed schedules beginning in May.

The amendment should also set a rotation so that each region goes first (and another last) once in every five presidential election years. The relative order of states would stay fixed during the three years after each presidential election. For example, in 2028 the Northwest could vote first, followed by the Midwest, Northeast, and so on in clockwise order. After four years, each region would move up in the rotation, with the region that voted second in 2028 going first in 2032. So in my illustration, in 2032, the Midwest would vote first on April 2, followed by the Northeast on April 23, and then the Southeast three weeks later, followed by the Southwest. Finally the Northwest, having voted first in 2028, would vote last in June of 2032. In 2036, the Northeast would vote first, followed by the Southeast, and so on.

Alternatives. Sabato, after collaboraton with other experts, suggests a similar division into four regions. Although 12–13 states is a lot of ground for candidates to cover before each regional primary election, this system is a workable possibility. However, he also argues that on each presidential election year, *a lottery* (held around January 1) should decide the order in which regions vote for that year.[41] The main advantage of this idea would be to make it harder even for wealthy campaigns to mount a lot of visits and events during the summer and fall prior to our presidential election years—as they now routinely do in IA and NH. Because campaigns would not know which regions will hold the first and second primary elections, they could not jump the gun and start campaigning in them earlier, and thereby elongate the full election to an absurd 15 months or more.

That is a good point, but the risk that one region might go eight presidential elections or more without its lotto ball popping up first, or that the same region might by chance get to vote first in two out of four presidential elections in a row, would diminish the perceived fairness of the amendment and reduce its chances of ratification. A fixed rotation guarantees each state its chance, once every 20 years, to do what IA, NH, NV and SC do now in winnowing the field. The prospect of big campaigns starting early in the first-voting region could be controlled by capping overall campaign spending (see amendment #5), or even by putting high taxes on early campaigning. Moving the first primary into April would also reduce the campaign length.

Some commentators argue instead for a single national primary across the entire country. But that is not necessary to solve the front-loading problem, given the options just described. It would doubtless increase turnout a lot, but at the price of eliminating valuable opportunities for less well-known candidates running smaller campaigns to rise through early primaries, as others are winnowed out. A single national primary would afford potential voters no chance to learn from the earlier primary races and their results.[42]

In one national primary, candidates would also have to mount all-out nationwide campaigns from the start, relying entirely on advertising blitzes and big rallies rather than smaller events, including direct contact with residents in early-primary states. This would favor the richest and already famous candidates, shutting out younger contenders and aggravating the outsized influence that wealthy donors have on the primary process.[43] In fact, holding a single national primary in the spring would merely turn it into the first round of a general election, with the November election then functioning as a runoff. There is no need for that once we have RCV in the November vote (see #1).

3. Open or Semi-Open Primary Elections: End Control by the Extreme Wings

The previous proposal for regional primaries with a fair rotation schedule would, if enacted, increase turnout substantially, especially in the regions voting first and second in a given presidential year. That's crucial: only about 33% of registered Americans voted in the 2020 primary elections, and that was the highest in decades.[44]

Even in presidential years, the most radical 20%–25% of registered Democrats and Republicans increasingly control the Congressional and presidential primary election outcomes, driving candidates toward the extremes and making legislative compromise less feasible when Congress meets. Given the effects on the nation, it is shocking to realize that only around 9% of Americans voted for either Trump or Clinton in the 2016 primaries.[45] This is explained by low turnout driven by the dominance of early primaries, the lack of RCV balloting, and the plurality winner taking all delegates in some states. Republican voters who disliked Trump largely split their votes between Governor John Kasich, Ben Carson, and Senators Cruz and Rubio. If even half of them had favored (say) Rubio as their second choice in primaries with RCV ballots, Rubio would have won 4.13 million votes to Trump's 3.38 million by the end of Super Tuesday.[46]

Because so many House and Senate seats are now "a lock" for one of the two dominant parties (see Figure 2.2), partly as a result of gerrymandering (see #4), the primary election becomes crucial in those districts and states. That's how we get Republican legislators who are unwilling to control drug costs to the point of blocking a cap on insulin prices for anyone not on Medicare (they did this during the passage of the Inflation Reduction Act in September 2022). It's also how we get Democratic legislators who support a mandatory single-payer health care system, rather than a "public option," that would allow people to keep their employer-paid health insurance. A desire to compromise with the strongly held convictions of other groups in order to get legislation done is not a serious concern for such candidates.

For such reasons, some political scientists suggest giving more influence to party leaders in selecting general election candidates, because they tend to "prefer moderate candidates over ideological ones."[47] Maybe "smoke-filled rooms" were not so bad, my family friend comments. But that also has its own risks, including keeping strong concerns among portions of the public bottled up and festering, out of view in national politics. I have no objection to leaders having a bloc of votes at their party's convention, but resisting the drive toward extremes also requires boosting primary turnout by broadening eligibility to vote in primary races. There are several possible ways to do this. In evaluating four main options,[48] we should look for one that maintains the idea of party as a political association but reduces the "barriers to entry" for new voters.

Four Options. (I) As the primary election currently works in most states, you can only vote in the primary for the party in which you registered a significant time prior

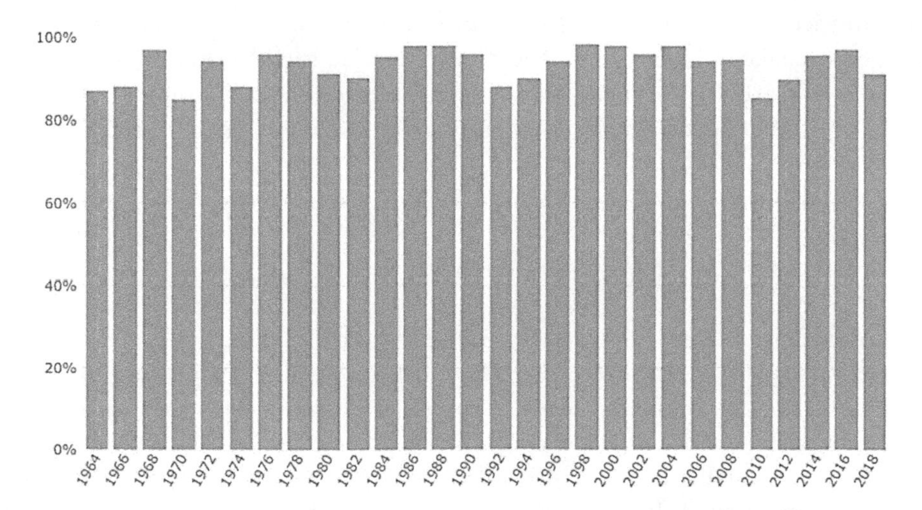

Figure 2.2 US House Reelection Rates

to the primary election date. But many Americans register to vote without affiliating with either of the big parties: a late 2021 Gallup poll found that fully 42% of voters identify as independent, although many may lean more Republican or more Democrat. That is a lot of independents who were at least uncertain about party affiliation when they registered and/or whose natural party "home" may be foreclosed by the two-party duopoly. They should have a voice in primary elections, especially when their House district and/or state is dominated by one of the big parties.

For example, if you are a Democrat resident in Idaho, which is heavily Republican overall, you can predict that the Republican nominee for an open Senate seat is very likely to win. Although your party affiliation matters to you, the Republican primary becomes the main event for such a "safe" seat—much as the Democratic primary for mayor of New York City was the decisive race for that office in 2021. The more heavily red or blue districts we have for Congress, state legislatures, and city government, the more primary elections become crucial.

In recent years, some states and localities have tried alternative primary systems to find a better way. The many permutations can get confusing, especially because the terminology is not totally standardized. It's helpful to distinguish the types, whatever we call them, by their main components.

(I) The traditional system in which you select among candidates who got on the ballot for your registered party (subject to state rules) is a "closed" primary.

(II) By contrast, an "open primary" usually refers to an election system in which

(i) a voter V who is *not* registered as a member of party P, because they are registered as independent or as a member of another party Q, can still opt to vote in P's primary.

(ii) without V having to register as a new member of the P party when voting;

(iii) but each voter can only vote in *one* party's primary race each election year.

This would obviously help Democrats in deep red districts and Republicans in deep blue districts to have a real influence, thereby promoting more moderate general election candidates. That is also true if, reversing (ii), such "crossover" voters must register with party P on primary election day in order to vote in P's primary. According to Ballotpedia, in 21 states, at least one party uses one of these "open" methods.

(III) A "semi-open" (or "semi-closed") primary is like an open primary except that condition (i) is more restrictive: (i*) only voters who are registered as independent can cross over to vote in party P's primary.

For example, if Mr. V (a voter) previously registered with party Q, he could not decide at the polls, or when receiving a mail ballot, to vote in P's primary instead of Q's. To do that, he would first need to re-register as independent some time before the primary election day or before a mail ballot is sent to him. States allow particular variations, but usually semi-open primaries also require that (ii*) once an unaffiliated voter V votes in party P's primary, they are registered as a P-voter. So, given (i*),

V cannot vote in Q's primary next time without first re-registering. Some states, e.g. California, have at times allowed each party to choose between open, semi-open, or closed primaries (see Figure 2.3).

(IV) There are also "blanket primaries" in which condition (iii) is altered so that any voter V can vote for one primary candidate C for each office on the ballot, regardless of V or C's party affiliations. For example, suppose V is a Democrat. In the primary, V can (if she wants) choose among several Democratic candidates for senator, and among several Republican candidates running for V's House district, and among Green Party candidates for governor. It sounds complicated; yet it is not hard for a well-programmed voting machine to keep track of such votes.

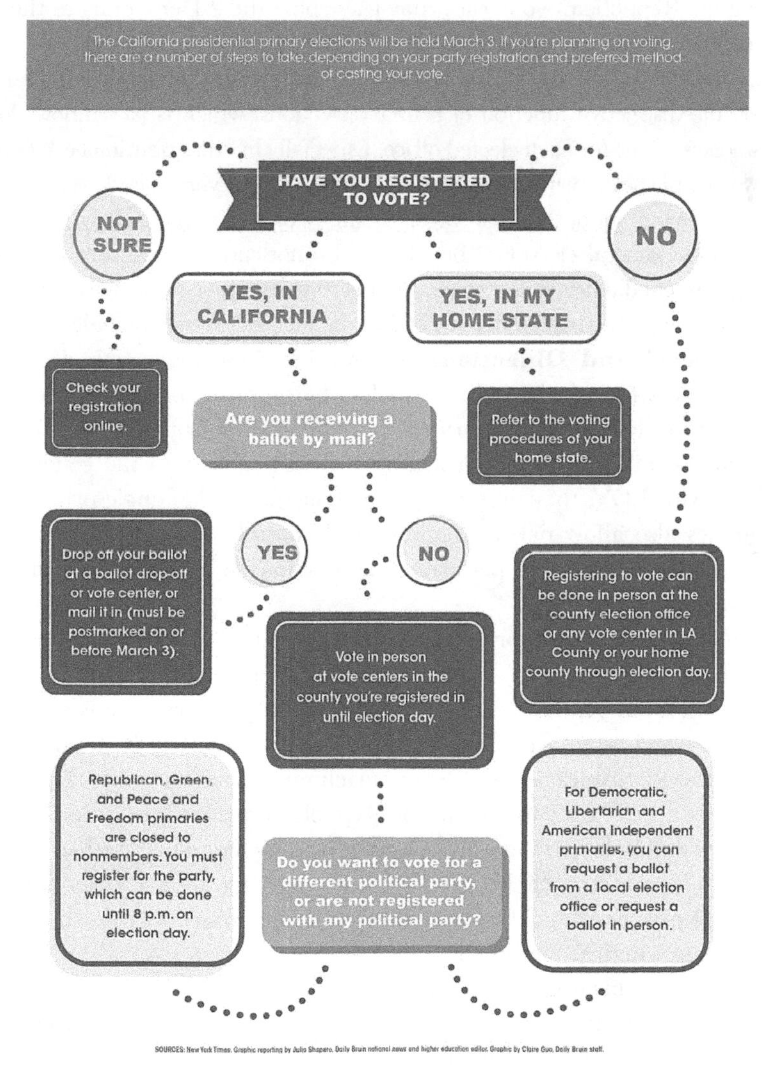

Figure 2.3 How to Vote in a Primary Election

The Supreme Court in 2001 rejected that blanket system, which had been used in California and Washington, as a violation of people's rights to free association in a party that can exclude nonmembers. But, oddly, the Court allowed Louisiana's *nonpartisan* top-two primary, in which the two candidates receiving the highest number of primary votes for a given office—regardless of their party—advance a runoff election if no one wins an outright majority for that office in round 1.[49] This is one version of so-called "jungle primaries," in which voters winnow out some *or all* candidates from each party. So in a top-two jungle primary, for example, the general election may only feature one Libertarian and one Republican, or two Democrats, for a given office.

Jungle primaries can be bad for at least three reasons. First, the ballots sometimes do not even tell voters what the party affiliations of candidates are. Second, they still have the spoiler problem. Imagine that 2 Democrats and 4 Republicans are running. By dividing the Republican vote, they may leave only the 2 Democrats in the top two places to compete in the general election.[50]

Third, a top-two jungle primary turns the general election into a runoff, and thereby gives up on the distinctive function of primary elections, which is to winnow down *each party's* candidates to one for each elected office. Especially in areas dominated by one party, the top-two nonpartisan primary will usually have the perverse result that third-party candidates are closed out of the final stage.[51] Some reformers suggest allowing the top *three* to proceed to the general election,[52] but this is also not enough to ensure a spectrum of alternative party candidates in the general election: voters may see only two Republicans and one Democrat (or the inverse) for key offices on the general election ballot.

The Proposal and Objections. Comparing these four methods, the jungle primary method is trying and failing to solve the problem that RCV is designed to fix. The open or semi-open primaries are less confusing but still encourage larger participation and allow a broad spectrum of small parties into the general election stage (where, with RCV, they pose no spoiler danger). Unlike jungle primaries, semi-open primaries also allow parties some level of control over their membership and candidates, which they need to perform their functions of gathering information and enabling collective action.

The main criticism of open primaries is that they can enable voters strongly aligned with party P to "raid" party Q's primary race in order to help elect a weak nominee for Q—a "poison pill" candidate. For example, if the primary race is close between a moderate law-and-order Republican (A) and a fire-breathing Republican (B) who promotes election conspiracies and wants to eliminate all social welfare programs, Democrats might cross over to vote in the Republican primary in order to nominate B, who will probably lose the general election to a Democrat. Or when a moderate Democrat has a primary challenger who advocates for totally open borders and abolition of all prisons, Republicans might raid that primary to help this non-viable far-left candidate win the nomination.

While that is technically possible, there seems to be little evidence so far that such raiding has happened to a large extent in open primaries. Still, in an age of mobs coordinated by social media propaganda, we should not entirely discount that possibility. Crossover is more likely if a major party P runs a candidate C who is utterly detested by eligible voters affiliated with other parties: some of them might then try to influence P's choice of nominee *to veto* that particular candidate C. That could happen spontaneously, whereas it would take a lot of coordination to raid P's primary in order to prevent P's most electable candidate from winning P's nomination.

The semi-open system is able to reduce these sorts of crossover threats. Few people would be organized enough to keep changing a party affiliation that resulted from voting in the last semi-open primary. The semi-open primary still reduces control by the fanatical party bases by allowing independents a vote in states with one dominant party. However, in states where one party is especially strong, a top-*four* system like Alaska's should ensure candidates from at least three parties in the general election, but it can also allow the top two from the dominant party to reappear in general (rather than winnowing them to one).

So I suggest that our amendment should mandate that primaries (a) be held on the same day for all parties in a given state; (b) use the open, semi-open, or top-four primary system, according to each state's choice; and (c) allow federal law to make adjustments needed to curb any large level of primary raiding, when these adjustments are narrowly tailored to that end. Over time, this will boost voter participation *on top* of what RCV brings by itself and result in generally more moderate nominees being selected to represent the larger parties in the general election.

Given the difficulties of this issue, critics will surely ask, shouldn't we simply leave it to each state, as we do now? The problems with this status quo are threefold:

- increasingly radical state governments may try to tailor the primary method to help their party's perceived interests;
- and/or these state legislators may want to keep primaries closed to protect more radical candidates in their party, including themselves; and
- such state legislatures might also adopt nonpartisan blanket or top-two "jungle" primaries to appear innovative while actually keeping third parties from becoming viable.

In short, if we make no change, soon Maxine Waters and Marjorie Taylor Green will look tame by comparison with new House members. Some national standard is necessary to resist rising ideological fervor and voter alienation, and to ensure fairness across all states.

It might seem that this can be achieved by ordinary federal laws, which are also easier to change if adjustments are needed later on. Unfortunately though, that route is not sufficiently secure. The two-party duopoly in Congress might decide to mandate a top-two primary to protect their dominance and blunt the effects of RCV. Or today's ultra-politicized Supreme Court might well decide to ban open or semi-open primaries, as with blanket primaries in the past, on the specious ground that political parties are just private clubs. That's why we need an amendment that explicitly recognizes the crucial public functions and responsibilities of political parties, so courts will help ensure that they serve public interests over the private advantage of party leaders and their big funders.

This is not to disparage the importance of private civic associations in promoting collective self-governance.[53] Rather it is simply to recognize that political parties are especially crucial organizations for informing, aggregating, and channeling the political concerns of citizens and smaller associations to which they may belong. When parties massively mislead their members and destroy national goods for their own short-term benefit, they need deep reform. That time has come.

4. Fair Districting: End Gerrymandering and Make Congress More Responsive

"Gerrymandered" electoral districts may be the most hated of all American constitutional problems, but solving it still involves some difficult policy questions. Many outrageous districts have their own famous names: the Earmuffs, the Octopus and Serpent, Goofy Kicking Donald Duck, and so on. This section goes beyond the weird shapes to the policy questions in a summary fashion that cuts through a lot of details—and most of the mind-boggling maps—that are usually offered to demonstrate the problem. I take this approach because the details often obscure the essential choices needed for a fair, stable, long-term solution (but more detailed explanations, including more district maps, are available on *TheDemocracyAmendments.org*).

Big Costs to the Nation. Consider three kinds of damage that gerrymandering does. (1) While I focus below on congressional elections, the effects of gerrymandering for statehouse districts are also dramatic. They allow a party controlling a slim majority in both chambers of a state legislature (a) to magnify its statehouse majority by redrawing its electoral districts, and (b) then use this enhanced control after a national census to gerrymander the state's congressional districts. A good example of this, as David Litt argues, is found in Wisconsin, where Republicans held 65% state assembly seats after the 2018 elections, even though Democrats won 53% of the votes.[54] Democrats did the same thing in Georgia during 2001.

(2) The gerrymandering of House districts then becomes a major cause of political polarization and gridlock because it produces so many "safe seats" in the general election. With district lines drawn to favor them, most House members can focus on their party base and ignore the general electorate in their districts.[55] In 2020, a *New York Times* analysis found that only 61 of the current 435 House seats were "battleground competitions"—a mere 14%. After all the gerrymandering in 2021, competitive districts are down to about 12.5% in 2022 (with only 7% being highly competitive).[56] The number would be even lower if New York had not been de-gerrymandered by state court order in 2022.

As many analysts point out, the decline in competitive districts partly reflects the "self-sorting" of Americans into bluer urban areas and redder rural areas. Even if all districts were *randomly* drawn, there would be a lot of uncompetitive ones in which people with similar political views are packed together.[57] But gerrymandering inflates the number of noncompetitive districts as they are redrawn once a decade after the national census.

Minimizing your opposition's chances by gerrymandering has become an advanced science aided by smart computer modeling.[58] For example, when they controlled the Texas statehouse, Democrats had drawn the districts to give their party 17 out of

32 congressional districts (53% of seats) in 2002, even though they received only 44% of votes.[59] By 2020, after two major rounds of gerrymanders by a Republican statehouse, Republicans won 23 out of 36 House seats (64%), even though they only received 53.4% of votes. In other words, their share of the vote dropped by almost 3 points; yet their share of seats won rose by 17 points—all due to the magic of computer-aided gerrymandering.

This technology has turned what was already a big problem into a true orgy of cheating. After the 2020 census, state governments redrew enough districts in precisely the shapes needed to flip at least five House seats *even if* turnout and voter choices had remained unchanged.[60] Everyone recognizes that this is dirty, much like tactics to rig voter registration (see #6), and it turns off moderate voters. As former Supreme Court Justice John Paul Stevens puts it, "whether liberal or conservative, candidates can be expected to adopt more extreme policies when competing within a single party" rather than against candidates from other parties.[61]

Republicans currently control more state governments and so do more gerrymandering, but Democrats also do it. For example, see Maryland's 3rd district, the "Praying Mantis," as it was in 2018 (see Figure 2.4). MD's new 2021 map was also rejected by a state court as excessively gerrymandered: it had 7 Democratic districts and 1 tossup, with no safe Republican district, although a third of MD voters are Republicans.

Figure 2.4 Maryland District 3 in 2018

(3) Gerrymandering also helps to make minority rule possible in the House of Representatives, which was intended to be controlled by the popular vote. For example, in 2012, Republicans won 53.8% of House seats while receiving 1.4 million less votes than Democrats.[62] Three times since 1950, one party has won an outright majority of all votes for House seats but still lost control of the House. This almost happened again in 2020.[63]

The American public is aware of the first two harms and is angry about them. In August 2021, the anticorruption group RepresentUS found that almost 90% of Americans disapprove of gerrymandering.[64] People can see that congressional and statehouse politicians are handpicking their voters rather than voters picking the politicians—a total inversion of democracy. Yet parties feel that, if the other side is going to gerrymander, they have to as well. In short, it is an arms race (with the structure of a "prisoner's dilemma").

The Limits of Districting Commissions and Federal Law. So then, why do we not just write an amendment mandating that independent commissions of experts handle all districting and be done with this nonsense? Such an amendment might well get ratified, and studies show that commissions generally do improve the situation. For example, California's commission has made more districts competitive in that state.[65] Currently, in 2022, only seven states give truly independent commissions the main responsibility to redraw statehouse *and* congressional district lines. In other states, the commissions are joint bodies of politicians, and/or they only draw state legislature districts, and/or they are only advisory or act as backups if the legislature fails to produce legal new maps.

Commissions can be made largely impartial if their members are selected by lottery from an expert pool or perhaps, as Sabato suggests, made up of retired judges.[66] But for this fix to be fair, we need commissions to be introduced everywhere, not in one state at a time. In 2022, California, Washington, Colorado, Arizona, and Michigan gave districting power to independent commissions, while no large red state did so.[67] And in 2014, New Yorkers passed a state constitutional amendment for fair districting, which courts enforced in 2022, reducing safe Democratic seats from 20 out of 26 to 15—enough to give Republicans control of the House in 2023–2024.[68] Thus Republican candidates now have a better chance in some large Democrat-controlled states, while Democrats' chances are minimized by unrepentant gerrymandering in all large Republican-controlled states.[69] As David Imamura argues, "[i]t cannot be that only blue states have independent redistricting processes while red states draw whatever lines they want. All states together must adopt uniform redistricting reforms."[70] Without a national standard, state-led reform amounts to unilateral disarmament by one side.

Congress *may* have the power to solve this problem by mandating independent commissions, at least for all congressional districts (if not statehouse districts). The "For the People Act" (FTP) passed by the House in 2021 would require each state's congressional districts to be approved by an independent commission made up of experts and ordinary citizens. So did Senator Joe Manchin's 2021 compromise proposal: "The commissions would each include five Democrats, five Republicans and five independents, requiring bipartisan approval for districts [...]."[71]

It would be great to solve this giant problem without needing constitutional change, but there are at least three big obstacles to that hope. First, the FTP formula for commissions would disadvantage smaller third parties. Second, a federal mandate for independent commissions would have to surmount a filibuster, which defeated the FTP and Manchin's draft bill. The same would apply to any updates needed to rein in unforeseen tactics by state governments to manipulate their state's commission (e.g. by spurious impeachments of members, etc.).

The third reason is the most shocking: the Supreme Court may soon hold that independent commissions, state courts, an even state constitutions cannot prevent a state legislature from drawing whatever congressional districts it likes. In 2015, Arizona's Republican party argued that the state's constitutional amendment (passed by a ballot initiative) creating an independent commission violates Article I, §4 of the federal Constitution, which says that "the Times, Places, and Manner of holding Elections for Senators and Representatives, shall be prescribed in each State by the Legislature thereof [...]," although Congress can "alter such Regulations." Their argument turned on a fringe theory, long rejected by most constitutional scholars, that "Legislatures" here refers only to one part of state government, giving them power "independent" of all other parts to draw district lines. The same argument would appear to allow state legislatures by themselves, without the governor's signature, to override any executive decisions made by state or county officials concerning how to count ballots under state law.

On the contrary, a lot of precedent interprets the word "Legislatures" in Article I to encompass a state's whole legislative processes,[72] because, of course, a state legislature only exists by virtue of its state constitution—and our framers typically used the term as a metonym for the state government[73] (this is an example of the vices of short constitutional text, see Desideratum 7). But AZ Republicans backing this outlandish "independent" or "absolutist" state legislature theory only lost by a 4–5 margin in a 2015 Supreme Court decision,[74] and the Court has moved farther right since then.

This theory, which may also have a major impact on presidential elections (see #12), will be tested in a pending case, *Moore* v. *Harper*, which began in 2021 when the North Carolina legislature drew new district maps and the NC supreme court rejected them for violating the state constitution. As in AZ, NC's Republican-majority legislature argued that their state courts have no right to limit their gerrymandering of congressional district lines. The Republican plaintiffs lost in lower federal courts; but in June 2022, the Supreme Court agreed to hear their appeal.[75]

Of course, this extreme tactic only increases the arms race: if the Court makes state legislatures "independent" of the rest of state government, despite 230 years of contrary interpretation, then Democratic-controlled statehouses can also destroy any and all checks and balances against gerrymandering in state law. Like NC's legislative majority, they can also use underhanded tactics to control any resistant state courts as well.[76] Even then, existing constitutional language should allow federal law to empower independent districting commissions or otherwise limit gerrymandering—unless the Court also rules that any attempt to limit gerrymandering by federal law violates the 10th Amendment.

No Constitutional Right to Fair Districts, Yet. This much is certain: the Supreme Court will not find any limit to gerrymandering in the current federal

Constitution. Over three decades, the Court has increasingly accepted gerrymandering for naked partisan advantage. While previous decisions held that federal courts could review this kind of gerrymandering, in *Rucho et al.* v. *Common Cause*, a case decided in July 2019, a 5–4 Republican majority on the Court opened the floodgates. Chief Justice John Roberts wrote that, although gerrymandering districts for one party's advantage might be unjust, federal courts will not even review district lines on that basis—*no matter how extreme* the gerrymander is.[77]

It has been a long road to this worst-case endpoint. Back in 1986, a majority of the Court ruled that each political group should have an *equal opportunity* to "elect representatives of its choice," which put political and racial gerrymandering on a par: both are unconstitutional when done primarily to reduce the "voting strength" of a racial group *or* a political party.[78] The Roberts Court now says the opposite.

As a result, a constitutional change is the only truly secure way to end gerrymandering at both the state and federal levels.[79] However, whether the commission fix is attempted by statute or amendment, commissions must use *specific parameters* that define fair districting in a democratic society. And there is no consensus on what those are: different state governments, commissions, and older Supreme Court cases point to different parameters. There are no value-neutral ways of defining fair districts: it is a substantive ethical matter.

Four Criteria. Here I will mercifully spare readers most of the geometrical intricacies and legal history that direct attention away from the key ethical questions involved in defining fair districts. But, beyond a few illustrations, you will have to trust me; those who want fuller explanations can find them on this book's online extension.[80] The main districting criteria that have emerged from experience, analysis, and legal argument generally reduce to these four:

- Proportionality: the percentage of the electorate supporting a political party is similar to its share of seats won for the next legislative term.
- Competitiveness: there are small margins of difference between political groups in a district, which typically produce close races (the opposite of safe seats).
- Compactness, contiguity, and traditional boundaries: regular district shapes, which may also respect county lines and natural boundaries such as rivers.
- Communities of interest: ethnic, religious, cultural, or economic groups with shared interests and some level of political cohesiveness, which may include minority racial groups who have historically often been victims of disenfranchisement.

Each of these criteria has intuitive appeal, as well as many supporters, and every critique of gerrymandering implicitly appeals to one of more of them. For example, when Litt calculates that gerrymandering currently gives Republicans at minimum a 20-seat head start in the race for the House,[81] he means 20 seats above their proportion of the national total of all votes for House seats. Let's clarify each of these proposed standards.

1. *Proportionality between the votes for each party and the seats won.* In 2020, North Carolina's district lines enabled Republicans to win 8 out of 13 House seats with 49.6% of the vote, while Democrats won only 5 seats (or 38.4%) despite getting 50% of the vote. This big disproportion arises from "packing" Democrats into a couple districts in which they

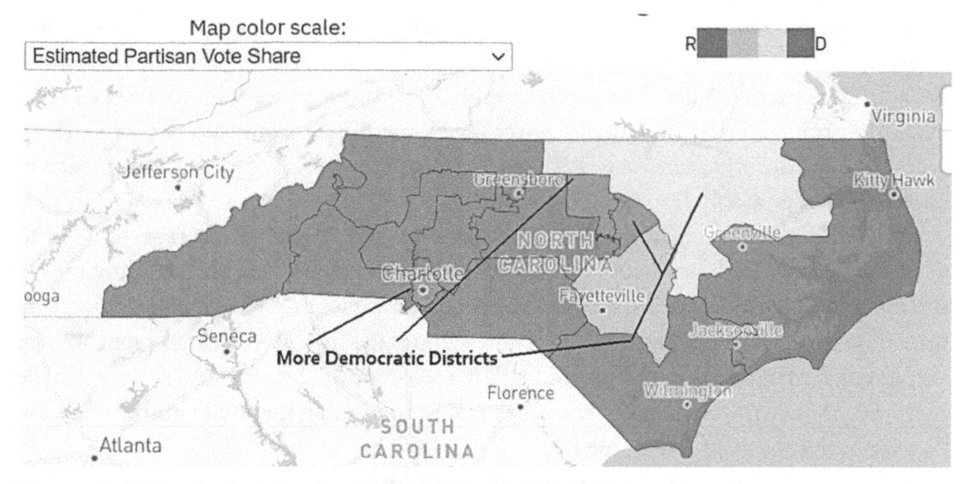

Figure 2.5 North Carolina Legislature's First Map 2021

have huge majorities and dividing ("cracking") other Democratic areas between two districts in other parts of the state. After North Carolina gained a House seat in 2021 due to the 2020 census, Republicans redrew the lines again to ensure Republicans at least 9–10 out of the 14 districts (roughly 70%). That map (see Figure 2.5)[82] was thrown out by the NC state supreme court for being so disproportionate in its effect, leading to the *Moore* v. *Harper* case. The NC court's much fairer map resulted in each party winning 7 of the 14 seats in November 2022.

This manipulation is possible because people vote by single-member geographic districts for the House of Representatives, as well as for most statehouse and country legislature seats. There are two main proportional remedies and variants of each:

(A) First, gerrymandering would disappear entirely if North Carolina took a *statewide* vote for its House delegation by "party list." Then a 50%–50% election result would translate into Republicans and Democrats each receiving half of the state's House seats. Each of these legislators could still be *allocated* to one of 14 congressional districts after the fact. But voters would be voting for their preferred party's statewide ranked list of candidates (a "slate"; see Table 2.3). In this method, which specific candidates are elected depends on how many total seats their party wins.

Table 2.3 Party Slate Proportional Representation

North Carolina	Candidates in Order of Rank from a Primary Race								
Republican slate	A	B	C	D	E	F	G	H	I
Democratic slate	J	K	L	M	N	O	P	Q	R
Forward Party slate	S	T	U	V	W				
Libertarian Party slate	X	Y	Z						
	Shaded candidates are elected proportional to the total vote for each party's list								

This system gives smaller third parties a chance. For example, in NC, if the new "Forward" Party received 1/14th of the vote (7.15%), it would win one seat. Adding RCV to this system would allow voters to rank whole slates if they wish to. For example, in this illustration, if the Libertarian party was ranked first by only 5% of voters, which is too low to win one seat, these ballots would be transferred to their casters' second choice, if any (probably the Republican slate).

Still, in smaller states, any party would need a substantial percentage of votes to get a single seat. In states with less than five congressional districts, rounding means the outcome could still be disproportionate because we cannot divide House members into fractions. For example, if Democratic candidates in New Mexico won 56% of the statewide House vote, they would still get two out of three House seats available there (66.7%) in a party list proportional election. (Increasing the total number of House districts reduces this problem; see #8).

In big-population states, the party list system yields more proportional outcomes than would large "multimember" districts combining three or four contiguous single-member districts. For in such multimember districts, rounding will again make the outcome significantly disproportional to each party's percentage of votes, just as in a whole state with only three or four single-member districts.

But a party list system also requires a way of rank-ordering candidates in each party's slate. A well-designed statewide primary election for each party can do this by allowing each voter to vote for one of the primary candidates or to rank several. In my illustration (see Table 2.3), A would be the candidate with the most Republican primary votes, B would be the runner-up in the primary, etc. Another more complex variation is feasible: in the general election, voters can vote both for a party and for multiple candidates. Then the party vote determines the percentage of seats for each party, while the votes for individual candidates determine their places in their party's slate. But either way, statewide at-large elections can be fairly confusing for voters new to such a system.

(B) So it is simpler for voters if (a) single candidates are still elected by voters in their district alone, but (b) a commission draws the district lines to produce a proportional outcome. In North Carolina, for example, it would be easy enough to design seven districts with more Republicans (say 58%–75% of each district population) and seven districts similarly full of Democrats.

This second way of bringing about a fairly proportional outcome by carefully tailored district lines would be more familiar than the statewide method, which might seem too radical to many Americans (see Desideratum 4).[83] More voters would also *like* their individual House member, given that they elected her or him by very wide margins. But while that might seem like a good outcome, it requires gerrymandering voters into likeminded or homogenous districts. This is not a recipe for vigorous contests and exposure to a diversity of viewpoints.

2. *Competitiveness.* Here we have come to the fundamental problem: vote-to-delegation proportionality can be in tension with the other vital criterion of competitiveness.[84] The reason is easy to grasp: when a lot of districts are competitive, a fairly modest swing in voter opinion, say by 3%–5%, can "flip" or alter the outcome in a lot of single-member districts. This large *threshold effect* in quite competitive winner-take-all districts

could be good for the country in some respects, because it would keep House members responsive and yield sizeable majorities in Congress that can move more decisively to enact their promised program.

Thus we cannot assume that proportional outcomes by themselves are the gold standard. Calling proportionality "representational fairness" or speaking of every deviation from it as an "efficiency gap"[85] only hides this dilemma. Votes cast for losing candidates are not fairly described as "wasted" in *close elections*: after all, they make the winning candidate aware of their vulnerability and encourage voters on the losing side to try harder next time (because with just a bit more, they could get over the threshold). For example, that a Republican almost won the race for governor of NY in 2022 is having an impact on NY policies. So beware of terminological pitfalls when reading about gerrymandering!

To illustrate, imagine that in NC, (a) each House member is still elected one district at a time (like now), but the state's 14 districts are drawn to be as internally competitive as possible, given the population's political leanings (as suitably measured at the time of redistricting). On this approach, with a population split nearly 50–50 by favored party, NC could draw a lot of districts in which there are nearly equal numbers of Republican-leaning and Democratic-leaning adults eligible to vote.

In that very unfamiliar but feasible situation, even an average 3% swing in opinion across the state could easily cause 10–12 districts to change hands. For example, Republicans could win 11 seats out of 14 (or 79%) with only 55% of the statewide vote, because they would net (say) a 1%–6% margin in 11 districts. This outcome would be quite disproportionate, but *not* because Republicans had gerrymandered 11 safe seats for themselves. Precisely the opposite: because they won 11 very "unsafe" seats, these Republican House members would know that their districts could easily return to the Democrats with a 3%–5% average swing in the next election. So they would be more likely to compromise with Democrats on a police chokehold ban, Medicaid expansion, or larger child tax credit for households earning under $70,000 a year. Obviously the same would hold in the reverse case where Democrats narrowly won (say) 10 out of 15 districts: they would be more moderate on cultural issues, such as sex education in elementary schools.

That would be a very good thing: the resulting NC House delegation would be hyper-responsive to the whole electorate in their districts. The lesson is that, while competitive districts definitely magnify the effects of small changes in voter sentiment, they transmit this effect into the federal system through *much more moderate* congressmen and congresswomen who are very keen to get good things done for their state. They have a mandate (as a party) and strong motives (as individuals) to govern effectively and compromise when necessary.

By contrast, on the statewide proportional method (A), it is easy to see that the five top Democrats and five top Republicans in their party's list, however it is made, will feel quite safe. That's because their party is almost certain to win at least 40% of the statewide House vote—equal to 5 out of 14 seats—no matter how the popularity of each party fluctuates over several election cycles. So, while the candidates ranked 6th, 7th, and 8th on their party's list after the primary would be worried and eager to appear bipartisan, at least 10 of the NC's House seats will be predictable in this system. The senior politicians holding them will take more extreme positions, because especially with closed primaries, the only voters they need to fear are radical primary voters who could push them farther down their party's slate.

This problem is worse in variant (B) with single-member districts drawn to yield a House delegation that is roughly proportional to the statewide vote margins. Just like now, many potential voters in the broad middle would be disillusioned, knowing that the general election outcome in their district is predestined by the packing of likeminded voters into these districts. If we are determined to make proportional outcomes the main criterion, the statewide vote by party list will be somewhat more competitive, especially in small states.

The proportional methods look a lot worse in this light: they can produce high numbers of noncompetitive seats even in states as evenly divided on political lines as North Carolina. Competitiveness and proportionality are inherently in tension, even if district lines are drawn by a commission. These ethically important criteria have to be balanced.

Still, our current gerrymandering system literally combines *the worst of both worlds*: it minimizes the number of competitive districts in a state *and* often yields outcomes that are wildly disproportionate in favor of party controlling the state government (and the districting). In sum, the fundamental evil of gerrymandering lies in using it to secure outcomes that are *neither* competitive *nor* proportional to the overall vote.

3. *Compactness and Contiguity*. What does all this have to do with district shapes, which are another common focus of public ire? The surprising answer is: *not as much as you think*. Like most Americans, I first became concerned about gerrymandering upon seeing bizarrely drawn districts. A classic example was North Carolina's 12th and 1st districts from a decade ago (see Figure 2.6). Obviously, both were gerrymandered to pick out precise groups of voters. In fact, both were drawn in 2011 to create majority-Black districts.

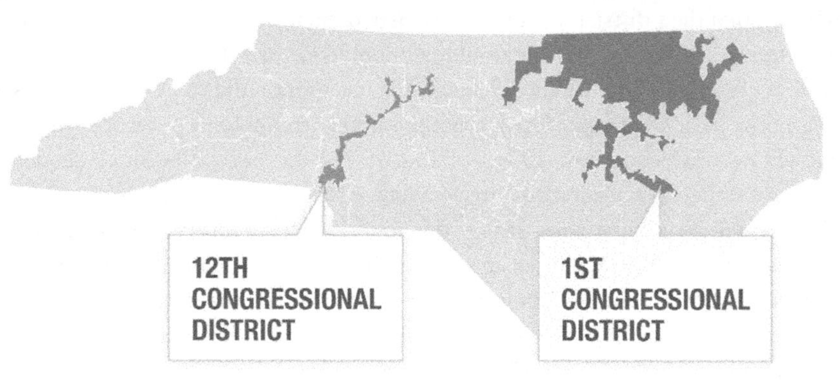

Figure 2.6 North Carolina's 1st and 12th Districts in 2011

They both *look* absurd, like Maryland's 3rd district (see Figure 2.4). In more technical terms, they are "contiguous" (with connected parts) but not "compact." To understand this, we need just a bit of math. Compactness had no precise definition in the 20th century, but today, experts usually measure the compactness of a district's shape (S) by comparing S to *the smallest circle* C that could contain all of S, as follows:

$$\text{Compactness of S} = \frac{\text{the area enclosed in S}}{\text{the perimeter of S}} \text{ divided by } \frac{\text{the area enclosed in C}}{\text{the perimeter of C}}$$

So if S is a circle, the ratio equals 1, indicating maximum compactness. By contrast, the old NC 12th was very noncompact, as we can see by nesting it within a circle (see Figure 2.7): this district's area is small compared to the circle's area, and the district's perimeter (total length of its edges) is huge, which usually indicates a lot of fine tailoring. But, while several states and districting commissions use compactness as a criterion, it is a very misleading one. Looking back at Figure 2.5, we see that NC's districts on the legislature's first proposed 2021 map are much *more* regular in shape than the old NC 12th: the Princeton Gerrymandering project rated the 2021 districts as slightly above the national average in compactness. And yet, as we saw, the outcome under them would be severely disproportionate *and* noncompetitive in most districts—the worst-case result, despite their compactness!

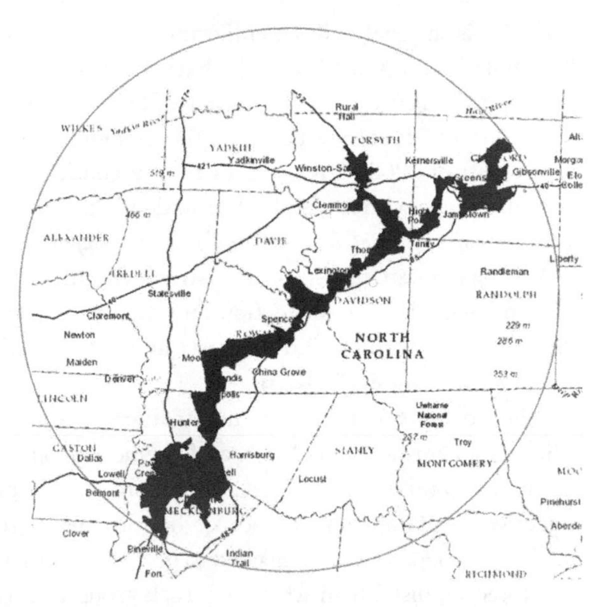

Figure 2.7 NC 12th District Noncompactness

So regularity in shape will guarantee neither competitiveness nor House delegations that are even moderately proportional to voter support for the parties. As Kristin Eberhard notes, depending on how a party's voters happen to be clustered or spread more evenly across a state, often the only way to get "fair representation" (i.e. proportional outcomes) while staying with single-member districts is to draw noncompact or "oddly shaped districts."[86] In North Carolina, one might have to divide some heavily Democratic urban centers to make six or seven districts in which (say) 55% of eligible voters lean Democratic. The same would be true if we wanted to make most of the 14 districts highly competitive: noncompact districts would be needed.

Two key points emerge here. First, highly irregular shapes only indicate that districts are being drawn with *some* goal in mind. But the goal behind the drawing is not necessarily unjust. Second, conversely, we cannot infer from district regularity or compactness that unjust gerrymandering is absent. In fact, manipulation of district lines is merely a tool that can be used for at least three different purposes:

(i) to make more competitive districts (unsafe seats); or
(ii) to make proportional outcomes more likely (through some safe seats)—whether for voters grouped by party or grouped by race/ethnicity; or
(iii) to make districts noncompetitive *and* outcomes disproportionate in favor of one party (and/or in favor of some other group).

Goal (iii) is the real evil; the tailoring of district lines is not always wrong in itself.[87] This evil explains some bizarrely shaped districts, like many of Florida's districts today. Noncompact districts set off our alarm bells because in our history, they have mostly been used to "dilute voting strength" of some group, in the language of the Voting Rights Act of 1965 (VRA). Let's briefly consider that legacy, which has associated irregular shape with racial discrimination in particular.

4. *"Communities of Interest" and Racial Groupings.* The fourth criterion would have us keep within single electoral districts certain "communities" or salient groups of residents who deserve protection and may have enough shared interests for them to elect someone with similar interests and concerns. This is what demographers call a politically "cohesive" group.

The trouble is that there are many different kinds of social groups—cultural, ethnic, religious, linguistic, age cohorts, and maybe economic classes—that might each want to control electoral districts in order to feel properly "represented." Each might have some objective social importance, too. Yet because these groups partly overlap, different and conflicting maps would be needed to give each of them control of some House seats.

Moreover, districts in which any such group is a significant majority would often be noncompact and cross country lines. At one time, it might have been plausible that the most important communities were largely defined by geographic boundaries such as rivers, mountains, coastal areas, or distinct ecosystems (e.g. arboreal forests or tropical bayous), which county lines may reflect. Such groupings were crucial for life in the past when it was hard and expensive to travel around large estuaries or communicate with people on the other side of a mountain range. But those barriers are less relevant today.

Likewise for contiguity: it reflects an old-fashioned belief that voters in a single district should live near to each other because they will share interests. That is much less obvious today. Unless "natural" boundaries pick out people with quite distinctive economic and/or social interests, it is unclear why rivers, mountains, etc. should still matter for fair districting.

Confusion follows from this proposed "communal" criterion and its "natural boundaries" cousin. Even if district-makers try to respect a given community's perceived desires, giving priority to any ascriptive group when districting is an ethical choice that affects society more broadly, for it embodies a judgment about which groups are most politically *relevant.* That can diminish people's autonomy by deciding in advance which group identities should matter most to them. It can also encourage insularity and single-issue tunnel vision. Do we really want experts to signal, through district lines, that voters should be more concerned to elect someone who "looks like them," or speaks like them, or prays like them, or trades and banks like them, or lives in a huge retirement community like them, rather than focusing on broader statewide or national issues?

At its worst, this could be a recipe for bigotry and/or a narrowminded focus on particular cultural interests. Rather than making diverse districts where people from different backgrounds must work together to be politically effective, the "communities of interest" criterion may encourage voters to follow whatever certain group leaders say, rather than making their own judgments after critical reflection (see *Shaw* v. *Reno* [1993] for related concerns). This may further encourage more people to "self-sort" into politically homogenous neighborhoods, which they are already doing, and thereby compound intolerance of political "others." More extreme identity politics and unreflective political tribalism are the exact opposite of what our nation needs.

That said, the US has a long history of disenfranchising Black, Hispanic, and Native American groups who have been frequent targets of violence, segregation, or other forms of social exclusion into the late 20th century. Thus federal courts have repeatedly cited the 14th and 15th Amendments as a basis for *reducing underrepresentation* of minority racial groups that results from districting lines. Before it was gutted (see #6), the VRA also protected racial, ethnic, and linguistic groups who are numerous, geographically proximate, and politically cohesive enough to constitute a majority or near-majority of a congressional district: their voting strength should not be "diluted" by cracking them into many districts or packing them into one district.[88] For example, in 2022, Governor Ron Desantis replaced maps drawn by Florida's legislature with his own district lines in order to "wipe away half of the state's Black-dominated congressional districts, dramatically curtailing Black voting power in America's largest swing state."[89] This is a truly egregious case of gerrymandering type (iii).

The VRA, then, aimed for more proportional representation of historically vulnerable groups in Congress, whatever their current party affiliations may be. This was one goal in North Carolina's 1st and 12th districts, as we saw, although the Supreme Court said in this case that more African-Americans were packed together than they needed to be in order to elect a black representative (they would have more voting power if spread between 3 or 4 districts).[90]

Another famous "majority-minority" (M-M) district was Illinois's "Earmuffs" around Chicago, which created a majority-Hispanic district. Likewise, Louisiana's district 4 (the "Mark of Zorro") during 1994–1995 was a thin irregular district on the northeast side of the state (Figure 2.8)[91] with a 63% African-American population at the time.[92] These special cases of gerrymandering show again that compactness is not a criterion of intrinsic importance in itself. District shapes are only *symptoms* of the underlying districting goals combined with the geographic location of various groups within a given state. And remedial assistance to increase minority representation in Congress and statehouses is arguably a good goal.

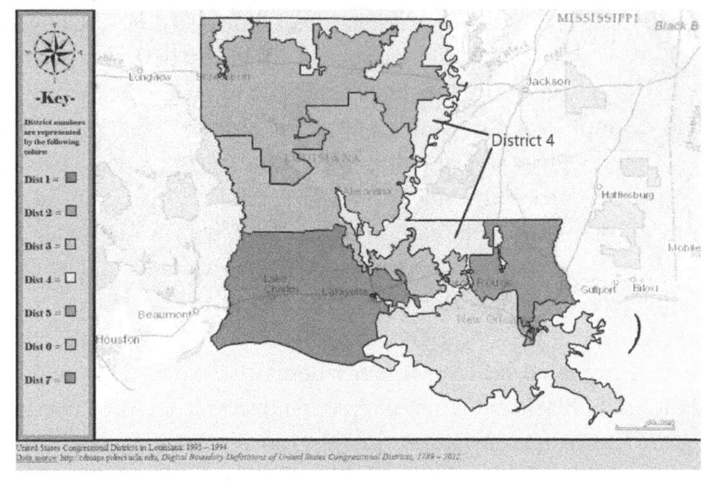

Figure 2.8 Louisiana's 4th District in 1994

But the truth today is that politicians involved in districting are mostly focused on the potential benefits to their own party, even if they claim that representation for ethnic or cultural groups is their goal. And since 2019, they no longer need to pretend to have more "noble" motives to draw safe districts for themselves and their friends. That's because of the Court's shocking ruling in *Rucho*, as described above. Now even a district insanely shaped to pack Black residents into a 90% majority might pass muster with this Court, if it were drawn that way for *political* reasons, e.g. to turn 2 majority-Democratic districts out of 4 into 1 out of 4.

The Proposal. So what is the best solution? Even independent commissions and district-drawing computer programs need to know which criteria to emphasize. This brief analysis implies that the Constitution should ban gerrymandering that makes a state's House districts both less competitive and less representative (proportional to vote margins for different parties), unless this is absolutely essential to preserve a minimum level of minority representation. Beyond that, I strongly believe that the increasing competitiveness should have priority.

Without serious competition, the two top parties turn into a duopoly—like rival street gangs who agree to hold residents hostage by enforcing monopoly control of "their" neighborhoods. By contrast, compactness and respecting county lines and/or natural borders are of no inherent importance; they are distractions from the truly vital goals of fair districting. Violations of compactness grab attention because they are symptoms of the deeper problem. Emphasizing these criteria can, at best, leave the impact of district lines to chance.

What about M-M districts with a majority of citizens from minority backgrounds? Probably the constitutional amendment should still allow Congress, through an updated VRA, to require that the number of M-M districts in a state not be less than half of what is possible, given its Black, Hispanic, Asian, or Native American populations. For example, if a state could in principle have four Black and/or Hispanic districts with enough irregular line drawing, then it must have at least two. Still, a lot has changed in the seven decades since the VRA. Might Americans in general be better off if more Republicans felt more need to win Black and Hispanic voters, and youth votes, while more Democrats were attentive to rural voters and military families? Ethnically homogenous districts do not promote that goal.

As long ago as the 1990s, Lani Guinier, a brilliant and vocal lawyer-advocate for increasing minority voice in our federal and state governments, argued that a "token" handful of Black and Hispanic representatives from M-M districts cannot by themselves easily overcome prejudices in "decision-making bodies."[93] Efforts to increase the number of representatives whose election depends on support from Black or Hispanic communities, while better than nothing, may simply give compact and cohesive minority communities an inattentive representative who relies on low-turnout primaries and political patronage to control their district like a personal fief.

In short, tokenism is no substitute for being able to form fluid coalitions with more potential allies and to cooperate with other segments of the population in order to advance interests that voters themselves, rather than districting algorithms, choose to prioritize. Such fluid coalition power requires *more competitive* elections, which are not guaranteed by putting a couple heavily minority-populated districts on the state map.[94] Still, this point cannot justify extreme moves like DeSantis's that dramatically reduce minority representation in Congress. His maps do not improve competitiveness either: FL votes for congresspersons in 2020 were 47% for Democrats and 52% for Republicans, but Democrats won only 8 out of the state's 28 heavily gerrymandered districts (or 28.5%) in 2022.

These examples suggest that competitiveness and outcomes proportional to party support among the electorate are the truly fundamental criteria for district lines, which should replace our current corrupt system. Proportionality is most easily achieved with a statewide vote for a House delegation, but it can be indirectly promoted by tailoring the boundaries of single-member districts too. Its main virtues are to increase stability, giving people some reliable basis on which to predict likely political outcomes in their region, and ensure that most voters will like their representative.[95]

Competitiveness is a more forward-looking standard. It gives people incentives to (a) change their minds in response to new arguments and events, (b) participate in public political discussions, and (c) vote based on their conclusions, because all of these things could make a real difference—especially if they can build fluid coalitions to bring other voters along with them. In an era when so many eligible voters are not yet affiliated with a party (see #3), competitive districts respect people whose minds are open and whose policy priorities are responsive to ideas and evaluations of options presented during the campaign. Delegations proportional to statewide support for parties will be harder to maintain via districting—especially in smallest 23 states, which have fewer than 6 districts each as new parties grow through RCV.

Thus my proposal favors competitiveness, but not to the extreme point that in a large state, a 3%–5% swing in votes could flip almost all districts from Republican to Democrat, or the reverse. Some limit to disproportional outcomes is needed to prevent unrepresentative supermajorities in Congress. This can be accomplished with a five-step recipe of this kind:

I. Congress will establish by law a suitable way of measuring popular support (Y) for each political party (P) with at least 7% of the electorate behind it in the decade up to and including each census year.

II. Let M be the margin between the two parties with the highest measured levels of voter support Y, averaged over 10 years. District lines should be drawn so that in states with 4 or more districts, at least half the districts (rounding down) have a margin no more than 5% or one-half of M, whichever is more.

III. When there are 8 or more districts in a state, for any party P polling Y% in statewide support averaged over the last 10 years, when Y is 25% or more, there should be, at minimum, a percentage of districts equal to half of Y (rounding down at or below half-percents) in which P is likely to have a 5% margin of advantage or more going into the next election.

IV. Among remaining district options that satisfy both of these requirements when they apply, the choice must be made by a nonpolitical state commission that draws maps according to the above criteria, whenever possible, and works to protect the interests of historically underrepresented minority groups.

V. Disputes about districting according to these criteria are heard by federal district courts but may be appealed to a national Fair Elections Court as the final arbiter.

To explain, §II imposes minimum levels of competitiveness even in fairly small states. In larger states, §III prevents states from cracking or packing significant political voting blocs to the point that these blocs can win no seats, or far fewer seats than their numbers would imply. The last two sections lay out how authorities will apply these criteria and resolve disputes.

Let's illustrate this recipe for fair districts with three different kinds of cases. First, consider Oregon, a state with 6 House members. Suppose the measured spread in the decade up to 2020 is 55% Democrat to 45% Republican: so M = 10%. According to §II, at least 3 districts in Oregon (half of its 6) must be competitive: they can have a margin of no more than 5% between these leading parties—even if this requires noncompact lines—in the year of redistricting (the 5% margin cap applies because it is equal to half of M). The other 3 districts can be less competitive. Although §III does not apply, because Oregon has less than 8 districts, the commission required by §IV would probably draw 1 Republic-leaning and 2 Democratic-leaning districts among these 3.

In North Carolina, assume that the spread is measured at 48% Democrat to 50% Republican in 2021: so M = 2%. According to §II, at least 7 of the 14 districts must have a margin of no more than 5% (which is more than half of M) between these two parties. §III then requires that 24% of the districts (half of 48%)—or 3 districts (rounding down)—lean Democratic by 5% or more. Likewise 25% of the 14 districts—or 3.5 rounded down to 3 districts—should lean Republican by 5% or more. These conditions give us 7 competitive districts, and 6 that are safer (3 for each party), leaving 1 district to the commission's discretion—probably to be an M-M district.

Now, instead consider a heavily red-trending state like Tennessee with 9 districts. Suppose the spread was measured at 60% for Republicans and 40% for Democrats; so M = 20%. Because the state leans so heavily one way, §II does not require draconian measures to make very close districts. It allows half of the districts, rounded down to 4, to have a 10% margin (half of M) or less. But §III requires that 20% of the districts (half of 40%)—which is 1.8 districts, rounded up to 2—be safer for Democrats, to the extent possible. There are enough Democrats to form at least a 5% majority in 2 districts. With 6 districts controlled by these conditions, the independent commission will have more discretion concerning the remaining 3. It could try to ensure that one district is majority-black, given that 17.5% of Tennessee residents are African-American.

§I and §III also allow smaller parties to grow by limiting cracking. Once a party gains 25% support in general elections in a state with 8 districts, it would get one relatively safe seat (0.125% of districts). In a state with 12 districts, it would win or be competitive in 2 seats unless its supporters are too scattered. Having seats in Congress would gain these smaller parties lots of attention. And these rules could also be extended to statehouse elections too.

In sum, this is a balanced formula. Unfortunately, this solution will take some time for voters to understand, but the issue is complex. It provides the sort of guidance that commissions and computer algorithms need if they are to produce fair districts in many different states of widely varying populations. A nationwide standard is essential to ensure that we do not end up with mostly safe seats in small states and mostly competitive districts in larger states, which would give an unjust edge to a party dominating more small states.

Variations are easy to imagine. One could emphasize competitiveness a bit more by lowering the maximum margin in §II from 5% to 4%. Or one could increase proportionality in outcomes by raising the minimum margin in §III to 6% or 7%. The main point is that we can devise a constitutional amendment that greatly reduces gerrymandering, based on a politically impartial set of objective standards that do not overemphasize superficial geometric parameters. If the House of Representatives is expanded (see #8), there would also be fewer states with less than 8 districts, which would make this kind of antigerrymandering formula even more effective.

The Define–Combine Alternative. I conclude this compressed analysis with a brief look at a proposal to draw new district lines every decade by a two-step process that is a bit like letting one hungry child cut slices in a small pizza, after which the other child picks the first slice. On this approach, the majority party draws the maps, but it has to draw *twice* the number of districts that the state's congressional delegation actually has, and it cannot draw any "donut" districts that completely encircle other districts in its proposal. The next largest party goes second: it combines neighboring districts in the majority's proposed map however it likes, until the number of districts is cut in half. These are then the final congressional districts for the coming decade.

This "Define-Combine" procedure ensures that the majority party can get much less advantage from districting. For example, when the minority party's potential majorities have been cracked, the minority can recombine them (although they cannot divide packed districts).[96] This fix works by enforcing bargaining under restricted parameters to produce the maps. This looks promising; although future analysis may reveal a first-mover or last-mover advantage in this process, such a flaw might be fixed by tweaking its conditions.[97]

However, Define-Combine would probably produce two-party compromises in which each receives a lot of safe seats. This would not yield the increased competitiveness we desperately need, and it would also shut smaller third parties out of the process. However, Define-Combine illustrates a way to reduce reliance on the sort of specific conditions that I laid out. It could even be used by commissions for districts left primarily to them under §IV of my proposed formula. Or an amendment could include a specific competitiveness condition like §II in my proposal and use Define-Combine for a state's remaining districts.

In conclusion, gerrymandering is one of the hardest issues to explain to the public and resolve in a way that should be widely acceptable. But expert analysis is finally yielding workable solutions. Luckily, the fundamental reforms needed to fix political campaigns and balloting are easier to explain. They are set out in the next two sections.

5. Campaign Finance and Election Spending Reform

The New Oligarchy. Leonard Leo is not a person whose name is known to most Americans. He was for many years co-chair of the right-wing Federalist Society, an increasingly powerful group that lobbies for particular conservative judges to be appointed to federal and state courts. His group groomed and promoted five of the six justices who overturned *Roe* v. *Wade* in 2022, allowing states to outlaw abortions, even with few medical exceptions. From the Federalist Society, to the White House short list, and finally to the Court is now the pathway.[98]

Barre Seid, a Chicago billionaire, is even less known, although he has reportedly made millions in secret donations to conservative groups over the years. In 2021, he gave $1,600 million in shares to Marble Freedom Trust (MFT)—a "dark-money" organization that does not have to report donations. Seid avoided up to $400 million in capital gains taxes in the process. Marble Freedom is run by Leonard Leo, who was at the time apparently its only paid employee.[99] Seid's gift is widely thought to be the largest single donation to an independent political group in history. Leo may use this fortune to fight laws and regulations designed to reduce climate change and to push the absolutist state legislature theory described above (see #4).

This is the kind of subterfuge that has made Americans across the political spectrum loathe the rising political clout of the richest few. Before the Covid years, a 2019 bipartisan poll found that a majority of likely voters rated "corruption in the legal system" as the nation's worst problem, above even health care costs, crime, or climate change. And 61% wanted major changes to our campaign finance laws along with more enforcement.[100] More than 67% of Americans also disapprove of the way that presidential and congressional elections—and increasingly statehouse elections too—spend ever-inflating amounts of money to flood airwaves with negative and misleading ads bankrolled by wealthy donors, lobbyists, and big corporations (see Figure 2.9), which are often not even disclosed in public records.[101]

People are right to be worried. As Sarah Chayes argues, kleptocracy is a creeping danger in America. After deregulation fever hit in the 1980s, "the lobbying profession

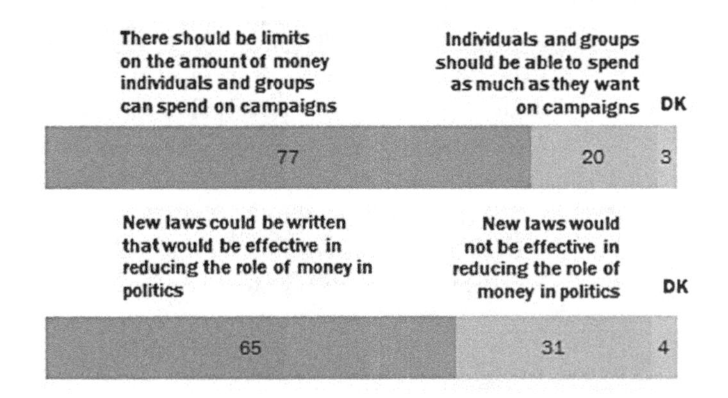

Figure 2.9 Strong Majorities Favor Limiting Election Spending

exploded, and industries began writing legislation for their own sectors; public services such as incarceration and war fighting" were partly turned over to contractors. In general, "the brakes on money in politics were released; and presidents began filling top regulatory jobs with bankers."[102] Contrary to Trump's promise to "drain this swamp," these problems worsened during his administration.

To understand what is happening, it helps to start with some distinctions. There are four ways to look at money in elections, and each is important:

- by *sources* of funds used for campaigns and "political activities" more generally (from individual donations, parties, political committees, public matching funds, etc.);
- by *types* of spenders—campaigns, corporations, unions, and other groups;
- by *targets*—types of election (presidential, congressional, statehouse, ballot question, etc.), or for direct influence on congressional committees and bureaus in the executive branch; or
- by *ways* of spending or what is purchased—advertising, registration drives, campaign tours, making a movie, or publishing a book, etc.

The charts in this section offer snapshots of these different aspects (and there is more on *TheDemocracyAmendments.org*). For example, consider how sources relate to spenders. Individuals (including candidates themselves) may give to every type of spender—specific candidates' campaigns, political parties, and independent "social welfare" groups (501-c-4s), whose primary purpose is not supposed to be political activities or lobbying (but often still is). They can also give to "political nonprofits" (527 orgs) that are primarily devoted to political advocacy.

Some sources can also spend directly on political activities, while others cannot; most can also give to other sources—but within a few limits. For example, an individual can pay to print a flyer and to hand it out. Parties can spend on organizing and also donate to specific campaigns, while corporations and independent groups cannot.[103] But corporations can contribute to political action committees (PACs) and to the independent groups, which do their political work for the big businesses—almost like contractors. PACs were formed in the 20th century as legal ways for businesses and unions to contribute to political campaigns: they are usually connected with particular businesses, nonprofits, or trade groups, and can give only $5,000 to each candidate during each election cycle.

By contrast, "SuperPACs" are not as linked to particular companies. Like political nonprofits and other independent groups such as Leo's, they do not give money directly to campaigns, and they supposedly promote views on "issues" rather than particular candidates. Currently, they can raise and spend money *without limit* from individual donors, corporations, independent NGOs, and other interest groups. SuperPACs are not supposed to "coordinate" with political parties. But it is usually pretty clear which side they support—and some SuperPACs promote a single candidate. All of the advertising, lobbying, and events they pay for are *in addition* to what official campaigns spend from their own well-heeled sources.

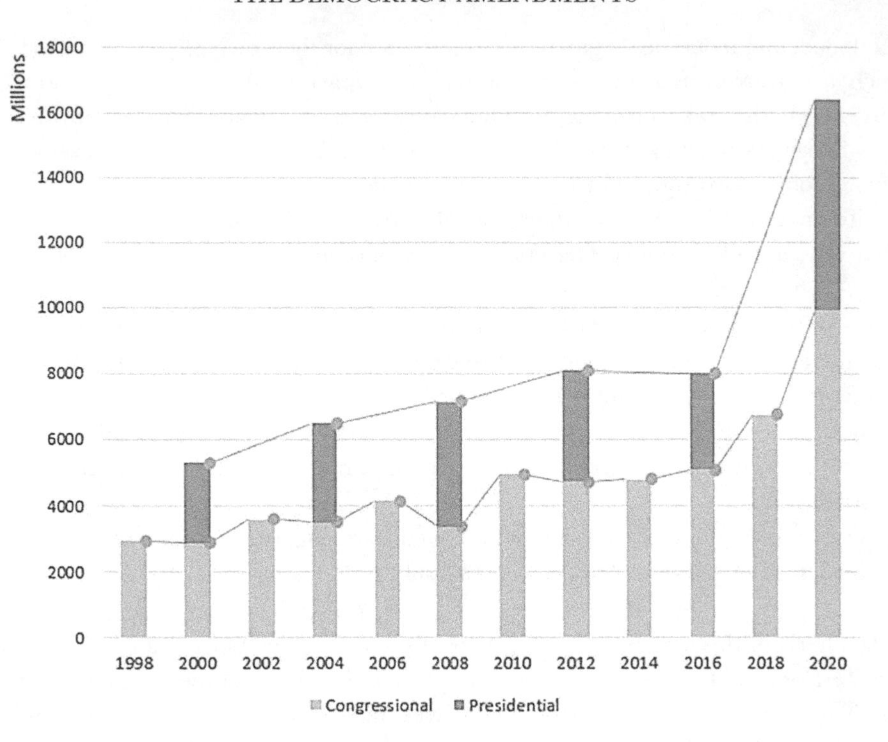

Figure 2.10 Spending by Campaigns, Parties, and Independent Groups on Federal Elections

Confused? If so, you are not alone. The myriad problems of campaign finance and money in politics today are hard for most Americans to understand, because they are hidden behind such a complex web of different kinds of entities. It's like a shell game.

The results, however, are quite evident. Figure 2.10 shows all inflation-adjusted election spending by presidential and congressional candidates, combined with separate or "outside" spending by political parties, PACs, SuperPACs, and other independent groups to influence federal elections. Total spending has more than tripled from 2000 to 2020! This is on top of steep rises in the last three decades of the 20th century. Billionaires account for $2.6 billion of the $14.4 billion spent in 2020. That's a handful of the absolute wealthiest Americans controlling almost *one-fifth* of the nation's entire election budget.

If we break out official *campaign* spending in congressional races, the costs rose from $343 million in 1982 to $2,286 million in 2020—almost a six-fold rise in 38 years.[104] This is an out-of-control arms race in which the richest 0.1% are battling to influence the federal government, while the rest of us are increasingly sidelined. OpenSecret's statistics on federal campaign dollars in 2016 and 2020 reveal that big donors and multimillionaire candidates' self-funding made up *over half* of the sources. Small individual donations by less wealthy Americans were not even one-quarter (see Figure 2.11).

The influence of the richest grows even larger when we add the money flowing into Leadership PACs, SuperPACs, and groups like Leo's MFT, which spend fortunes on television and radio ads, mailers, online messaging about hot-button issues, and attacks on candidates (including even elected judges) who don't do their bidding. Total

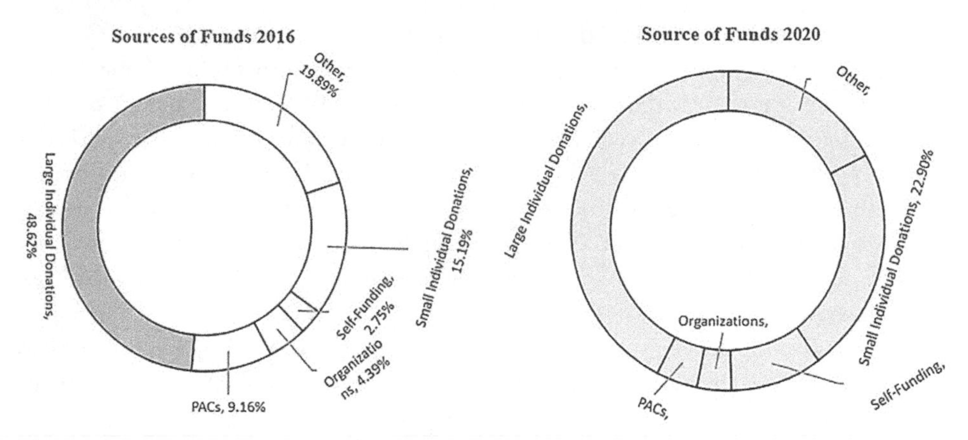

Figure 2.11 Official Campaign Spending, 2016 and 2020

outside spending by such entities was an enormous $3.3 billion in the 2020 presidential election, almost double the 2016 figure. And often these PACs and social "issue" groups can twist an incumbent's arms in Congress without spending one dollar: just the prospect that they might fund a primary or general election opponent is enough to induce terror and obedience.

Monetary Leverage. The result is what I will call "monetary leverage," namely the ability of people to use large amounts of wealth to shape law and government policy to their liking. Consider four among thousands of sickening examples.

(1) In his stunning book, Adam Cohen describes how leading Republicans in Congress came to Las Vegas to pay homage to Sheldon Adelson, the billionaire casino magnate.[105] Adelson had donated over $92 million to their party, conservative candidates and PACs, and to other groups in 2012—more than the next 9 largest individual conservative donors combined.[106] This should worry anyone, including many Republicans, who may not benefit from policies that specifically help casinos.

(2) Members of Congress seek out assignment to committees with leverage over laws that affect big donors, because these jobs reap rewards. As David Litt puts it, "if you're on the financial services committee, you can expect huge contributions from banks," and if your committee covers agriculture, "you can expect Monsanto to come knocking."[107] In 2017, three former members of Congress—two Republicans and one Democrat—explained how much fundraising a congressperson must do for their party ("party dues") in order to chair important committees. And even without that perk, congresspersons often report having to spend over 20–25 hours a week calling or visiting with donors:

> These demands to raise money take legislators away from doing the people's work, incentivize members of Congress to seek campaign cash from the interests they regulate, and elevate fundraising skills over policy knowledge when it comes to who controls legislation. Furthermore, [this practice] strengthens a small elite of Washington-based powerbrokers.[108]

(3) Some of the most influential donors and lobbyists represent drug-makers,[109] military suppliers, banks, high tech, and big box stores. In 2022, Home Depot donated more than any other company to the so-called "sedition caucus" of 2020 election deniers. But big financial firms, their lobbyists, and PACs and SuperPACs that they support may have the biggest influence. This is why private equity and hedge funds run as partnerships have for years paid a tax rate much lower than everyone else's: Congress carved out a loophole specifically for them, famously leading investor Warren Buffet to remark on how unjust it is that his effective tax rate is lower than his secretary's.

After more than a decade of reform efforts, it looked like this $14 billion giveaway to the richest 0.01% would be ended in the Inflation Reduction Act of 2022—until Senator Kyrsten Sinema (D-AZ) insisted on keeping the loophole for "wealthy hedge fund managers and private equity executives."[110] Earlier she had also opposed any increase in marginal tax rates for top earners. *The Wall Street Journal* notes that "Ms. Sinema has received roughly $2.2 million in donations since 2017 from individuals and committees in the securities and investment industries, more than from any other sector."[111]

(4) On a much broader scale, large donors and their lobbyists work overtime to secure tax dodges and massive subsidies for certain businesses at our collective expense. Consider what we might call the Mother of all Plutocratic Wins, namely the December 2017 tax cut law pushed by Trump, Treasury Secretary Mnuchin, and House Speaker Paul Ryan. It was billed as a way to lower everyone's taxes and bring profits from multinational corporations back to the US. Instead, most of the savings went to the wealthiest companies and individuals, while taxes on middle-class families with high mortgages and state taxes went up (see Figure 2.12). As Cohen reports, after this law was signed, 60 "profitable Fortune 500 companies paid no taxes at all, including General Motors, IBM, and Netflix" in 2018. Adelson's casinos saved $670 million.[112]

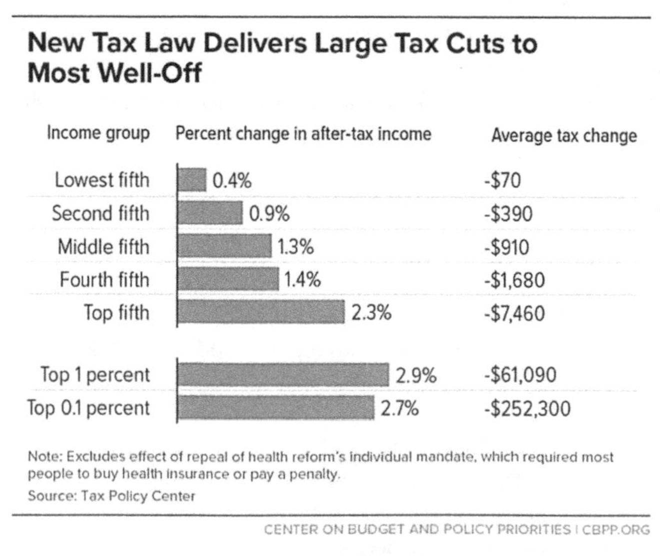

Figure 2.12 Tax Cuts in the December 2017 Tax Law

The result of such influence campaigns has been rising income inequality, corporate "rent-seeking" (special protections), dangerous financial speculation, and opportunities galore to externalize costs onto the public—all through favored treatment by the government.[113] The system produces government not "for the people" but instead for elites who capture larger shares of the economic pie, even when the total pie shrinks in recessions. The saddest aspect of such cases is that they no longer shock us.

Evaluation: Corruption, Leverage, and Access. In sum, monetary leverage is a huge problem in America today. Leverage or strong influence on legislation is what hedge fund managers have through Senator Sinema, and conservative American bishops have through Leonard Leo and his protégé, Justice Samuel Alito. Leverage arises from the interaction of several factors, including at least

- who can contribute to political campaigns, and how much;
- what spending is allowed on political advertising by campaigns and by other groups or legal entities;
- how much public funding is available for political campaigns;
- whether free time on mass media is given to qualifying political campaigns; and
- what the relation is between individual candidates and their parties.

For example, in nations with parliamentary proportional representation, there is much less focus on candidates as individual personalities than there is with US single-member districts and two senators per state; so individual campaigns are small in most parliamentary democracies. This is why a third of the Organisation for Economic Co-operation and Development (OECD) nations have no limits on campaign contributions: most of them have parliamentary systems *and* strict limits on political advertising. The US is nearly alone in having an open sluice gate for election spending by independent groups, weak limits on contributions to political campaigns, little public funding for campaigns nor much free "air time" (mass media presence), and as much advertising as available funds will allow.[114] This has huge impacts because, on average, Americans watch about three hours of TV (and/or online shows) with ads every day.

We have to evaluate campaign donations, advertising by third-party groups, and other spending by corporations to influence legislators within this larger context, which helps explain why most politicians are virtually *forced* to seek large amounts of campaign funding and SuperPAC support. It is not because they go into government to become ultra-wealthy or to lick the boots of billionaires; in fact, most of them could make much more money in the private sector. Rather, their predicament is like that of someone running a small business who has to pay one local mafia family for protection against another.

This is a crucial point that many Americans do not understand: the private gain, and thus corruption, is mostly on the side of the donors. Neither Justice Alito nor Senator Sinema took *bribes* to enrich themselves; it is not like they are stashing millions of campaign dollars in their private bank accounts or receiving free title to a private

Alpine resort home from big businesses. It's their job in government, which only pays $174–270k, that depends on wealthy supporters.

As Lawrence Lessig (once an avid Reagan supporter) explains in *Republic, Lost*, our campaign finance laws and lobbying practices promote a culture of friendly acquaintance and informal interdependencies among legislators, appointed federal officials, the donor class, and their lobbyists, who provide "research" and "analysis" to members of Congress and executive branch officials. In most cases, reciprocity develops tacitly, rather than through explicit quid-pro-quos: legislators and regulators develop a sense of *indebtedness* to these elite individuals who have given them so much "help."[115]

This is not bribery in the most familiar sense, but it is definitely a kind *access* that you and I do not have. Ask yourself: in the last decade, how many opportunities have you had to sit down and speak one-to-one with your representatives in state government, much less your House member or senators, for a good 30-minute chat? They have spent many hours discussing issues that affect your family with deep-pocked influencers who do not even live in their districts or states. As Lessig says, "[a]cess is power." Even if a member of Congress is already disposed toward a lobbyist's position on an issue, that lobbyist focuses the member's attention on specific details that help the lobbyist's paymaster.[116] In other words, lobbyists mold the agenda to focus on the pet priorities of specific industries, multimillionaires, unions, and trendy cultural groups, while the biggest national problems get less legislative attention.

And as we have seen, it pays. Like a thousand Lilliputians tying down Gulliver, in 2021, corporations that would have paid higher taxes or lost business to green energy startups lobbied like crazy against the Build Back Better bill, which was *the main legislative promise* on which Biden was elected.[117] Ten industries spent at least $700 million on this hatchet job[118] to block the will of a majority of voters—with help from former aides to Senator Joe Manchin who now work for big lobby firms on K Street.

This omnipresent pall of big-donor dependency continually blocks key priorities for which electoral majorities thought they were voting. Whether Republicans or Democrats wins, reforms promised by candidates get lobbied to death by groups whose clients might get less money or attention if these reforms passed. Who could expect anything else when members of Congress have to spend over a third of their time raising money rather than working on legislation? As Al Gore summed up the situation a decade ago,

> not since the 1890s has US government decision making been as feeble, dysfunctional, and servile to corporate and other special interests as it is now [...]. The subordination of reason-based analysis to the influence of wealth and power ... has led to catastrophically bad policy choices [and] sclerotic decision making [...].[119]

In fact, "lawyers representing corporate lobbies" often now participate in the "actual drafting sessions" to write laws on Capitol Hill; similarly, many "state legislatures [...] routinely rubber-stamp laws that have been written [...] by corporate lobbies."[120] And it has only gotten worse since Gore wrote this. The next section explains why.

One Constitutional Challenge: Free Speech. So how did the wall between money and state collapse in a nation where, in 1853, the Supreme Court directly rejected dark-money attempts to influence legislation by corporate lobbyists?[121] Two causal factors in the framework for monied leverage stand out as crucial: insufficient limits on campaign and third-party spending, and the "personalization" of corporations for 1st Amendment purposes.

Over the years, Congress has occasionally made serious attempts to stop the campaign finance arms race by limiting campaign contributions and spending. The 1971 Federal Election Campaign Act, updating earlier laws, established a small level of public support for presidential general elections campaigns, later extended to include primaries (a provision that became moribund in 2008).[122] This law, along with 1974 additions after the Watergate scandals, established strict financial disclosure requirements and several kinds of caps:[123]

A. individual campaign contributions and independent spending to support a candidate: $1,000 per primary election and per general election;
B. individual contribution to a state political party committee: $5,000 per election; and $20,000 per year to a national party committee;
C. individual contributions to political action committees (PACs): $5,000 per election;
D. individual total contributions to candidates, parties, and PACs: $25,000 per year;
E. a candidate's personal donation to their own campaign: $25,000 for House races, $35,000 for Senate races;
F. political party spending on behalf of their candidates: $10,000 in House campaigns and $20,000 in Senate campaigns;
G. PAC contributions to a candidate running for office: $5000 per election;
H. PAC spending to help a clearly identified candidate: $1000 per candidate;
I. a ceiling on general election advertising spending by a campaign: $70,000 for a House seat and $150,000 for a Senate seat (or, if larger, 12 cents per eligible voter);
J. Presidential campaigns: $20 million in general election spending and must accept public election financing and its restrictions on private donations.

No doubt most Americans would be astonished to learn that we once had such sensible limits in place, like most other mature democracies on Earth. In our time, Biden's campaign raised over $1 billion dollars in 2020; Trump spent $66 million of his own cash on the 2020 race; and infamous freshman Congressman George Santos (R-NY) funneled over $700,000 from his company to his campaign. Yet, the 1974 limits were not *very* restrictive, and many of them were increased in 2001. Within these rules, wealthy donors and their family members could collectively give many thousands to a single campaign, and large sums to PACs that support their favored candidates, and yet more to their favored party at the state and national levels, which also supports their candidates.

So what happened to these sensible limits? First, as Caroline Fredrickson explains, big corporations began to directly lean on executives and other employees to make large donations to their PACs, and the number of PACs and corporate lobbyists started their rapid rise.[124] Then the Supreme Court's 1974 ruling in *Buckley* v. *Valeo* stuck down parts of limits A, C, and D, and all of limits E, H, I, and J as somehow unduly limiting people's free political speech. The rejection of spending limits was crucial because ultimately donations to campaigns, parties, and PACs do not give the doner much leverage if they cannot be spent on advertising, stumping on the campaign trail, and organizing (e.g. registering supporters). *Buckley* freed the richest individuals and organizations to spend enormous amounts in (indirect) support of candidates and parties during the election season, as long as their advertising and advocacy is not pre-planned (nod, wink) with official campaigns.

The central flaw in the Court's argument, as John Rawls pointed out in his damning critique,[125] is that it equated spending money with "speech." When our first federal Congress wrote the Bill of Rights, political parties did not even exist and no one imagined billionaires blanketing the world with television and internet ads, direct mailers, and bots driving deceptive messages to our phones and emails. Because we have finite attention spans, these advertising blitzes can drown out everything else.[126] In democratic elections, freedom of political expression surely cannot mean that our richest citizens can buy a "voice" *many millions* of times larger and louder than the rest of us can afford.

This view has thoughtful critics who still care about the unjust leverage problem. Richard Hasen, for example, argues that freedom of the press could be reduced by caps on elections spending, because publishing (in print or online), or making and airing a movie, can be a kind of expenditure to help a campaign or support a candidate's policy priorities.[127] Moreover, new candidates need to spend more to challenge congressional incumbents, who have built-in advantages (including some federal money to mail constituents).

This objection requires a three-part answer. (i) First, we must distinguish two main ways of spending to win elections. Spending that mass-distributes content that is free to viewers through *high-traffic venues or communication routes* with very limited space—an ad on the evening news hour, a Facebook popup appearing on millions of users' screens, a billboard hanging over the entrance to a major bridge, or a pile of pamphlets blocking every front door in town—is distinct from producing a book, movie, webpage, or podcast. In the latter category, you get the content only if you take further steps (buying the book, clicking to play to podcast, etc.). By contrast, content in the first category comes up directly and *crowds out* a hearing for other people's speech in the same high-visibility public spaces. Just as we would not allow a wealthy political group to reserve the town square for rallies on *every* available day by auctioning use of the square to the highest bidder, we should not allow wealthy groups to dominate the airwaves and internet ads.

An amendment could easily protect the second kind of (voluntarily received) political speech while allowing federal law to limit the first (involuntarily received) kind for purposes of reducing inequality in political voice. For example, there would be no limit on publishing a book about a candidate, printing up flyers to hand out in town, or releasing a documentary about a political issue near to an election. There would also be no limit on emails or phone calls that people agreed to receive by signing up for a campaign's or political advocacy group's update lists. It does not matter if the borderline between these categories of communication is slightly fuzzy; that is true of many important distinctions in law.

(ii) Building on this key distinction, it is clear that spending caps should be strictest on advertising and other free-to-viewer content referring directly to candidates or their campaigns, especially during election seasons. Limits could be higher on advertising that only discusses "issues" without naming, showing, or directly alluding to candidates. Similarly, limits can be much higher on spending to hold rallies or events that people can attend if they wish to meet candidates or their surrogates. It is really advertising in high-traffic venues on which people rely that should be the main target of caps.

(iii) But is this fair to candidates challenging well-known members of Congress? Hasen reports that social scientists find little evidence of campaign contribution limits increasing incumbents' advantage. However, an amendment to fix campaign finance should specifically cap campaign spending by incumbents at a slightly lower level (perhaps 90% of the challenger's cap) to level the field a bit. In both cases, sources still need to be limited as well, so that one or a few very wealthy donors do not "own" or control challengers. This burden on challengers can instead be offset with more public financing.

For example, like Lessig, Hasen recommends a federally funded $100 voucher, available every even-numbered year, for each registered voter to give to a candidate, party, or interest group of their choice. In other words, once you register to vote, you could give $50 of your "federal campaign coin" to a candidate contesting your House district, $20 to a presidential candidate, and $30 to a political group you support (e.g. the League of Women Voters). The federal government would then give $50, $30, and $20, respectively, to these entities that you chose. This would generate millions of dollars in small donations for the campaigns of new candidates.[128]

Moderate caps on individual donations still allow campaigns and political advocacy groups to combine donations by many individuals to fund advertising and issue advocacy. The goal should be to prevent most of the money coming from a few very influential persons and businesses. As Hasen notes, even with limits on outside group spending of $3,000 per election district and $150,000 nationally, Canada still has "open elections [...] with robust political competition." There is plenty of free political speech in Canadian election seasons.[129]

In sum, free speech rights have limits that are partly a function of their purposes, which, for the framers of our Constitution, included instituting "republican government." In a republic, some limit on spending to broadcast one's views to large audiences during campaign season is essential to give others a fair chance. In the *Buckley* decision, then, the Court majority totally violated the original intentions of James Madison, Thomas Jefferson, and others who brought the Bill of Rights to fruition.

A Second Constitutional Challenge: Corporations as 'Persons.' Federal legislators tried to pick up the pieces of our campaign finance rules shattered by *Buckley* with a series of small measures, culminating in the famous McCain–Feingold Bipartisan Campaign Reform Act of 2002—a product of seven years of unrelenting work to overcome Senate filibusters. This landmark law restored modest limits on campaign spending by national political parties and prohibited "issue ads" paid for by for-profit and nonprofit corporations that name candidates during campaign periods. It reversed a Federal Election Commission (FEC) ruling that allowed unlimited "soft money" donations to political parties for "party-building activities."

The attack in federal courts began almost immediately. Even though this modest law to rein in the campaign finance arms race was supported by senators representing over 70% of the entire nation, the Supreme Court eviscerated part of the law by expanding the range of ads funded by corporations and labor unions that could escape McCain–Feingold limits.

Then the biggest hammer dropped. On January 21, 2010, the Court decided *Citizens United* v. *FEC*. Their 5-4 decision eliminated the limits on "independent" election spending (including advertising) by big groups, corporations, and unions, including multinational companies with board members connected with foreign governments.[130] Talk about activist judges!

In possibly the worst majority opinion since *Plessy* v. *Fergusson* approved racial segregation as "equal," Chief Justice John Roberts argued that corporations of all kinds are "persons" with the same 1st Amendment speech rights as you and I. Most Americans recognize that this assertion is patently absurd.[131] Kristin Eberhard reports that over three quarters of Americans oppose *Citizens United* and the deluge of attack ads that it unleashed. They despise the fact "that their government is bought and paid for" thanks to the twisted illogic of Roberts' effort to rationalize plutocracy.[132] As Fishkin and Forbath put it, this decision weaponized the 1st Amendment, which was meant to protect the weak against censorship, into "a tool for dismantling egalitarian forms of self-government."[133]

Of course, corporations have been "persons" in one artificial legal sense for centuries; this simply means that as a collective entity, they have legal rights to do things that are necessary for a market economy to function, such as making contracts. A corporation needs a legal status in order to act as a collective entity and protect its members; and this status implies entitlements. For example, corporations have some privacy rights to keep communications and proprietary data privileged. But that does not mean your supermarket should have the same 5th Amendment protections against self-incrimination as you do. Nor can Saks Fifth Avenue have a conscience and freely exercise it by going to pray in church, any more than a company running hospitals can exercise the 1st Amendment right to peaceably assemble in the city park for a protest march. Corporations cannot be taken into police custody, and when the 5th Amendment refers to a "person held to answer for a capital crime," it is not talking about entities like Purdue Pharmaceuticals which—although it killed many thousands of Americans—could not literally receive a lethal injection for mass murder. Thus the popular bumper sticker, "I'll believe corporations are persons when Texas executes one."

The Bill of Rights, in short, is entirely about *actual human beings* ("natural persons"). It does not mention corporations, although the power to make laws concerning them is implicit in the Commerce Clause of the Constitution.[134] A right to "corporate speech" is a pure invention of Justice Lewis Powell, a radical anti-worker corporate lawyer appointed by President Nixon.

As Gore notes, the *Citizens United* decision directly conflicts with Republican President Theodore Roosevelt's prescient argument that the US should "prohibit the use of corporate funds directly *or indirectly* for political purposes."[135] It also contradicts earlier opinions by Republican-appointed justices Sandra Day O'Connor and William Rehnquist, who recognized that limits are needed to give everyone an opportunity for political speech during in debates, in presentations to courts, and in other contexts.[136] We do not allow a few individuals to buy up all the speaking slots in public hearings by massively outspending others in a millionaires' bidding war: why is election advertising by corporations and independent issue groups any different?

The results of *Citizens United* were predictable. As shown in Figure 2.13, independent spending just on congressional races by political groups, corporations, and their PACs—outside of what is contributed to official campaigns for the House and Senate—rose from a modest $42 million in 2008 to over $800 million in the decade after *Citizens United* (a 19-fold or 1,900% jump). Party and party leadership PAC spending rose from roughly $275 million to over $1200 million, for over $2 billion in total independent spending on 2020 congressional elections[137] (just 5 Senate races cost over $100 million each). And this does not include independent spending to boost presidential candidates (which are included in Figure 2.10). In this environment, what chance is there that Congress will substantially strengthen antitrust laws to rein in oligopoly powers of giants such

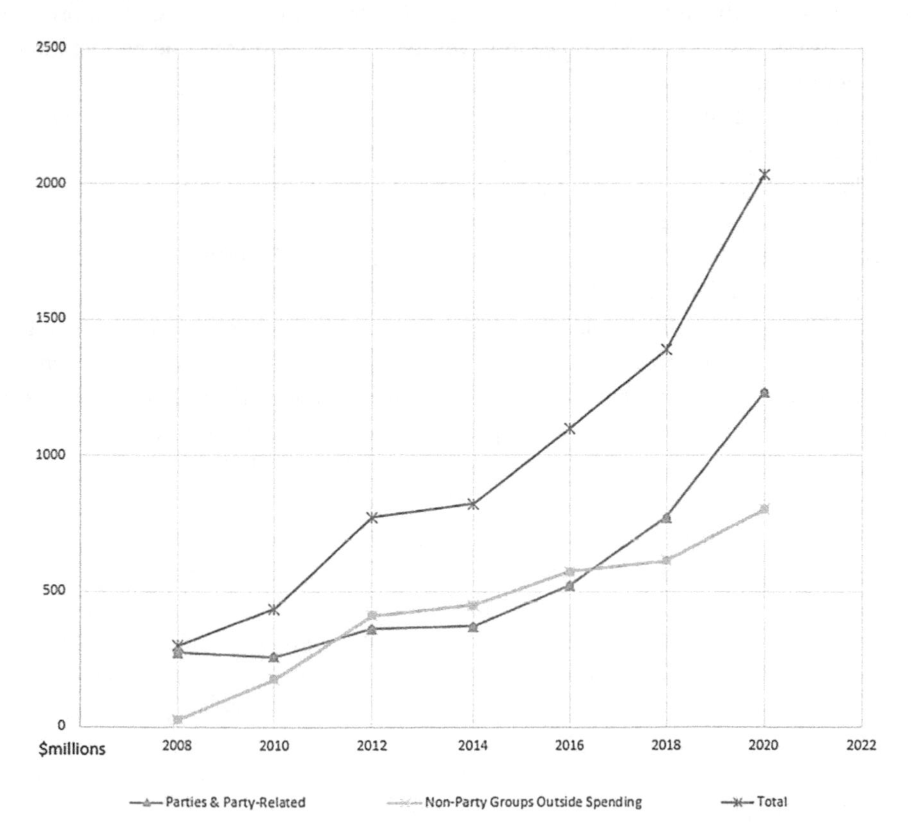

Figure 2.13 Independent Expenditures on Congressional Elections

as Microsoft, Google, Facebook, or Amazon—even if a large majority of Americans support such reforms?

Thanks to Roberts & Co., corporations and their owners are also increasingly directing a lot more cash into elections for state offices, including elected judgeships, which get less media attention (see #14).[138] This can be a cheap way for them to score big by blocking regulations and lawsuits that would protect public interests, and to influence redistricting once per decade after the census.[139] One study found that the "interest group activists" who contribute to state legislative candidates and run "independent" ads to support them explain about 25% of liberal shifts and 9% of conservative shifts in statehouse votes from 2000 to 2012. Their influence has only increased in the last decade, as state governments have been captured by national party politics and become less responsive to views of state residents.[140] Gifts from well-funded lobbyists are addictive: the Republican leadership in my original home state of Pennsylvania keeps blocking a vote on banning gifts such as expensive vacations given to state lawmakers.[141]

Finally, *Buckley* and *Citizens United* made it virtually impossible for candidates to enter presidential primary races without the backing of billionaires. As Ari Berman reported, in 2012, "not a single member of Congress was elected without donations" from the richest 0.01% of Americans, i.e., the wealthiest 1 in 10,000.[142] Incumbents' advantages also expanded, which further reduces the number of competitive seats. For example, in the last midterm election (2018), House incumbents spent more than 4 times as much as their challengers on average, and Senate incumbents spent about 7.5 times more.[143]

To be clear, I am not asserting that for-profit businesses, unions, and nonprofits should be banned from *all* election spending. On the contrary, civil society actors can play valuable roles in checking any government overreach by providing another center of power that can balance populist sentiment and entrenched bureaucracies.[144] Corporate donations to campaigns through PACs, and to SuperPACs for independent advertising, simply have to be limited.

The Proposal. The trends since 2010 urgently need to be reversed: allowing all the political leverage that money can buy is not a sustainable trajectory. As Hasen puts it, our Constitution cannot be "a suicide pact;" but by allowing the richest to "transform their vast wealth into vastly superior political power," the Roberts Court threatens "democracy itself."[145] Because of this, most analysts believe that an adequate solution is possible only through a constitutional amendment.

Writing in 2015, Hasen hoped for a solution by appointing justices who are less ideologically extreme on campaign finance issues. Now that hope is clearly in vain; it could be decades before the Court would overrule *Citizens United* on its own, and we do not have that long. Yet Hasen rejected the idea of an amendment as impossible and likely not to be specific enough to balance free speech with political equality (or with limits to inequality in leverage).

His stance is a great example of what happens when we despair of the amendment route: it unwittingly makes us serfs begging for scraps, contorting our efforts to fit the Court's perverse dicta.[146] This is the wrong way to approach systemic breakdown in government: the Supreme Court ultimately serves the American people, not the reverse. Millions of Americans working together for a constitutional new deal should *overrule* the Court on this issue. To address Hasen's points, the needed amendment has to be more specific than Tom Udall's resolution, which simply said that "Congress and the States may regulate and set reasonable limits on the raising and spending of money by candidates and others to influence elections" (and legislative outcomes).

The language I suggest, which is developed partly from Udall's proposal and another on *WeAmend.us*, divides up the components for maximum clarity. Its first article sets out a central principle and addresses the *donation side* of our monetary leverage system by proposing a cap on individual contributions to any of the three main kinds of political agents in our system. Article II turns to spending by political campaigns and parties, giving Congress discretion to set caps (subject to judicial review) in this area. It would also reduce the incumbent advantage and combat the leverage of big donors through the kind of small-donation transferrable voucher that reformers of many partisan stripes have recommended. The third article completes the *spending side* of the equation by capping independent political expenditures by corporations, SuperPACs, unions, and "social welfare" groups. It would end corrupt lobbying, enhance opportunities for challengers by allowing Congress to require some free air time for serious candidates, and protect freedom of the press.

I. The United States is a deliberative democracy in which every citizen has an equal right to political participation. To this end, the right to spend money on political activities, as defined by federal and state law, is not unlimited and may be subject to viewpoint-neutral limitations. In particular,
   (i) each adult's personal spending to advocate for specific candidates, legislation, and similar political activities, whether by contributing funds or donations in-kind to political campaigns, political parties, or independent political and social advocacy groups, are subject to an annual total cap across all such activities set by Congress, which shall not be less than *one-tenth* of the real median US household income [= about $7078 in 2021] nor more than *one-fifth* of the real median US household income [= about $14,156 in 2021];[147]
   (ii) All donations over $1000 in value to political campaigns or to independent groups conducting political activities must be publicly disclosed.
   (iii) Only citizens and legal residents who are 18 or older may make such contributions and expenditures for political advocacy, as defined by federal law. No foreign sources are allowed to purchase any political advertising whatsoever in American media, or make any contributions to political partics, campaigns, independent groups, or corporations that spend more than $2,000 a year on political activities in the US.[148]

II. Political spending by political campaigns, political parties and their committees, and independent groups are subject to annual caps, and to further caps during election periods, set by federal law.
   (i) These caps must be set at levels commensurate with reasonable opportunities for candidates from all backgrounds to compete.
   (ii) Caps must be at least 10% higher for challengers than for incumbents.

(iii) There shall be a federally funded voucher of not less than $50 that each registered voter can freely allocate to, or divide among, the campaigns, parties, or registered independent social advocacy groups of their choice, to be used only for legitimate campaign expenses, including *truthful* political advertising.[149] These vouchers may be in addition to campaign matching funds established by law, and are not taxable.

(iv) Congress may set equitable conditions for candidates, parties, and independent social advocacy groups to be eligible to receive voter-directed federal vouchers, including modest evidence of candidates' electoral viability. Misuse of voucher funds is a federal felony.

(v) Congress will regulate mass media news channels or programs, as defined by law, to assure minimum standards of fairness and balance, factual reliability, and freedom from influence by foreign governments in election coverage and political reporting.

III. Corporations, workers' unions, and other associations are not natural persons and do not have the same basic rights as natural persons. Their rights of political advocacy are limited in the following ways, unless Congress by law institutes stricter limits:

(i) Associations of people other than political parties, including corporations, unions, and political action committees, may contribute to political campaigns and to political parties only §I funds that they gather through voluntary individual donations in ways regulated by law.

(ii) Independent spending on political activities, including advertising concerning issues before Congress or to support one party or political position during election season, are defined in statute as political expenditures that do not go to campaigns or to political parties. Total independent spending by corporations, unions, social welfare organizations, and other associations and advocacy groups may be limited by law.[150]

(iii) Nor may lobbyists or their agents, as defined by law, make or arrange any donations or in-kind assistance to political parties, campaigns, or political action committees. Lobbyists are limited to providing information and advice on policies to Congress and federal officers.

(iv) The federal government may by law require every mass media channel, forum, or platform with large audiences to provide a reasonable minimum level of free time or space during the general election for candidates for elected federal and state offices who achieve sufficient levels of support among the entire electorate, as defined by law, during the primary election.

(v) Nothing in this amendment shall be construed to prevent Congress and the States from protecting the fairness of electoral processes and limiting the influence of private wealth on legislation and administrative decisions in government.

(vi) Nothing in this amendment shall enable Congress to abridge the right to petition, or to offer documents or content advocating political positions to the public, which people may voluntarily open, search out, or purchase on their own initiative, in contrast to paid political advertising that appears directly in prominent, high-traffic venues, as defined by law.

An amendment of this breadth would work a revolution in American politics. It would probably cut total election spending to a third of its current size or less, thus freeing members of Congress from the endless rat race of wooing multimillionaires. It would also make the public more powerful than all private lobbies. Public funds to match small private campaign donations have been successful in elections for state government.[151] The voucher would be even more powerful, because people would not have to spend any of their own money to direct their voucher to a candidate for federal office, or to other political–social issue groups. Even at the lower $50 level per voter, total voucher donations could top $2 billion every 2-year cycle—enough to rival private donations. This would open up elected offices to many potential candidates who are currently shut out of primary campaigns for lack of big donors. Combined with more competitive House districts (see #4), there would be fewer incumbents who go unchallenged just because they have raised a massive war chest before the campaign even begins.[152]

The Pew study noted earlier (Figure 2.9) suggests that there would be very wide support for several provisions in this detailed amendment. It would create a framework within which effective federal laws on campaign finance and advertising become possible, and greatly expand opportunities for new candidates who are not owned by the donor class. And the individual voucher would give states a new incentive to increase registration rates.

Note that Article III, unlike some more strongly worded amendment proposals,[153] still allows corporations to play a role. Some popular proposals would not allow corporations to spend anything "to influence the outcome of public elections."[154] Instead, my amendment would permit Congress to set spending limits under which corporations could support political positions during election season. I would recommend a cap of perhaps $80,000 per year for large corporations with subsidiaries, and lower caps for smaller businesses, on a sliding scale set by statute.[155] Big companies and civil society actors may have useful points to make in political debates. They just cannot drown out the vast majority of the public or gain thousands of times more access to legislators. More generally, we can strongly limit the influence of big donors, SuperPACs, and outside groups without requiring perfect equality in each person's political influence.

Finally, this amendment protects publishers of print, video, and online political content. And by mandating a minimum fair-and-balanced standard for mass media, we would finally conquer the pandemic of lies, heavily slanted coverage (propaganda),[156] and bot-driven misinformation that are poisoning American politics. Recall that until the late 1980s, the Fairness Doctrine for mass media only required a modicum of balance across a channel's or forum's different shows and coverage, not a breadth of viewpoints within each individual show. Free speech flourished under this standard.[157]

Vouchers as an *Alternative* to Amendment? There are different possible versions of the voucher idea to empower everyone, no matter what their financial means, to allocate a small amount of money as they wish for political advocacy. Usually this is paired with the idea that campaigns can accept these vouchers only if they agree to strict limits on amounts they will accept from any individual donors and corporate PACs. The "For the People Act" takes a similar approach by offering to match small donations under $200 by $6 dollars for every $1 donated (for candidates who accept spending limits that this entails).[158]

Yet without hard limits on big donations and on the spending side, campaigns that get many massive donations bundled together by lobbyists from several wealthy individuals and/or PACs may simply opt out of a federal voucher program in order to avoid the strings attached to them. Some candidates, like Bernie Sanders, will accept voluntary limits on big donations as a point of pride. But many others will not, and some may use millions in personal wealth on their own campaign, or on a close relative's campaign.

Moreover, as Mann and Ornstein argue, without a constitutional amendment that allows limits on independent advertising by the ultrarich, corporations, and outside groups, public financing to match small donations will not be enough.[159] That's because campaigns and independent issue groups will use advertising to get more vouchers. Small donations have increased in recent years, as our two dominant parties moved into permanent fundraising mode. But they are often raised by messages pushing ever more extreme positions and scare tactics. As Lessig says, "[e]xtremism [...] pays, literally," even though it horrifies moderate potential voters.[160]

My approach mitigates that problem by requiring campaigns and groups taking voucher money to use it only for truthful communications (see §II clause [iii]). Then an allocatable voucher can motivate a lot of moderate and/or less politically active Americans who presently donate nothing to campaigns. After all, it would only take a few clicks to donate.

In sum, only through an amendment can we reverse the fundamental wrong of *Citizens United* and end the system of lobbying in Washington D.C.[161] Until then, Congress should do what it can to counter the influence of big lobbies and dark money funneled through independent political groups. But the American public clearly wants a more fundamental reform to end the excessive political influence of the wealthiest that is making them even richer at the expense of most other segments of the nation.

6. Constitutional Voting Rights: Fair and Accessible Elections with Integrity

Voter turnout in the US is historically lower than in many other developed democracies (see Figure 2.14 and Figure 1.4), and this is partly due to the ways that states make it hard to vote. The first five constitutional revisions outlined above would all increase public interest in voting as the number of viable political parties rises, more districts become competitive, and parties become more responsive to ordinary-income voters rather than very wealthy backers. But that will not help enough if people cannot easily register to vote, cast a ballot, and trust the ballot counting.

Many Problems. Political scientists note that the US is unique in lacking clear countrywide standards in elections for national offices.[162] It must be obvious that the US now desperately needs basic national standards establishing simple, easy, and reliable ways of registering, voting, and counting ballots. This is not hard with 21st-century technology, but it requires investment, well-trained and well-paid poll workers, and impartial administration by election experts. The Supreme

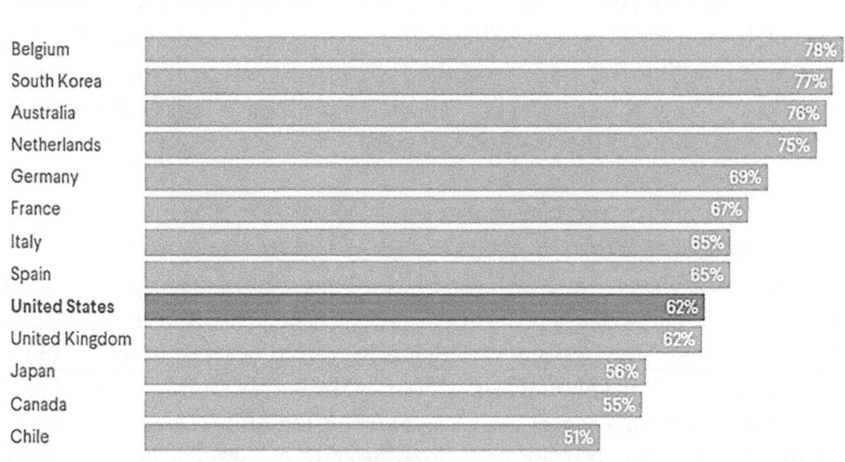

Figure 2.14 US Voter Turnout vs. Other Democracies

Court has complained before that even different counties within the same state use varying voting and counting methods, but the Court has done nothing to stop these inequalities.[163]

Any good-faith attempt to resolve these difficulties with voting rights has to start from one fundamental principle: democracy depends on *cooperating* with others who disagree with us, at least for a time, on some policy questions. That cooperation requires fair rules for everyone that foster trust. Without such rules, we have no peaceful way to manage deep differences of opinion. Widespread violence and even dictatorship are the only alternative once we reject fair election processes in a drive to win power *at all costs*. Consider five serious problems to which this drive has led.

1. Since 2020, our country has turned a dark corner, with relentless attacks on the election systems and the underpaid staff running it, including thousands of Republican and Democratic officials just trying to do their jobs. Propaganda spreading lies about ballot boxes being dumped and conspiracies about election managers seem to some operatives like a great way of riling up supporters and raising money. But these tactics are self-destructive in the long run for obvious reasons:

- impartial umpires will quit;
- if you legitimately win, the other side will no longer accept that; and
- if some kind of manipulation of the vote count really does occur, people in the party benefiting from the abuse will not believe it—because of all the "crying wolf" we have endured.

Once cynics sow enough doubt for strategic purposes, most people on all sides will think the game is rigged.

2. The pillars holding up our temple of democracy are also being sledgehammered by state governments and the Supreme Court. While the Voting Rights Act was originally a product of the civil rights movement in the 1960s, Congress renewed it in 2006 by rare overwhelming margins. A total 92% of the House voted yea, and Senate reapproval was *unanimous.*[164] Yet, with breathtaking antidemocratic hubris, in June 2013, the Court gutted Sections 4 and 5 of the new VRA anyway, removing the need to clear election process changes with the federal watchdog.

Immediately after, several states embarked on crusades to make registering, voting, and fair vote-counting harder.[165] For example, as Cohen notes, Alabama started to require photo IDs to vote—and then closed 31 offices issuing driver's licenses, mostly in its 8 counties with more Black residents.[166] It doesn't get much more cynical than that. The argument for such abuses is always that otherwise thousands of ineligible people will vote. But as the Levinsons note, an exhaustive review by Trump's own commission found less than 10 certain cases of voter fraud among 136 million votes in 2016.[167]

3. Still, if it ends the strategic promotion of conspiracy theories about the vote, it may be worth requiring proof of residency and an official ID or birth certificate to register, and a photo ID to vote in every state—*if* this is part of a fair overall package of measures to rebuild trust our elections. But that works *only* if documents are easy for everyone entitled to them to obtain without a lot of costs and difficult paperwork. County registrars should even help residents to get such documents. It helps if the state accepts ID cards from employers and colleges at the polls, perhaps along with a piece of mail addressed to the resident. But some states now accept only a *government-issued* photo ID.[168]

Of course, if you own a car and drive legally, this will be easy. But many city residents do not need to drive, and/or lack the income to own or lease a vehicle. Statistics on licenses by ethnicity are in short supply, but one 2012 study found the following percentages of adults without a valid driver's license or other government-issued photo ID: black 13%, Hispanic 10%, other/mixed race 11%, white 5%.

What about other government-issued ID? Many states offer this, but often with a lot of hoops to jump through. Texas, for example, requires your birth certificate or marriage license, your social security number, thumb prints, an appointment at a driver's license office, a $16 fee, and possibly further documents—all to get a state ID that *might* allow you to vote if you can also register (that's a separate process).[169] I wouldn't be surprised if a DNA sample comes next. It is very hard to see how this is compatible with the 24th Amendment passed in 1964, which explicitly banned a "poll tax or other tax" as a precondition to vote. Even a $20 fee to get a birth certificate as a precondition to get a $10 photo ID that is needed to register and/or to vote really violates that constitutional law.

4. However, the far bigger problem, as election experts argue, is badly conducted purges of voter rolls. Of course, voter rolls need to be kept up to date; ours are not, because, unlike most democratic nations, we do not have one national database of registered voter information connected with other public records from coroner's offices, Departments of Motor Vehicles (DMVs), Social Security, etc. This flaw almost never leads to voter fraud, but it offers an excuse for shocking abuses. Here are a few quick examples.

The most impactful purge was conducted in Florida before the Gore vs. Bush election that we considered earlier (see #1). Litt vividly describes how, early in 2000, Florida Governor Jeb Bush's team hired a contractor who purged from FL voter rolls over 67,000 people it claimed were deceased or felons barred from voting. Many of them had simply been conflated with people of similar names. "A conservative estimate is that 12,000 eligible, registered Florida voters were taken off the rolls, about half of them African-American."[170] That is a very big deal in an election decided by 537 votes when the Court bizarrely stopped the recount halfway through.

Since then, Ohio purged over 115,000 people for not having voted in six years, and then found that over 18,000 were purged by mistake. These were engaged citizens; over 10,000 of them voted in the 2020 election.[171] Similarly, in 2017, Indiana tried to remove registered voters who shared a first name, last name, and birthday with someone registered in another state, without even trying to mail them a letter to check. This unreliable method would have removed tens of thousands of Indiana residents (e.g. some who had moved to Indiana while forgetting to de-register in their previous home state). When federal courts blocked this purge, Indiana tried to do it again in 2020.

And in 2017, Georgia Secretary of State Brian Kemp removed a whopping 1.5 million people for missing one or two elections and not responding to an inquiry postcard that looked like junk mail. This would not have been allowed under the VRA, but the Court permitted it by a 5–4 vote. Over 70,000 of those disenfranchised re-registered to vote in GA within two years;[172] probably another 30,000 still lived in GA.[173] Kemp also closed over 200 polling places, mostly in poor or minority neighborhoods, before winning the 2018 race for Governor by only 55,000 votes (a 0.4% margin). If these examples aren't enough, Cohen also reports that independent groups are suing poor counties to purge voter rolls, knowing these counties lack the money for a court fight.[174]

5. Finally, a few states have taken to blocking voter registration forms by demanding perfect agreement with DMV and Social Security records. As Bentin Mock explains, if a voter or registration drive volunteer puts "Tom" as a first name for a person listed as "Thomas" on his driver's license, the state will toss out the registration without even notifying the would-be voter. In Georgia, on July 4 of 2018, 51,000 attempted registrations were on hold for this reason, "with 80 percent of those being African-Americans, Latinos, and Asian Americans."[175] As Litt points out, non-white names are more likely to be misspelled by a worker transcribing info from registration form into a database, with the shocking result that 70% of registrations held up by "match" conditions in 2018 where non-white. Florida tried the same thing in 2018, with the absurd result that it rejected *more than half* of all registration attempts in the lead-up to that election![176]

Beyond these five most glaring problems with US elections, there are many others. States may make it nearly impossible to conduct legal registration drives; or toss out mailed ballots for a signature written with a shaky hand after morning coffee; or change precinct lines close to an election; or make it hard to get an absentee or mail ballot; or reduce the number of polling places and then let lines to vote become hours long (Georgia, Florida, and Texas are infamous for this outrage[177]). After the VRA was gutted by the Court, "13 southern states closed 1,688 polling locations between 2012 and 2018."[178]

As Litt argues, lines longer than an hour really reduce turnout and affect non-white voters far more often.[179] In some cases, polls even close with people still waiting. A 2019 study using cell phone data showed that "voters in predominantly black neighborhoods waited 29% longer, on average, than those in white neighborhoods [and] were also about 74% more likely to wait for more than half an hour."[180] Clearly, this could affect outcomes in close votes.

Like a game of "gotcha," state laws with such results put more pressure on voters to navigate an increasingly hostile obstacle course in order to cast a valid ballot.[181] Yet even when they result from incompetence and underfunding rather than from intentional malice, these problems erode trust in election outcomes among many centrist and lefter-leaning voters. Similarly, loose standards for mail ballots in bluer states erode faith among some independents and many righter-leaning Americans.

Sane people across the country need to demand that all such faith-eroding tactics stop before the election system collapses. We can build a system that boosts trust in election outcomes among all voters, but only if we have the courage to accept a repaired system's results. This would force political parties to win by convincing more voters on the issues, rather than by rigging the voting process to exclude those they have not persuaded.

As I emphasized in the Introduction, no party can use such shameful methods for very long and survive as a democratic institution. Mass lies, coordinated manipulation of one's own supporters, specious challenges to ballot counts, and slimy attempts to confuse and repel potential voters will eventually consume the whole system in which political parties operate. If we do not overcome this existential challenge by peaceful reform, then the future will belong to the mass-murdering tyrants in Russia, China, and elsewhere, rather than to our children, grandchildren, and their democracy-loving friends around the world.

A Ten-Point Fix. So what solutions would a sane compromise require? Most of the problems just summarized should in principle be fixable by ordinary federal laws. Uniform national requirements that could win bipartisan support must include measures that make registering and voting easier, along with safeguards that lay to rest fears about vote tampering or registration by illegal aliens. A viable solution recipe needs all of the following ingredients.[182]

(i) *Election Day and Early Voting.* Make Election Day a national holiday with its date fixed on the first Tuesday in November. Every state should also offer at least two early in-person voting days on the two weekends prior to the election. States should receive federal block grants for all election expenses, conditional on hiring professional staff and accepting best practices concerning ballot design and voting machines.

(ii) *Accessible Voting.* States must make an in-person polling center or drop box, which were introduced for safety reasons,[183] available within 4 miles of everyone's residence (with exceptions for the most sparsely populated areas). States should also make available enough voting booths and staff so that no one ever has to wait longer than 30 minutes on Election Day. Voters must be notified both one month and one week prior to early voting days if their polling place has changed. A ballot cast in the wrong precinct should still count for every federal and statewide election.[184] [NB: mail ballots make this mistake nearly impossible.]

(iii) *A National Standard for Voter Registration.* Establish multiple ways to register to vote, including documents proving residence that can be submitted online, by mail, or in person at town, county or state offices such as DMVs *and local post offices.* Citizens can obtain supporting documents such as a birth certificate for free.[185] Eligible persons may also register on the day of an election at their polling place when they have reliable photo identification, and immediately cast a provisional ballot, which will be counted once their registration is confirmed. Anyone whose registration is rejected must be notified in writing and has the right to appeal at the state's expense. States may not de-register anyone based solely on their having the same name and town of residence as a disenfranchised felon, or the name and birthday of someone registered in another state, or for having missed votes in the last six years.

(iv) *A Frequently Updated National Voter Registry* can be managed by an independent federal commission, with paper backups to prevent tampering.[186] The general presumption must be that people report their identity and residence honestly (the state has the burden to prove them wrong). But the registry should also flag any inconsistencies with public information, death certificates, or tax filings that declare residency, and then follow up with the registrants to resolve any uncertainties about their status. This system would help especially when people move, e.g. by ensuring that they are deregistered in their previous state or county. It could send email and paper mail messages to every registered voter in January of an election year, describing their status in the national registry, and provide a website where they can correct any mistaken information and explain inconsistencies.

The registry could also send every voter (who does not opt out of this feature) a free federal photo ID card bearing the registry information, good for two years at a time, which must be accepted as sufficient proof of identity when someone comes to the polls or votes by mail. If we want to minimize both fraud and inadvertent errors, this is the fairest reliable way to do it. Note that this would not be a *requirement* for every American to carry a federal photo ID: it would be entirely optional, but also backed by a reliable national registry.[187]

(v) *National Vote-by-Mail and Precinct Standards.* The law should make it easy for registered voters to request a mail ballot but prohibit states from sending them automatically to everyone unless an emergency warrants this. In every state, ballots *postmarked* by Election Day should be counted for up to ten days afterwards. They should be counted in every state on a rolling basis as they arrive. It is hypocritical not to start counting mail ballots until Election Day and then complain that the election results are slow.

It should also be free to mail ballots, and the US Postal Service should give them priority with tracking, so their transit can be checked by voters using a number retained from a tear-off portion of the ballot. An email or text message confirming receipt should go to each person when their mail ballot is received; this can alert voters if someone else mailed their ballot without their consent. No one except a close relative, home aid, or immediate neighbor (in the same building or on the same street) should be allowed to mail your ballot for you. And voters should be able to confirm that their mail ballot was counted by checking a state website.

Mail ballots also should not be rejected for a stray pen mark or single typo (e.g. a letter in their address). This does not happen to people at polling stations. Signature matching should not be used; people sign differently depending on the pen, time of day, recent work with hands, and many other factors. Instead, the voter's identity could be confirmed with a unique PIN, provided separately from the federal ID card, which each voter enters on their mail ballot.

If a voter's mail ballot is rejected at the counting center, they should receive an email to this effect, and have a chance to "cure" their ballot within three days by confirming their identity as the sender with answers to a few simple questions.

(vi) *Photo ID.* In a spirit of compromise, federal voting law should require valid photo ID to be presented by anyone voting in person. But adequate IDs should include any federal photo ID or passport, a state driver's license, other state ID, dated employee photo ID card, high school ID with documents confirming the bearer's age, and dated college student ID cards. Images of such IDs saved on phones should also count.

(vii) *Double-blind Vote Counting.* Voting machine results, paper ballots, and mail ballots should routinely be counted twice, with any significant discrepancies between the counts examined in more detail. Poll watchers (without guns) from the largest parties could inspect these results, observe proof-of-identity checks during in-person voting, and watch the opening and processing of mail-in and drop-box ballots, as long as they keep a respectable distance and avoid threatening acts. An impartial judge should be available in each county to rule quickly on trouble at vote-counting centers, and on ballots whose status remains disputed after an apparent voter is contacted for confirmation and given the chance to respond by text, email, or letter. At the national level, a special Court of Elections staffed by judges with senior status should be available to settle larger disputes quickly.

(viii) *Clear, Easily Understandable, and Reliable Ballots.* Voting machine screens and paper ballots should make it clear how to vote for each candidate (e.g. no confusing arrows), and make it easy to see each candidate's affiliation. Voting machines should not be connected to the internet and should produce paper records. Paper ballots can be useful backups if the machines at a polling station fails.But confusing "butterfly" ballots and punch card systems (of "hanging chad" infamy[188]) should not be allowed.

(ix) *Intentional Deception of Voters is a Felony.* Paid advertising, mail, and social media posts intended to discourage groups of people from voting, mislead people about their voting opportunities, or scare people away from polling places should be a federal felony, punishable by not less than a $50,000 fine and five years in prison. To stymie another form of dirty trickery, candidates with names similar to anyone else on the ballot should be clearly separated and distinguished (with emphasis given to their party affiliation). Anyone who offers or accepts bribes in order to run for federal or state office, for example to siphon off votes from a similarly named candidate, should be subject to a minimum of five years in prison and banned from ever holding federal office.

(x) *Automatic Recount Standards and Protections for Vote Counters.* Every state should be required to recount any election within a 0.5% margin of victory. But any party filing suit to protest a vote-counting procedure, final tally, or recount should have to pay a $500,000 fine if the suit is ruled by a three-judge panel to be frivolous or based on no plausible evidence. Threatening nonpartisan poll workers or public employees involved in vote counting should be a felony with a minimum sentence of five years in prison.

This recipe is fair to all sides. It addresses several Republican concerns about mail ballots and voter IDs, while adapting the most defensible ideas from Democrats, and promoting the main goals of the VRA that was renewed by such a huge supermajority in 2006. An *Esquire* poll suggested that 56% of Republicans supported similar measures in the "For the People Act" (which got filibustered in the Senate).[189] Senator Joe Manchin's own compromise proposal included points (i), (ix), parts of (ii) and (iii), and stronger versions of some provisions, such as automatic registration at the DMV unless you opt out when getting your license.

These ten points do not include everything that many Democrats want, such as universal mail balloting, no photo ID at the polls, voting rights for all convicts once out of prison, or automatic voter registration (which most other industrialized democratic nations do use).[190] The ten points also meet Republican requests to prevent potential abuse of mail ballots, ensure accurate voter rolls, and restore confidence in vote counting processes.

Why an amendment, then? This ten-point recipe should be enacted through ordinary federal law. Call it the new "Voting Integrity Act" (VIA). But even if a national standard like this finally passes both chambers of Congress, there are three big problems with relying on such a statute alone.

First, we have seen what happened to the VRA. Over the last two decades, our high court has rejected one part of the VRA after another, until almost nothing remains. The Court could just as easily rule that one or more parts of the ten-point VIA violates states' rights to set the terms of their elections.[191] This danger arises from the fact that, believe it or not, Americans do not yet have a true constitutional *right to vote.*

Congress traditionally has authority to regulate federal elections based on Article I §4 of the Constitution, and this was affirmed in a 2013 Supreme Court decision.[192] But we cannot trust the Court to interpret this federal authority as robust enough to support all parts of the ten-point fix. The Constitution refers to voting in the 15th, 24th, and 26th Amendments, but the Court has interpreted them so as to leave states enormous latitude in deciding who is eligible to register, how one registers, when and where people can vote, how ballots are structured and counted, etc.

Second, anything like the ten-point VIA requires the cooperation of state officials to work. But in recent years, the Court has repeatedly ruled that federal authorities cannot "commandeer" help from state officials. This is a broader problem—deserving its own amendment—that now makes it harder to enforce federal rules on immigration, firearms, gambling, and many other issues.

Third, without an amendment, rival political parties could alter the rights and protections in the envisioned VIA in bizarre ways to enhance their power. A constitutional right to vote would give courts a clear direction in checking such manipulations, thereby reducing perverse incentives to mess with voting rights rather than doing the work to persuade voters on the merits of one's policies.

For these reasons, many scholars studying voting laws have concluded that a general right to vote and minimum requirements for fairly run elections needs to be made explicit in US constitutional law, as they are in most other developed democracies. Only such a constitutional revision can ensure that minimum national standards would be the same for everyone in the country, which is what an *equal vote* really means. However, the needed amendment can be much simpler than the ten-point plan. A detailed analysis by *Demos*, a public interest NGO, suggests clear clauses like the following:[193]

I. The people of the US are guaranteed a representative democratic system of government. Every citizen of the US of legal voting age with no felony conviction has the inalienable right to a free, equal, and secret vote in all federal, state, and local elections.
II. Registration through a national voter registry shall be easy, free of monetary costs, and free from discrimination, in intent or effect, on account of race, ethnicity, gender, language, socioeconomic status, age, religion, or place of residence.[194]
III. Every registered voter has the right to vote on a ballot that is easy to understand. Access to the polls shall be free of material obstacles, such as harassment or intimidation at the polling place, lines of more than 30 minutes, long distances to voting sites or drop boxes, misleading instructions, and late changes to voting locations or procedures, unless such changes are clearly warranted by a state of emergency validly declared for nonpartisan reasons.
IV. Every citizen has the right to reliable and secure methods of voting, including access to mail ballots, integrity in the vote-counting process, and election officials whose impartiality and security are protected by law. Congress will establish and fund a federal Court of Elections that will have final appellate authority to decide disputes about candidates' eligibility to run, elections processes, challenges to ballots, and returns in all federal elections.
V. Congress shall have the power to enforce these measures by law, including through the mandatory assistance of state officials.

The special tribunal for elections proposed in §IV is common practice in many democratic nations and would relieve our regular federal courts from the mounting political pressures (and costs) that they face. This independent body could also take over certification of presidential election results (see #12). It could be staffed by lottery from a pool of willing federal judges and justices who have reached their constitutional term limits or retired early (see #9), and/or perhaps other retired officials. Conservative scholars have proposed that this court consist in four judges chosen by the four majority and minority leaders of the Senate and House, together with three more judges elected unanimously by these four.[195]

Enshrining an equal right to vote in the Constitution is vital for symbolic reasons, but also because federal judges only *balance* rights that they find within constitutional language. Without this status, the right to vote can too easily be overruled when construing other explicit rights.[196] It is crucial to put the burden on state officials and the anticipated national registry to make opportunities for registration and voting easy, rather than requiring eligible citizens to negotiate a minefield of tricks to register and ultimately cast a ballot. We do not tolerate "buyer-beware" scams in the marketplace; likewise, "voter-beware" is no way to run a democracy.

Of course, election integrity is important: we should make sure that voters are who they say they are, that they are voting where their primary residence is, that they do not vote more than once in the same election, and that if a mail ballot with their name is returned, it was filled out by them. But the state has the burden to make it easy for people to meet these reasonable conditions. This is on a par with the often-cited point that it should be easy for most people to file a tax return without lots of expensive expert help. Just as states offer fairly simple webpages that are sufficient for most people to file a state tax return, so they should have secure and easy webpages for voter registration as well.

This proposal would not force states to restore voting rights to felons who have completed their sentences, but leaves it open that Congress might establish a standard on this matter. This is a large compromise, given that in 2020, over 3 million felons who have completed their entire sentence, including probation or parole, were still barred from voting in their states—often due only to old fines they are too poor to pay.[197] That's more than the entire voting-age population of Oklahoma, with its 5 House members. The US is the only democratic nation "in which ex-prisoners may be permanently disenfranchised,"[198] and the only one that leaves it to subnational units to decide on the length of disenfranchisement. It is worrying that the fraction of US residents who are barred from voting has increased from roughly 3.5% in 1980 to over 8.8% in 2020.[199]

The draft amendment also leaves open whether any noncitizens should be allowed to vote for any offices. It was fairly common in the past for states and/or cities to grant legal alien residents certain voting rights, and a strong case can be made especially for long-term residents holding green cards. The US was home to almost 13 million "legal permanent residents" (green card holders) in 2022, who form 3.9% of our national population—more than the smallest 13 states combined! Many green card residents are married to an American, and come with special advanced skills; they fill 40% of our high-tech (STEM) jobs. Some have aided our military in overseas operations, or are protected victims of human trafficking. They are counted in censuses to establish how many House members each state gets. For comparison, if even half of them who have been legal residents longest could vote, they would exceed the number citizens eligible to vote in Virginia or Massachusetts.

But a viable amendment would doubtless have to compromise on this point. It could explicitly limit enfranchisement of legal aliens, continue to leave it entirely to the states, or (say) let Congress give votes in federal elections to green card holders resident in the US for 5 years or more. Citizenship matters, and more conservative Americans might want a (near-) total ban on noncitizen voting.[200] In general, overreach on both extremes should be reined in by a consensus voting rights amendment.

Finally, this kind of amendment would greatly relieve pressures on state officials to warp election processes for partisan reasons. Once it becomes illegal to engage in incredibly unjust tactics, the arms race in voting process manipulation ends: state officials can no longer be asked to put their party over their conscience. We teach our children to *win fairly or not at all.* Squeezing out a few more hollow victories by making registration and voting harder, threatening officials, and lying about election returns, is not worth the spiritual damage it does. And it betrays all American service personnel—from 1776 to the Iraq and Afghanistan wars—who gave their lives in order to establish and protect democratic institutions on this Earth.

7. End the Filibuster: Make the Senate Work as the Framers Intended

The first six amendments we have examined all concern fixing our elections. That it requires six distinct constitutional reforms to root out the evils which have produced ossified two-party dominance just goes to show how deep the rot is.

But, while anything close to proposed amendments #1–6 would transform our elections and political parties root and branch, this is still not enough to ensure that Congress actually enacts the priorities for which its majorities are elected. Only such responsive outcomes show people that their vote really makes a difference, and allow them to learn from past policy mistakes. Yet both the House and the Senate have internal problems that could block the benefits of election reforms #1–6. These are the topics of amendment proposals #7, #8, and #21.

How the Filibuster Harms the Nation. The filibuster is now well known to more Americans. As we saw, it requires 60% of the Senate, not 51%, to pass most legislation except budget bills (which the Senate exempted some time ago out of sheer necessity). Most people do not realize, however, that the filibuster appears nowhere in the Constitution. It is merely an internal Senate rule—one among many that the Senate readopts by simple majority every two years at the start of a new session.

But among congressional rules, the filibuster has the great distinction of being totally contrary to the main goals of the document produced by the 1787 constitutional convention. Even worse, under the tyranny of the minority that it creates, the Senate has almost completely ceased to function. This is a disaster because in many respects, the Senate was designed to be the heart of our system. Until the Senate's filibuster rule is ended, the US government will remain on life support.

Consider just one of the filibuster's myriad recent effects. On November 30, 2021, a highly disturbed student shot multiple people at the public high school in Oxford, Michigan, killing six. It was the third mass school shooting within three months and just one more in a long pattern of shootings at schools and big events. But the Senate has given up trying to address the glut of unsecured high-power weapons in more households, which is enabling these mass shootings—and massively driving up security costs for all of us in the process.[201]

Things were different a decade ago when Adam Lanza used four of his mother's many semiautomatic guns to kill 26 people, including 20 children, at the Sandy Hook Elementary School in Newtown, Connecticut. After a memorial service and speech by a visibly distraught President Obama, it looked like the Senate might finally strengthen gun laws. Two months later, a bill to expand federal background checks to cover gun show sales was introduced with bipartisan support in the Senate. Polls showed that almost 90%

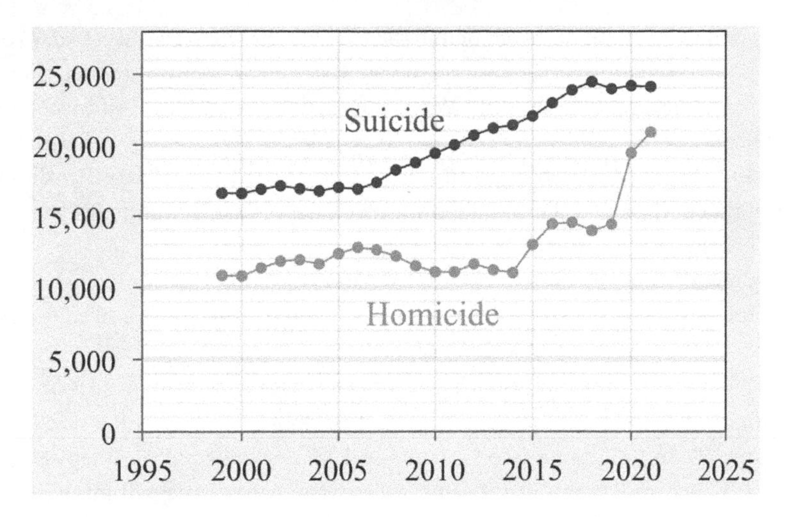

Figure 2.15 Gun-related Deaths in the United States

of Americans favored closing the gun show loophole. This modest bill did not try to renew the lapsed federal ban on large-magazine weapons that was in effect from 1994 to 2004—without preventing any hunters from enjoying their legal sport. Gun violence has increased since that time (see Figure 2.15).[202]

On April 17, 2013, the gun show background check bill was approved in a vote by 55 out of 100 senators, despite fierce lobbying against it by the almighty National Rifle Association (NRA). But it still did not become law, because 60 senators first had to vote for "cloture" to end debate before proceeding to a final vote on the bill itself. Although this sounds confusing, it means that the Senate must take a supermajority vote in order to hold a simple majority vote on almost all bills. This bizarre rule allows a minority of 41 senators to kill proposed laws by postponing a final vote on them indefinitely. That is 41 senators, not senators representing 41% of the American public.

In the gun show case, the 45 senators opposing this background check bill, including 4 Democrats, came mostly from more rural states with smaller populations: they represented less than 38% of all Americans at the time. Control by such a small minority is possible because every state, despite their massively varying population, has just 2 senators (see #24).

Of course, we want major legislation to have broad support across the country; so maybe more rural states with smaller populations deserve some extra protection—some affirmative action, in short, so they are not always outvoted as a bloc. But they would have that and more in a Senate run by simple majority votes: the smallest 26 states, which are home to less than 25% of the American people, would still control 52 Senate seats (see #24). Instead, the filibuster gives their senators *even more power* in the Senate. Talk about greedy.

I do not mean that the filibuster is mainly used by Republicans from more rural states with smaller populations. On the contrary, Democrats frequently filibuster when they are in the Senate minority. In addition to blocking gun show background checks, Republicans have filibustered to block equal pay for women, a $10 national minimum wage, citizenship for residents brought into the US illegally when they were very young,[203] an easier path to forming a trade union, a cap and trade system to reduce greenhouse emissions, and voting rights bills.[204] Yet Democrats have used the filibuster to block Trump's border wall, a bill to force "sanctuary cities" to cooperate with Immigration and Customs Enforcement (ICE), and (sadly) to block chokehold ban legislation—on the excuse that it did not go far enough (but really to prevent Republicans from looking good on the issue of excessive police violence).

Still, given the Senate's composition, 51 senators often represent much less than 51% of the population. And the filibuster often *further* reduces the portion of the population whose voice in the Senate can block legislation.

Today's kill-everything filibuster is also a far cry from the famous instances of yore when a long string of senators kept holding the floor in rotation for weeks on end, reading pages from the phone book just to block some major pieces of legislation from advancing. This is the "talking filibuster" that many Americans still imagine—a kind of ongoing protest that would grip the country's attention.

The most famous talking filibuster began on March 9, 1964 when the Civil Rights Act to protect Black Americans from segregation was introduced in the Senate. It lasted three months until a June 10 vote limited debate and led to its passage. Because the Act was revised during this period to reduce the provisions that its Republican and dixiecrat opponents most disliked, the outcome reinforced the myth that the filibuster encourages compromise between the two major parties.

In fact, that was uncommon even in the 1960s because filibusters were very infrequent, and the parties' main incentives in that period already required some give and take. Then and now, party leaders want to block landmark initiatives by their opponents. But in the past, leaders also needed to get something positive done to report back to constituents even when their party was in the minority. That meant compromising often enough to maintain bipartisan relationships so members could occasionally call in favors across party lines. That incentive no longer operates: few senators now feel any pressure to compromise with the other party.[205]

This explains why the filibuster was rarely attempted before the 1970s except on the most explosive issues like ending segregation and promoting racial equality. It was seen as a tool to be used *very sparingly*, because it stopped all other Senate business, used up a lot of goodwill, and sometimes generated public outrage. For example, in 1917, a group of 12 isolationist senators blocked a bill to arm US merchant ships against increasing attacks by German submarines. These senators were pilloried in the press, and President Wilson's public criticisms forced the Senate to adopt the first cloture rule allowing 2/3^{rds} of the Senate (67% of senators) to cut off debate.

Relative to that margin, the 1975 rule change that required "only" 60% of the Senate to proceed to final votes sounds like real progress. But appearances can be deceiving. Five year before, in 1970, the Senate also changed its rules so that other business could proceed on the Senate floor even while a bill was being held up by a filibuster. That crucial change meant that senators no longer had to speak interminably to filibuster a bill. This had the unintended consequence of *dramatically lowering the social costs* that senators had previously paid for filibustering: they were no longer enraging their colleagues by stopping all other Senate action indefinitely. Thus after 1975, a mere 41 senators could filibuster a bill forever without having to speak about it at all: they merely had to *threaten* an actual filibuster marathon to table a bill.

This disastrous rule change effectively made the filibuster *automatic* for everything except budget bills and (since 2017) Supreme Court confirmations. All other legislation now needs 60 votes before full Senate debate on it can even begin, let alone end. As Mann and Ornstein note, no other democratic legislature in the world has such a hurdle, let alone in a body already so hugely misproportioned to population.[206]

Predictably, filibusters and cloture votes rose from barely a couple times per term in 1917–1918 and 24 times per term in 1975–1976 to over 330 per term in 2019–2020 (see Figure 2.16). And the true numbers of legislative initiatives stopped by filibusters despite support from a majority of senators is *far larger* than this graph suggests, because

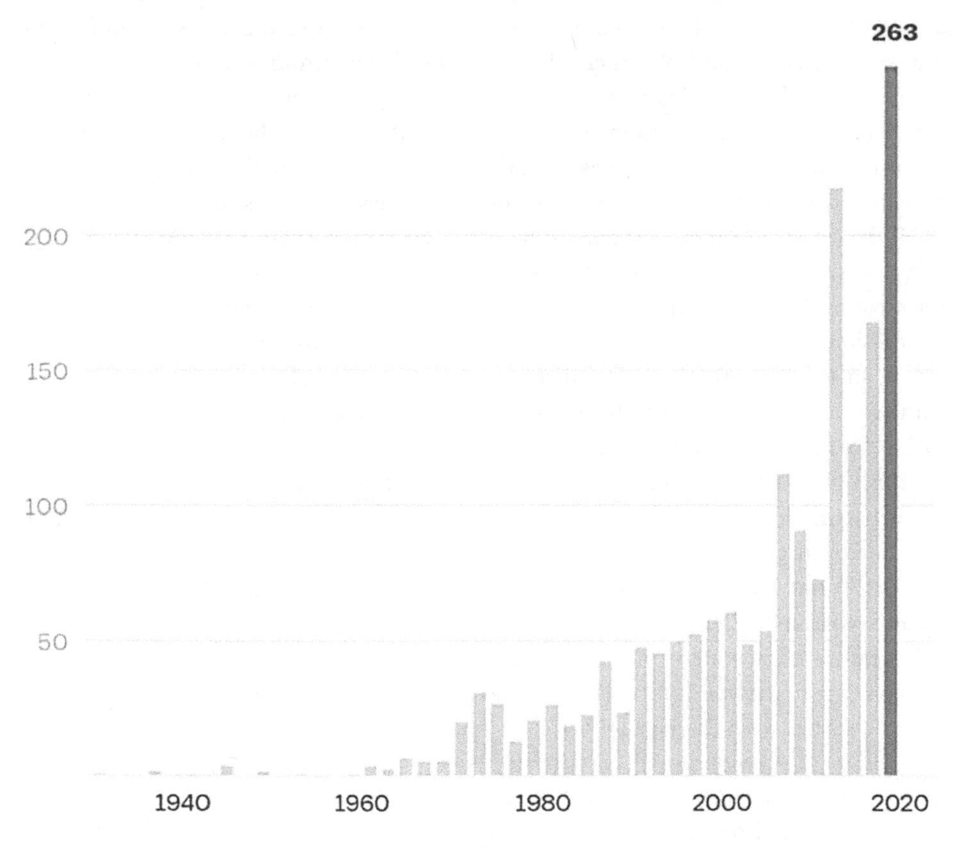

Figure 2.16 The Rise of the Filibuster Threat

it became pointless in most cases even to put committee-approved bills on the Senate schedule when they did not already have 60 or more likely supporters.

So much for the quaint notion that the filibuster inspires valuable deliberation or facilitates the great public arguments though which the Senate sometimes educated Americans in past generations. Long gone are the heady days when Daniel Webster eviscerated John Calhoun's claim that states should be able to "nullify" federal laws, and Henry Clay begged his colleagues for compromise to prevent civil war—and their speeches were read out loud in public squares and schools across many states.

In its present mode, the automatic filibuster makes minority rule by 41% of the Senate routine. Unsurprisingly, this has become the single greatest cause of gridlock in Washington D.C. As real-world problems such as rising urban crime, inflation, health care, gun control, weather disasters, tech monopolies, and a broken immigration system all fester unresolved for decades, resentments build, and the country never moves beyond divisive stalemates (see ch.1).

This provides an opening for partisan forces that feed on division: they demonize sane efforts to solve these problems and portray them as life or death struggles in order to drive turnout from their base. As rivalry around these tough issues rises and people dig in, the chance to resolve them through rational compromise is lost. The national interest depends on finding viable solutions, but the party's interest is served instead by demagoguing the issues with incendiary rhetoric. As the chokehold ban and gun show filibusters show, today's politicians do not want to deprive themselves of a "wedge" issue on which they can fundraise by passing an effective law to address it.

This perverse result of the filibuster is especially evident in the political wars over health insurance from the early 1990s on. As noted in the Introduction, Obama tried for most of 2009 to build a compromise on health insurance reform; he made many concessions to Republicans in the process, such as giving up on a public option. Then, in January 2010, a Republican won the special election in Massachusetts to fill the seat left open by Ted Kennedy's death, campaigning mainly on the promise to be "Number 41" and stop everything in the Senate. So the Democrats had to go through a torturous process of making Obamacare into a budget bill to pass it with a simple majority. Not a single Republican senator voted for it, despite all of Obama's efforts.

Not What the Framers Intended: The Filibuster Violates the "Grand Compromise." The filibuster survives today because myths persist that it serves some noble purpose intended by our founders. The truth is the exact opposite. This section reviews three common errors that help sustain popular attachment this arcane Senate rule, no matter what damage it does.

1. The most widespread erroneous belief is that we need the filibuster to be a "republic" that does not allow "absolute majoritarianism." This is an elementary mistake. To Madison, Adams, Jefferson, Wilson, Hamilton, and other leading theorists of the time, the "republican principle" meant simple majority rule by wise elected representatives. As Taylor et al. argue, citing *Federalist* 14, "democracy" referred to people meeting to legislate directly, as in ancient Athens, while a "republic" referred to people governing indirectly by electing representatives.[207]

So it was not majority rule in Congress, but rather direct democracy by plebiscites unlimited by individual rights, that our framers rejected in embracing "republican government."[208] Most of them also held that tyranny of *the minority* had to be avoided for government to be effective.[209] Moreover, it would be one thing to require a 60% majority of voters to enact a federal law by direct national plebiscite (see #21); requiring 60% of elected senators is something else entirely.

The main critics of the 1787 constitution who contested its ratification also wanted democracy via elected representatives, along with constitutional guarantees for individual rights. Many of these critics were upset that Senate, even without a filibuster, gave too much weight to smaller states. Adding a filibuster rule, which had not even been imagined, would have increased the injustice of the Senate's design in their eyes.

In modern history, the central and cogent objection to unlimited majority rule in legislatures has been that majority rule itself has moral grounds in the equal value of each person's capacities for autonomy. Those capacities entail individual rights that elected bodies like Congress cannot legitimately violate (because that would nullify the basis of democratic right to collective self-rule). This, in a nutshell, was Abraham Lincoln's argument against Stephen Douglas's infamous doctrine that a state convention or legislature may establish slavery in their state by a majority vote if they want to. Lincoln's solution was the 13th Amendment banning slavery. Neither Lincoln nor the authors of our Bill of Rights envisioned supermajority thresholds in Congress as the way to correct Douglas-style bare majoritarianism.

Moreover, in recent decades, a simple majority of the Senate often represents much more than a simple majority of American *people*. For example, in the Senate elected in 2020, the 50 Democratic senators represented roughly 57% of Americans. A rule requiring approval by senators who collectively represent 60% of *the nation* to pass bills on certain topics, such as basic rights, might be worth considering. Instead, the filibuster means that 59 senators potentially representing *over 85%* of the people are not enough to enact a law. No wonder, then, that the filibuster was largely invented by a man whose primary goal was to destroy the work of our framers by restoring state vetoes over federal laws. This man was John Calhoun, a radical proslavery crusader who aimed to prevent the federal government from steering the nation.

2. This brings us to the second myth. Many incautious filibuster-defenders have revealed the depth of their ignorance by saying that the filibuster was part of our founders' design for "limited government." To score well on a US history exam, you must know that the main reason why the convention met in 1787 was because the existing system under the Articles of Confederation barely worked. It was caught in endless gridlock precisely because it required 2/3rds of states—9 of the original 13—to pass laws on most national topics.[210]

For example, in 1784, Thomas Jefferson (himself a slave owner) won support from a majority of states meeting in the Congress of Confederation for a bill to ban slavery after 1800 in *all* new states that would be formed west of the original 13.[211] Imagine how this could have changed our history: slavery might have died out by the 1840s (especially if the five original southern slave states eventually adopted Jefferson's proposal to ban enslavement of anyone born after 1800). But in 1784, Jefferson fell *one state short* of the necessary 2/3rds to pass his Land Ordinance. In effect, his proposal to stop the spread of slavery and thus encourage its gradual abolition was filibustered.

This tragedy illustrates a basic and obvious truism of collective action: the more a procedure for making binding decisions deviates from simple majority toward unanimity, the less power it has to coordinate members of the group participating in the decision. The Congress of Confederation, in short, was too much like the UN Security Council to do much for our young nation. It was a one-chamber body in which each state had an equal vote. In other words, it was like the Senate created in the new constitution, except in the crucial respect that the Senate would operate by *simple majority* in voting on all but a few enumerated topics.

This was essential to the new design because it added two more hurdles: bills had to pass the House and avoid a presidential veto (and eventually survive judicial review as well). Had the framers retained the previous 2/3rds threshold for decisions in the Senate, their new plan would only have *increased* the difficulty of passing needed laws. The convention met to do the opposite, namely to make federal governance possible and effective. Indeed, Madison defends the simple majority threshold for a quorum because without it, "the fundamental principle of free government would be reversed" by allowing a minority in Congress to block legislation.[212]

Thus the filibuster directly conflicts with the framers' central goal of eliminating the 2/3rds requirement to pass ordinary laws. As Adam Jentleson explains, in writing the constitution at the 1787 convention, our founders judged that "supermajority thresholds should be reserved" only for votes on treaties, impeachments, overriding a president's veto, and constitutional amendments. "On all other matters, the delegates were clear that the Senate was to be a strictly majority-rule institution." In 1789, the first Senate adopted 20 rules, *including* a key rule from the English Parliament called "calling the previous question"[213] by which a simple majority could end debate when it had clearly gone on long enough. This rule was omitted from the 1806 Senate rulebook written by Vice President Aaron Burr on the mistaken belief that it was no longer needed. For the presiding chair could cut off senators who had gone off topic for hours.[214]

And so they did until Calhoun, then presiding as Jackson's VP, weakened the custom by refusing to stop harangues that were irrelevant to the bill under discussion. Calhoun recognized that filibusters would operate as a procedural trick to smuggle a new kind of minority veto into the constitutional system. A handful of times from 1841 to the Civil War, Calhoun and his allies used the tactic of holding the floor for days on end leading up to a recess, e.g. to stall bills on banking or block admission of new free states. But even then, senators accepted that a filibuster could only delay, not kill, a pending bill.

After the Civil War, these delaying tactics returned, eventually prompting senators to seek rule changes. The profoundest of these was a bill to restore the traditional "previous question" rule. It would have passed the Senate in 1891 and spared this nation much agony if only its backers had not made a fateful procedural miscalculation.[215] So the filibuster survived, returning to prominence in 1917, as told above. Rule 22 allowing cloture by a 2/3rds vote was supposed to be the remedy.

Instead, this supposed remedy formalized the same threshold that had existed in the Confederation Congress! To appreciate just how outrageous this is, recall that many delegates from large states at the 1787 convention almost walked out when Connecticut and Delaware insisted on getting the same weight as Virginia and Pennsylvania in the Senate (see #24). It is absolutely clear that if small states had additionally insisted on including a supermajority threshold for all Senate votes, the large states would never have accepted the grand compromise, and the federal government would not have been established.

By analogy, imagine that you concluded a difficult deal to purchase a new machine at a huge price, only to discover on receipt that the seller had removed a most vital part. The filibuster is like that: it reneges on the main concession that small states made in 1787 in exchange for two senators per state.

Calhoun's betrayal enabled later southern segregationist senators who openly praised "white supremacy" to block several civil rights bills with potential majority support in the Senate from 1877 to 1964. They built up the false ideology that the filibuster is essential for the right of minorities—that is, minorities *of states.* They misportrayed motions to end discussion of a bill and proceed to a vote as violating their right to "free debate," even though they were not seeking to extend real debate on a bill's merits at all. Beneath all this bs, they had one aim: to block social equality across racial lines. As Jentleson sums up, "[i]n the eighty-seven years between the end of Reconstruction and 1964, the only bills that were stopped [as opposed to delayed] by filibusters were civil rights bills."[216]

Thus by allowing filibusters and betraying the Madisonian principles on which our Constitution was based, the Senate blocked progress on our worst social problem for decades. Although they ultimately failed to preserve racial apartheid and disenfranchisement of Black Americans, the dixiecrats succeeded in infecting the heart of our federal system with Calhoun's lethal pathogen. With the filibuster now mainstreamed, that infection is killing the federal government, just as Calhoun hoped.

3. In light of this history, we can also dismiss a myth popularized by some lawyers that the filibuster rule is allowed because the Constitution says each chamber of Congress can make its own rules (see Article I §5). To test this argument, let us imagine that the House of Representatives decided to adopt an "internal rule" that, from now on, they will give each state delegation an equal vote on all motions, thus effectively turning the House into the Senate. It is pretty obvious that such procedure would be unconstitutional, as it would undo the grand compromise. The same would be true if the Senate decided that from now on, it would give each senator between 1 and 60 votes, based on their state's population size, to cast for or against each bill. For example, senators from New York could have 30 votes each, while senators from North Dakota had 1. It would be an amusing experiment for the Senate to enact such a rule that made it operate by proportional representation like the House: the Supreme Court would probably decree it unconstitutional within a few hours!

So no, the Senate cannot adopt just any internal rule it wants. The filibuster is unconstitutional on exactly the same basis as votes proportional to state populations would be in the Senate: it violates the convention's main compromise. Congressional rules are limited by the letter and implicit norms of the Constitution. The House and Senate could not, for example, adopt some clever procedure to override a president's veto by a 51% majority, when the Constitution specifies a 2/3rds threshold for this, or decide to certify presidential election results by flipping a coin. As Jack Rakove notes, agreeing with Jentleson, the filibuster has effectively become a decision rule of the sort that is banned by the Constitution's explicit list of *exceptions* to simple majority decisionmaking.[217] "Originalists" should be the first to recognize this.

The Proposal and Alternatives. The filibuster is most likely to be removed by the Senate changing its offending rule at the start of a new session in January. At the least, as several conservatives have proposed, the Senate might go back to requiring "talking filibusters," perhaps with a limit of one speech per member, or with a total time limit.[218] But again in 2021, the Senate majority held back out of fear that once their opponents have the majority without a filibuster, they will pass extreme and highly destructive laws. This is main reason cited by Senators Manchin and Sinema for keeping the filibuster going even for voting rights bills (which could easily be exempted).

This attitude amounts to rejecting democratic faith in the people. On the contrary, if a few highly ideological laws do pass when the filibuster is gone, *the people will learn*, just as they do with bad state laws and in parliamentary systems. It is much better for Americans to see the majority's will enacted and come later to recognize that some enacted policies were mistakes. The only alternative to such a process condemns voters to conclude that carrying elections is useless and the whole system is rigged—perhaps by some suspect group (add here your favorite conspiracy *de jour*). That is ultimately far more destructive than passing a few bad laws in the Senate.

No wonder, then, that most state governments do not allow filibusters. Simple majorities rule without disastrous results.[219] Some 43 state legislatures either limit total debate time on a bill and/or allow a simple majority to end debate by calling the question.[220] I checked West Virginia and Arizona: neither allows filibusters. In the AZ and WV state senates, 51% can enact their platform in the knowledge that voters will hold them accountable for making bad laws. That is much better than doing nothing on urgent social, economic, and environmental problems!

Yet even if our federal Senate eventually musters the courage to eliminate its filibuster rule, some version of it could always be resurrected under a jaded new procedural guise by a latter-day Calhoun. The only permanent fix is to ban filibusters explicitly in the Constitution and emphasize that Congress does not have unlimited discretion over its rules. The amendment can be simple in this case:

I. Filibusters are prohibited in both houses of Congress: debate may be extensive in time, but not unlimited. A simple majority is sufficient to open debate on a bill. In the Senate, debate may extend to 50 hours on a bill, unless the Senate adopts a lower time-limit, or Congress sets a lower limit by law, or a simple majority extends the time for a particular bill or resolution to ensure that every senator who wishes to speak on it has had at least one hour to do so. Then a motion to call the previous question can be approved by a simple majority.

II. No member of Congress may place holds on legislation or appointments. Internal Senate and House rules may never be used to bring about procedural results that violate the intent of the Constitution as amended. Within these limits, Congress may by law determine rules for proceedings in both chambers.

While Republican leaders have tried to sell the filibuster to their supporters in recent years, I believe this amendment would have considerable support among most Americans. A recent poll found that only 38% of voters preferred a 60% rather than a 51% threshold (and that's despite the influence of the three myths debunked above).[221]

Introducing this amendment as part of the broader agenda of constitutional reforms could also push the Senate to pare down the filibuster—e.g., by exempting bills concerning voting rights, election finance, and approval of new states from filibusters. That would not be enough to allow major legislative breakthroughs on many real-world problems, but it would be a good start.

8. A Proportional House of Representatives: Restore the Framer's House

While the high costs of the filibuster are becoming better known, the House of Representatives has a different problem that is not yet widely discussed: its 435 members are *far too few* to do the job that our founders intended. For comparison, Britain has about one-fifth of the US population but they are represented by 650 members in the House of Commons. Canada's population is about 11% of ours, but their House has 338 members.

In 1787, our federal constitution established 65 House members apportioned to states roughly according to their populations (about 58,000 Americans per member). They expected this number of congressmen to rise after the first national census in 1790. And it was raised to 105 by a 1792 law. Thus in March 1793, each member of the newly elected House represented about 37,080 people (by the 1790 population count). Given a population of about 328 million in the 50 states, each House member in 2023 represents over 756,321 people on average—*20 times more* than in 1793.

This has happened because rural-dominated Congresses of the past, fearing rising city populations, stopped increasing the size of the House after 1911, and eventually people forgot that the number of House members is supposed to increase with population. In 1911, each House member represented about 212,019 residents: to get back to that ratio, we would need 1,552 House districts. And to get back to 37,080 people per House member, we would need a whopping 8,873 House districts!

Don't worry, I am not proposing to turn the House into a complete zoo with many thousands of congresspersons. But we do need to fix several problems that have arisen from 112 years without an increase in the total number of House districts.

Injustices Resulting from an Inadequate House. A House stuck forever at 435 is big trouble for at least four reasons. First, the lower chamber of the US legislature was supposed to be the part of government closest to ordinary citizens—a function that has only become *more* important over 250 years, as the franchise was expanded to every adult citizen and senators grew more distant from the people with rising state populations. With House districts now including three quarters of a million people on average, it is much harder for us to communicate effectively with our representatives or meet them at public events. And many who hold safe seats choose not to make public appearances at all, although they still spend lots of time meeting with big donors (see #5).

Second, large-population states that already suffer dramatic underrepresentation in the Senate can also lose out in the House, contrary to the framers' intentions. For example, California has roughly 68 times more residents than Wyoming but only 52 times more House members. Similarly, Texas's 38 House members each represented about 782,376 people in 2022, while Rhode Island's 2 House members each represented 530,754 people. That means each person in Rhode Island has 32% more weight in the House than a Texan—*on top* of having 28 times more weight in the Senate!

This occurs because every state must have at least 1 House member, and there are only 435 to go around—not enough for the House delegations from each state to vary smoothly by state population, especially when three states have less than 1/435th of the national population. Because congresspersons do not come in fractions, the *steps* between possible House delegation sizes produce large variations in residents-per-House member. A state just below the threshold population needed to get one more House member will have a lot less weight per capita than a state that is just above that threshold.

For example, Delaware's people now have the *least* weight in the House per person: one member represents 989,948 people (by the 2020 census). Montana, by contrast, has only about 9% more residents (1,085,004 total), but it now gets two House members who each represent about 45% fewer people than Delaware's representative does. Ergo each Montanan has *almost twice* the weight in the House as a Delawarian. In fact, if Montana selected its congresspersons by lottery among adults eligible for 45 years, each would have roughly a 1 in 10,333 chance of becoming a congressperson—similar to the chance of winning with a Pick 4 lotto ticket. Vermont and Nebraska are doing well too. As a result of these steps (see Figure 2.17), many states have a ratio that is much higher or lower than the national average for all House districts (in statistical terms, a large deviation). This problem will only get worse over time until we add more representatives.

Third, the injustice caused by disproportionate representation in the House spreads to the presidential election, because in the Electoral College (EC), each state's number of electors equals the number of its House members plus its two senators. The lack of sufficient House members for large states compounds the advantage that smaller states already have in the EC because of their two senators. Until we get rid of the EC (see #12), only enlarging the House will mitigate this problem.[222]

Finally, too few House districts makes gerrymandering worse. A larger House would mean more diversity in congressional districts that each elect a single member. Greg Blonder imagines the situation with a House of around 1,700 members:

> Rural conservatives, disenfranchised in the shadow of a more populous liberal city, can finally elect one of their own. Progressives, by winning new urban seats, promise to erode the old white male club. Independents, appealing to smaller groups of voters disgusted with mainstream politics, will flourish outside the two-party bubble.[223]

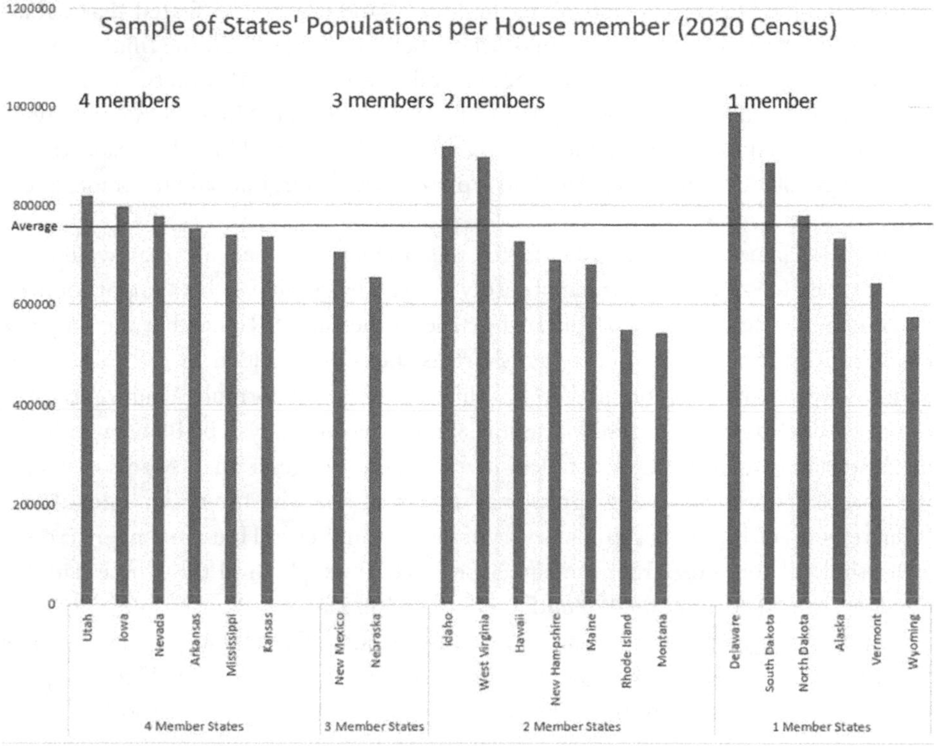

Figure 2.17 House Delegation Steps in Voter Weight

In particular, districts representing different parts of cities and suburbs would become possible, potentially overlapping with distinct "communities of interest" (see #4). Thus even without other reforms, the evils of gerrymandering would be reduced by a larger House.

Possible Solutions. Several of the Constitution's original drafters *and* its critics tried to save us from a House of Representatives becoming increasingly out of touch with ordinary Americans. The committee that hammered out the "grand compromise" recommended an explicit "one representative for every 40,000 inhabitants;"[224] but the convention was delayed on this point by worries about whether other criteria such as a state's wealth should be involved in apportionment of House members, and whether/ how to count enslaved persons (see #12).[225]

Some delegates also aimed for one representative for every 30,000 inhabitants. Famously, this was the one thing that George Washington requested on the record at the constitutional convention.[226] And in the *Federalist Papers*, Madison assured readers that the main goal of the ten-year census was to "augment the number of representatives" when reapportioning them to the changing populations of each state.[227]

But Article I §2 of the completed 1787 constitution phrased the number as a ceiling rather than a floor threshold: the House could not be *larger* than one member per 30,000 residents (e.g. no districts with only 25,000 residents).[228] This language was a compromise among delegates like Mason who argued that "some permanent and precise standard was essential to fair representation" in the House, and others who feared that a fixed number like 30,000 might in time make the House too large.[229] So the final language implied that 1 : 30,000 was the target ratio, while leaving some flexibility for Congress to decide the exact ratio.[230] Recognizing this loophole, the Massachusetts ratifying convention asked for an amendment saying that the House could not be *smaller* than 1 member per 30,000 until there were 200 representatives. Virginia said the same, as did critics in several other states.[231]

In 1789, James Madison tried to fix the problem with a rule that would still prevent the House from becoming absurdly large. The result was his "Apportionment amendment," which is actually the first article in the Bill of Rights, but the only one never ratified (it always fell one state short as states were added in the early years, and it was eventually forgotten). Perhaps this is because the formula Madison tried to develop from Virginia's suggestion was unclear. But recent analysis by Blonder, building on historian David Kyvig's detailed investigation, suggests that Madison meant the number of residents per congressional district to rise with the nation's population in increments of 10,000 per district every time the number of House members crossed a threshold of 100—e.g. from 1 member per 50,000 people until the House had 200 members, and then 1 per 60,000 until there were 300 members, and so on.

Following this formula today would give us a House of 1,722 members, with about 192,480 residents per district—notably close to the 1911 ratio when the House stopped growing.[232] Because Madison's article is technically still open for ratification (see #25), one strategy to jump-start House reform would be to renew the ratification drive among states.

Alternatively, Congress could just adopt a new specific House size by law as it did many times before the 1920s. In deciding on a number, it could look at other democratic nations around the world. For example, each member of the UK House of Commons represents about 92,000 people.[233] Drew Desilver found in a 2017 study of apportionment that the US has by far the worst population-to-legislature ratio among all developed democracies in the OECD—a group of 37 leading democracies with free markets (see Figure 2.18).[234] Our ratio is almost *triple* the nearest other nation (Japan), and we would have to enlarge our House more than fivefold to 2,180 members to approach the OECD average.[235]

Relative to that benchmark, conservative commentator George Will's suggestion of 1,000 members seems modest.[236] In 2023, 1,000 districts would leave us with about 329,000 people per district on average, 56% higher than the 1911 ratio. But this would be enough to significantly reduce all four problems caused by an inadequate House.

More modestly still, in November 2018, *The New York Times* editorial board published an opinion piece taking up the finding that, in developed democracies, the size of the legislature (or its larger chamber) tends to be roughly the *cube root* of its population.[237] Although it has a Pythagorean ring, there is nothing magical about this formula; it is only an average. But the number of House districts remained close to the cube root of the US population until about 1954.[238] Today, it would imply a House with 692 members—enough to make a dent in the problems noted above.[239]

A First Draft Proposal. But whatever formula you favor, experience since 1911 suggests that we can no longer rely on an ordinary law to fix this problem. Even if

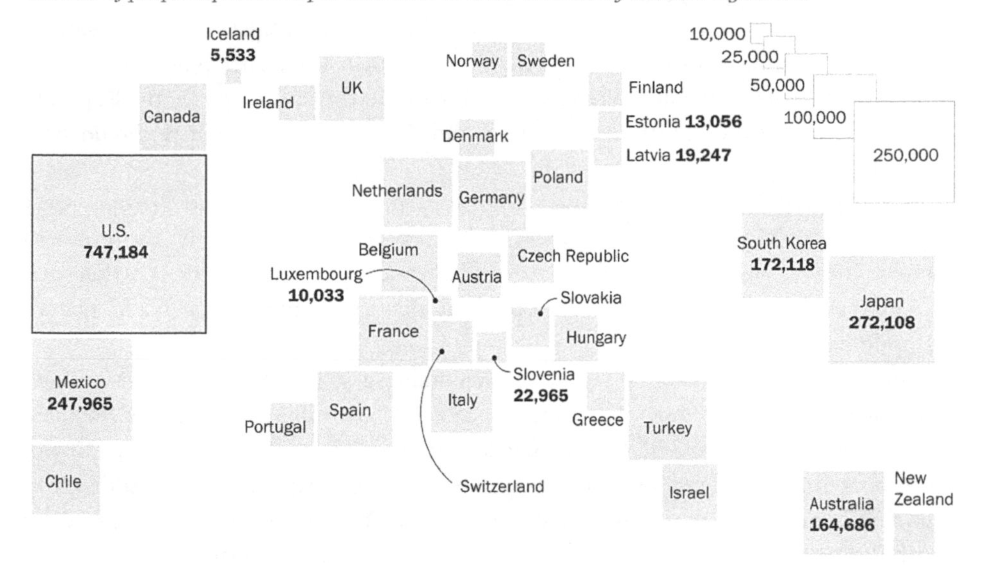

Figure 2.18 Ratio of Residents to Representatives in OECD Nations

Congress passed a one-time increase to (say) 700 members, the House might stay stuck at that size for another century. Or suppose the cube root rule was enacted in statutes to provide for gradual increases over the decades. This would lead to a constant battle, with later congressional majorities seeking to block coming increases that they think will be disadvantageous to their party in the short run.[240]

As Madison realized, it would be much better for the nation if the apportionment rule was settled in the Constitution, as it almost was in the 1790s, through an amendment. Among the options surveyed, the cube root rule would result in about 483,000 constituents per House member in 2023, which is too much. We need to ensure that representatives or their proxies (see below) meet frequently with groups of their constituents.

Blonder was therefore on the right track with his corrected version of Madison's Apportionment amendment. However, it is too complex to be easily understood and trusted. If we instead fixed the number of congressional districts at the cube root of *twice* the US population, we would have about 876 districts for our 2022 population,[241] which is closer to Blonder's result. This would mean about 378,000 residents per House member—still 30% more than in 1911, and well above the OECD average, but enough to reduce gerrymandering and smooth out disproportions between states.

To ensure some access to your representatives, the amendment should also specify that each House member must hold at least two question-and-answer events open to constituents every year, and engage in at least one televised general election debate.

The same should be required for every senator. Incumbents should not be able to hide from the people they represent.

Finally, the amendment should say that, within each state, the number of residents in each of its House districts should be equal up to a 0.1% difference. The same should apply to its statehouse districts. This is close to the rule given by the Supreme Court a half-century ago in *Baker* v. *Carr* and *Reynolds* v. *Sims*. But it should now be made explicit in the Constitution.[242]

A Weighted Vote Alternative. However, I have found that most people greet the idea of doubling the size of the House with severe scorn: they focus on the proposed increase in *politicians* rather than in *districts* and *access* for the people. Critics say that such an expansion would be obscenely costly, and that these politicians would not all fit inside the Capitol building.

For the record, actually the costs of maintaining 876 House members without reducing the staff per member would only be about $1,500 million a year in 2021 dollars. That would be a tiny 0.000317% of total federal spending in the last normal (pre-Covid) fiscal year—that is, about $3.17 out of every $10,000 the government spends. Adding two high-tech bombers to our air force could cost more than this, and so could adding security detail for every member of Congress in an era of rising political violence and shootings. What Medicaid spends in three months—a lot of which recently has gone to hospital care for unvaccinated people sick with Covid—could fund 876 House members *for a century*.

And a more responsive House would repay its meagre costs a thousand times over. It makes little sense to run a government that spends over $4,500 billion in a lean year and *not* be willing to pay $1.5 billion to make sure that the politicians allocating all this spending are really listening to us, the American taxpayers. The same thing goes for the physical size of the House chamber and offices: this is the last thing we should be worrying about (for more on this issue and costs, see *TheDemocracyAmendments.org*).

Still, my family friend might be right that more House members would mean more "pork" spending, especially now that "earmarks" are back in the budget process (see #22). Given this, and the unpopularity of adding more than a few House members, it's lucky that there is a less "personnel-intensive" alternative. We could fix the House size at 435 plus 1 for Washington D.C. (see #11), but give *weighted votes* to all House members, with those representing more people getting slightly more votes. Weighted votes are used in many board elections by company shareholders and in various international organizations. They could easily be used in Congress too.

For example, say we doled out total of 5,000 "member-votes," as well as 436 actual representatives, to the 50 current states and D.C. in proportion to their populations. This implies about 1 member-vote per every 66,289 Americans represented in 2020—close to the 1789 ratio in the first federal Congress. Dividing the population of each state by 66,289 gives you each state's share of the 5,000 member-votes, which would in turn be divided among their actual House members as illustrated in Table 2.4 (for 16 sample states). These are the *weighted votes* that each representative in the House would cast in committee and in whole House votes (rounded to one decimal point).

This method makes the votes that each House delegation has closely proportional to their state's population without adding House members. For example,

Table 2.4 Weighted Votes in the House of Representatives

State	2022 House Delegation	State Delegation's Total Member-Votes	Each Member's Weighted Vote
California	52	596.44	11.5
Texas	38	439.67	11.6
Florida	28	324.91	11.6
New York	26	304.74	11.7
Washington	10	116.24	11.6
Maryland	8	93.19	11.6
Minnesota	8	86.08	10.8
South Carolina	7	77.21	11.0
Oregon	6	63.92	10.7
Oklahoma	5	59.73	11.9
Utah	4	49.35	12.3
New Mexico	3	31.94	10.6
Idaho	2	27.74	13.9
Montana	2	16.36	8.2
Delaware	1	14.93	14.9
Wyoming	1	8.70	8.7
Washington D.C.	1	10.40	10.4

California would have about 68.5 times as many member-votes as Wyoming, and it has 68.5 times more people. Similarly, in this system, Montana would have 9.5% more member-votes than Delaware for its 9.5% more residents (rather than having twice Delaware's weight). The differences in weighted votes for each House member seen in the last column of Table 2.4 corrects for the disproportions in House delegation sizes (illustrated in Figure 2.17).

Still, as mathematically cool as it is, this system has three drawbacks. First, each House members would still represent 12 times more people than in 1911, which makes it hard for them to meet with many constituents. Second, because the number of single-member districts would remain the same, gerrymandering would not be reduced by this reform.[243] Third, votes reported in decimal points might confuse the public for a while, even though the math works fine.

Assistant Representatives. The first drawback can be reduced by another innovation: each House member could employ four *part-time Assistant Representatives* assigned to one quarter of their congressional district, each with about 189,400 residents (in 2021 numbers). This is fairly close to the 1911 ratio. These surrogates would be like House members in training and could represent the diversity within each district better than any single member can. They would not vote in Congress; their job would be solely to meet with constituents. As part-time positions with only a couple staff members in their home state, these Assistants would be quite inexpensive too.

Of course, these ideas can be combined with a larger House as well. For example, we could have 600 districts, 1,800 member-votes apportioned across the states, and three Assistant Reps per House member. Arguably such Assistant positions could be created by statute—although it would require an amendment for them to fill in for incapacitated House members (see #19). The weighted voting method would also require an amendment.

These points reinforce the position that restoring the House to its original function really requires constitutional change. Madison was right: we should follow his wisdom and take strategic calculations and partisan advantage out of the equation entirely. Only an amendment can ensure that members of the House of Representatives remain in close contact with interested constituents.

9. Eighteen Years on the Court Is Enough: Democratizing Judicial Confirmation

The Recent Travesties. Ruth Bader Ginsburg was an American icon. Perhaps the leading female jurist of her generation, she is one of the most important campaigners for women's rights in American history, next to figures like Susan B. Anthony, Elizabeth C. Stanton, and Sojourner Truth. We might one day see her face on our currency.

Ginsburg's early legal career was dramatized in the movie, *On the Basis of Sex*, showing the first case in which a US Court of Appeals overturned a law for giving women and men unequal treatment. But far more important is the 7-1 decision (with only Scalia dissenting) authored by Ginsburg three years after she was appointed to the Supreme Court. In her majority opinion, she wrote that policies treating men and women differently could only be justified by highly compelling public interests.[244] In practice, this meant legal equality for women in almost all cases, doing some of the work that the Equal Rights Amendment of 1972 would have accomplished, had it been ratified.

It is perhaps not surprising that a woman of this much tenacity, who rose in what had been an entirely male-dominated field, was not receptive to the implied question that Barack Obama left unstated at their polite lunch in 2013. This meeting is now the stuff of D.C. legends. Obama arranged it, according to staff members, in order to gently discern whether Ginsburg might retire while he still had a majority of the Senate on his side. Even though she was already 80 years old at the time and had twice recovered from cancer, she clearly let this "young man" know that she was not going anywhere if she could help it. She finally succumbed to cancer in September 2020 during Trump's last year in office, about seven weeks before he lost the election.

What happened next is well known. To replace Ginsburg, President Trump nominated probably the most fundamentalist religious jurist ever to serve on Court: Amy Coney Barrett, a young and obscure law professor at Notre Dame who had served 3 years on the appellate court for the Seventh Circuit. She was best known for being part of a "charismatic" ecumenical group, the People of Praise, who hold that men are divinely ordained to lead households. Hardly the most legally qualified candidate, she would not have even made the top 50 in a list determined by law school deans.

But whatever one thinks of Barrett's views or talents, the biggest outrage in her lightning confirmation is procedural. To explain it, we have to go back to mid-February

2016 when Justice Antonin Scalia—until Barrett, the most conservative member of the Supreme Court in the last half-century—died without much warning. With almost 9 months to go before the November election, Obama fully expected to appoint Scalia's successor. In bipartisan spirit, he intentionally selected a moderate and fairly old nominee, Merrick Garland who many Republican senators had praised in when he was appointed chief judge of the prestigious D.C. Circuit Court in 2013.

Yet the Republican majority in the Senate shocked the public by refusing even to hold hearings on Garland's nominations, despite their constitutional duty. They claimed that a president should not fill a Supreme Court vacancy this "close" to an election. There is no rule in the Constitution saying that nominations may be ignored if they are made during a presidential election year. Republicans claimed that stonewalling was justified by dixecrat Senator Strom Thurmond's old practice of halting Judiciary Committee confirmations of judges to federal circuit courts during the summer recess.[245]

March 16, when Garland was nominated, is not generally regarded as "summer." And after Ginsburg's passing, Mitch McConnell did not consider late October too "close" to the upcoming election. When senators voted on party lines to confirm Barrett a mere *nine days* before the 2020 election, the hypocrisy was thick enough to cut with a knife. For, in 2016, Republicans had held Scalia's seat open for more than *a year* until Trump could be inaugurated.. So when he was confirmed to the Supreme Court in April 2017, Neil Gorsuch, another conservative Catholic, could fairly be accused of receiving stolen goods.[246] He accepted the nomination even though he had published a 2002 opinion piece criticizing the Senate for delaying judicial confirmations for partisan gain.

Gorsuch had been recommended by Justice Anthony Kennedy, famed for halting the Florida vote recount in December 2000, and (with Roberts) for destroying election finance limits in *Citizens United* (see #5 and #6). Kennedy may also have hand-picked his own successor, Brett Kavanaugh, yet another very conservative Catholic. This reportedly resulted from meetings between White House attorney Don McGahn and Justice Kennedy that were more successful than Obama's meeting with Ginsburg. Perhaps getting to pick two new justices was sufficient to persuade Kennedy to retire during Trump's term?[247]

If so, that is a dangerous precedent: what is to stop justices in future from exchanging their retirement for the president issuing some executive order, or the congressional leadership passing some law that the retiring justice wants? Could we soon see justices receiving large "retirement gifts" from SuperPACs, or even from foreign dictators?

That is how Senate Republicans and Kennedy's bargain enabled Trump to appoint 3 justices in 4 years, while Obama—like Bill Clinton and George W. Bush—was able to appoint only 2 justices in 8 years. The Democratic minority in the Senate could not stop Gorsuch or Barrett because Senate Republicans removed the filibuster for Supreme Court nominees in 2017. Democrats had done away with the filibuster for lower court nominees in 2013 because Republicans were constantly filibustering Obama appointees to the federal district and appellate courts, which had not been common practice.

This part of the story is much less well-known, but very important. Once McConnell took control of the Senate in 2015, the Republican majority "shut down the lower court confirmation process" during Obama's last two years. This left Trump a massive 88 vacancies on federal district courts, 17 vacancies on the circuit Courts of Appeal, and one empty Supreme Court seat. In Russell Wheeler's estimation, this sheer obstruction of so many lower court nominees has "ratcheted up the contentiousness and polarization of an already broken confirmation process" so much that total stonewalling of nominees from the other party may become the norm, leaving judicial staffing shortages with serious consequences.[248]

The other result is a series of Court rulings, from endless gerrymandering and unlimited corporate dollars in elections to abortion, and expanded gun carrying in public, that have deviated ever farther from big supermajorities of public opinion. However, my concern here is not with quality of the Court's decisions or the advantages one party has recently reaped. It is about the means used, not the goals.

The Problems to Fix: Manipulation, Loss of Public Faith, Overly Long Tenures. The tactics seen in these recent appointments have huge costs for the republic, lowering trust in the Court that we need to serve as a bastion of stability when entering a period of likely constitutional crises. Once the umpire is widely perceived as biased for one team, their authority to arbitrate disputes and motivate compliance erodes. And after a gunman was arrested near Justice Kavanaugh's home in 2022, concerns that a justice might be assassinated are rising.

From the mid-1980s to June 2022, Gallup polls show public confidence in the Supreme Court declining from 56% to 25% (see Figure 2.19).[249] And no wonder. Any impartial observer would have to conclude that the Court nomination process has been completely hijacked: all semblance of impartial procedure is gone. Democrats have also pulled seat-stealing stunts, albeit quite a long time ago.[250] Moreover, they blocked Robert Bork when Reagan nominated him in July 1987 by outrageously defaming him in a "personal and mean-spirited" public relations campaign[251] (but Bork at least got his hearing, and Reagan was able to fill the vacancy with Anthony Kennedy).

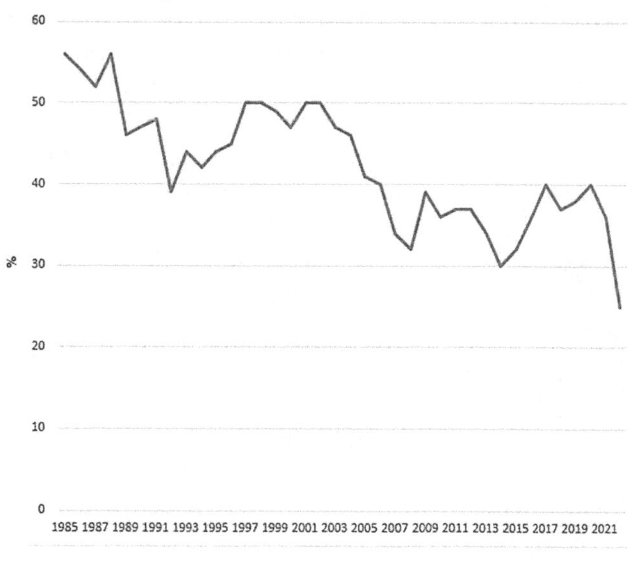

Figure 2.19 Decline of Public Faith in the Supreme Court

Out for revenge after the Garland travesty, some Democrats in 2020 talked incautiously of "court-packing" or adding seats to the Supreme Court after Biden's win. This awful idea would only invite another mutually self-destructive arms race: after both parties try this a few times, we could have 30 or 40 Supreme Court justices.

But clearly something needs to change: a system in which seats on the Court depend on a death lottery, delayed retirements, deals with older justices, and appalling shenanigans in the Senate is no longer working. It is making appointments far more politically divisive than they need to be, and leading to public disgust when the confirmation process dissolves into an unrestrained brawl.

Here is another way to analyze the problem. If we look back to the beginning of John Kennedy's term, we will find that Republican presidents gained *almost double* the justices per year in office that Democratic presidents did (Table 2.5). And this is counting Justice Goldberg, who was appointed by John Kennedy but became the US Ambassador to the UN only two years later. Looked at as an average, Republican presidencies yielded 2.00 justices for every four years in the White House, while Democratic presidencies yielded only about 1.20. If Biden appoints only one in his first term through 2024, which looks likely, the Democratic yield will fall to 1.06—roughly *half* the Republican yield.

My complaint is not that fate is unfair to Democratic presidents. Even allowing for contingencies of disease and retirements among justices, such a massive disproportion has other causes—such as blocking Garland, and the determination of justices (and judges on the nine circuit courts) to retire when a president of their own party is in office. Such strategic retirements tend to make majorities on the Court self-perpetuating, because justices keep angling for replacements who hold opinions like their own. In fact, not a single justice has retired from the Court during the term of a president hostile to their political leanings since Abe Fortas in 1969 (who Nixon, with William Rehnquist's help, forced out of office through a high-pressure smear campaign).[252] The natural number—without the manipulations of the Nixon and Trump years and a few justices staying on into their 80s—looks to be a little under 2 justices per 4-year term.

Table 2.5 Supreme Court Appointments per President

Presidents	**R-Years (Approx.)**	**D-Years (Approx.)**	**Republican Appointees**	**Democratic Appointees**	**Average by President**
Kennedy		4		2	0.500
Johnson		4		2	0.500
Nixon	5		4		**0.800**
Ford	3		1		0.333
Carter		4		0	**0.000**
Reagan	8		4		0.500
GHW Bush	4		2		0.500
Clinton		8		2	0.250
G. W. Bush	8		2		0.250
Obama		8		2	0.250
Trump	4		3		**0.750**
Biden		2		1	0.500
Totals	**32**	**30**	**16**	**9**	**0.403**

No matter which party benefits in one period of time, such a wide variation between the impacts of each presidential election massively distorts the relation between the judicial and executive branches. The democratic accountability of the Court is not compatible with 8 strategically timed retirements in the last 53 years and 0 vacancies in 4 out of 11 presidential terms since Jimmy Carter. Nor is it compatible with senators blocking appointments for years or rushing through fanatically partisan appointees three weeks before a presidential election. It is also odd, to say the least, that 5 out of 9 justices should be conservative Catholics in a nation in which not even 15% of adults are conservative Catholics.

Let's sum up the five perverse incentives created by this warped system. First, presidents are trying to appoint younger and thus generally less qualified nominees. The last two justices appointed were only 48 and 51 years old at the time, and may thus serve over 30 years. Second, justices increasingly want to stay past their prime, in addition to timing their retirement for partisan benefit; the average retirement age is up to 81. Until the 1960s, the average length of service was "around fifteen years," but "the average tenure of justices who have left the Court since 1970 has been roughly 26 years" (and climbing). Third, there is the constant temptation to change the number of justices, which has varied between 6 and 10 in American history.[253] Fourth, there are morally dubious stratagems to get justices to retire. And fifth, we have rising obstruction of appointments, especially at the appellate and district level. If nothing is done, we could soon see a hostile Senate refusing to vote on a president's appointments for two years or more.

Noting all these problems, the bipartisan Presidential Commission on the Supreme Court recently backed term limits as a way to regularize both the length of tenure and the regularity of appointment. Justices need to be protected from arbitrary removal by elected politicians. But 49 states do not think this requires lifetime tenure on their state supreme court.[254] Shady deals to get justices to retire are more likely when so many justices seem to conflate life tenure with "eternity."

The Solution. A fair procedure would fix the number of Supreme Court justices and their terms, as most American state constitutions and systems in other OECD nations do. To prevent the radical disproportion we found, the new procedure should ensure that every presidential election has have the same weight on the Supreme Court. This is the goal stressed by conservative law professor Stephen Calabresi in his co-authored 2005 essay arguing that we should set an *18-year term* for Supreme Court justices[255]—a proposal that could easily be extended to the circuit Courts of Appeal as well. Combined with staggered start dates for justices, this system would reduce all the perverse incentives.

Thus many jurists and lawyers across the political spectrum have come to favor the 18-year solution with 9 justices,[256] which is highlighted on the nonpartisan website *FixTheCourt.com*. Higher numbers have been proposed, but 9 works mathematically with an 18-year term. A recent study by the Constitution Center published in the *Atlantic* found a very wide consensus on this proposal among conservative, centrist, and liberal scholars. In the Center's "Constitutional Drafting Project," both the conservative and progressive constitutions agreed on the main components of this fix.[257] Public opinion is similar: a July 22 poll by AP-NORC found that over 67% of Americans favor term limits for the Court.[258]

My version simply adds further commonsense language to address irregular vacancies and Senate holdups. To prevent a future Congress from altering the terms or number of justices, the fix must take the form of a constitutional amendment along these lines:

I. Nine justices will each serve 18 years on the Supreme Court, with their terms staggered so that one justice retires on April 20 of every odd-numbered year. This avoids election years and gives newly inaugurated presidents 3 months before they must nominate a new candidate. The public will elect the president knowing that he or she will fill exactly two vacancies during a 4-year term.

II. Congress may determine by law whether justices completing their 18-year term can serve an additional period, if they wish, on special federal courts such as military courts, the FISA court that approves surveillance orders, the special Court of Elections (see #6 and #12), and others. However, retired justices may not hold any other paid job after their retirement from the Court, whereupon they will receive their full annual salary and benefits for life. Gifts they receive may be capped by law.

III. For justices serving on the Supreme Court at the time that this amendment is ratified, staggered terms will be phased in through a lottery conducted by an impartial panel as prescribed by law. On April 20 of the next odd-numbered year, one justice will be selected to retire in 2 years, one to retire in 4 years, one to retire in 6 years, and so on up to the justice selected to retire 18 years hence.

IV. Irregular Vacancies:

(i) When a vacancy on the Supreme Court occurs other than through the scheduled biannual retirement of one justice, except when due to an attack, it will be filled through selection by lottery among all judges who presently serve on the federal circuit Courts of Appeals, have served there for at least 6 years, and are less than 62 years of age. The judge thus selected becomes a member of the Supreme Court immediately without further confirmation, but with a mandatory retirement date identical to that of the justice whom they are replacing.

(ii) Any justice who is assassinated or incapacitated by an attack must be replaced with a judge from a federal appeals court who is generally affiliated with the same political party as the victim, through a process detailed in statute.

(iii) Congress may by law determine whether such interim appointees are eligible for reappointment if their term on the Supreme Court is less than 6 years, and also provide for interim appointments of justices during national emergencies affecting the federal courts or the ability of Congress to meet.

V. When the Chief Justiceship becomes vacant, the President shall promote any current Associate Justice who has served 8 years or more to the Chief Justiceship, with confirmation by the Senate. Thus no one will become Chief Justice immediately upon their confirmation to the Court, and no one will serve as Chief Justice for more than 10 years.

VI. When the President appoints a candidate for the Supreme Court, the Senate must vote on this appointment, by simple majority, within 3 months. If the candidate is rejected, the next candidate appointed by the President must

> receive an up-or-down vote by the Senate within 2 months. If that candidate is also rejected, the third candidate appointed by the President must receive a final Senate vote by simple majority within 1 month of the appointment. If this candidate is also rejected, then the vacancy is filled by lot from among all judges on the federal circuit bench who are under 62 years old, just as in cases where a justice dies, retires, or is impeached before their term ends.

In addition to establishing term limits and a regular schedule for appointments, this system would ensure that a hostile Senate cannot block a president from filling a vacancy for more than 6 months. If senators block three appointees in a row, they risk getting a justice from a federal Appeals court whom they may dislike.[259] Justices will occasionally retire or die before their term ends, but there would no longer be a political incentive for them to time their retirement when their preferred party controls the White House. If they do, their successor will be chosen by lottery and only fill out the remainder of their term. So they could not use retirement as a bargaining chip.

Of course, this system would increase the importance of judges serving on the appellate courts. However, the same system could in principle be applied to them, so that each president replaces 2 judges out of 9 on each appellate court within a 4-year term, and a district court judge is chosen at random if an appellate judge dies or vacates before their term is up. Given that appellate judges might be younger, perhaps they should have more options after retirement. But we still need to insulate federal judges from all kinds of financial and other political incentives, which was a primary purpose of life terms. This will be accomplished in the new system by prohibiting them from taking any other paid job outside the judiciary and limiting gifts to them while ensuring their salary and benefits for life.

There are plenty of possible variants on the system outlined here that could be considered. For example, we could add that no one under the age of 45 should be appointed to the Supreme Court, and phase in the terms for current justices by giving the shortest remaining term (2 years from the phase-in start date) to the oldest justice and the longest (18 years) for the youngest justice, etc. But an amendment prescribing a lottery for the phase in, as in §III, may be easier to ratify.

Some reformers would also like to see the Supreme Court increased to 11 or even 14 justices in order to make rigid blocs among them less likely.[260] Blonder argues that a Court of 14 justices is more likely to represent "an average political position," and make it easier for a justice to recuse themselves when appropriate, while an even number promotes compromise.[261] But any number of justices higher than 9 raises mathematical complications (see *TheDemocracyAmendment.org* for analysis).

Other variations concern what happens when a seat on the Court is vacated before the justice's term is up. Instead of selection by lottery from among appellate court judges, we might have a panel of experts—retired justices, previous attorneys general, and/or law school deans—select a candidate from the Appeals courts to fill out the remainder of that justice's term. Or the independent panel might select 3 candidates among which a joint congressional judiciary committee could choose one. While there is probably no perfect solution for these irregulary vacancies, the main goal is to keep the president out of the process when they are not replacing a justice whose term is ending on the regular schedule. The president should only get 2 appointments in 4 years, barring some massive state emergency (see #19).

Some authors have also argued that Congress can establish an 18-year term on the Supreme Court without an amendment by rotating justices to lower federal courts and/or to special courts after that period, or by establishing a tradition of publicly promising to retire after 18 years when a justice is being confirmed.[262] But both these approaches seem too unreliable for such a central part of the federal structure: the temptation for Congress to change the term or rotation, or for the Court to invalidate it, or for individual justices to concoct reasons to renege on their retirement promise, are too great. An amendment, by contrast, would bring stability. There are other important questions about the way that the Court operates, and whether its jurisdiction is too great. It is best to address these in issues in a separate amendment—see #23 on judicial review—given the strong bipartisan consensus that makes an amendment on the term and rotation one of the lowest-hanging fruits for constitutional reform today.

10. Robust Civics Education: A National Standard to Empower Citizens

As we saw in the first chapter, beyond all the problems in our federal institutions and the way political parties now operate, some challenges arise at the level of individual citizens, who often understand too little of the issues and the functions of the federal government to exercise democratic power responsibly. This mass ignorance makes people easily manipulable by scare tactics, by appeals to vices such as group-based hatreds, and by outright deception and misinformation. This is even more likely when partisan attempts to demonize mainstream journalism drive people toward unreliable fringe sources. As the authors of one national survey say,

> Without an understanding of the structure of government, our rights and responsibilities, and the different methods of public engagement, civic illiteracy and voter apathy will continue to plague American democracy.[263]

This is no exaggeration. A Pew Research study showed that Americans who get most of their news from social media are less than half as likely to demonstrate political knowledge.[264]

The Antidemocratic Challenge. As in the past, some critics of democracy today seize on such findings to argue that popular government with free elections cannot produce good results, because people are so wedded to the beliefs and hostile emotions that make up our political ideologies: they will sacrifice lots of material gains to maintain such attitudes. For example, the US increasingly needs immigrants to fill some low-wage jobs and to pay into the Social Security system; but many Americans refuse to believe this, even when presented with hard economic evidence. In other words, wishful thinking on political and related economic issues is strongly motivated by people's sense of identities, loyalties, and self-image. Bryan Caplan, for example, concludes that "rule by demagogues" who confirm our shallow dogmas and bigotries is "the natural condition of democracy."[265]

This view that "the masses" are bound to be politically "deplorable" has a long history running from Plato's *Republic* to today's scholarly defenders of rule by experts (epistocracy). Annual Annenberg Center studies show that efforts to teach civics have made improvements in recent years. Yet less than half of Americans can name all three branches of government (see Figure 2.20), and it does not get much more basic than that.

Certainly the epistocratic idea was common among several founders involved in writing our original Constitution—although Madison and other federalists still strongly defended answerability to the people as a bedrock requirement of just government. In particular, the Platonic view was a key reason for rule by representatives, who were expected to be highly educated,[266] as opposed to direct democracy (see #7), and for basic rights as limits to majority rule. But as Ilya Somin argues, we should not assume that the "vastly disproportionate" political "influence" of wealthier Americans, who tend to have higher levels of education and political knowledge, is always good for the nation.[267]

While there is no room to fully engage with these arguments here, they miss a key point: when a system drives high turnout based on something other than extreme partisan motivation—such as civic duty—politicians have incentives to educate and appeal to a wider range of moderate constituents who have little ego invested in one party's totalizing narrative. Flaws in our federal structure give politicians perverse incentives to cultivate civic ignorance rather than educating constituents on issues.

That said, I strongly agree with Caplan that familiar cognitive biases deriving from *desires to believe* things for reasons other than their correctness can cause majorities of voters to err.[268] Worse, expert campaign consultants have made a science of knowing how to identify and exploit such forms of wishful thinking on political topics (see ch.1). And worse still, as Caplan argues, profit-driven medias largely "show viewers what they want to see and tell them what they want to hear."[269]

This explains why probably over half of all stories on Fox News, CNN, and MSNBC during the last 7 years have focused on Trump and people attacking or defending him, related scandals etc.—as if little else of importance were happening in the world. Drama, conflict, and colorful personalities sell, while evenhanded analyses of social facts and testimony from natural science do much

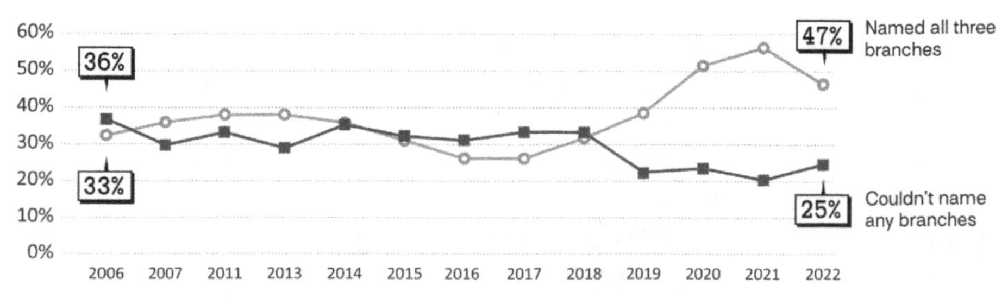

Figure 2.20 Americans' Basic Civic Knowledge Over Time

worse in grabbing viewer attention. By flattering viewers' errors, wishful thinking, and paranoias, emotive mass media companies feed vicious cycles of confirmation bias and expanding blind spots.

Here is the heart of the problem: American mass medias are the most advertising-driven in the world, with a gargantuan $285 billion spent on ads in 2020 (for reference, that is three times the cost of Obamacare subsidies for health insurance).[270] As long as advertising has this much power in controlling coverage, most popular medias are certain to favor misleading content that sells, rather than educating their viewers. Unlike the more balanced TV news sources on which most Americans relied in the 20th century, and that the British get from BBC channels, the internet "has made it easier for people to seek out news that confirms their existing beliefs."[271]

And there are other reasons why it may seem to many citizens that it is not worth the time or effort to acquire social, historical, or economic knowledge relevant to political decisions. Somin suggests these factors[272]:

- an individual person's vote has almost zero chance of changing any election beyond the township level;
- their political knowledge or contributions make almost no difference to the total quality of public discussions about political issues;
- if most others are not trying hard to consider objective evidence relevant to political questions, why should you spend the time and effort to do this?

To these, we can add the systemic causes of alienation (reviewed in ch.1) that reduce engagement: If elections brought big results, more people would care.

In fact, there are several theoretical problems with Somin's (game-theoretic) claim that voting is not worth even its (hopefully small) costs. People may vote out of a sense of duty, to express opinions to others through the total number of their candidate's votes; to increase the size of candidate's mandate to govern; to be part of a winning majority; to build stronger showings for a party they like even if their candidate loses (which we saw is a good reason for RCV balloting); and more.[273] The desire to "stick it" to the other side could also be a big factor for some voters.

Still, Somin is correct that keeping informed about who represents them, what Congress is doing, and facts relevant to big issues of the day involves work and time that people could spend on their own household (or on entertainment). Thus I see two other reasons why even highly educated people are ignorant on basic points, such as who their governor is, or which party has a majority in the Senate:

- it is so easy in this area to *free ride* on the fraction of the public who do seem to care about politics, and who know at least a few things about the issues and which party is doing what;
- it appears likely to most people that the situations in which they live and work will pretty much go on as they presently are, no matter who wins elections.

In other words, political laziness is motivated by a false sense of security. That changes when a hurricane wipes out their community, or a massive currency devaluation triggers a great depression, or their children are drafted into a war. But many Americans have been comfortable for a long time, and do not see big politically-driven problems or threats coming—at least for their family. Their mindset is like the first-class passenger on the luxury ocean steamer, *Titanic*, who asks "why should I waste my time volunteering an hour per day on the 'Iceberg Lookout' team, when the ship seems to be going along fine and there are so many more entertaining opportunities?" So it is also, sadly, with the ship of state.

For Deweyian Democracy. However, none of this means that we should abandon the principle of equal voting rights or stop trying to increase voter turnout, as some epistocrats suggest.[274] Instead, we should reform the structural factors that are driving so much "rational ignorance," low-quality media, indulgence in unreliable socially destructive beliefs, and free riding on politically active people.

In defending rule by a knowledgeable elite, Jason Brennan argues that, even though democratic government usually produces better results than oligarchy or dictatorship, other systems we have not yet tried might perform much better still.[275] That's right, but notice that *one* recipe we have not tried is the following combination, which I will call "Deweyian Democracy"—after John Dewey, who argued over a century ago that both formal education and diversity in shared social life could be designed to enlighten participants:

1. elections that matter, in which the majority effectively enacts its main campaign promises (so it pays to be engaged) (see #7);
2. easy registration and voting (see #6);
3. voter-funded or "publicly owned" elections with less partisan advertising (see #5);
4. mass medias like the British BBC that employ fact-checked journalism to educate their audiences, rather than aiming primarily at profit through high ratings;[276]
5. restrictions on lying by politicians (see #15) and incentives for politicians to inform rather than manipulate voters;
6. a robust civics education curriculum for all citizens;
7. incentives throughout adult life to learn objective information relevant for political decisions; and
8. ongoing social encouragement not to be "a dupe," but instead to build social and political knowledge, and enjoy sharing it with others.

This approach accepts that an informed electorate is a crucial public good—much like parks and roads.[277] It is not something that a for-profit media market is going to produce spontaneously; rather, it needs to be coordinate by government and civic associations, including endowment-funded journalism. The first three items in my Deweyian list are among the goals of amendment proposals #1-8 and #12, while proposals #14-15 in the next chapter promote the fourth and fifth components of Deweyian Democracy. This section focuses on its last three components.

Let's start from one piece of good news: psychological research finds that a strong majority of voters "do not choose their political views based on narrow self-interest:" they are concerned about the nation's progress, or at least about the welfare of large groups, rather than only their private economic or material gains.[278] Civics education can build on this basis, which includes common concerns for justice, especially if we alter social norms so that it is no longer *considered cool* to indulge in lots of fact-free wishful thinking on topics relevant for public policy. Just as social movements have made bullying and "toxic" forms of machismo much less popular than they once were, we can tie more social status to minimum levels of political sanity.

Civics education is also our best counterweight to the distorting influences of addictive social media, rage-promoting algorithms, deceptive advertising, and slanted partisan "news." As Dewey argued, the viability of democracy depends on the social understanding and sympathies of large numbers of voters. Beyond ensuring that every American knows elementary facts that enable them to assess major political issues, a sound civics program can resist many forces that seek to profit from sowing rancor, hate, and lies that objective social science refutes.[279]

The best antidote to this kind of mind-control is to teach students the canons of sound reasoning, how mass medias work to profit from manipulating them, what verifiable evidence requires, and the structural causes of embittered political rivalries that now threaten our most fundamental institutions. Hard social facts and truths about real-world problems do not line up with *either* extreme-left *or* extreme-right beliefs: teaching them to students will shock people on both poles out of their increasing dogmatism and immersion in fantasy worldviews.

A Curriculum Outline. But for this solution to work, civics education has to be a serious core subject with the same highest-priority status as high school History or Algebra. It cannot be a little co-curricular activity on the side, or a 1-credit "engaged learning" project tacked onto another course, focused on a visit to a county office or to a meeting of the state assembly. Every high school student needs two semesters of detailed training in civics and critical thinking that covers a lot of key facts and concepts, as well as teaching them *how* to think rigorously about political subjects, so that they are more immune to deceptive tactics and outright lies.[280] Such a course could survey some big issues at stake in current federal politics as illustrations, but focus on fundamentals needed to evaluate policy choices, including:

- which parties have controlled the House, Senate, and presidency in the last 30–40 years, and their main economic and social policies;
- an outline of major changes in tax laws, including changes in top and bottom rates, types of taxes, average tax burdens, and resulting federal revenues, in the last 70 years;
- a thumbnail history of our current federal deficits and debts, drivers of annual deficits, and their economic effects;
- our six or seven largest entitlement programs, and future projections of their sinking trust funds;
- the largest 10 to 15 items in our annual federal budgets and budget myths (e.g. direct foreign aid is less than 1%; interest on the national debt is nearing 8%);[281]
- a short primer in basic economics relevant for policy, e.g. main causes of inflation, how recessions happen, supply chains, forms of stimulus and monetary policy, and their usual effects;

- the economic definition of public goods, externalities, and causes of market failures, including "rent-seeking" activities, oligopolistic behavior, missing or unequal access to information, and pooling risks via insurance;
- a basic outline of our foreign policy from the 1970s on, including war spending figures;
- how to interpret basic statistics, charts, and figures without being fooled;
- an introduction to informal logic and critical thinking, along with review of common fallacies, and how to find *reliable sources* on the internet.

A student should leave this year-long sequence knowing, for example, that Reagan's tax cuts, like George W. Bush's, produced enormous federal deficits. But they would also know about rising federal debt, unsustainable projected increases in entitlement program spending, and threats to the Social Security trust fund. They could distinguish regular income from capital gains and estimate the (fairly large) effective tax rate paid by a family earning $1 million annually, when state and federal taxes are included. They would know the difference between a million and a billion in the federal budget and be able to describe some of the largest programs it funds.

Our civics graduate could also distinguish regular income tax from payroll taxes and approximate the total level of public assistance received by a low-earning 2-parent family of 4 who get the earned income tax credit, child tax credit, reduced school lunch, Medicaid coverage, and rental assistance or public housing. They could estimate roughly what food stamps and federal college aid provide, and what they cost each year. Our graduate could also say something about why college and health insurance have costs have increased so much, and how our defense budget compares to the military budgets of other large nations.

Of course, many states already have some civics requirement, but their content is far weaker than the thorough curriculum just outlined. Usually Civics is one semester or less, and it may consist mostly in specific group research projects. There is movement in the right direction: some 17 states now require students to pass the US citizenship exam, which includes basic facts that all immigrants must learn to earn citizenship. That's good, but this test is not very robust. Sample questions include:

- Which of these three is not part of Congress—the Senate, the House, or the Supreme Court?
- Who wrote the Declaration of Independence—King George, John Adams, Thomas Jefferson, or George Washington?
- Who becomes president if both the president and vice president die?—the commander in chief, the Speaker of the House, the Chief Justice, or the Secretary of State?
- How many justices are there on the Supreme Court: 11, 6, 9, or 12?
- Who was president during the Great Depression and World War Two—Herbert Humphrey; Franklin Roosevelt, Theodore Roosevelt, or Ronald Reagan?

Students should all know this sort of stuff even before entering high school. There are some harder questions, and thankfully students have done better on the citizenship test in 2022: in PA for example, over 84% passed. But this test still does not cover even 10%

of the topics I listed as essential. Similarly, high school American history courses will not routinely cover more than 10% of what a robust civics curriculum requires.

A minimum nationwide standard is also needed to ensure that state or local officials do not politicize the curriculum that provides such a crucial foundation for maintaining the democratic government on which our entire way of life depends. My outline does not favor the left or the right: it would only familiarize students with the most basic facts about our government, without all the partisan riffs on contested cultural and historical topics. Veterans' trauma awareness and LGBTQ+ awareness are important, but understanding the causes of gridlock and partisan polarization, budget deficits, recent legislative initiatives on infrastructure, foreign policy challenges, and what federal benefits Americans receive is even more important—and students will not get much of this from social media.

After all, the federal government is a truly enormous set of common projects that we collectively undertake. Many Americans will pay well over a $1 million into it during their lifetimes, or $2 million if we include all payroll and state taxes—another thing that students should learn in high school civics. Everyone ought to have some handle on the main things the government does in our name and with all that money, including welfare, farm subsidies, other transfer payments, and what national and global macroeconomic forces federal spending and borrowing interact with.

Such a standard of civic understanding will also make high school graduates more resistant to the "snake oils" of our day—internet scams galore, misleading advertisements, fake stories coming from bots funded by foreign tyrants, and so on. This national requirement need not increase the total number of required high school courses. Rather than requiring two full years of US History, as many states do, we can change that requirement to three semesters (in my school, AP US History was *one* year). We can also reconsider our *eight* required semesters of gym. Physical health is important, but so is the health of our body politic.

A national standard will also ensure that all young adults share some common ground, and help to restore mutual understanding and solidarity across all states. As Reich says, civics education should teach students to transcend dogmatism, humbly recognize their fallibility, and bridge ideological divides. Above all, it must cultivate the virtue of putting the common good above one's personal material gain.[282] This issue is so important that its solution needs to be enshrined within our Constitution. I have found that most Americans across the political spectrum agree with this, and many would support an amendment along the following lines:

I. Every high school student in the US shall take at least one full semester of Civics, which shall include the basic history of our tax law and current tax burdens, objective information on the federal budgets, entitlement programs, other major federal programs and recent policy issues, and the fundamentals of economics necessary to assess proposed policies on all such matters in a responsible manner.
II. Every high school student shall take at least one full semester devoted to critical thinking, basic patterns of cogent reasoning, common fallacies, statistical literacy and how to read charts and graphs, how to recognize expertise in specialized areas, and identification of reliable sources on the internet.

Such a requirement would be extremely popular as long as the courses focus on "just the facts," not partisan spin. If necessary, its bipartisan credentials might be further enhanced by adding a third section empowering Congress to ban really outrageous political activism in high school and college classrooms,[283] and to outlaw very narrow ideological (even if unwritten) litmus tests in hiring and promoting people in teaching, academic research, and journalism. The public has a direct interest in this because we rely heavily on these fields for objective expertise and education.

It goes without saying that such a robust national civics requirement cannot remedy all the deficits in our high school curricula. It would help a lot, for example, if we spent less time on world history from the Stone Age to World War I, and instead insured that every student had at least one course devoted to the main historical developments in (say) 7–8 regions of the world during the last 60 years.[284] Given globalization, it would also help for every high school student to spend at least one summer working and/or studying abroad. But these are topics for another place.

Objections and Supplements. In response, Brennan and others contend that "civics education doesn't work." Although nothing close to the curriculum I'm recommending has been tried, he will consider this irrelevant, because the problem is that "[m]ost citizens have no incentive to remember the civics information they learn in school."[285]

There are many ways that smart democratic government could counteract this tendency. Somin considers rising proposals to encourage adults over 25 to participate in "citizen juries" or "deliberative polls," which are like retreats in which ordinary folks receive summary information on a big political issue (e.g. immigration, health insurance, or the topic of a pending state ballot initiative) and then discuss it with expert facilitators. Their results can be published as sources of reliable information.[286] Brennan also notes Caplan's intriguing suggestion to offer a short national test that any voter can take shortly before a general election, getting $1,000 for scoring 90%–100%, $500 for getting a score between 80%–89% and a $100 for 70%–79% correct.[287] Game-show style competitions for bigger cash prizes might also be worth trying.[288]

The federal government could also offer citizens vouchers for one free continuing education course per year on civics and current issues, which would be revised biannually by a panel of experts randomly chosen from a pool of qualified and willing experts. And scholars who study ways to promote stronger social solidarity have long advocated creating a national public service program.[289] While usually envisioned as something that young people could do for a year right after high school or college graduation, it could instead include a paid option for service later in life. The civics education amendment could explicitly ensure that Congress has the power to create such a program.

Finally, the epistocratic skeptics may also be missing something crucial: people *love to share* what they know (comprehension of important information is the ultimate public good—giveable to others with little cost to oneself). Once every American aged 18–23 has had two semesters of Civics and Critical reasoning, and they often share what they have learned with older folks, we may pass a kind of tipping point. Beyond this threshold, it may become so uncool to be clueless and constantly get corrected by young adults on political topics that older adults will have to do better. I think this is already happening, albeit in a haphazard way: young people on average seem much better informed about at least some social issues (the trendier ones) than they were 20 or even 10 years ago. This may invert the situation we have today, in which immersion in fact-free delusion and conspiratorial nonsense is literally paraded by many as a badge of honor.

In sum, robust civic knowledge and global awareness can no longer be a luxury for a few; they need to take priority in American secondary education and should be mainstreamed in our society as an important basis for social respect. In time, these reforms would fundamentally transform our political discourse and mood. A new era of accountability and public enlightenment would follow—exactly the opposite of what YouTube ideologues and mortal enemies like Putin are planning for us. There is nothing so dangerous to dictators and entrenched special interests than a large majority of voting citizens who understand what their government is doing and why.

Chapter Three

SOLUTIONS II: FIFTEEN PROCEDURAL AMENDMENTS TO STRENGTHEN DEMOCRACY AND THE RULE OF LAW

The first ten amendments outlined in Chapter Two form the core of a centrist reform agenda that has been coalescing for at least a decade, as more and more Americans across the political spectrum realize that bold action is needed to save our republic. This chapter is devoted to further amendments to make the presidency, Congress, and our federal courts function more efficiently and responsively. All but two of them are "procedural," i.e. about how different parts of the government work. They would not settle substantive issues about what a working government should do about, e.g. a basic income, global security, abortion policies, or stronger anti-monopoly laws.

Several of next 15 proposals, although not all, will seem familiar from political dialogue in recent years. Most range from quite uncontroversial to only moderately controversial. In particular, the elementary "good governance" proposals (#13–19) are very "low hanging fruit." They all address basic gaps in our federal governing processes which leave room for a myriad of misfortunes that can be prevented with straightforward additions to our constitutional text. A national push for new amendments would do well to start with these kinds of reforms.

By contrast, my proposals on the Electoral College (EC), the Senate, and the amendment process itself will be more controversial, and probably cannot be ratified in the near future without being linked to other popular reforms, despite their great significance. The treatment of each topic in this chapter is briefer than in Chapter Two, partly because some have been the focus of insightful and recently published books. However, readers who would like more detail on these proposals can find it on *TheDemocracyAmendments.org*. Although amendments 11–25 are all vitally important, they rank slightly lower than the "top ten" in urgency for our system's survival.

11. Representation for Washington, D.C., Puerto Rico, and Permanent Territories

The first topic for this chapter concerns a national disgrace that results from contingencies of American history: according to the 2020 census, there are over 4 million US citizens who have no representation in Congress because they live in Puerto Rico, Washington D.C., or other US territories such as the island of Guam.

And some 55,000 of those born in American Samoa (a chain of Pacific Islands) are US "nationals" but not birthright citizens.[1]

For comparison, the population of Washington, D.C. is larger than both Wyoming's and Vermont's, and it has almost the same population as Alaska. Puerto Rico's 2020 population exceeded that of 20 states. Together, D.C. and Puerto Rico are home to almost as many residents as Wyoming, Vermont, both the Dakotas, and Alaska all *combined.* Yet, these 5 states collectively have 10 senators, while D.C. and Puerto Rico have zero.

As a result, over 3.1 million Hispanic, black, and Pacific Islander Americans have no representation in Congress, and at least 2.8 million of these have no voice in the presidential election either. Given our history, that ought to be the end of the debate: it is simply wrong to disenfranchise innocent Americans who want to participate on an equal footing with all others.

This section focuses mostly on Washington D.C., because Puerto Rico can become a state through a statehood "enabling act" passed by Congress and signed by the president without a constitutional amendment. And from the 1980s through 2020, the Republican Party platform has consistently supported statehood for Puerto Rico.[2] Still, Puerto Rico's case should be considered with D.C.'s because the island's status is another big structural flaw that makes our federal system less democratic. The disposition of D.C. and Puerto Rico, together with other territories, concerns a bedrock principle: no part of this union should be left without equal citizenship and equal voice.

Puerto Rico Statehood. Puerto Rico became part of the United States by forcible colonization in 1897. After a 1952 federal law made Puerto Rico into a "commonwealth" with a special territorial status, support for statehood increased over time on the island, as connections with the mainland rose and the option of independence became less viable.[3] In just the last 10 years, Puerto Rico has voted *three times* for statehood on different ballot questions. In 2012, 54% voted on the first question against continuing the commonwealth arrangement; and 61% of those answering a second question voted for statehood, as opposed to full independence or "free association" (a weaker form of independence). But due to blank ballots in the 2012 vote, another referendum was held in June 2017. Statehood won by 97% in this vote, yet turnout was marred by boycotts.

Thus, a third referendum was held on the general election day in November 2020. Turnout was high, even though the island has no vote on presidential candidates. The ballot question was clear and incisively bivalent: *statehood—yes or no.* Statehood won by a clear 52.5%, confirming the 2012 result. Moreover, the voters also elected a governor from the New Progressive Party, which has statehood as its central plank, although advocates for an autonomous (semi-independent) status still have strength in the island's legislature.

This was not a landslide, but the margin for statehood was roughly double Biden's margin in the nationwide popular vote, despite the fact that residents of Puerto Rico know they will pay more federal taxes if it becomes a state. The margin would have been even higher but for false narratives that the island would have less "independence" as a state. On the contrary, remaining a territory leaves Puerto Rico entirely at the mercy of the federal government: in a series of the so-called "Insular" cases, clearly racist in their initial motives, the Supreme Court has allowed Congress to legally discriminate against the island's residents in federal laws and government programs. Puerto Rico's government can only decide issues that federal law happens to leave to it, whereas states have strong rights under the Constitution, which makes them legally equal to all other states.

The clear victory for statehood in the very reliable 2020 election is not surprising, considering how badly Puerto Rico has suffered under its second-class legal status in the last two decades. Federal law encouraged overreliance on borrowing by the island's government. Austerity needed to pay off these debts, combined with federal subsidies to mainland businesses shipping food and other consumer goods into Puerto Rico, have hindered its economic growth.[4] The increasing ferocity of hurricanes driven by global warming has dramatically eroded the island's capacity for self-help. All these factors have driven a staggering 26% of the island's residents to leave over the last 22 years.

Hurricane Maria alone, which hit the island in September 2017, did over $100 billion in damage and killed almost 3,000 people. This hurricane was the nation's biggest natural disaster in 100 years. And after Hurricane Fiona hit in September 2022, much of the island was again without power, running water, or accessible roads for weeks. Puerto Rico needs major infrastructure upgrades to survive the growing impacts of climate change. With investment and debt restructuring, it could become a jewel for environmental tourism, farming, and retirement communities, as in parts of Florida and the Keys. But without the 2 senators and 3–4 House members that Puerto Rican residents deserve, their plight is largely ignored by the rest of the country.

Rectifying this national shame only requires a new federal law, and a bill permitting Puerto Rico to take a binding final vote on statehood passed the House in December 2022. But this case raises deeper questions about the status of territories and statehood in the Constitution—which we also see in the plight of American Samoans. First and foremost, an amendment should require that residents of *all* US territories should be legally equal in their basic rights, and have some voting representation in Congress, along with a say in presidential elections and in any ratification of later amendments.[5] Most of our allied nations give some representation to outlying territories that they still administer. About 4% of French citizens, for example, live in one of its 13 "overseas territories," such as the island of Martinique. France gives them 27 deputies in its National Assembly (about 4.7%), and 21 senators (about 6% of the upper chamber).[6] Because American constitutional law lacks such a provision, statehood really is the only way for Puerto Rico to gain any democratic voice at the national level.

Second, the fact that there are only 435 House seats to go around under current apportionment law deters members of Congress from giving 3–4 House districts to Puerto Rico, because their states might then lose a seat. This disincentive would be reduced by an apportionment amendment setting the number of House seats at (say) 1,000 or the cube root of the US population + 100 (see #8).[7] Third, Puerto Rico statehood could be part of a bargain to give congressional representation to D.C., which probably does require an amendment.

Representation without Statehood for Washington, D.C. Statehood has long been proposed for Washington, D.C. as well. A 2016 referendum showed that an overwhelming majority of the district's residents believe that they deserve federal representation (see Statehood.dc.gov)—although making D.C. a state is not the only (or best) way to accomplish this. The main arguments for giving D.C. 2 senators and 1 House member are that

- Basic justice requires representation in Congress. Jonathan Turley, a lawyer famous for defending Trump in his first impeachment trial, wrote that "[t]here is universal agreement that the current nonvoting status of the District is fundamentally at odds with the principles and traditions of our constitutional system."[8]
- The district's population is 52% Black and Latinx, making it likely to increase minority representation in Congress.
- Unlike Puerto Rico, D.C. could not request independence, and its residents already pay full federal taxes: so they currently suffer taxation without representation, which was a key reason for our Revolutionary War against Britain.
- D.C. is not economically weak. A 2016 analysis points out that 21 states relied on federal money for more of their budgets than does the District government.[9]
- Washington, D.C. is the only capital city in any democratic nation whose citizens do not have *any* representation in the legislature. For example, Australia's capital district of Canberra, which was ceded from other states much like D.C., has roughly 453,000 residents compared to D.C.'s 690,000. This Australian capital district elects 3 Australian House members out of 151, and 2 senators out of 176.
- In 1978, both the US House and the Senate already passed a constitutional amendment—the District of Columbia Voting Rights amendment—to treat D.C. *as if it were a state* for Congressional representation, election of the President, and Article V functions. But this proposal was not ratified by enough states within the 7 years it allowed.[10] As Akhil Amar explains, by the late 1970s, "Black voters had decisively migrated to the Democratic camp, and Republican politicians were loth to give their rivals two new Senate seats and at least one House seat."[11]
- When Congress created the federal District pursuant to Article II §8 of the Constitution, federal leaders intended to give District residents equal representation but got stopped by controversies about slavery in D.C. After the Civil War, District residents did briefly have full voting rights, but the desire to disenfranchise free black Americans migrating there moved Congress to disenfranchise them again.[12]

There are also no plausible arguments against representation for D.C. When the Constitution was written, it gave the federal government direct control over the envisioned new "federal district" because the Continental Congress had often been harassed or even threatened by local forces during and immediately after the Revolutionary War.[13] That motive is long gone: there is no chance now that any state or local government will threaten federal officeholders in the capital, many of whom safely maintain a local residence in Virginia or Maryland.[14]

The *only* real motive today for denying D.C. representation in Congress on a par with the 3 smallest states is that polls predict the District would elect Democrats. While partisan calculation has played roles in admission of new states before, mere consistency has eventually compelled people to admit that a territory has met the objective qualifications set by tradition.

Not so any more. Conservatives cynically call for D.C. residents to vote in Virginia or Maryland because these are already blue(ish) states. So their proposal is simply vote dilution—in a context where small states currently give *them* a huge edge in the Senate. Here is a feasible response: federal law could allow each eligible full-time D.C. resident to choose *any* other state in which to vote as if it were their state of residence: it would be interesting if 400,000 D.C. voters decided to vote with Wyoming to elect its congressional delegation, or went instead with Florida or Texas to help swing their large numbers of presidential electors.

But the more fundamental error here is short-term thinking. As noted in Desideratum 3 , after a set of constitutional reforms, our parties will no longer be the same ones we know today. The District's demographics have been changing and there's a good chance, if ranked choice voting (RCV) is adopted, that D.C. residents could elect senators from some new third party within a decade.

Consider this comparison: if 19th century Democrats had not pressured Virginia in 1846 to "retrocede" or take back the southern corner of the District that originally included Arlington and Alexandria—all so they could continue the slave trade there—then Virginia would probably still be a red state today. Trying to calculate whether basic reforms will strengthen the *current* Democratic or Republican party is myopic. These changes are on a different level than short-term political tactics—a level where only experience and fundamental principles are sounds guides. The right question is always: will a proposed reform strengthen my nation by fulfilling the pledge of "liberty and justice for all?"

However, there is a big problem with simply making D.C. a state. The 23rd Amendment, passed by Congress in 1960 and ratified in 1961 with Nixon's support, gives "the district constituting the seat of government of the United States" 3 presidential Electors (Puerto Rico lacks even this much). As a result, many scholars think that making D.C. a state by ordinary law would require reducing "the seat of government" to the National Mall, perhaps including a few surrounding streets with federal office buildings. Would this leave the residents of the White House by themselves to elect 3 presidential Electors? Or would "the seat of government" be gerrymandered to include just a few hundred prized households near the Mall?[15]

Obviously, this is not what framers of the 23rd Amendment intended. The 1978 D.C. Voting Rights Amendment would have solved this problem by repealing the 23rd Amendment and folding D.C.'s 3 electors into the broader reform of treating the District "as though it were a state" in elections and representation, with 1 House member and 2 senators. This obstacle could also be cleared by an amendment establishing a national popular vote for the president (see #12), which would supersede the 23rd Amendment. But without such a constitutional fix, simply making D.C. a state leaves the fate of 3 electors ambiguous, making it likely that the Supreme Court will reject a D.C. Statehood Act.[16]

This view implies that an amendment is needed to make D.C. a state. In that case, though, it would be easier to ratify an amendment that uses the 1978 approach of treating D.C. only as though it were a state, so that its distinct status is maintained.

The Proposal. I therefore suggest an updated version of the D.C. Voting Rights Amendment that also addresses the status of other non-state territories. Hopefully consideration of this amendment would additionally prompt swift action to normalize the status of Puerto Rico, which polls suggest would be a "purple" state.

I. The District's Special Status.
   (i) While the District constituting the seat of government cannot become a state, that District is granted representation in the Senate, the House of Representatives, and presidential Electors on the same basis as if it were a state.
   (ii) This includes as many representatives in the House of Representatives as this District would be apportioned if it were a state; but these representatives will be in addition to the total currently apportioned among the several states.

II. The addition of new states to the Union shall never diminish representation of current states in the House of Representatives.

III. The locally elected city government of Washington, D.C. is also treated as a state government for the purposes of constitutional amendments, and Congress cannot direct its decisions on matters concerning amendment or calling a convention.

IV. Anyone born in any Permanent American territory lying outside the several states has birthright citizenship. Permanent residents of such territories are collectively granted representation by one voting member in the House of Representatives, one voting senator, and two presidential Electors, who are in addition to the total number of congresspersons and electors set by federal law.

§I is an equitable solution to the disenfranchisement of D.C.: it bans D.C. statehood but provides for representation of D.C.'s residents in Congress without any other state losing a House member as a result. Likewise, §II ensures that Puerto Rico statehood would increase the total number of House districts, rather than taking any from other states. §III clarifies the independence of the D.C. government for Article V purposes, as mentioned in the 1978 amendment resolution. Section IV is also an inherently fair solution for other non-state territories: given that their aggregated population is less than Wyoming's, one senator should be enough. This could also be a "deal-sweetener," because these territories are home to many retirees and military personnel who presently tend to vote more conservatively.

In the same spirit, we should consider a few conceivable variations that might pave the way for such an amendment. Obviously, §IV might be removed for treatment in a separate amendment if it proves to be an obstacle. Republicans might also demand that D.C. receive only 1 senator and 1 House member. These compromises would be bitter badges of explicit inferiority for naked partisan ends. A more attractive alternative might be to *combine* D.C. residents with all Americans residing in non-state territories other than Puerto Rico,[17] which would remove the need for Article IV. This would form a more "purple" electorate of about 1.1 million people (larger than Montana and Rhode Island) represented by 2 House members and 2 senators.

On the other hand, Puerto Rico statehood might be added to the amendment to balance representation for D.C., given that Puerto Rico is likely to vote more centrist or Republican in the immediate or foreseeable future. This would be tricky, because it would have to ensure the island's self-determination—perhaps by requiring a final decisive vote for statehood or independence.

12. Direct Election of the President

One member of Congress has aptly described the Electoral College (EC) system—the bizarre indirect way in which Americans elect our president—as "a creaky, shadowy place filled with hidden doors and booby traps galore, the perfect jagged battleground for a lawless demagogue [...]" The problems of the EC rival the evils of gerrymandering for their fame and divisiveness.[18] Among my students, I find that eliminating the EC is usually the first constitutional change they propose.

It is easy to see why. The president and vice president represent Americans as a whole, not state groupings of people. A direct national election would also be *much* cleaner and simpler. When all votes for presidential candidates are added up across the entire nation, we get much wider margins between the top two candidates (see #1). This would make claims that the election was "stolen" even less plausible than they are today.[19]

Direct election of the president and VP by a national popular vote is *not* a left-liberal idea. Around 63% of Americans preferred it to the EC in a July 2022 poll by Pew Research.[20] Presidents Nixon and George H. W. Bush have supported direct election, and strong majorities of Republicans in Congress supported it in votes during 1969 and 1970.[21] Conservative scholars today also endorse it,[22] and believe it could be good for future Republican candidates, given that both leading parties will campaign differently after this fundamental reform.

A direct popular vote would allow more time for vote-counting, which is really needed as people increasingly prefer mail ballots. Without electors as intermediaries and the December 8 deadline for states to certify their electoral votes, recounts or even an actual runoff could go until mid-December if necessary.[23] And a special Court of Elections (see #6) fills a dangerous lacuna in our current system: it would resolve disputes within any particular state about their election returns—with detail on how the court works to be specified in enabling statutes—without having to involve the Supreme Court.

Yet, I have left the EC for 12th in the list of priorities because I think the top ten amendments described in Chapter Two are even more important, and because ending the EC system may be hard to pass and ratify as a stand-alone amendment. After both G. W. Bush and Trump were elected without a majority in the national popular vote, many Republicans now assume—quite wrongly—that the EC is essential for their party's success (see #3).

It is also dangerous for the president and VP, as the only elected officials who represent the whole country, to be selected by a minority of voters nationally. It is even worse for them to be determined mostly by swing voters in just a handful of states. This perception stirs resentment, undermines faith in our system across the country, and makes a mockery of the United States on the world stage. The huge swing-state effect may bring ballot manipulation and violence to several states in the 2024 and

2028 elections unless the EC system is changed to ward off disaster. And, as I detail below, includes other perils unknown to most Americans today that could trigger a profound constitutional crisis and weaken the nation for decades.[24]

The Lapsed Original Purposes of the EC. The task of defending a direct national vote in place of the EC is simplified because this has already been done in Jesse Wegman's definitive 2020 study titled *Let the People Pick the President*, and in Alan Johnson's book, *The Electoral College*. And Alex Keyssar's *Why Do We Still Have the Electoral College?* offers a very detailed history. These works explain how the EC was finally adopted at the 1787 constitutional convention after delegates cycled between at least 15 other possible methods for selecting the president.[25] John Feerick, a leading scholar of the EC, notes that Madison, Wilson, Morris, Carroll, Dickinson, and others at the convention argued for direct election of the president by analogy with the direct election of governors in several states.[26]

In fact, direct election by national popular vote was almost adopted in the convention. It only failed by 5 states to 6.[27] As Keyssar describes, Madison in particular argued for direct election of the president as a basis for the executive's role in the separation of powers.[28] A main argument against it was that voters across the nation would not have sufficient information on enough presidential candidates, given the limits of travel and communication at the time. Today, these problems are long gone. But our founders hoped that the EC would serve five other purposes, every one of which is now defunct and/or now poses great dangers that did not exist in 1787.

First, the electors would be wise men in each part of the country who would know local candidates for the presidency, when the people at large could not possibly know much about them. But the idea that impartial electors would deliberate *within* their respective states—they were never tasked with meeting together as one national body—ended barely 12 years after the convention, when political parties began to control states and their electors.[29] Still, the hopeless notion of electors deliberating occasionally encourages a couple electors to go "rogue" and vote contrary to their preelection pledges.[30] In some states, electors could even run as independents pledged to no candidate; this was common in the first few presidential elections.

Second, like the indirect election of senators that we abolished a hundred years ago, the electors were supposed to give state governments a role in choosing among presidential candidates. Today, every state instead uses a popular election to select its presidential electors, and most Americans do not even realize that in early years, several state governments directly chose their electors.[31]

This forgotten specter may be about to return when the Supreme Court decides *Moore* v. *Harper* in 2023 (see #4). The Court may approve the fringe and debunked "independent state legislature" theory, which would allow willing statehouse majorities to select their state's presidential electors directly, even if their state's law says otherwise. In fact, that is precisely what White House lawyer John Eastman and other Trump lawyers tried to get Rusty Bowers, longtime Republican Speaker of Arizona's House, to do after the 2020 election.[32] Trump himself pressured Republican leaders in the Michigan and Pennsylvania statehouses to throw out their popular votes and directly appoint Trump electors instead.[33] And the Florida state government was preparing to award its electors to Bush after the election of 2000 if the (partial) recount had not gone Bush's way.[34]

Three justices in the *Bush* v. *Gore* decision said the state legislature has this power. And the Court in 2020 cited an ancient case from 1892 holding that citizens has no constitutional "right to vote for presidential electors;" on the contrary, legislatures have "the broadest power of determination" over who becomes an elector.[35]

Some jurists assure us that, once a state's law says that the popular vote determines its electors, the state's legislature cannot unilaterally override its popular election results.[36] I am less optimistic: it is easy for a statehouse majority to insert conditions into state law saying that the legislature reserves its right to pick electors if there seem to be "problems" with the popular vote. For example, the constitution of Texas says that, if the governor declares the presidential vote in doubt, the legislature meets in special session to select that state's 38 electors.[37] Such a debacle is possible in 2024 or 2028. The Electoral Count Act reforms enacted in December 2022 make it harder for Congress to challenge a state's certified results,[38] but do not require states to follow their peoples' popular votes for electors. And the Court could reject the Act's provision giving each governor final authority to submit their state's slate of electors.

Third, the framers expected that in most presidential elections, no candidate would gain an absolute majority of electors. Then the House would select among the top electoral vote getters, conducting a kind of runoff, with each state delegation having an equal vote.[39] As more states started to conduct a popular vote among white men to select their electors, the likelihood of the presidential election going to the House declined, leaving another forgotten danger.

Fourth, the EC included a compromise with slave states, which infamously got to count 3/5^ths^ of their enslaved populations in the census figures determining their number of House members—and thus their number of electors.[40] For example, following the 1800 census, South Carolina received 5 House members for its 199,440 white residents and 3 House members for its 156,151 enslaved African-Americans. Given these 8 House members and 2 senators, South Carolina received 10 electors for the 1804 presidential election. Thus, 30% of its electoral vote rewarded SC for enslaving people. By 1823, at least 6 of Virginia's 22 House members, and a quarter of its 24 electors, were due to its enslaved population. Nationwide, at least 9% of electors were due to nonvoting enslaved residents in 1793, declining to about 6% of electors from 1851 to 1860.[41] Although these electors may only have swung one presidential election in 1800, the 3/5^ths^ rule certainly reduced incentives for states to emancipate.

One might think that this bonus to slave states in the House and EC ended when slavery was outlawed by the 13th Amendment.[42] But actually, from roughly 1880 to 1970, most southern states made it hard or nearly impossible for their black residents to vote, and yet got to count them fully (not by 3/5^ths^) in their census numbers.[43] This egregious tactic would not have worked if the presidential election were decided by a national popular vote. So the desire to suppress the African-American vote was a strong motive against replacing the EC in the 20th century.[44]

This point generalizes to *any* way of suppressing the votes of some groups: as Keyssar puts it, the design of the EC is "such that states did not lose any influence in presidential elections by imposing restrictions on the right to vote."[45] If some state found a legal way, say, to strip the vote from people over 70, or people holding master's degrees, that would leave their still-enfranchised residents with more power in the presidential election via the EC. Today, millions of disenfranchised felons, legal noncitizen residents, and illegal aliens are counted toward each state's census numbers, thus boosting its number of electors, even though these residents cannot vote. By contrast, a national popular vote is an incentive for each state to raise its overall voter turnout for maximum impact in the national total.

Of course, this problem is not unique to the EC. A state's strength in the House is also unaffected by the percentage of its residents who are eligible to vote, or registered, or who actually turn out to vote—whereas these percentages would be vital if states had to compete with each other in electing a national slate of House representatives or a national slate of senators. An amendment to improve apportionment (see #8) could also specify that each state's share of House members depends on the number of residents eligible or registered to vote.

Fifth, the EC was meant to give small states extra weight through their equal number of senators, for which states receive two electors. As the national territory, population, and size of the House expanded, this "small state bump" declined. The only elections it flipped were in 1876, 1916, and 2000.[46] Today, the largest 12 states control 282 electoral votes, which is a majority of the EC.

But the growing malapportionment among states in the House (see #8) is pushing the small state advantage in the EC up again. For example, in 2024, Vermont with its roughly 623,000 people will have 3 electors (= 2 senators plus 1 House member), while Idaho with its roughly 1,861,000 residents will have 4 electors (given its 2 House members). That means every Vermont voter has *more than double* (about 224%) the weight in the presidential election that every Idaho voter has (see Figure 3.1).

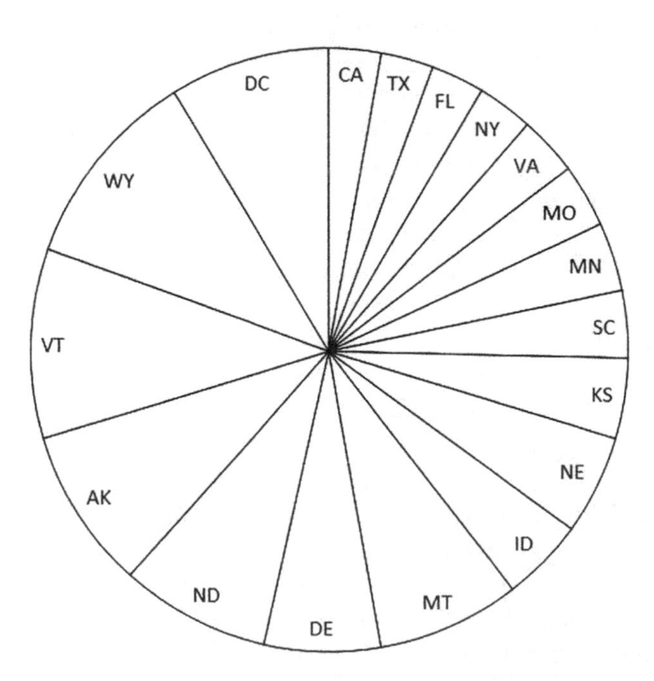

Figure 3.1 Relative Weight of Voters by Sample States in the Presidential Election

More generally, by combining the distinct misapportionments in the Senate and House (see Figures 2.17 and 3.6), the EC helps states that already have enormous extra weight in Congress. North Dakota, for example, has about 259,000 people *per elector*, while New York has about 719,000. Given their huge advantage in the Senate, small states like Wyoming, Vermont, Montana, Rhode Island, and the Dakotas hardly deserve a bump in the EC *as well*. Why should each Alaskan have three times the weight of each Floridian in electing the president? Likewise, Delaware already has the same number of senators as Texas, which has 30 times more residents. Yet on top of that, Texas's 38 presidential electors are only 13 times as many as Delaware's 3 electors.[47]

If a coming presidential election ends up being decided by 5 to 10 electors, these misproportions could determine it, effectively cheating larger states with lesser influence per capita. As long as the EC remains, this problem can only be reduced by increasing the size of the House (see #8).

The EC's Ten Main Contemporary Problems. Let's now integrate this problem of misapportionment with the largest harms and dangers arising from the EC system today. To summarize the findings of many in-depth studies briefly, it helps to distinguish and summarize in one list all the root problems, their interconnections, and their negative effects with a few illustrative examples.

i. *Winner takes all:* Because 48 states and Washington D.C. award *all* of their electoral votes to whichever candidate wins their statewide popular vote, they cancel out "all popular votes for the losing candidates" in their state.[48] For example, votes for Trump in New Jersey and votes for Biden in Texas had *zero weight* on the outcome in November 2020, because individual votes for presidential candidates are not aggregated in a national sum.

ii. Because the national sum of presidential votes does not matter, big differences in turnout between states have no effect on the electoral vote tally. For example, in 1964, turnout in Connecticut was more than *twice* the turnout in South Carolina, but the majority winners in each received the same eight electoral votes.

iii. Because states do not hold runoffs in their presidential elections, their electoral votes often go to a candidate who only wins a *plurality*, not an absolute majority, of votes for president in their state.[49]

iv. These problems, along with the small-state bump can *deny* the presidency to a candidate who wins a plurality of the popular vote. This has happened at least four times in our history: 1824, 1888, 2000, and 2016.[50] It almost happened again in 1948 with Dewey vs. Truman; in 1960, with Kennedy vs. Nixon; and in 2004, when a switch of just 59,301 votes in Ohio would have handed the presidency to John Kerry while leaving him below Bush in the popular vote. Worst of all, in 1876, Tilden probably won *an absolute majority* of the popular vote but still lost the contested electoral vote to Hayes.

v. Due in part to problem (iii), in 16 other elections, the EC system has produced a president who *won* with only a plurality rather than an absolute majority of the national popular vote—most recently, Bill Clinton in 1992 and 1996. The EC can also deny the presidency to a candidate winning a plurality of the EC and of the national vote (as in 1824).

vi. If no candidate wins an absolute majority of the electoral votes, the president is elected by the newly elected House of Representatives from among the top three electoral vote-getters, while the Senate elects the vice president.[51] Worse, in such a "contingent" election, the House votes as if it were the Senate—i.e. with only *one vote for each state delegation* (e.g. Texas and Vermont get equal say).[52] This has happened only twice in our history: in 1800 and 1824. But it almost happened again in 1968 when the rabid segregationist George Wallace ran precisely to "peel off enough electoral votes from both Nixon and Humphrey to prevent either from winning a majority." In the House, Wallace's followers could have acted as kingmaker and extracted steep concessions from the eventual winner.[53]

vii. As noted, disputes about the validity of electoral votes in a particular state can control the outcome, and these must be decided by federal courts and/or Congress.[54] In 1876, a congressional commission ultimately picked the president by awarding 20 contested electoral votes to Hayes.[55] After the 2020 election, the so-called "fake" electors for the losing candidate tried to submit unelected slates of electoral votes from Georgia, Pennsylvania, and Michigan. The revised Electoral Count Act may deter such efforts. But if an "alternative" (unelected) slate is submitted by some wayward governor, public confusion and upset will be tremendous.[56]

viii. If disputed electoral votes or deadlock in counting them leaves the nation with no president-elect by the Inauguration Day (January 20), the vice president-elect would serve as acting president.[57] But if electoral votes for the VP are also disputed or the Senate is deadlocked in choosing the VP, then the Speaker of the House becomes acting president on January 20. This could lead to more than one person claiming to be president,[58] and give supporters of the Speaker an incentive to prolong a deadlock in counting electoral votes.

ix. And there is uncertainty about what could happen if the leading presidential or vice presidential candidate (or both!) dies, or withdraws, or is revealed to be a traitor between the election and the meeting of the EC.[59] The death or incapacity of elected electors during the same period is also a potential problem (which state law could address with surrogates).

x. Finally, as mentioned, "faithless" electors (not to be confused with "fake" or invalid electors) have played a role in a few elections.[60] Today, 32 states and Washington D.C. have laws requiring electors to vote as they pledged, and in a unanimous 2020 decision, the Supreme Court said that states could enforce such laws. But in several of these states, the penalties are small, and votes for presidential candidates by faithless electors could still get certified. The very real prospect that a few faithless electors could swing a presidential election[61] threatens to plunge the nation into chaos at a time when doubts about election integrity have already created a powder keg.

Many of these root problems are not widely understood: most Americans only know about the main *effect* of the EC, namely that a candidate who loses the popular vote can win the presidency (iv). Others like (vii) and (viii) were largely "invisible administrative" potholes that have come into view with the attempt to manipulate the electoral vote after the 2020 election.[62] With the full list in front of us, it should be clear that a national popular vote for a presidential ticket is the simplest solution. But this breakdown of flaws also allows us to distinguish the evils that are due to the EC system by itself from those that arise partly from other constitutional flaws.

Five Fixes that Keep a Modified EC: All Inadequate. (1) As noted earlier, the small-state factor and malapportionment would be nearly eliminated if the size of the House of Representatives raised to 700 or higher, thus making each state's number of electors more proportional to its population (see #8). This would also be the result of Larry Sabato's favored amendment to distribute between 74 and 100 extra presidential electors to the 38 largest states proportionally to their population. Then, for example, despite Bush getting all of Florida's electors in 2000, Gore would have won the presidency by 307 electors to 305, reflecting his 540,000 lead in the national popular vote.[63]

Such an amendment would reduce the chances of the presidential election being thrown into the House and the upheavals this would produce. But people living in the 12 smallest would see nothing for them in such an amendment, whereas everyone eligible to vote would get a new opportunity with a direct national vote for the president and vice president. And, like other ways of trying to improve rather than jettison the EC, Sabato's proposal would not prevent the Supreme Court from decreeing that state legislatures can directly pick their state's electors, no matter what state law says about how they are selected.

(2) Further, ranked choice ballots in the presidential election (see proposal #1) would largely eliminate problem (iii) and reduce problem (v): one candidate would be likely to win an outright majority of each state's popular vote through the RCV automated runoff before receiving its electoral votes. So the winner of the EC would be more likely to have an outright majority of RCV-adjusted popular votes nationwide as well.

But RCV might eventually help a few third-party candidates to become strong enough in a few states to win all of their electoral votes. That could mean that no candidate would have an outright majority of the EC. Then, we have a dilemma. If the third-finishing candidate could authorize some of their electors to switch to one of the other candidates (see x), there is a risk of corrupt deals. If they cannot do this, then it goes to a contingent election in the House. If you thought January 6, 2021 was bad, try to imagine the scenes if House delegations were directly picking the president for the first time in over 200 years!

(3) At least the problem of California and Wyoming each having one vote as the House selects the next president could be remedied while keeping the EC. An amendment could direct the newly elected House, when no one has won an absolute majority of the EC, to select a new president by each House member casting one vote (perhaps with a runoff round) rather than by one vote per state. Madison himself suggested this amendment in response to Jackson losing in the 1824 election,[64] and Sabato also supports it.

Yet, none of these ways of improving the EC system can solve problems (i) and (ii). *These are the true heart of the issue*: by running the presidential election indirectly through

51 jurisdictions, however their ballots are designed and their votes are aggregated, we recreate all the familiar problems of single-member congressional districts *within* the presidential contest. In this context, state lines function like fixed gerrymanders in a two-step process where each district gives all of its points—which vary imperfectly relative to population—to one of the candidates, who becomes president with a majority of these points.

Because of problem (i), solutions (1), (2) and (3) leave the worst overall effect of the EC unresolved: presidential campaigns would still focus mostly on just 8–12 "swing" states, the others being largely foregone conclusions. Solutions (1)–(3) also retain the second-worst effect (iv), namely that a candidate receiving fewer popular votes than their main rival can win: diluting the small-state bump reduces but does not eliminate this danger.

To see why nothing short of direct election by national popular vote can fully solve both these most glaring and harmful effects of the EC, let's briefly consider two other potential ways of patching up the EC system, which were used by several states until the 1830s.[65] Both attempt to reduce problem (i), and they have come back into vogue as people look for ways to improve the EC.

(4) *The District Method.* A state choosing to use the "district method" distributes its electors one per each congressional district, with its remaining two electors going to the statewide plurality winner (who could be decided by RCV in future). Maine and Nebraska are the only states currently splitting their electoral votes this way. This is an alternative to the plurality winner taking *all* of a state's electoral votes.

Unfortunately, though, the district method only imports the dramatic effects of unlimited partisan gerrymandering of congressional districts into the presidential vote. Imagine if a presidential swing state like Florida or Ohio decided (by state law) to adopt the district method for electors: district lines would become so vital that officials might resort to bribes or even hitmen in desperation to rig those lines to their party's advantage.

Due to gerrymandering and accidental groupings of more liberal and conservative voters, this approach can actually exaggerate the gap between the electoral and popular vote: Bush would have beaten Gore by 38 rather than 5 electoral votes in 2000 if the district method had been used nationwide. Trump would still have won in 2016 despite Hillary Clinton's 2.8 million lead in the popular vote. Most shockingly, Romney would have beaten Obama in 2012, even though Obama won almost *5 million* more votes nationwide![66] That would have made Obama only the second candidate in history after Tilden to win an outright majority of the popular vote and still lose the EC.

These perverse results would be much less likely if the number of congressional districts were doubled or tripled and a constitutional anti-gerrymandering formula were adopted (amendments #8 and #4). But until then, the district method version of the EC is even worse than the status quo. It only moves the "wasted vote" problem to the district level: only likely swing districts would matter to candidates.

(5) *The Proportional Method.* This version of the EC is not dependent on a fix to gerrymandering because it awards a rounded share of a state's electoral votes to each candidate based on their share of their *statewide* popular vote. It can also solve

the faithless elector threat (x) if each state's electoral votes are automatically awarded to candidates based on their proportion of the vote in that state without human electors being involved (but the absolutist legislature danger would remain).[67]

Critics note that the proportional method would lead to third parties winning more electoral votes, bargaining with larger campaigns to transfer their electors, and potentially throwing the election into the House (see vi).[68] In fact, this would have happened in 2016: if every state had awarded all its electoral votes proportionally, the electoral vote would have been split 266 for Clinton and 267 for Trump, with 6 electors pledged to other candidates.[69] However, RCV ballots would reduce the chances of this happening, especially if candidates have to score above (say) 10% of the popular vote on the first round to win even one elector in a state with 10 or more (otherwise ballots for them would be transferred to the voter's next choice, if any).

Yet, RCV cannot fix the proportional method's rounding problem. As long as 26 states and D.C. have 6 or less electoral votes, a candidate's electoral vote share in smaller states can only be *crudely* related to their share of the state popular vote. For example, in Rhode Island in 2016, Trump won almost 39% of the vote. But RI only has 4 electors, who cannot be divided into fractions. So, Trump would probably have received only 1 of the 4 electors (or 25%), depending on the exact rounding rules. These would have to be complex to account for votes going to third parties, thus further confusing the public. And different statehouse majorities might keep changing those rules in an effort to boost their party's favored candidate.

As a result, the proportional method can easily allow the popular vote winner to lose the presidency. It only reduces this chance if the size of the House or number of electors is massively increased to make each state's electors more proportional to its population. For example, as with "member votes" for House delegations weighted by population (#8), imagine that the states and D.C. divided up 5000 electors (or electoral points). This would solve the rounding problem, but it could raise the chance of third parties winning enough electors to throw the race into the House, even with RCV.

What if we combine several of these EC-compatible fixes? Believe it or not, even if RCV, a larger House, and anti-gerrymandering standards were all in place, and other constitutional changes needed to remediate (vi) and (viii) were made, then both the district and proportional methods would *still* have serious flaws. In particular, problem (ii) would remain: if turnout varies widely between states (or districts), a candidate might win 6 of 11 electoral votes in Massachusetts by getting 1.3 million actual votes there, while her opponent wins 6 of 11 electoral votes in Tennessee via 0.7 million actual votes there. This would not change much if MA had 106 electoral votes and TN had 104 (closely reflecting their relative population sizes). As a result, the national popular vote could still deviate significantly from the national EC outcome.

People usually become enthusiastic for the district and/or proportional versions of the EC because they can be adopted by state law without a constitutional amendment. But this hope ignores another big danger: if they are introduced *one state at a time*, these methods function as unilateral disarmament by unsuspecting popular movements, or as tricks to undermine one party. Just as gerrymandering reform that is restricted to liberal and moderate states only makes the (current) Democratic party weaker (see #4), states that adopt the district or proportional method without it being a national requirement for *all states* usually weaken their impact on the overall presidential race.[70] This can make it more likely that the winner of the national popular vote loses in the EC, making problems (iii) and (iv) in the EC system even worse.

The same holds for trickery. As with rounding rules, as long as there is no uniform system for all states, parties controlling particular state governments can move back and forth between the three known EC methods for their party's perceived benefit. Perhaps they can even invent clever new ways to rig their state's electoral slates.

For example, demographic changes predict that a Democrat could win a plurality or majority of the presidential vote in Texas within 18 years. When that happens, Republicans across the nation will be astonished to realize that now the EC system makes their party (given its current stances on issues) very unlikely to win the presidency. Anticipating this, the Republican-controlled majority in Austin will suddenly decide that the district or proportional method is "much fairer" than winner-take-all for its presidential electors. That way, when the reckoning comes, the Republican candidate may get 16 or 17 of Texas's 38 electoral votes rather than 0. But when Democrats take control the statehouse, they will switch Texas's presidential vote back to winner-take-all. The same, of course, could happen in reverse if Michigan or Wisconsin trend more conservative.

Imagine the fury and alienation that these games will produce when they cause a candidate who wins the national vote by 4, 5, or even 6 million votes to lose the presidential election. The district and proportional methods can only make a bad situation even worse unless they are *mandated universally* for all states. But that requires a constitutional amendment, when the advantage of these methods was supposed to be to avoid that need. If we do have to amend the Constitution to fix problems (i)–(x), then the simplest option is the direct national vote. It is analogous to the method that we already use to elect governors, and that virtually every other developed democracy on Earth employs. Direct election it eliminates any need for the bewildering complexities, pitfalls, and potential for trickery that are involved in alternatives (1)–(5).

The Proposal, Three Objections, and Replies. At this point, we should ask whether there is any good motive for trying to make the historically tainted EC system work by patching up some of its many flaws, while potentially creating new problems, as alternatives (1)–(5) do? The main answer has always been the myth that the EC protects small states from being "swamped" by large ones.

In fact, small states already have ten times the extra protection they could ever deserve in the Senate, and in our ancient process of ratifying constitutional amendments as well. Nor do small states share unique interests that need protection from national majorities: in reality, about half of them are "red" and half are "blue" today.[71] As George Edwards points out, most farms are actually in large states, and agriculture subsidies to them are already so out of hand that presidents from both parties try to restrain them.[72]

There are only three objections to direct election of the president worth considering. The first is that it would weaken our two-party system, as third parties gain importance.

But as I have argued throughout the first two chapters, the dominant two parties no longer serve national interests; instead, they are increasingly cannibalizing the system on which we all depend. So the rise of other parties in direct presidential elections would be an improvement, not a liability. With RCV, there is no danger of spoiler candidates preventing a clean win in a direct election: one candidate is likely to win an outright majority, or something close to it, in the national vote for the White House. Nor, based on experience with our races for governor, are we likely to see many presidents winning by less than a 45% plurality.[73]

Second, critics argue that a close nationwide vote would spark court challenges in hundreds of counties across the nation demanding recounts everywhere. But this allegation has things backwards. No city or county would have a decisive swing influence when all popular votes are summed up across the country. The national vote margin is extremely unlikely ever to be less than 300,000 in a nation as big as ours, especially with RCV, whereas the margin in Florida after the 2000 election was a statistically irrelevant 537 votes: a coin flip would have been fairer than what transpired in that case (see #1). Congress can also enact clear standards for mail ballot tracking, double-blind ballot counting, automated recounts in close counties and states, and stiff penalties for frivolous lawsuits based on no hard evidence, especially if we adopt a Voting Rights amendment (see #6).

Instead, it is the EC system that is destabilizing the nation by making the outcome turn on close votes in a few swing states. This is the motive for spurious legal challenges, fraudulent allegations of mass voter fraud, state laws tailored to reduce participation by disfavored groups, and criminal efforts to corrupt election officials—all to flip the crucial swing counties in swing states that decide the EC outcome. Far from "containing" the fights to a few locations, the EC system has made these fights so toxic that they are killing democratic processes in the United States. If we do not move to a direct national vote, federal courts may be inundated with lawsuits that cost counties and states hundreds of millions of dollars in every presidential election.

Third, there is the refrain that presidential candidates in a direct election would only visit large cities and focus advertising campaigns there, while ignoring rural areas.[74] In truth, however, candidates already do that—*because of* the EC. As Wegman explains, candidates will waste little time or money on states where they start out already 7–9% ahead or behind in the polls. That often leaves only 10–13 states (or less) worth fighting for. In 2024, these will again be Wisconsin, Michigan, Ohio, Pennsylvania, North Carolina, Virginia, Georgia, Arizona—and maybe Maine, New Hampshire, and/or Florida. Most of the more rural states are the least visited, both because they are "safe" states and they have few electors. As a FairVote event tracker showed, by the end of October, 33 states had not hosted a single campaign event featuring either main candidate in the 2020 election (see Figure 3.2). That was consistent with the elections in 2016, 2012, 2008, and 2004, when 34 states did not host either main candidate for a general election event. TV ads for presidential candidates were also concentrated in the same 12–13 swing states.[75]

So the presumption behind this "flyover" objection to a direct national vote is baseless. It would actually be an improvement if candidates "only" visited big

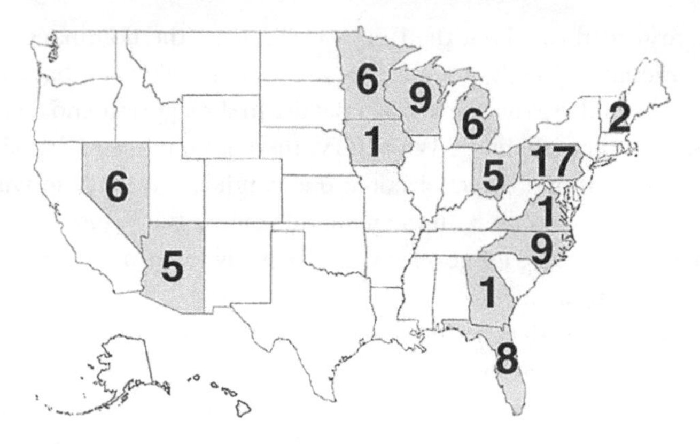

Figure 3.2 Main Candidates Campaign Events in 2020

cities across the nation during the general election. Because every vote would count toward the national total in a direct election, winning a million more votes across 30 currently "safe" states—including many smaller and rural ones—could well mean winning the White House. Not only Dallas, Seattle, New Orleans, Denver and St. Louis, but also Louisville, Omaha, Jackson, Billings, Birmingham, Indianapolis, Memphis, Santa Fe, Knoxville, and many smaller cities would be on the campaign routes.

That is a key benefit of an amendment to institute a national popular vote for the presidency: by solving problem (i), (ii), (iii), and (iv) simultaneously, unlike the proportional or district methods, a direct election with RCV would produce *a far more competitive campaign across the entire nation*: every vote in every state would matter. Voter engagement and turnout would rise, because now a few more votes for a Republican presidential candidate in New York might offset a few that she lost to a Democrat in Texas. As a result, presidential candidates would have to appeal to more moderate voters everywhere. This bigger turnout would also cause more congressional races in presidential years to become competitive, further loosening two-party domination. Undecided citizens in previously "safe" states would suddenly have a strong reason to learn more about candidates' positions and cast a vote.

In addition, advertising spending would also be more evenly distributed across the nation. If this change were combined with modest controls on campaign and third-party spending for advertising (see #5), current swing states and swing cities could see dramatic reductions. All these salutary effects combined might be like awakening from an evil spell that has held the nation in its grip for over a century. Citizens in Ohio, Georgia, and Arizona could breathe the free air again, while potential voters in Kansas, Oregon, Alabama, Oklahoma, Minnesota, and maybe even Alaska and Hawaii would be amazed to discover that presidential candidates care about them. I'm certain that most Americans would love this new process.

Because presidential campaigns would have so much ground to cover, candidates might also designate two or three of their most likely cabinet members and send these proxies to events across many states. But if we still worry that nationalized campaigns will only focus on 15–20 big cities, we could add clauses that directly prevent this. §II in this draft amendment provides one feasible example:

I. Election of the President and Vice President shall be by a plurality of a national popular vote. All citizens over 34 years of age are eligible to run for these offices, including individuals who have been naturalized citizens for at least 15 years, as long as they all fulfill basic disclosure requirements in federal law.
II. Candidates whose names appear on the general election ballot in 10 or more states and the District of Columbia must spend at least two days in each of 25 states, and hold at least 10 events open to the general public outside of the nation's largest 30 cities by October 20, or risk being disqualified. They can be excused from fulfilling this requirement only for reasons of injury, illness, or other emergency by appeal to the federal Court of Elections.
III. The President and Vice President must run as a single slate on ballots that allow voters to rank up to four slates, including one write-in slate, if they wish.[76] These choices will be processed in an automatic runoff as provided by federal law. No person can run for President or Vice President on more than one slate; nor for any other federal or state office at the same time.[77]
IV. The ticket receiving the highest total number of votes after the automatic runoff wins [perhaps plus a contingency provision for low plurality winners: see below].
V. On January 2 of the year following the election, any disputes about any jurisdiction's reported election returns that still remain unresolved by methods established in federal law will go to the federal Court of Elections for final resolution by January 9. On January 10, the Court of Elections will certify the results, which Congress and every state shall respect.
VI. Congress has the power to enable these provisions by federal statute.

§I eliminates the antiquated constitutional clause that bans naturalized immigrants from running or serving[78] (and thereby eliminates its potential conflict with the 20th and 25th Amendments), while also making room for financial disclosure requirements (see #15). §II addresses the common worry about campaigns focusing only on the largest cities. It would also help prevent too many minor party candidates from distracting attention, and thus allow voters to focus on a manageable number of options. But this requires a mechanism to handle emergencies that give candidates good excuses for not fulfilling the event distribution requirements.

§IV allows the plurality winner of the national popular vote to take office; but with the RCV clause in §III, the winning ticket will usually garner an outright majority.[79] This keeps Congress out of the process of picking the winner. But over time, if the United States developed four or five major parties due to RCV (see #1), there might be rare cases in which the plurality winner has a fairly low proportion of the national vote for the presidency. The amendment could include a provision for that contingency.

A spectrum of such provisions is suggested by the history of debates over altering or replacing the EC. I will mention three promising ones that Congress has considered in the past. The first is similar to Senator Birch Bayh's original plan: if the plurality winner does not secure at least 40% of the popular vote, then a joint session of the new Congress, with each member casting one vote, decides between the two slates with the most nationwide votes. A second option proposed that if no slate secured 40% of the popular vote, but the plurality winner would also have also secured a majority of electoral votes, then that candidate would become president; otherwise the House, voting as individuals, would select among the top slates. A third proposed to combine a direct popular vote with a requirement to win "at least one third of the states."[80]

Such a contingency provision could confer greater legitimacy on the winning candidate without needing actual electors or electoral votes to be counted. In the remote case where a candidate wins the plurality of the national vote by less than 40% and would not have a majority of electoral votes under the old system, perhaps an actual runoff election should be scheduled in mid-December and inauguration delayed by a few weeks if necessary.

Finally, §V of my proposal refers to the Court of Elections mentioned in the Voting Rights amendment (see #6), which would take political pressure off the regular courts and Congress. Here again, we can imagine variations worth considering. For example, perhaps Congress should still have a vote on January 11 (rather than January 6), during which agreement by 60% of both chambers would be enough to amend the Court of Elections' certified results. This would insure against some serious miscarriage of justice in the Court.

The Interstate Compact. There is one last alternative that deserves mention because it has been so widely touted: namely, the proposal for an agreement among states that collectively have 270 electors or more to award all their electors to the winner of the national popular vote. This creative proposal is an attempt to avoid the need for a constitutional amendment. It is possible in principle because the Constitution (in Article I §10) allows interstate compacts with approval from Congress—and, as we saw, states are not compelled to allocate their electors to the winner of their in-state popular votes. But, much as we might hope this approach can work, I consider it very unlikely.

While the push for the popular vote compact gained ground for many years, it has been stuck for some time at states totaling 195 electors;[81] the additional 75 electors needed would require several other more conservative-learning states to join the compact. Even then, it would have to be approved by Congress, which would currently require 60 votes in the Senate. Numerous challenges in state courts would follow, and the Supreme Court might still find that the compact violates Article II of the Constitution (as altered by the 12th and 20th Amendments).

If it survived such judicial challenges, the compact's real test would come when

- a candidate A narrowly wins a (current) swing state S, such as Michigan or Georgia, but
- their rival B wins more votes nationally, or even wins an outright majority of the national vote;
- and S's electoral votes would put A over the top in the EC.

Would officials in state S follow their compact and award their electors to B instead? This would confuse many voters in S, because the EC system misfocuses attention on each state as *the relevant aggregator*: so it would look to residents of S who voted for A like their (in-state) "majority" was being robbed in favor of B.

The pressures to renege on the compact in such a case, or to help the candidate favored by the statehouse majority, would be huge, and the compact's enforcement uncertain. Candidates might mount a 50-state campaign only to find that one or two states in the compact changed their law to back out of the scheme in late October, putting the EC and its swing states back in charge. Or Congress and an incumbent president expecting to lose the national popular vote could rescind their approval of the compact late in the game.[82]

In sum, the process of presidential elections is too important to be left to uncertainties—as it now is, and still would be under the interstate compact. We need a clear process, fixed in the Constitution, which overcomes collective action problems among states. At best, approaching the 270 threshold for the interstate compact might spark renewed enthusiasm for the sort of amendment I have outlined.

The Main Obstacle: Short-Term Thinking. The effect of an amendment to elect the president directly through a national vote would be exhilarating: an election run under this new system might restore public confidence in democratic values. So why on Earth, then, did our parents' or grandparents' generations not replace the EC long ago? The answer is not really the lobby power of smaller states that get an influence-bump from the EC. Rather, for over 150 years, the biggest obstacle to reform has always been the enormous extra power that *current swing states*—and swing cities within swing states—gain from the EC. Both major parties and their presidential candidates cater almost slavishly to these few parts of the country that will decide the election, often to the detriment of national interests. But that gives those swing sections an incentive to keep the EC.

As Wegman tells, this is exactly what defeated the push for direct election of the president in 1969. After heroic work by Birch Bayh and his allies, the House of Representatives passed an amendment abolishing the EC by a huge 339 to 70 majority (over 82%) on September 18, 1969—a fact that every American should learn in high school (see #10). It looked destined to pass the Senate as well and probably gain ratification *until* the ardent racist Strom Thurmond and his allies convinced (ironically) leaders of minority groups in northern cities that this amendment would diminish their influence. In New York City, for example, these groups could turn the statewide vote for the president, and NY state was back then the largest swing state in the nation. These local leaders persuaded more northern senators to join dixiecrats in opposing the amendment, which failed in the Senate in September 1970.[83]

Thus these few big city leaders half a century ago condemned their grandchildren to live through two elections that handed the White House to the popular vote loser (in 2000 and 2016), two others that almost went that way (in 2004 and 2020), attempts to manipulate electors in December 2020, and more of the same to come until we restart Bayh's titanic effort almost from scratch.

The root cause of this historic disaster is short-term thinking in swing states. Their leaders should understand, as the NY case shows, that they will not have swing power for very long. In an era when people's sense of identity is less tied to places and their jobs are likely to take them across state lines multiple times during their lives, the EC is not in their long-term interest. The temporary advantages it gives to a few states result from the confluence of state boundaries and demographic changes that no one controls: as Litt puts it, the EC's "effects are basically random."[84] Surely it is nuts to keep a *randomizing module* in our process for selecting the highest elected office in the nation.

Republicans must also realize that they do not need the EC to win the presidency. It is a fallacy to infer from the elections of 2000 and 2016 that Republicans would have lost without the EC, because neither G. W. Bush nor Trump (nor their rivals) ran a *truly national* race for the popular vote everywhere in America. For this reason, it is even misleading to call them "popular vote losers," because they were not trying to win the national popular vote. So, *we cannot know* what would have happened if direct election had become law before 2000. When the system is fundamentally altered, the parties and their candidates will behave quite differently (see Desideratum 6).[85] Thus, we should put unreliable assessments of short-term advantage aside and end this EC mess once and for all.

That could happen in two ways. First, scrapping the EC might become part of a larger compromise package of constitutional reforms. Second, when Texas flips into the Democratic column, many Republicans may be eager to consider an amendment for direct election. During that brief historical window, Democrats will again be tempted to keep *their* new-found advantage by maintaining the EC and extracting revenge for 2000 and 2016. They should resist that devil's bargain, put aside self-serving and short-sighted pleas from the swing states of that decade, and take the historic opportunity to bequeath to all our descendants a fully democratic presidential election.

13. Commonsense Limits to the Pardon Power

I turn now to a series of reforms that are needed to strengthen the rule of law and ensure greater integrity among all elected and appointed federal officials. Unlike some of the previous amendment proposals, these are topics on which there is already growing consensus across the political continuum that deep changes are needed. I begin with one that concerns both the danger of corruption and reasonable limits to the executive's check on judicial decisions.

The reasons for limiting the pardon power are obvious. The potential for abuse by pardoning friends or relatives, or dangling a pardon to silence potential witnesses against a sitting president or vice president, has been all too evident for some time. Some of Trump's 73 pardons during the waning hours of his presidency were shocking because they rewarded close allies guilty of serious crimes. The most egregious of his pardons freed Paul Manafort, who had worked directly for the pro-Russian puppet leader of Ukraine, Viktor Yanukovich, who tried to overthrow Ukrainian democracy in early 2014 with Putin's aid.[86] Manafort, who served for a time as Trump's campaign chairman, was convicted for laundering money from uncertain "offshore" sources through $22 million in New York real estate. But other recent presidents such as Clinton and G. W. Bush have also pardoned political cronies or commuted their sentences, despite their being under investigation by special prosecutors. Clinton, for example, pardoned his half-brother for cocaine trafficking. And President Biden could pardon his son Hunter Biden, who is under investigation for fraud. This is an equal-opportunity hazard, whatever party the president belongs to.

There are several good reasons to retain some pardon power. Miscarriages of justices can happen and mercy has its place when convicts have reformed, or when their unique circumstances were not accounted for in mandatory sentencing guidelines. In cases of widespread insurrection or civil disobedience, the power to issue a general amnesty may help resolve a conflict that is tearing the nation apart. Lincoln used pardons selectively to promote healing during and after the Civil War; and other nations have found pardons useful in bringing rebels into peace negotiations. Andrew Johnson also proclaimed a general amnesty on Christmas Day, 1868, with 14 excepted classes, such as generals in the confederate army and officers in the confederate government. But he also granted over 12,600 pardons to individuals in these classes (conditional on taking an oath of loyalty to the Union and never again engaging in slavery). Some of these cases were quite controversial at the time.

The same applies in a lesser way to widespread civil disobedience and civic strife. Jimmy Carter used a general pardon to end legal disputes over Vietnam draft-dodgers that would otherwise have dragged on for years.[87] Franklin Roosevelt holds the record for presidential pardons, largely because he received so many requests from thousands of people convicted on alcohol crimes during Prohibition.

Public safety might also benefit. In extreme cases, presidents may offer pardons to a criminal whose help is absolutely essential to stop a major threat to national security. But some limits are required for good governance: an almost-absolute pardon power is an outdated vestige of monarchy that few of our nation's governors enjoy. For example, no one should get a pardon for making big donations to a political party or campaign.

Most importantly, it is essential to limit the president's power to pardon family members and high federal officials, especially when their testimony in fraud or corruption cases might tend to impugn the president or their administration. Without this limit, the pardon power undermines the capacity of the Justice Department, special prosecutors, congressional inquiries, and even impeachment proceedings to deter serious abuses of office.[88] That has nothing to do with judicious mercy or helping the nation to move forward after a crisis.

Likewise, most Americans would be shocked to learn that presidents can and have issued *preemptive* pardons to people for crimes for which they are not yet charged.[89] This power could invite confidents of the president to commit brazen crimes with a guarantee of impunity,[90] whether the proactive pardon came after or even before the crime. Crimes committed with a president's prior knowledge, election tampering, and other crimes warranting impeachment should be unpardonable—by both later presidents and governors (if state crimes were involved). Such potential abuses could be prevented or significantly reduced by the following sort of amendment:

I. Limits on Close Affiliates
   (i) The President cannot pardon himself or herself, or any close family members as defined by federal law, or any of their current or former cabinet members, or high-ranking advisors in the President's administration or election campaigns, as defined by federal law.
   (ii) Nor may a President pardon anyone who has contributed resources to their campaigns or to their party in amounts above thresholds defined by law.

II. Limits for Crimes in Office
   (i) No high-ranking federal official, as defined by law, can be pardoned for a crime committed in the course of exercising powers of their office, unless a pardon is first recommended by an independent Commission of Pardons established by federal law to consider these and other pleas for clemency.
   (ii) In deciding on recommendations, the Commission will consider whether the crime for which pardon is sought involved attempted or actual serious abuse of official powers or privileges, which generally defeat a case for pardon.

III. Limits on Crimes Cited in Impeachments
   (i) No President, Vice President, cabinet official, or judge impeached for, in part or whole, certain serious felony crimes, may be pardoned for those crimes.
   (ii) Nor may a President issue any pardons for persons who are being considered in active impeachment proceedings, until their resolution in acquittal.[91]

IV. No one may be pardoned upon conviction for crimes involving corruption that were first investigated by special prosecutors appointed by the Department of Justice or Congress.

V. No pre-emptive pardons
   (i) No one may be pardoned for a crime for which they have not yet been charged.
   (ii) All pardons must be published in open public records, unless compelling security reasons prevent it.

VI. Congress may, with two-thirds of both chambers concurring, reverse any pardon within one year of it being issued.

§II partly follows the model in several states that limit governors to pardons recommended by an impartial commission. Arguably its scope could be extended to include close associates and friends of the president or vice president, but this set would be harder for Congress to define in statute than "close family members" and high-ranking officials.

Similarly, the ban on preemptive pardons in §V prevents pardons from disrupting investigations; and §IV ensures that the president cannot buy silence in serious corruption cases by promising pardons after prosecution. Reformers have also advocated that documents related to pardons issued should be made public. But then ordinary law must be able to carve out limited exceptions.[92] Finally, §VI deters highly questionable pardons during a president's final days in office.

The goal throughout is to strengthen the other "good government" reforms recommended below, which could otherwise be undermined by the pardon power. Ideally, once Congress established how the federal Commission of Pardons is staffed, almost all presidential pardons would go through this regular channel, making the whole process less politically charged. It is also worth considering whether the amendment should ban all presidential pardons in the lame-duck period following a presidential election. This would allow voters to take account of a president's pardons on Election Day, but it could also block pardons needed in emergencies.

Why not simplify the amendment to say only that Congress may by law establish limits and/or conditions on presidential pardons? This is an example of the dilemma discussed in Desideratum 7. The advantage of short language is that Congress could rectify later problems not anticipated when writing the pardon amendment. The main disadvantage is that later congressional majorities could tailor the limits on pardons for their political convenience—and for their opponents' inconvenience—with presidential consent. This seems unwise, given the vital role of pardon limits when fighting corruption in government: some hard rules are needed.

My suggested language balances these approaches by giving Congress some latitude in specifying the limits, or adapting them as future threats demand, without giving it unlimited power to do whatever it likes with pardons. Detail in the amendment also prevents federal courts from frustrating main goals of the reform through creative reinterpretation. The same points apply to the anti-corruption measures in the next three sections. In my view, distrust in our federal government has reached such critical levels that detailed and strong new constitutional language is needed to restore public trust.

14. The Integrity of All Federal Officeholders: Anti-Corruption Standards

The call to reduce corruption across our federal government is probably the single most frequent demand made by Americans of all party affiliations. But our Constitution lacks several commonsensical standards of good governance, including basic rules to prevent conflicts of interest and elementary disclosure requirements. Just as there is supposed to be some separation of "church and state," we need constitutional walls between Congress, executive offices, big business, capital markets, and foreign influencers.

What protections we currently have are provided in statutes that later congresses or courts can alter or overturn, and in congressional "ethics" rules that almost never entail very strong penalties for their violation. For example, Charlie Rangel (D-NY) was "censured" by a supermajority of the House in 2010 for 11 ethics violations, but he kept serving until his retirement in 2017. Paul Gosar (R-AZ) is still in office after being censured in 2021 for making a death threat: he tweeted a video showing his face on a cartoon character stabbing to death a character with Alexandria Ocasio-Cortez's face (D-NY). And despite falsifying much of his history before his election in 2022, Congressman George Santos (R-NY) is unlikely to be expelled unless he is convicted of a felony. Expulsion in either chamber requires a two-thirds vote: thus Congress has expelled only two members (both Democrats) since the end of the Civil War. Clearly self-policing is not working.

The powers of mega-corporations and lobbyists with many personal connections on the Hill, who regularly try to "capture" important administrative bureaus that are supposed to enforce federal regulations, will not be sufficiently controlled by limits on campaign donations alone (see #5). There is a growing "revolving door" between congressional and federal executive offices and corporate entities with large material stakes in the decisions that these offices make.[93] At last count, 449 former members of Congress are currently registered lobbyists for powerful organizations; and this does not include those in law firms that serve big corporations which benefitted from the former member's work in Congress.[94]

It was not always this way. Gore notes that in the 1970s, before big-money lobbyists changed how the federal government works, "only 3% of retiring members of Congress gained employment as lobbyists; now [in 2012]... more than 40% of retiring House members become lobbyists." In the same period, corporate PACs increased 20-fold, and expenditures by lobbyists jumped 35-fold.[95] In one study, Hasen found that "half of retiring senators become lobbyists, and [...] lobbyists who used to work for a senator see their income fall by nearly a quarter when that senator retires."[96] Another study running from 2017 to 2019 found that 50% of retired or defeated members of Congress became lobbyists, with another 9% selling their influence to a business or trade group.[97] Similarly, an independent watchdog discovered that, between 2008 and 2018, "380 high-ranking Department of Defense officials and military officers became lobbyists, board members, executives, or consultants for defense contractors within two years of leaving the Department."[98]

This should be stopped completely. The purpose of working in Congress, the Pentagon, and other federal offices is to serve the nation, not to build a list of contacts that one can monetize afterwards. Legislators and regulators in federal offices should not be able to move immediately into paid positions with the very companies, nonprofits, unions, or other powerful groups over which they exercised federal oversight. We need stronger general standards that establish bright lines between these realms. I propose all of the following measures—stated here briefly to clarify the main idea in each without trying to provide precise constitutional language:

I. A 10-year gap between serving in the House or Senate and serving as a paid lobbyist, as defined by law, after serving in Congress. A 5-year gap between serving Congress or the executive branch as a senior staffperson, as defined by law, and working as a paid lobbyist.

II. A minimum 7-year gap between serving in the House or Senate and holding a paid position in any corporation or nonprofit organization that reaped substantial material benefits, as defined by law, from legislation on which one worked in congressional committees.

III. A minimum 5-year gap between working in any high executive or military office, as defined in law, and working in any corporation or nonprofit organization that has a close relationship—as defined by law—with the federal offices in which one worked.

IV. An Insider Trading ban

   (i) To avoid conflicts of interest, all members of Congress, all executive leaders at the cabinet or undersecretary level, all federal judges, and their legal partners and children, must hold all their assets over $10,000 per person in blind trusts managed by persons with no privileged access to information from federal sources that might give undue advantage in investment decisions.

   (ii) Congress must set rules for its members to recuse themselves from decisions in which their spouse's or childrens' employers, immediate relatives, or business partners have a significant and direct material or financial stake.

   (iii) The same recusal rules apply to the federal judiciary. And Congress may extend recusal requirements to other high executive officials if it so choses.

V. The President, Vice President, and cabinet members may not materially profit from any relationships with members of foreign governments, or with corporations having a significant level of foreign ownership, as defined by law, for a period of ten years after they leave office. This applies to accepting gifts of any kind from the same entities or their agents. Congress has the power to set similar standards for generals and admirals in our armed forces.

VI. No federal lawmaker, officer, or judge may take trips sponsored or paid by any for-profit or nonprofit corporation, entity, lobby, or foreign government during their term in office and for at least 5 years after their federal employment ends.

VII. Intentional violation of these conditions is *a felony* carrying a mandatory minimum prison sentence to be established in statutes, and a lifetime ban from employment in any capacity in any level of government.

The reforms in §§ I–III would end the revolving door. For example, generals could not retire and go to work immediately for a big defense contractor. There are some limits in federal law that require one- or two-year gaps, but this amendment would toughen such limits and apply them to the highest executive officers, members of Congress, and our justices.

The blind trust requirement has been promoted in recent reform bills and petitions in Congress. As E. J. Dionne put it, "politicians should not be stock traders."[99] But experience shows that Congress will never police its own members adequately: we must constitutionalize the ban on insider trading that our legislators sometimes violate despite a recent act outlawing it.[100] Similarly, §VI should already be enacted in statute, but it is not. Instead, even federal judges have been taking corporate-sponsored trips for years—and might even overrule laws forbidding such junkets.[101] Influence through lawmakers' spouses, children, and their partners is also important.[102]

Again, such provisions look more detailed than the constitutional clauses we are used to. But they are badly needed to force clear and commonsense anti-corruption standards into every part of the federal system, and ensure that judges will not block them.[103] These explicit standards would still leave plenty of specifics to be filled out in enabling statutes that can adapt to changing circumstances. But it is not enough for an amendment simply to state a short and abstract anti-corruption principle and leave all of the details to Congress and the courts. Too much self-regulation is not safe.

15. Qualifications, Disclosure, Honesty and Professionalism Requirements for Office

While the bright lines described in the previous section would establish arms-length relationships between legal regulators and regulated parties, the individual officeholder's character is also crucial. The Constitution should enforce minimum qualifications for major public offices, and protect civil servants trying to uphold federal laws, which is essential for integrity throughout the executive branch—with all its many contemporary powers and functions.

Although massive public trust is invested in our high political offices, their only eligibility requirements currently concern age and citizenship (and some reformers recommend relaxing these[104]). It is downright crazy that we do not have any substantive credential requirements and/or background checks for some of the most powerful jobs in the world. Minimum financial disclosures are also needed to ensure the integrity of high officers like the president and federal justices, protecting them from blackmail or undue influence—especially by hostile foreign powers. After years of massive hacks, China's dictatorial regime possesses personal information on 80% of Americans.[105] Christopher Porter and Brian Finch speculate that "China is gathering the pieces needed to create in the US a version of its omnipresent surveillance state."[106]

Given such threats, we need to set a minimum bar for all candidates and applicants. For many offices, this may safely be done by statute. But for positions like the president or leading roles in Congress or the federal judiciary, any such requirement would surely face serious legal challenges unless it had an explicit constitutional foundation. Likewise, our existing federal anti-nepotism statute does not clearly apply to White House staff; it could easily be rejected by a federal judge,[107] given attempts to push the radical and dangerous doctrine that there can be no statutory limits on presidents' authority over anything or anyone in the executive branch.

We also increasingly need a basic honesty requirement for elected officials who currently abuse their privileges not just to distort a few facts for partisan advantage, but even to spread mass lies that can be extremely harmful to the public, to faith in our elections, and to the credibility of our institutions. Ordinary citizens can legally misuse their free speech rights by intentionally spreading falsehoods for political purposes, but virtually everyone is bound by standards of honesty in their jobs—and can be dismissed for a pattern of lying to customers or bosses. This includes most civil servants, and it should be no different for federal politicians: if they want to lie to the public, they should find other employment. Running and holding office should require accepting certain basic standards of decency, which can be summarized in the following sort of provisions.

I. Candidates for the offices of President, Vice President, member of the federal judiciary, member of Congress, and cabinet positions, including the National Security Advisor must
   (i) disclose to the public the most recent ten years of their personal tax returns and their spouse or partner's tax returns, their family's assets and liabilities, and tax returns of any businesses in which they or their family have a majority stake—or all such tax returns if less than ten years of returns have been filed;[108]
   (ii) pass a federal background check for security clearance ensuring that they are at no substantial risk of blackmail or manipulation, as defined by federal law;
   (iii) and have no felony conviction within seven years prior to their assuming office.

II. Candidates for the offices of President and Vice President must release their college records, if any, and any records of bankruptcy pertaining to a business that they directed.

III. Members of Congress, federal judges, and cabinet officers convicted of a felony during their time in office must resign their offices immediately and take no other job in government or lobbying, at any level, for at least seven years.

IV. The President may not appoint to any position in the federal judiciary, cabinet, or other high executive office, any member of their immediate family, as defined by law. Family members already serving in such positions before the President's election may continue in their job if approved to do so by a joint committee of Congress, as prescribed by law.

V. (i) All federal judges and executive officers below the cabinet level must have credentials relevant for the expertise needed in these positions, as defined by federal law and enforced by the federal Office of Personnel Management.
(ii) No administration may subvert, for political or personal gain, the ordinary procedures of executive departments that are needed to maintain professionalism and expert work on issues crucial for the national interests and fair, impartial, execution of our laws.

VI. Federal and state elected officials, candidates for elected office, election campaign leaders, judges, and political appointees in government have a solemn duty of honesty to the public and to their colleagues. By seeking and holding office, they agree to be liable to felony charges for a long train of lies and misrepresentation on matters of serious public concern, including well-established facts bearing on issues that confront policymakers, or about their own qualifications, history, actions, actions of those whom they supervise, and actions of other lawmakers and public officials, especially in their public roles.[109] Conviction for gross dishonesty in government may not be pardoned.

VII. Congress has the authority to enable these provisions by appropriate statutes.

These straightforward conditions would help assure minimum levels of integrity and competence in the most powerful positions within the federal government. Just as Trump should not have made his daughter and son-in-law Special Advisors in the White House, John Kennedy should not have appointed his brother to be Attorney General. Nor should Eisenhower and Franklin Roosevelt have given family members paid close advisor positions. This basic anti-nepotism principle holds no matter what we may think of the family members' performance in office (e.g. Robert Kennedy probably helped to prevent a nuclear war during the Cuban Missile Crisis).

Nor can we rely solely on partisan confirmation processes: a relatively clean financial record and ability to pass federal background checks for security clearance are absolutely essential in an era when hostile foreign regimes are amassing big data on all our current and prospective federal officials, and the danger of cyber-blackmail is growing exponentially each year.

Beyond that, a constitutional requirement for relevant credentials is the only sure way to prevent presidents from filling important oversight and law enforcement bureaus with unqualified cronies and potentially even ex-cons, which is a recipe for corruption. §V would also ensure professional conduct in executive offices, protecting officerholders from political pressures to misuse their authorities and powers (also see #16 §IV).

Finally, the commonsense honesty standard in §VI would tend to suppress every other means of corruption across the federal government, and go a long way toward restoring public trust.[110] For example, it would ensure that a politician like Santos who tells a series of lies during his campaign can be removed by judicial proceedings without a two-thirds vote in the House. It would also stop our politicians from collaborating with bad actors, foreign and domestic, who chose misinformation campaigns to secure outcomes that they could never get through fact-checked journalism and arguments based on objective factual merits.

Note that the crime of protracted and systemic lying to the public would be prosecuted only rarely, like sedition, in extreme cases like Santos's—not for a couple random half-truths or minor fibs. But this check would transform the tenor of our politics. In Britain, a prime minister can be ejected for lying about a couple parties that broke Covid lockdown rules. Here, we tolerate long-term lying on matters of a thousand times greater significance, and these lies are amplified by partisan mass media. It demands far too much of ordinary citizens to expect them to punish such dishonesty at the ballot box even though they are constantly subject to increasingly Orwellian deluges of deception from every direction. Democracy has some necessary background conditions, and freedom from mass brainwashing is clearly one of them.

This proposal does *not* violate or alter the 1st Amendment, because the free speech principle in our Bill of Rights does not prohibit honesty requirements on the job. Imagine a doctor who claimed that his free speech rights allowed him to tell a patient to drink a lethal substance because it is good for her. Such a doctor would rightly be seen as a criminal and prosecuted if the patient was injured. Why should the standard be lower for the person holding the highest political office in the world, or their cabinet members, or their campaign managers? Just think, for example, of Rudi Giuliani criss-crossing the nation in 2016 telling big crowds that dispossessed and traumatized Syrian refugees fleeing genocide were probably terrorists.[111] It should be illegal for such poisonous libel to be repeated continually by a senior campaign official. Anyone in federal and campaign offices should be treated like trustees or fiduciaries with solemn responsibilities to the people they serve: lie to those depending on you, and lose your job.

16. An Independent Department of Justice and Professional Civil Service

Recent years have also made crystal clear how much pressure the White House can put on Justice officials to investigate, or not investigate, particular matters and persons. Because clear constitutional protections are lacking, officials looking into 100 classified emails held on Hilary Clinton's private server or investigating potential connections between Trump campaign officials and Russian agents were widely attacked and vilified by party leaders.[112] The same applies to Federal Bureau of Investigation (FBI) agents just following orders in recovering top secret documents and 26 boxes of presidential records that Trump intentionally withheld for a year, despite requests from the Archives, at his Florida residence. Similarly, FBI officials who searched Biden properties for more classified material should be protected.

Attorneys General, FBI directors, and Special Prosecutors have also been fired or pressured to resign for political reasons, and pressured to attack election returns without material evidence of election fraud. Nixon, Trump, and other presidents have also occasionally tried to force the Department of Justice to file charges against their perceived political opponents. This is not an idle concern: in the past, other presidents have also encouraged the FBI to "discredit and disrupt" political movements or leaders they did not like, including Martin Luther King. There needs to be an arms-length relation between the White House and the Justice Department.

In other areas too, career civil servants who are trying to do their job professionally have been condemned as members of an (imaginary) "deep state" simply because they were more loyal to our system of law than to a charismatic chief executive or a particular party. Somehow a fake elector is clean, but a county election official impartially following ordinary practices for ballot counting is construed as a part of a "deep" cabal of hidden illuminati, and hounded out of her job and home.[113] Such allegations are used to justify replacing expert career professionals with uncredentialed super-partisans and yes-men.

These kinds of duress are the very lifeblood of kleptocratic regimes around the world. As Mickey, Levitsky, and Way argue, "[e]lected autocrats [...] purge career civil servants and replace them partisans."[114] When cronyism rules in this way, it bleeds the nation of its human capital, betrays the people at large, and eventually erodes impartiality in the courts as well. Our Constitution ought to include the strongest defenses possible against slides in this direction. Pressures intended to corrupt nonpolitical federal officials, especially in law enforcement, demoralize the career experts that we badly need to make a sound federal system work. These trends drive away highly talented people who should be defended against corruption at the top.

To fix this, we must strengthen checks *within* the executive branch and reverse our march toward an ever-more imperial presidency. This is entirely consistent with the framers' hopes: the separations between the three branches were never intended to be the *only* checks and balances. Within the legislature, the House and Senate check each other; likewise, there should be checks on presidential powers within the executive branch.

Some framers at the original convention and in the first federal Congress meeting in 1789 anticipated this when they argued for a "council" or cabinet who are not subject to dismissal at-will by the president, but instead would be more directly answerable to Congress.[115] Today we urgently need to ensure independence in the Department of Justice and provide legal cover for experts and career professionals serving in all federal departments. The following provisions would achieve that, while also reassuring the public that no clandestine cabal or "deep state" is illegally working to undermine their elected leaders or to defraud the people.

I. The Department of Justice and all its bureaus must operate as nonpartisan organs aimed at upholding the Constitution and enforcing the laws of the United States. While the President and congressional committees may refer evidence of criminal wrongdoing to the Department of Justice, they may never order that particular parties be investigated or charged, or threaten or dismiss Justice officials for not complying. Doing so constitutes a felony.

II. Protection from Arbitrary Dismissal.

(i) In order to ensure that the Department of Justice can investigate serious crime within any branch of government, the Attorney General and Director of the FBI shall be appointed to terms of 12 years, and be no older than 62 when appointed. Once they are confirmed by a 55% majority in the House of Representatives, they cannot be dismissed by the President alone.

(ii) The President can recommend removal of these officers to the Senate Judiciary committee. Their removal requires concurrence of 60% of the whole Senate.

(iii) Whenever either of these positions is vacant, the Senate shall recommend to the House one out of three nominees named by the President. If this nominee fails to gain approval by a 55% majority in the House within three months, the Senate may in turn recommend one of the remaining two of the President's nominees. If this nominee is also rejected by the House within three months, the President may submit a new list of three nominees to the Senate, with the process repeating until the positions are filled.

(iv) If the President refuses to name three nominees within two months of a vacancy in these positions, the Senate must recommend its own nominee for confirmation by the House. Congress may by law provide for cases not covered by these permutations.

III. Special Prosecutors.

(i) Whenever significant evidence arises concerning possible felony crimes by the President, the Vice President, or any cabinet officer, the Attorney General shall appoint a Special Prosecutor, who will begin immediately to investigate the allegations. If the Attorney General declines to appoint a Special Prosecutor, Congress may, by a 60% vote in both houses, appoint its own Special Prosecutor.

(ii) No Special Prosecutor may be dismissed by the President or Attorney General while conducting their investigation. But Congress shall by law establish a process whereby the appointment of a particular Special Prosecutor may be appealed by the administration. Special Prosecutor investigations may not continue for more than a year. They must be adequately funded, but Congress can set reasonable limits to their budgets.

(iii) A Special Prosecutor's subpoenas may not be refused, even on pain of self-incrimination, except for the most compelling reasons of national security, as defined by law.

(iv) In their final report, the Special Prosecutor may recommend impeachments, or directly file charges against accused persons, thereafter turning over their case to federal prosecutors. Any officer of the United States may be prosecuted for alleged felonies while in office and required to leave office if convicted. However, the President may not be prosecuted for any crime less severe than manslaughter, assault, or treason while still in office. This limited immunity ends once the President leaves office.

(v) The President, Vice President, cabinet officers, Speaker of the House, and majority leader of the Senate are not subject to civil lawsuits while in office (for a maximum of ten years of immunity).[116]

IV. The Civil Service.

(i) While political appointees answer to the President, the nation depends on a professional and impartial civil service in all executive bureaus of the United States. Therefore no official below the level of undersecretary or its equivalent may be dismissed without clear cause involving dereliction of duty or ineffectiveness in their job, as defined in relevant statutes. Major reorganizations that result in significant staff reductions, as defined by law, must be justified by clear public interests.

(ii) However, federal employees may not unionize, and dismissal for cause is presumed to be legitimate until proven otherwise.

(iii) The independence of the civil service demands impartiality in conduct and execution of the laws together with an arms-length relationship with all businesses that have a profit-based interest in the interpretation of laws or regulations promulgated pursuant to federal law.

V. Congress has the power to implement these requirements by statute.

By denying the president authority to dismiss the Attorney General, FBI Director, or special prosecutors whenever they wish, §II of this amendment would empower the leaders of our Justice Department to safeguard integrity throughout the federal government. Of course, these officials can also abuse their power,[117] so (ii) provides a way to remove them for dereliction or abuse.

Some reformers instead propose that the Attorney General be elected separately from the president and vice president. After all, in almost every state, the governor does not appoint the state Attorney General.[118] Their separate election, however, would turn the national Attorney General into a political stepping-stone, whereas we need the head of the Justice Department and the FBI director to be as *apolitical* as possible.

Together with the requirement for professional credentials (see #14 above), §IV would protect rank and file civil servants and their offices from political manipulation. Cabals in the executive branch could no longer operate by purging faithful professionals who refuse to abuse their offices in pursuit of the private interests of corrupt superiors. But provision (iii) ensures that "dead wood" can be weeded out, and reorganizations can be undertaken [compare #22).[119]

§I extends our constitutional ban on "bills of attainder" to executive orders that someone be charged and tried. §III would ensure that special prosecutors are empowered to unearth corruption without being stymied by misuses of executive privilege or even by an Attorney General who refuses to bring criminal charges that are clearly warranted by the findings. Constitutionalizing the status of special prosecutors overcomes the argument that only impeachment can check presidential actions.[120] Clauses (iv) and (v) resolve long-standing questions about immunity from prosecution and civil lawsuits for the highest officers and congressional leaders.

While the language I suggest could be varied and perhaps made leaner, the goal throughout this amendment should be to strengthen the rule of law by rejecting the extreme "unitary executive" doctrine that ordinary law cannot enable executive officers to check the president's will. However, the amendment also recognizes that the president's limited immunity is necessary for stability and security, with impeachment as a final option if that immunity is abused.

17. Clear Standards and an Impartial Process for Impeachments

This brings us to the fraught topic of impeachments, especially of a sitting or former president, along with related investigative powers of Congress and executive privilege. It should be obvious that the impeachment power has not worked as our founders hoped. In fact, it may be the least successful aspect of the 1787 design that survived the Civil War and Reconstruction. In 230 years, the House of Representatives has impeached federal officials only 21 times—or 22 if we count Richard Nixon, who resigned before a full House vote on his case. The Senate convicted only 8 of these officials, all of them federal judges.

Only 4 presidents have faced impeachment proceedings; only 3 were impeached by the House; and only Nixon was forced from office (because he correctly expected conviction). No president has ever been removed by Senate conviction after impeachment by the House. But there have been many presidents who were quite bad at their jobs, even if they weren't criminals. At least two or three were truly terrible at being president (Warren Harding, it is said, focused mostly on golf and poker). And a few more proved, while in office, to be highly unethical and even criminal men.

The founders in 1787 modeled our impeachment process on Great Britain's, where the House of Lords tried impeachment charges. But the Lords were not elected, and therefore could be freer from political parties. By contrast, US senators have been directly elected for over a century now, and selected by political parties before that. No wonder that the Senate has almost never been able to rise above party politics when trying impeached presidents.

Even if the threat of impeachment has deterred some potential crimes, Congress has not applied even remotely consistent standards for it across time. Andrew Johnson, tried in 1868, survived by one senator even though he had abused his office to block congressional efforts to empower freed Black Americans, and he probably bribed at least one or two of the senators who voted to acquit him. By contrast, Bill Clinton was impeached for perjury concerning a sexual relationship and minor obstruction of justice—not obviously the kind of abuses that warrant impeachment,[121] which clearly did exist in Nixon's case. Donald Trump was impeached twice on serious charges of corruption, obstructing justice, and inciting insurrection, but he construed the disputes as merely matters of partisan rivalry rather than deep violations of constitutional principles.

This is all very damaging to our system. House impeachments and Senate trials have publicized important facts, and thus educated the public to an extent. But in a situation where the nation is bitterly divided along party lines reinforced by highly partisan medias—the vicious circles noted in the first chapter—the civic costs of impeachments have enlarged: the Trump impeachments further deepened emotional rifts in the nation without removing Trump or barring him from office. This is not to critique the impeachers, who felt they had to act, but simply to note an important social fact. The unfortunate result is that impeachments may become frequent, now that these extraordinary proceedings have been sucked into the self-reinforcing vortex of hyper-partisanship. For example, Republicans might impeach Joe Biden in order to get more publicity for evidence of money laundering and shady foreign deals on Hunter Biden's stolen laptop.

If impeachments become frequent publicity tools, the broad public's faith in their importance and fairness will be further eroded. The record in recent years will also convince future presidents that almost all members of their party in Congress will stick with them, even if they are obviously guilty of gross malfeasance in office (with or without an actual felony). In this situation, because virtually any president will have more than a third of the Senate with them, they will all believe they can never be convicted no matter what they did to get impeached.[122] We can also expect executive officials to flout congressional inquiries during impeachment hearings, and extend claims of "executive privilege" to the Moon and back.

When impeachment is trivialized this way and rendered toothless, the risks to the nation are serious. One day we might really need impeachment to work for the Union to survive. In that desperate hour, public confusion about what "high crimes and misdemeanors" means will also work against us. This problem is not alleviated by the oft-repeated platitude that impeachment is "political as well as legal," because a president can be impeached for breaches of trust that are not "crimes" listed in criminal codes.[123] Although true, that formula provides little guidance. If we keep a revised impeachment process, at least its standards must be clarified.

Those standards must also be realistic for the kind of process that we select. This is not easy: creating an impeachment process that can really work, with impartial standards that cannot easily be misused for unnecessary political crusading, seems to be one of the toughest constitutional challenges there is. A blue ribbon commission should study the salient alternatives and make a recommendation for an amendment. But I will briefly sketch two quite different approaches to consider.

The Criminal Model. The first option is to make impeachment, at least for the president and vice president, more *like* a criminal trial conducted mostly by the judicial branch, even though the relevant offenses need not all be felonies. Impeachment would then have four stages, corresponding to finding probable causes of impeachable wrongdoing, investigation, indictment (being "charged"), and trial. This process could allow more than one avenue for finding probable causes that trigger an independent investigation (see §III below for suggestions).

This process would also require more substantive criteria for impeachment. There are three likely categories of harms or wrongs here:

- Familiar felony crimes such as perjury, fraud, grand theft, arson, rape, and murder;
- Systemic use of deception, pressure on officials to act illegally or otherwise abuse their powers, and other immoral methods for personal or political ends (see #16);
- Gross incompetence in office, terrible judgment, and/or a long train of dereliction of duty that threatens the national good.

Technically, a president could be impeached for any and all of these under current practices. But in 2012, Sandy Levinson rightly worried that impeachment for gross dereliction or personal dysfunction has moved beyond reach: because the idea of "high crimes" has been "captured by lawyers," legislators and the public now understand it as requiring "criminality rather than incompetence." So presidents will assume that they could only be impeached for "flagrant crimes [...] (and possibly not even then)."[124]

Ten years later, history has vindicated this concern. But Levinson's parenthetical possibility is surely the biggest worry now. If that is right, then our highest priority should be to create an impeachment process which at least makes it very likely that a president guilty of serious felonies and/or systemic deception and corruption in office (the second category of impeachable offenses) is likely to be impeached, convicted, and removed and/or barred for life. In other words, by giving up on the third category of harms, we might at least generate strong deterrents against wrongs in the first two categories.

This was essential to the founders' intention, because systemic corruption emanating from the White House infects other parts of the government by suborning officials to violate or not enforce the laws, or to hide major lapses in planning or execution of policies. Above all else, the threat of impeachment was meant to prevent the president and/or their cabinet from mafioso behavior, such as extorting fealty by corrupt means or pressuring officials to violate their oaths of office. As Hamilton said, impeachment should focus on "those offenses which proceed from the misconduct of public men, or, in other words, from the abuse or violation of some public trust."[125] That is why the original impeachment clause explicitly mentions "treason" and "*bribery*" before the infamous "other high crimes" phrase.[126] Such tactics, typical of dictators and drug lords, are worse than incompetence by which a president may fail to protect the national good. These points suggest the following sort of amendment:

I. A President may be prosecuted for crimes after their term ends or they are removed from office through impeachment.[127]

II. Impeachable offenses include bribery, blackmail, and serious felony crimes; systemic efforts to encourage insurrection; systemic attempts to spread lies about election processes; a substantial record of efforts to corrupt federal or state officials, or members of Congress for personal, political, or material gain; a prolonged pattern of actions evincing gross disregard for democratic values and the rule of law; broad and ongoing refusal to enforce laws vital to the national interest; misuse of the military, treason and other strategies aimed at securing advantages to known enemies of the United States, whether foreign or domestic, as detailed in statute.[128]

III. Probable cause for impeachment on any of these grounds may be found by the Attorney General, a Special Prosecutor appointed to investigate corruption allegations [see #16], a resolution of the House of Representatives, a resolution of the Senate, or a federal court when trial of persons for other crimes produces substantial evidence of grounds to impeach a federal official, as defined by law.

IV. Prosecution.

   (i) When probable cause for impeachment is referred by any of these sources, it will be considered by a Special Prosecutor selected by lot from a pool of retired district attorneys organized by federal statute. The prosecutor may dismiss the case for lack of evidence, or call a federal grand jury to hear evidence and decide whether to issue articles of impeachment.

(ii) The judge overseeing the grand jury will be selected by lot from a pool of willing and able retired federal judges or federal judges who have taken senior status.

(iii) When a grand jury meets to consider impeachment, the Special Prosecutor's subpoenas and discovery orders may not be resisted by claims of executive privilege; but the suspect also has the right, through their counsel, to submit evidence and call witnesses, as provided by federal law. All the evidence and the grand jury's findings are made public at its conclusion, except evidence deemed by the presiding judge to be a national security risk.

V. If the grand jury votes for impeachment by a three-fifths majority, the case is tried by a special Court of Impeachment consisting of nine judges selected by lot from nonelected state supreme court judges, or by another method as Congress may provide by law. Conviction requires a two-thirds majority of the judges. The accused may appeal to the Supreme Court only on grounds of severe abuse of power by the Court of Impeachment.

VI. Conviction results in removal from office, loss of federal benefits, and a lifetime ban on holding any position in government at any level. Whether or not the accused was convicted, evidence arising during the grand jury hearings or subsequent trial may also be used as a basis for separate criminal prosecution.

VII. Conviction on articles of impeachment may never be pardoned.

The leading idea here is to employ groups of people who are not from Congress in deciding whether to pursue possible articles of impeachment, to issue articles of impeachment, and to convict or acquit the impeached official. State supreme court judges, in my view, could come closer to the sort of impartiality in trying federal impeachment cases that Hamilton was hoping for, which the Senate clearly cannot furnish. Specifying nonelected judges will also give states some incentive to avoid the corruption that attends elected state judgeships. While a grand jury can hear evidence and decide whether a trial is merited, the final decision to remove a president or other senior federal official will remain too political for an ordinary jury to decide.

An alternative proposed by some "radical democratic" or populist scholars is to resist corruption among elites in the national government through a standing "Tribunate," elected by small local assemblies, that would initiate and/or rule on impeachment cases. But this would involve a big constitutional change to set up thousands of local popular assemblies (see #25).[129]

The No-Confidence Model. Overall, it seems likely that impeachment run this way would have real teeth and be widely perceived as fair—or at least as much less tainted by partisan motives than the current process is. It would also prevent articles of impeachment being brought frequently or on weak material bases. But even if so, this still leaves the problem of president who is grossly negligent in a national crises or a tremendous liability to the nation, without being evidently guilty of impeachable crimes (especially as redefined in my proposed §II with a focus on corruption), or so mentally impaired that their cabinet could suspend them under the 25th Amendment.

For such cases, Levinson makes the intriguing suggestion that presidents be removable through a two-thirds vote of "no confidence" in the president by Congress convening in extraordinary joint session (i.e., by any mix of 357 senators and representatives, assuming all present).[130] A more demanding variant would be to require two-thirds of such a joint session, including at least 60% of both chambers. While no-confidence votes are a familiar feature of parliamentary systems, they would integrate differently with the US system, because the VP would probably become president as soon as the president is removed.[131] This prevents opponents of the president's party from abusing the no-confidence process just to install a president of their own party.

This is a great idea, because it would offer a rapid way to get rid of a derelict president whose harms cannot wait for the next election, and without going through a long impeachment process. There is one wrinkle: Levinson worries that no-confidence might apply not just to the president, but also to their VP and cabinet, if most of the administration is an intolerable danger to the nation. So he suggests that the no-confidence motion in the joint session could apply to the president and VP simultaneously *if* it also names the person who would act as president for the term's remainder.[132] While interesting, that approach would open the possibility of cabals between different groups in Congress. Perhaps it is better, albeit a bit more chaotic, to require that a second no-confidence vote apply to the VP once they have become president, with a successor to them named in that resolution.

Which of these two models is better? Levinson envisions the no-confidence process as a supplement to the current impeachment process, which would remain unchanged in the Constitution.[133] Given the latter's toothless state, it would be better in my judgment to replace the current impeachment process with something like the quasi-criminal prosecution process described above, *and* also add in a limited no-confidence procedure. While Congress would then lose most of its role in impeachment, it would gain a better way of checking the president and administration. Adopting both these constitutional changes together would clearly constrain presidents more than they are now. But that may be justified, given the perception that presidential powers have increased significantly in recent decades.

Levinson's proposal has the advantage of avoiding all the complications that, as my criminal model illustrates, come into designing a new impeachment process, while preserving a way for Congress to get rid of a horrible chief executive. And his no-confidence procedure by itself might be easier to get ratified. But if the impeachment process were also amended, it would offer a backup way to remove a criminal president who is still supported by more than 40% of Congress. This dual system would also emphasize the important difference between criminal corruption on the one hand, and disastrous policymaking and/or refusal to do the president's job on the other.

18. Congressional Oversight Powers and Foreign Interference in the Political System

There are still two more areas in which stronger barriers to corruption are needed. We have to block and deter rising threats of interference by hostile foreign regimes and ensure that official misconduct can be discovered and forcefully addressed. The independent Justice Department described in proposal #16 is crucial to that end, but Congress also plays a role.

None of us wants congressional committees to focus most of their time on endless hearings that only inflame partisan passions. It would help if more investigations were handled by independent commissions of the sort that effectively investigated the 9/11 attacks. For decades now, going back at least to the infamous "Whitewater" hearings on Clinton that found virtually nothing, long-running investigations in Congress can distract from other important work. Sometimes they really are necessary if something terrible has occurred. But inquests that look like personal attacks just further divide the nation and fuel conspiracy theories. Unfortunately, that happens often enough that even when a bipartisan committee *is* fairly investigating very serious issues, it can be misconstrued as mere "witch-hunting."

This dilemma may recede when other reforms end the domination of Congress by the two-party machine. Then multi-partisan groups in the House and Senate will be able to empanel independent commissions when needed. For example, a commission might have worked well for the January 6 inquest, as long as it had real subpoena powers.

But even if the most politically incendiary hearings are passed to independent panels, when really necessary, congressional committees will remain indispensable checks on the executive branch. These committees cannot exercise their oversight functions unless they too have enforceable subpoena and referral powers. They are not meant to be either courts or prosecutors, but they must be able to compel testimony.

This problem might be addressed by a new federal law limiting claims of executive privilege. But once again, federal courts could simply reject such a law if it is not given a clearer constitutional basis in an amendment. I therefore recommend language along the following lines:

I. Limits to Executive Privilege.
   (i) Congress, its committees, and independent commissions to which it delegates proper authority, have the power to compel testimony and discovery of evidence by subpoena.
   (ii) Officials in the executive branch may refuse to comply with subpoenas on grounds of executive privilege only when authorized do to so by the sitting President, and only then in cases where such privilege claims are essential and narrowly tailored to securing national public goods.
   (iii) When Congress, its committees, or its authorized independent commissions reject a claim of executive privilege, the case goes to the federal Court of Appeals for the first circuit for expedited review, unless Congress by law provides another avenue for speedy and impartial disposition of such disputes.

II. Contempt of Congress is a Crime.
   (i) When either the full House or full Senate vote to hold a witness in contempt of Congress or in contempt of a duly authorized independent commission, the case goes to the Attorney General for possible prosecution.
   (ii) Conviction on charges of contempt may not be pardoned and carries a sentence proportional to the wrong as prescribed by law, starting at one year in federal prison.

III. When hearings and investigations by a House or Senate committee or by an independent commission find clear evidence of crimes, the full House or Senate may, by a 55% vote, refer the matter directly to a grand jury meeting under the auspices of the District Court for the District of Columbia. The court will assign a special prosecutor to hear relevant evidence before the grand jury.

That, to use my grandmother's expression, would put the fear of God into them. Clad in such constitutional armor, Congress and duly authorized independent commissions would be able to restore balance with an executive branch that has grown increasingly prone to thumb its nose at demands for reports or testimony, and at congressional oversight more generally. As presidential powers to act through executive orders have inflated in recent decades, it is crucial to ensure that Congress can check executive overreach, especially when it threatens to corrupt multiple executive offices or bureaus.

The proposed §III would also empower Congress to bypass the Attorney General in extreme cases where corrupt officials or civilians in league with them probably deserve to be indicted. This power would be used sparingly because of the (small) supermajority requirement of 55% to refer a case for prosecution. But it is needed in cases where the Department of Justice may be protecting administration insiders, who may thereby get away with contempt or other crimes.

There is a newer kind of threat on the horizon as well: through unprecedented levels of cyberhacking, brutal foreign dictators seek leverage over US officials and clandestine influence in our political processes. It is not for nothing that the tyrannical regime in China has conducted a decade of cyberthefts to gather data on all federal employees. Similarly, the enormous Russian "SolarWinds" attack in 2019 took information from thousands of government computers.

Then there is election "interference"—way too mild a term for the outrages it covers. Russian troll farms have flooded western social media sites with propaganda to swing opinions and encourage violence. When Russian operatives hacked into the DNC and then into the laptop of Clinton's campaign manager in 2016, they performed a cyber-version of the Watergate break-in, even if not coordinated with any American.[134] This is far worse than spy balloons. If intrusions and theft on these scales had been undertaken by conventional methods in the 20th century, they would have been treated as grounds to declare war. But today, they are quickly forgotten by the public.[135]

The principle here is clear: we must prevent foreign regimes from manipulating future American elections, candidates, and elected officials, even if that requires hard power. The privacy of campaign communications has to be protected for the process to be viable, and integrity requires that no candidate for federal office encourage foreign regimes to hack their political opponents. We can reduce the chances of compromised candidates and campaigns with these additions to the Constitution:

IV. The privacy of all political campaign communications shall be protected by law, except where those communications show evidence of a crime and are legitimately subpoenaed by American authorities.[136]

V. Stolen Information and Foreign Influence
   (i) Political campaigns may not knowingly use information stolen by any source. This shall not be construed so as to impair the right of journalists to publish information received from unnamed domestic sources whose identities they must protect.
   (ii) Political campaigns that knowingly receive or use information stolen from other campaigns, or stolen from the private communications of candidates and their staff, may be disqualified from election by the Court of Elections as specified in statute.
   (iii) Political campaign officials who knowingly collaborate with foreign governments or their proxies, accept assets from foreign interest groups, or encourage foreign agents to steal privileged information from rival campaigns or interest groups, or to sabotage political rivals, are guilty of treason and subject to criminal punishment accordingly.

VI. Blackmail of government officials and cyberattacks on American campaigns, candidates, or election systems by foreign powers or their agents will be treated as acts of war. The President is responsible to use all necessary measures, up to and including kinetic reprisals, to deter such attacks.

VII. Documents and information duly classified as secret may not be declassified without the President's written order to the cabinet. If three or more cabinet members object, the Senate Select Committee on Intelligence shall decide the matter by majority vote.

The new language in §V concerning treason would make clear just how seriously we take collusion with hostile governments and their cronies by any American political campaign. Our framers were rightly concerned about political abuse of treason charges; but the danger of foreign manipulation of our campaigns and officials is now so great that the definition of treason needs to be expanded.

Likewise, §VI is needed to ensure that foreign powers aiming to manipulate American elections will receive heavy penalties, potentially even including a conventional military response: this kind of precommitment greatly enhances the deterrent. It is now clear that no other deterrent may be sufficient, and this is not a problem we can address adequately with ever-increasing cyber defenses alone. The costs of cyber-security should be put on the attackers, not the defenders.

We should consider using the same kind of strict precommitment to stop ransom attacks and kidnappings by making it a felony with prison time to pay ransoms. That would be painful at first, but hackers and foreign agents will have little to gain from ransomware attacks on American companies, cities, counties, hospitals, colleges, utilities, etc. if ransoms cannot be paid.

Cryptocurrencies, despite their popularity with naïve libertarians, are also doing untold harm. Aside from enabling ransomware and encouraging speculative bubbles that cost Americans many billions annually, they erode central bank control over money supply and interest rates, which are essential tools to fight inflation. And they fuel heinous criminal networks, trafficking in weapons and people, and corrupt regimes. But ordinary law is sufficient to ban ransom payments and the use of cryptocurrencies.

Finally, §VII seeks to clarify for the public that declassification is an executive order that no president can do on their own or in secret. When national security is urgently at stake, it is appropriate for there to be a legislative check on declassification.

19. Emergencies in Government and Emergency Powers

On September 11, 2001, in addition to hijacking the commercial airliners that hit the World Trade Center towers and the Pentagon, four terrorists hijacked United Flight 93 out above western Pennsylvania and turned it toward the nation's capital. Because this attempted attack came after the three other aircraft crashed into their targets, a few passengers were able to discover what was occurring via Airfone. In response, 33 incredibly brave souls aboard Flight 93 stormed the cockpit and overwhelmed the terrorists, but not before one of them crashed the plane into the ground just east of Somerset in central PA.

The independent bipartisan 9/11 Commission concluded that the terrorists' target for Flight 93 was probably the White House, although other sites in Washington D.C. were possible. But through extensive research, Bill Sternberg concluded that the Capitol building and Congress were actually the final target chosen by Osama Bin Laden's network. Imagine the devastation such an attack by planes or drones could cause if there was little warning time to evacuate that building while Congress was in session.

This brings us to the difficult topic of emergencies. As Elizabeth Goitein writes, "unlike the modern constitutions of many other countries, which specify when and how a state of emergency may be declared and which rights may be suspended, the US Constitution itself includes no comprehensive separate regime for emergencies."[137] It only indicates that Congress or the president (it's unclear who) can suspend the ordinary entitlement of persons detained by authorities to a judicial hearing or jury trial (*habeas corpus*).

Clearly, as 9/11 showed, there are awful situations in which the president or acting president would need emergency powers. Yet, all the way back to ancient Athens and Julius Caesar in Rome, history is replete with democratic systems that have collapsed through a chief executive declaring or receiving constitutionally unspecified emergency powers and then abusing them. The Weimar Republic ceding dictatorial power to Hitler is the most famous example, and Venezuela is the latest case.

We can distinguish these problems from a related one concerning mass casualties in government. Experts have for years recognized that our system is vulnerable to collapse during a big emergency, such as attacks that killed large percentages of Congress and/or other federal officials. Prior amendments and statutes tell us what happens if the president and VP are both killed, and what the order of succession is beyond the House Speaker as well (although this law is still imperfect). But other kinds of disasters are not covered and uncertainty could lead to rival people in the decimated government claiming various authorities—the very last thing the nation would need in a crisis caused by a big bombing or terrorist attack.

Continuity through Nightmare Scenarios. Starting with the second problem, Levinson rightly argues that we need some mechanism to rebuild Congress and/or the Supreme Court in the event of mass casualties in these bodies. An amendment is needed because the Constitution currently requires elections to fill open House seats, which is too slow after a mass casualty event, and it requires half of each chamber of Congress for a quorum. And there is no constitutional provision for replacing completely disabled or comatose House members or senators who have not resigned.[138]

To fix this, Levinson refers to the draft amendment prepared by Brookings and the American Enterprise Institute, which would allow Congress to specify in law a procedure for replacing members quickly in an event where over 25% of either chamber were injured, killed, or otherwise unable to serve.[139] I recommend lowering these thresholds to 10%, given that this number of casualties would usually be enough to swing control of the House or Senate.

To remove any partisan political motives for such a horrific attack, the law passed pursuant to such an amendment should specify that persons of the same political party as those killed or rendered incapable of serving will substitute in for them until the next regular election, at latest. A good method would be for each member of Congress to have an approved list of alternates (of the same party) ready to step into their place, much like alternate jurors.[140] Two or three alternates could be rank-ordered, or the member's home state governor could choose one person off their list during the emergency. For example, if the "assistant representatives" I described in the proposed amendment for the House (#8) were approved, one of them could automatically fill the seat of a murdered, missing, or severely injured House member.

A comprehensive emergencies amendment should also include a similar continuity system for senators, so that governors cannot replace a deceased, captured, or comatose senator with someone from a rival party. This would also deter plots, such as kidnapping or murdering ten senators in order to flip Senate control.[141] Earlier (see #9 §III), I suggested a similar method to ensure that a Supreme Court justice killed in an attack would be replaced by a judge of the same political affiliation to serve as long as needed, or for the remainder of the murdered justice's term.

If we do not trust the president or Congress to accept the replacements specified by ordinary laws immediately after a massive attack, specific procedures could be written into an emergencies amendment—with a further provision for unforeseen permutations, in which case the actual or acting president could use improvised solutions on a temporary basis to ensure that Congress and the Court can function. This brings us to the question of the executive branch's emergency powers more generally.

States of Emergency. In over two centuries of legislation, our laws have accumulated many authorizations of specific emergency powers for various situations that the executive branch gets when the president or Congress declares a national emergency. A recent Brennan Center study reported at least 136 such authorizations in existing law waiting to be triggered. They need to be reviewed, pared down, and consolidated,[142] but there are problems related to this. In addressing them, our guiding principle should be that, for democracy to endure, emergency powers must always be *temporary and reviewable.*

First, existing law provides that, when both chambers agree, Congress can vote to end a president's declared emergency; but the president can veto that act. Probably, emergency-ending joint resolutions should not be subject to the veto (see #20). The National Emergencies Act (NEA) makes declared emergencies sunset after a year, but a president can renew them indefinitely at will, even after losing an election (and it seems that ongoing declared emergencies can even continue into a new administration). Goitein found in early 2019 that 30 states of emergency declared in past years are still technically continuing, mostly from sheer neglect: Congress had not met even once specifically to vote on them, as the NEA requires.[143]

To fix this, an emergencies amendment should specify that states of emergency are not renewable by the president beyond some time period—say 6 months—without an *affirmative* simple majority vote by Congress. Following a suggestion by Bruce Ackerman, we should require higher thresholds beyond this, such as

- 60% of both chambers must agree to extend an emergency declaration beyond a year;
- 67% of both chambers to extend it beyond two years;
- and three-quarters (75%) of the House and Senate for annual extensions beyond three years.

This would ensure that powers under a particular emergency cannot continue indefinitely without bipartisan (or multi-partisan) approval.[144] If such requirements are only set in ordinary law, they do not bind future majorities in the legislature, which could simply rescind these conditions and allow a popular president to continue emergency rule indefinitely.

Second, there are no clear constitutional limits on the sort of *problems* that can justify emergency powers, or on *specific powers* that Congress might allow the executive to use in dealing with legitimate emergencies. For example, could a president decide to suspend the entire Bill of Rights? Could they postpone a federal election, as Lincoln contemplated doing but eventually rejected in 1864?

Fixing this problem requires limits to emergency authority set in the Constitution, which would also strengthen the Supreme Court's hand if it needed to intervene to stop a fledgling American dictatorship. Of course, as the early days of the Civil War showed, the president might have to exceed their official authority, however specified, in sufficiently desperate predicaments: law cannot anticipate all contingencies. But even if a president is granted general or unspecified emergency authority, at least basic rights to life and bodily integrity could be constitutionally protected—much as there are modality constraints on methods in warfare, such as bans on chemical and biological weapons.[145]

Similarly, based on historical experience, the Constitution could limit the "causes" or grounds for temporary emergency powers to invasion or massive cyberattacks, insurrection or rebellion, large-scale natural disasters, public health crises, and possibly conditions of severe economic meltdown or social chaos on a mass scale. To justify national emergencies, they must either threaten central organs of the government itself, or be widespread, fast-moving, and highly destructive in their potential effects. And truly extraordinary justifications should be needed to postpone elections (for at most a year).

Regarding means, the Covid experience suggests at least that emergency powers should include an ability to coordinate corporate and state government resources when this is essential to meet a threat like a pandemic. For in such situations, refusal to cooperate by a few state governors could make it impossible to prevent enormous harm to the whole nation, or to large parts of it (e.g. a very lethal virus spreads through "weakest link" states). Overcoming such collective action problems might require temporarily suspending some limits on federal authority over what are normally state matters.

The president's military powers are a related and complex issue that I will not try to tackle here. But in case the 25th Amendment process is not rapid enough to block (say) a rogue order for a chemical or nuclear strike, it would be smart to add a constitutional option for our top military commanders to protest what they judge to be unconstitutional orders not justified under the president's emergency powers—whether the emergency declaration is authorized by a congressional resolution or not.

So I suggest that, by their majority vote, any 2/3rds of our military chain of command—i.e. the Secretary of Defense and the (currently eight) officers who form the Joint Chiefs of Staff—have the right to appeal to the Supreme Court any apparently illegal order issued under color of emergency powers before obeying it.[146] If the Court agrees with the Chiefs, it would countermand that order, and at its discretion, also suspend the president's emergency powers pending further review. As 9/11 showed, there may not always be time for such a process. But it could prevent a completely unhinged president from planning to misuse our vast military capacities in extreme ways during some future crisis.

20. It Is Too Hard to Override Vetoes: Lower the Threshold

The previous six amendments were all focused on basic standards for stability, good governance, and the prevention of corruption. Now we can turn back to the rising tide of gridlock that was partly addressed by earlier proposals (especially ##1, 3–5, and 7). Because our system contains so many incentives against compromise and so many "hurdles" that enable uncompromising agents to block federal action on fraught issues for decades, the presidential veto threat makes our system even more anti-majoritarian and less likely to respond well to real-world problems.

In the original Virginia Plan introduced at the 1787 convention, the president would only have been able to veto laws if a majority of a small council (or cabinet) agreed.[147] Maybe this was a good idea: as the power of the presidency has grown over our history, presidents have vetoed and threatened to veto many more bills in the last 150 years. Our first sixteen presidents up to Lincoln vetoed a grand total of 36 bills, and let 23 lapse by neither signing nor vetoing them for ten days extending into an adjournment of Congress (the "pocket veto"). But from 1865 to January 2023, there have been 1482 actual presidential vetoes and 1043 pocket vetoes—far more than our framers imagined.[148]

On the surface, it may not look like the veto has been overused in recent presidencies (see Figure 3.3). But do not be deceived. These numbers leave out hundreds of *veto threats* that stopped legislation without an actual veto being required. The number of *effective*

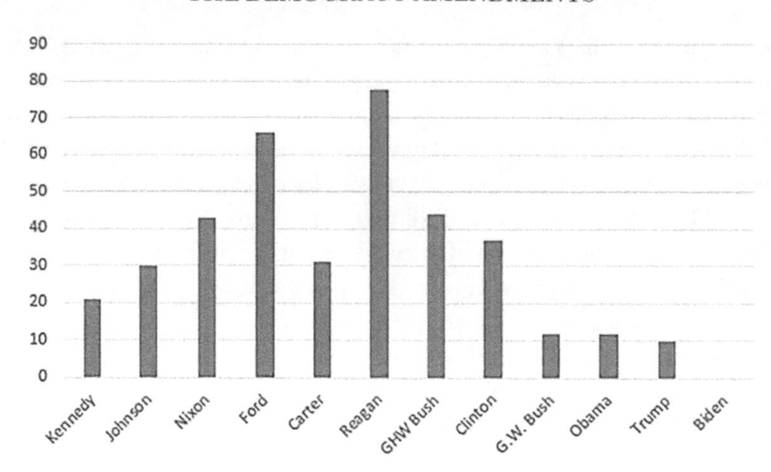

Figure 3.3 Presidential Vetoes

veto threats is hard to quantify, especially given that some may not be issued publicly. But at least on paper, G.H.W. Bush threatened about 310 bills; Clinton threatened approximately 390; George W. Bush threatened a mere 132; and Obama held the veto axe over at least 500 bills.[149]

Moreover, the decline in actual vetoes since Reagan results partly from the huge rise in filibusters after the No-Talking-Required rule for filibusters was adopted (see #7). Congress has become so much less productive, as the other drivers of gridlock set in, that presidents had many fewer bills to veto. So whenever the filibuster is finally abolished, we can expect to see vetoes and veto-threats rise again.

Do we need the veto at all? Many other democratic nations do well enough without it, and passing both chambers of our Congress would remain a high hurdle even without the filibuster (most other developed democracies do not allow their upper chamber—let alone a minority of it via filibuster—to block bills forever).[150] However, the president is generally seen as the one officer truly answerable to the whole electorate—and they will really be that, once they are directly elected (see #12). This may be a good reason for the president to retain a veto as a check on a legislature that is (for now) entirely elected by states and districts rather than nationally.

However, the veto power should still be reduced. The most straightforward way is simply to make it easier for Congress to override presidential vetoes. Leaving aside pocket vetoes (which give Congress no chance to override), less than 7.5% of actual vetoes issued by presidents have been overridden by the required 2/3rds majority in both the House and Senate. These included some very important pieces of legislation, such as the 2020 anti-money-laundering provisions in a Defense act that Trump vetoed,[151] and the Comprehensive Anti-Apartheid Act of 1986 that Reagan vetoed.

This heroic override, led by Senators Richard Lugar (R-IN) and Edward Kennedy (D-MA), enacted sweeping sanctions that forced South Africa to end its policy of racial apartheid. By 1991, Nelson Mandela was released from prison, the African National Congress was legalized, and negotiations for a new constitution were begun. But it took more than a year of hard fighting in Congress to get the anti-apartheid law enacted.

More valuable bills could be saved from the presidential axe if we lowered the high 67% threshold for overrides to 60% in both chambers, with this amendment:

I. A bill that passes Congress with at least three-fifths of both houses concurring is not subject to presidential veto.
II. When a President vetoes or fails to sign a bill duly approved by Congress within fifteen days of its passage, Congress may reconsider the bill until its session ends. If three-fifths of both chambers concur, the bill becomes law.

This reform would allow pocket vetoes to be overridden and help promote more bipartisan compromise legislation. Its benefits could be further extended by altering §II to say that three-fifths of Congress meeting in *joint session* is enough to override a veto. In other words, 60% of all 535 senators and House members together would suffice to sustain a law that had already passed both chambers separately. This would blunt the effects of small-state domination in the Senate when it comes to veto overrides.

On the other side, we could also consider giving the President a limited line-item veto on budget bills to help rein in our federal deficits. This idea, which has been frequently proposed in recent decades, is briefly considered in the #22 below.

21. Loosen Congressional Leaders' Control, Reduce Gridlock, Move Appointments

Another roadblock in our long obstacle course for new legislation includes the leadership in both chambers of Congress. They have near-total control of the agenda, checked only by capacity for their caucus to vote them out of leadership and the need to reach agreement with some powerful committee chairs. These chairs in turn can block many non-appropriations bills almost indefinitely. This has become a big a hurdle both for bills and appointments.

Agenda Liberalization in the House. In the past, control of the agenda was not used so vigorously to exclude all ideas from the other party. Both the majority leader in the Senate and the Speaker of the House would protect bipartisan compromises reached in committees, even if many in their own party disliked the deals made by committee chairs. Legends in Washington D.C. say that in 1981 and 1982, Speaker Tip O'Neill (D-MA) allowed the Republican minority to bring several of their proposals to a full floor vote because he thought the proposals on which Reagan ran and won should have a fair chance in Congress.[152]

In D.C. today, that attitude is almost inconceivable. In a famous 2004 speech, Speaker Dennis Hastert (R-IL) rejected an important bill to overhaul the nation's intelligence bureaus, which a clear majority of the 435 House members would have supported, because a much smaller majority of his 229 Republican members, including one committee chairman, did not like it. In 2003, he blocked a Medicare revision bill for the same reason.[153] If closely adhered to, this "Hastert rule" requiring a *majority of the majority party* to pass bills makes serious compromise much less likely. With the slim majority that Hastert had after the 2002 midterm elections, it meant that a mere 115 members of his caucus—less than 27% of the House—could block any action.

So in practice, later Speakers have sometimes had to violate the Hastert rule to get urgent legislative work finished. For example, in January of 2013, Speaker John Boehner had to pass a law to avert automatic tax increases and budget cuts mandated by prior legislation: it passed with 85 Republicans and 172 Democrats voting for it—a strong 59% of the House, and yet Boehner was called a traitor for doing this. He also courageously passed the Violence Against Women Act renewal in 2013 with only 38% of his members supporting it. Such cases illustrate that significant progress can often be made by combining votes from both parties. But the majority party caucus is rarely "rolled" this way except on must-pass bills or cases where the leaders see that blocking a bill could spell electoral disaster.[154] The compromises with a few extremist members that Kevin McCarthy made to become Speaker in 2023 may make passage of bills needing Democrats' support even less likely.

Democratic theory recognizes the peril of leaving agenda control entirely in a few hands,[155] and dubious practices like Hastert's only prove this point. A recent example is Senator Kristin Gillibrand's very important Military Justice Improvement Act, which was introduced in 2019 to reform the way our military addresses sexual assault allegations. Senate leadership refused to bring it to the floor even though it was approaching 59 cosigners. Its key provisions were also excluded from the December 2021 law to reauthorize military spending. Finally in December 2022, key provisions of Gillibrand's bill were passed as part of the annual Defense spending authorization.

As such cases show, the public could benefit if members outside of leadership have some real opportunity to get proposals with wide support on the agenda, whatever the leaders say. In parliamentary systems, this is often accomplished by allocating a few days of debate to what are called "private members' bills." These bills sometimes get enacted because they articulate positions that substantial numbers of legislators from all major parties support, even if the leaders do not want them considered. And even when voted down, such bills can help focus new attention on important issues that have been sidelined by party leaders.

Short of moving to a parliamentary system, we could allow something similar in our House by an amendment allowing petitions among members to force a floor vote on a legislative proposal:

I. When 55% of members the House of Representatives sign a petition in favor of a draft bill more than three months before the next Congress begins, the Speaker of the House must schedule at least four hours of debate on that bill and hold a full House vote on its final form, following any adopted amendments, within one month of the petition being validated by the Clerk of the House. If it passes the House, the Senate must hold a full vote on the same bill within two weeks. If the Senate amends the bill before approving a new version, the House must hold a floor vote on the amended version within the next two weeks.

This provision would be a constitutional version of the "discharge petition" rule: it would ensure that "members' bills" would get a real opportunity in Congress, including bypassing filibusters. But some limit on how many of them can be considered per term should be added—e.g., perhaps 3–5.

Spear has proposed instead that representatives in the House be allowed to introduce motions putting a bill on the House agenda, and requiring an immediate simple majority vote on such motions.[156] But that would go too far in giving members power to fill the whole agenda, and thereby negate the entire committee process of editing draft legislation. House and Senate leaders and committee chairs need some coordinative power to keep regular order. However, committee chairs should not be able to permanently block votes on bills that most committee members support, as they often do (a privilege that gives them extraordinary and excessive power in Congress). In this case, ordinary law could solve the problem by, say, allowing a petition by 60% of committee members to force a vote to pass a bill out of their committee.

A similar way for senators to force a vote on bipartisan legislation could operate in the Senate. In fact, such a provision might make ending the filibuster more acceptable to more senators. For without Senate members' bills, the majority leader's power would be enlarged when the filibuster ends. Of course, even if this amendment applied to both chambers, leaders in the House and Senate would still have several tools to discipline members who introduce or support bills that the leaders dislike. But at least occasionally, enough members would be prepared to incur leadership wrath in order to achieve great breakthroughs for their nation.

Plebiscites: Referenda and Public Initiatives. Public petitions offer another possible way of democratizing the congressional or national legislative agenda. But they are not without problems.

Imagine that you are at the Motor Vehicles office renewing your license when the clerk asks you whether you would prefer a moose or reindeer as a pet. You might have a preference (the reindeer is much easier to handle). But why this question, of all things? Well, the clerk explains, the state is asking everyone this question for the benefit of a reindeer herder who is friends with the governor. Irritated, you think, "if only they had asked us whether we wanted mortgage assistance for first-time homebuyers," which would really help you. Petition signature drives and state ballot referenda can feel like this sometimes.

Many American states have forms of direct democracy, including "popular initiation of legislation" by public petitions, popular initiation of state constitutional changes, and referenda on ballot questions initiated by the legislature and/or by public petitions. Yet, unlike our states and unlike many other developed democracies, our federal system includes none of these pathways for national law.[157] Should we add some?

At the national level, Congress could place proposals on the federal ballot for voters to approve or reject. But for voters to make law by such a national referendum would require an amendment (especially if the process did not require the president's signature). Initiatives are a different story: it is hard to imagine a fair and viable process by which citizens could petition to put a question on the ballot or to place a draft bill on Congress's agenda for mandatory consideration. To avoid Congress being overwhelmed by petition proposals, a significant threshold of public support would be needed—perhaps 8% of all registered voters, or 5% of registrants in every one of at least 30–35 states, to put an item on the House and Senate agendas.

These numbers sound low, but they imply 10–16 million signatures. It is hard to imagine an impartial apparatus to collect and verify that many. And voter initiatives that directly place a bill on the next general election ballot, so it could be enacted by voters without any congressional action, would surely need even higher numbers of signatures, e.g., perhaps 10% or 12% of all registered voters.

Moreover, at the state level, we see that petition drives are usually controlled by big-lobby advertising, although such spending could be limited (see #5). Richard Ellis, a critic of popular initiatives, points out that initiative drives tend to be driven by well-funded groups focused on their own pet issue that may not rank high among most voters' priorities at all.

Thus, the moose–reindeer problem. Why should millionaire investors and weed lovers get to put a question about marijuana on your state ballot, when more people might have preferred a question about local control of zoning laws? This is an important question even if you happen to favor legalizing marijuana when accompanied with strict penalties for driving buzzed. The public initiative fix risks trading one kind of elite agenda control (in the statehouse) for another kind by social trendsetters with the money to push petition drives. At least legislators are attuned to issues that rank higher with (many of) their voters.[158]

The better option is for Congress to put ballot questions on the federal ballot with the promise of giving attention to proposals that have already built strong public backing over many years. But that does not overcome the agenda-control problem, and the wording of any ballot question and the explanation appended to it can have large effects on the outcomes.[159]

A State Check on Congress, and a Congressional Check on States. Given the problem with national voter initiatives, I suggest a method for state governments to have some collective influence on the federal agenda. Imagine the following:

> II. Whenever, within a two-year period, two-thirds of the states approve the same resolution proposing a bill for consideration by Congress, both the House and the Senate must hold final votes on that proposal within three months of the resolution being certified as valid by the President.

Such a provision would appeal to believers in states' rights and provide another viable way to diversify control of congressional agendas by circumventing committees and majority leaders in Congress. It would be strongest if it did not allow the House and Senate to amend statehouse initiative bills before a first vote on them. If the bill in exactly the form submitted by the states was rejected by at least one chamber, then it could be reconsidered with amendments that might enable it to pass.

This sort of approach makes creative use of the national–state relationship in our federal system, but through a more *productive* kind of check that does not increase gridlock. This is better (and less extreme) than allowing 2/3^{rds} of states voting together to veto a federal law, as some have proposed. Similarly, while several founders at the 1787 convention wanted a federal veto over state laws, we could instead allow Congress, by a simple majority, to put two bills per term on the agenda of every state legislature for mandatory consideration.

An analogous possibility is to add a section allowing each chamber of Congress to have some influence on the other's agenda. §I suggested requiring a couple members' bills passing the House per term to get an up-or-down Senate vote. The amendment could also allow House leadership to place one House-approved bill per year on the Senate's agenda for a vote not subject to filibusters. Senate leaders could have a reciprocal power to force a full House vote on one Senate-passed bill per annum.[160]

Nominations and Cabinet Officers. In the Senate, leaders also have the power to prevent final votes on nominations, which they often use against a president from another party. That power would remain even if the filibuster were ended. But in recent years, this tactic has created large backlogs of empty leadership positions in the executive branch after Republicans gained a majority of the Senate during Obama's second term (and see #9 on judicial vacancies).

Once Trump was in office in 2017, the opposite problem arose. Rather than appointing cabinet officers who could overcome filibuster threats and gain Senate approval, Trump instead used many "acting" officials who need no Senate confirmation, and who would be loyal only to him. Thus several large departments were run by unqualified political cronies who might not have received Senate confirmation by the Republican majority. For example, the Department of Homeland Security had no permanent professional leader during migrant surges in early 2020, and the Department of Health and Human Services was not well prepared to respond to the coronavirus crisis. A straightforward remedy can be modeled on the requirement outlined earlier to vote on presidential nominations to the federal bench (see #9 §VI):

III. Nominations to Cabinet Positions.

(i) The Senate shall vote conclusively on all nominations made by the President, excepting those to the federal judiciary, within no more than four months from the date of the appointment, unless a duly declared emergency prevents their vote.

(ii) Any appointee on whom the Senate fails to vote within four months is automatically confirmed.

(iii) But any office that requires Senate confirmation and is left vacant by the President for more than six months may be filled by an appointee selected by a resolution of the House of Representative and confirmed by the Senate. Such a nominee takes precedence over anyone later nominated by the President for the same position. And the Senate must act on the House's nominee within two months, or during the remainder of the congressional term if that is less than two months.

(iv) Once confirmed, an appointee nominated by the House cannot be removed by President within one year after Senate confirmation, or when a new President is elected, or in cases of national emergency as defined by law.

This would put an end to the stalling, and to "holds" by which individual members of the Senate can bottle up forever a particular nominee they dislike. The third clause would ensure that the President cannot unilaterally nullify existing laws that empower various executive bureaus by refusing to appoint someone to lead them.[161] This would also strengthen the proposed requirement that high officials be qualified for their office (see #15).

Together, these three reforms would have wide appeal, because they reduce gridlock and make the federal government more responsive. But they would require a constitutional change to be secure.

22. Federal Budget Guarantees

Beyond the measures to reduce gridlock described in the previous two sections, there are specific problems in the budget process by which Congress now annually approves and allocates over $5,800 billion. These acts decide on the scope of hundreds of federal programs—most with many working parts. The gargantuan size of our federal budget makes it a hard job, but the recent tactic of resorting to sweeping "omnibus" spending bills, which are put together mostly by party leaders and committee chairs and often passed at the 11th hour, is very far from ideal. The old phrase "sausage-making" hardly does it justice.

The best-known outrages in the federal budget come from the practice of "earmarks," by which particular congresspersons add money for specific projects that usually benefit cities, counties, or local organizations in their districts—which thus avoid having to compete for federal grants. Examples include the infamous $452 million "Bridge to Nowhere" in Alaska, an odd $1.6 million for "equitable shellfish aquaculture" (shellfish farming) in Rhode Island, and Senator Graham's $121.8 million for an aircraft maintenance hangar at a South Carolina Marine Corps base. Reportedly by its high water mark in 2006, earmark spending hit roughly $26 billion a year. That's more than the entire $25.9 billion in Pell grants for college tuition spent in fiscal 2021.

The House and Senate both changed their rules in 2011 to ban this widely condemned practice that has funded a lot of dubious projects. But while it is easy to multiply apparently absurd examples, defenders argue that earmarks help "grease the wheels" to get legislators to compromise on important bills. Following this logic, against strenuous objections from many quarters, leaders in both parties agreed to reintroduce earmarks in 2021. They were used to get the giant infrastructure spending bill of November 2021 passed and funded in a March 2022 bill.

These direct appropriations to special interests in their home state help members of Congress raise campaign donations from people associated with earmark beneficiaries.[162] Thus earmarks might reek less of corruption in a world where campaign finance was controlled through constitutional reforms (see #5) and small states did not have so much extra power (see #7, #8, and #24) to rake in pork projects at higher per-capita rates. Maybe then earmarks would be worth their costs in a legislature where every member is elected locally rather than nationally.

Either way, though, the focus on earmarks misses much larger problems with our budget process. Total earmarks were never more than a tiny fraction of the federal budget. For example, the omnibus spending bill for 2022 contained at least $5 billion in earmarks, whereas all federal outlays in fiscal 2022 totalled $5,852 billion (a thousand times the earmark spending). In comparison, the big 2009 stimulus law included about $13 billion in pet "pork" projects.[163] That's "real money" (in D.C. insider-speak), but it amounted only to 0.37% of federal spending in 2009.

Similarly, Biden's infrastructure bill contained roughly $5.7 billion of earmark projects, including $22 million that Senator Manchin won for a water treatment plant in West Virginia, along with approval of more leases to drill for oil in the Gulf of Mexico. But earmarks are less than 0.48% of the total $1,200 billion spending in this law.[164] In fact, there are four other much bigger problems with all recent federal budgets that get less attention:

A. The House and Senate often fail to complete regular federal budget bills on time; they make large parts of the federal government operate on "continuing resolutions" for months, or bicker their way into a government shutdown.
B. Some members of Congress seem increasingly willing to use the prospect of a default on the federal debt itself as a bargaining chip—a *very* dangerous tactic, given that a default would ruin our credit, massively hike interest on our colossal federal debt, devalue the dollar, drive up the cost of imports, and probably trigger a global recession.
C. The federal budget is full of programs with little demonstrated effectiveness that roll over from year to year without requiring specific reauthorization: continued spending at roughly the same level is the default assumption. This drives inefficiency in bureaucracies with more incentives to enlarge themselves than to produce public goods.[165]
D. And because legislators are answerable to current rather than future voters, they have incentives to pay for too much of our annual federal costs through deficit borrowing, which our young Americans will have to pay with massive interest later on.

For example, in fiscal 2019, largely due to tax cuts (see #5), Trump's Congress ran a whopping $985 billion deficit. The deficit skyrocketed yet further during the Covid years because of stimulus checks to American families and businesses. Unless there are more tax increases and spending cuts, large annual deficits will continue adding to the national debt year after year (see Figure 3.4 from the Congressional Budget Office—borrowing added to the national debt each year is the gap between the two trend lines after 2001). Our country looks a lot like a household with an ever-growing credit card debt.

While there is much that congressional leaders could do immediately to improve their flawed budget process, it seems clear that they need some new constitutional incentives. One popular response is to recommend a balanced budget requirement similar to those found in several state constitutions.[166] That might be unwise, given the need for extra spending in emergency or near-emergency situations—a new war, a new pandemic, or a financial crash that could lead to a second Great Depression without significant stimulus spending. But we also cannot keep loading our children and grandchildren with over $500 billion in new debt added every year, driven partly by mandatory entitlement programs that are on unsustainable trajectories.

I therefore suggest measures that would impose fiscal discipline without going all the way to a balanced budget amendment (which would probably require multiple exceptions). Following conservative authors, I suggest requiring a dispositive *4-year budget resolution*, adopted within four months of the president's inauguration, that sets binding

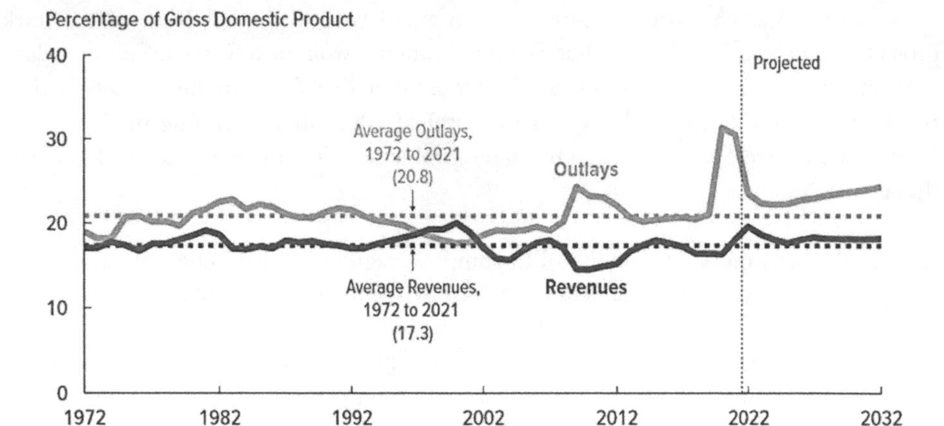

Figure 3.4 CBO Long-Term Budget Projection of July 2022

tax revenue targets and any new borrowing. This resolution, with a special constitutional status, would thus control total spending (appropriations bills) for the presidential term. We could also limit earmarks to 0.5% of all federal spending.

To work well, this approach may require giving the White House a bit more power than it currently has in budget-making, even though presidential power needs to be reduced in other cases (see #16–#18). The following illustrates a feasible way to do this via new constitutional requirements:

I. The Controlling Budget Resolution.
   (i) By the end of May in the year after a presidential election, the House of Representatives must complete a four-year budget resolution determining all major sources of revenue and a borrowing limit based on Congressional Budget Office projections. Barring a declaration of economic emergency by the President, no more than 10% of revenues in the four-year budget can consist of borrowing from any source.
   (ii) All appropriations bills for four fiscal years, starting on June 1 following the budget resolution, must fit within its terms, unless Congress by law authorizes adequate new sources of revenue *other than additional borrowing.*
   (iii) If Congress fails to raise revenue sufficient to cover program expenses required by current law, given the borrowing limit set in the controlling budget resolution, the President must reduce expenditures across all programs to stay within this aggregate limit.
   (iv) After an annual appropriations bill is reconciled and approved by both chambers of Congress, the President may, by line-item veto, reduce spending on particular programs by up to 15% of levels set in the bill for such programs, if all such reductions together amount to no more than 5%

of total appropriations in the bill. The bill, so altered, becomes law within 30 days of the President's signature, unless, during that time, both chambers of Congress revert any of the President's reductions by 60% majorities.

(v) Earmarks may not total more than 0.5% of all federal spending in any appropriations bill, although Congress may set lower limits.

(vi) The President may reorganize executive agencies and departments to promote greater efficiencies, unless both the House and Senate revert these changes by a simple majority vote, which is not subject to the President's veto [compare #20 §IV].

II. Congress must complete all general appropriations bills by the end of each October. In the event that Congress fails to meet this deadline, spending on programs for which appropriations are incomplete remains at the same nominal dollar levels as during the prior fiscal year.

III. Full Faith and Credit.

(i) At no time may the Government of the United States of America ever default on payment of its legally incurred debts.

(ii) If Congress fails to authorize increases in taxation necessary to avoid default, the President is required immediately to increase taxes and decrease spending as necessary to avoid any default.

IV. Regular Program Audits.

(i) All statutes, regulations, and programs that involve federal spending must be reauthorized every 15 years, on a cycle set by law within two years of adoption of this amendment. If not reauthorized, spending on such programs must wind down to zero within two years.

(ii) Before it is reauthorized, each program involving more than $50 million in spending, adjusted for inflation, must be evaluated by an audit of its effectiveness, efficiency, and possible overlap with other federal programs.

(iii) Each federal department as a whole, including the Department of Defense, must also be audited by an independent commission, which makes recommendations to Congress, on a 20 year rotation.

§I reflects some proposals in "The Conservative Constitution" commissioned by the National Constitution Center.[167] I have included a limited version of the line-item veto.[168] This would help prevent Congress from forcing the administration to spend more on certain programs and purchases than the relevant departments even request, all to benefit particular special interests or states.

For example, this has often happened with US Defense budget which, even recognizing rising threats from China and Russia, is by far the most bloated creature of government on Earth. Like the big slice of cake your aunt gave you despite your asking for a small one, the $768 billion National Defense Authorization Act (the annual NDAA) signed by Biden in December 2021—which made up about 44% of all discretionary federal spending—was even $35 billion *more* than the White House and Pentagon had requested in their budget proposal.[169] For comparison, this extra gravy ladled onto the Defense budget almost equaled all federal spending on science ($37.8 billion) in 2021.

§IV incorporates suggestions by Philip Howard, Senator Rick Scott, and others to prevent automatic renewal of federal programs without serious assessment of how well they are performing. The goal is to prevent programs that accomplish little from continuing simply through inertia.[170] While many of our federal departments are enormous, an evaluation of each once per 20 years should be feasible if Congress establishes a rotation. The same goes for particular programs once every 15 years. Controls of this kind can reduce "principal-agent" problems that arises from bureaucracies defending their own indefinite continuation with little public benefit.

§I (vi) also includes part of Howard's suggestion that presidents be able to reorganize executive offices to give individual officers more discretion and thus responsibility, while rewarding achievements and efficiency.[171] Congress would also have much stronger incentives to complete a regular budget if anything like §II were added to our Constitution: if it failed to act, spending on every program would decline in inflation-adjusted terms.

§III would stop dangerous shenanigans with the debt ceiling. It is worth considering an overall limit to the federal debt, such as 100% of annual GDP, that could only be temporarily exceeded during emergencies. All these conditions operating together would bring us much closer to balanced budgets over the long-term. Instead, as things are now, our federal debt is on a path toward collapse and/or default (see Figure 3.5[172]), which would plunge the nation into a deep economic depression.

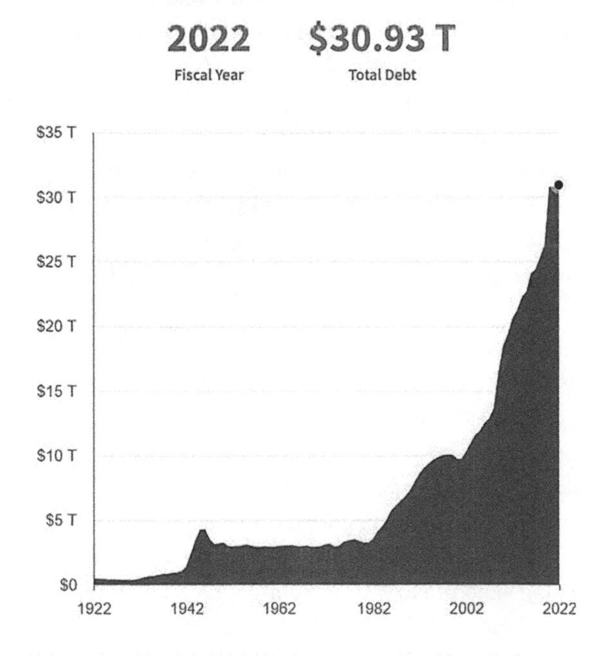

Figure 3.5 Rapidly Rising US National Debt

23. Improve Judicial Review: Rational Bases and a Remand Option

The amendments considered so far address many points on which the public is upset with the federal government in general and Congress in particular. But one major complaint has not yet been considered, namely the widespread sentiment that the federal judiciary's powers have grown too large. Many Americans believe that at least some of the issues decided by courts would be better left to legislators who are more directly accountable to voters. The objection that "unaccountable" judges are "legislating from the bench" would be reduced by tying the Supreme Court and appellate court appointments to presidential terms, as proposed above (#9). But we also need to clarify how judicial review should work.

In defense of the judiciary, it is partly because Congress has become so ineffective that reformers have increasingly sought relief in courts, prompting judges to pick up the slack. This pressure would decrease with constitutional reforms to improve our elections and make Congress more responsive (see #1–8, #11–12, and #21). Yet even then, a few relatively simple reforms could further improve the relation between our legislative and judicial branches.

In particular, while bare majorities should be enough to interpret or apply ordinary laws or change past rulings in federal courts, many critics want to require supermajorities for the Supreme Court to invalidate a law (in whole or part) as unconstitutional. This is not surprising, given the Court's many efforts to undo democratically made law in recent years.[173] Yet that would significantly reduce the Court's power, tilting the balance quite a bit toward Congress.

I suggest instead giving the Court another way to make invalidation on constitutional grounds rarer. This would involve introducing a third option besides accepting or rejecting parts of a law or regulation, and clarifying some bases for evaluation of statutes. I offer these proposals in summary form here:

I. Remand to Congress.
  (i) The Supreme Court may, upon thorough review of a statute, decide *neither* to uphold the statute as constitutional *nor* to reject it in part or whole as unconstitutional, but rather to remand it for reconsideration in Congress, with objections and problems noted.
  (ii) In that case, both chambers of Congress must, during their next term, either revise the law or take a new vote on its current form.
  (iii) If Congress leaves the law unchanged, which does not require the President's approval, then the Supreme Court may decide to take up the presenting case again, or instead to apply the unchanged law as reaffirmed by Congress.

II. To be constitutional, every statute must be supported by substantive public reasons relating to public or common goods beyond the mere preferences of interest groups. Laws and executive orders with no rational basis beyond naked partisan advantage are thus unconstitutional.

III. Holistic Assessment.

(i) Federal courts must give considerable weight to the literal meaning of constitutional text, long-established precedents, and the legislature's original intent in forming laws.

(ii) But the Constitution as amended is also rooted in principles, such as basic human rights, liberty within the rule of law, the common good, and moral requirements of democracy, which together constitute the spirit of our laws. These principles should inform the decision of cases when existing constitutional language does not immediately determine their disposition.

The new option created by §I gives the Supreme Court a way to register objections without going as far as invaliding a law. The justices could instead force elected members of Congress to consider the issue that the Court would otherwise have to decide for them. If Congress fails to remedy apparent problems, such as infringements of individual rights that are not necessary to defend compelling public goods, then the Court can still strike down the offending law on reconsideration. In many cases, though, this procedure might produce a compromise between our legislature and the high court.

Compare this to the popular alternative of requiring 6 out of 9 justices (or, e.g., 8 out of 13 in an enlarged Court) to strike down a law as unconstitutional, and a similar supermajority for an appellate court to invalidate a law.[174] Such a reduction in the judiciary's check on Congress may make sense once our legislature is restored to responsiveness and effectiveness through other amendments. But the remand option is a less radical step. If we believe it is not enough to address the objection that judges are "legislating from the bench," we could also give Congress an option to restore a law that was struck down by anything less than a unanimous Court. This could be done, say, by passing the law two more times with an election intervening, or by a 60% majority both chambers.[175]

§II embodies a bedrock principle of civic republicanism: government exists to secure common goods, including individual rights.[176] When a legal provision manifestly has no plausible relation to any public good or national interests, federal courts can weed it out of our system. This is what theorists call a *minimal rational basis test*. As Cass Sunstein explains, it is basically Lincoln's principle that might does not make right applied to law. Legitimate law cannot be based on naked power, preference, or will; it must be grounded in public reasons.[177] Our founders took this principle for granted and assumed it was implicit in the Constitution. But today, we need to make it more explicit.

It would not require much for a law or policy to pass this rational basis test. Even many (although not all) "earmark" projects could pass it, because courts do not have to *agree* with its goal to uphold a law: they merely have to agree that legislators sincerely intended a goal related to public goods when writing the law. So this constitutional requirement could be invoked to strike down a provision only rarely.

But it would establish a crucial limit: provisions that are clearly intended for nothing but a pure partisan advantage, such as making it much harder to vote in one county than another, are unacceptable (this was also Justice Stevens' main objection to partisan gerrymanders: see #4). Similarly, distinctions that only serve some narrow interest group with no national benefit, such as tax exemptions for a few thousand hedge fund managers, could be overruled. This could reduce Congress' propensity to run deficits to subsidize tiny fractions of the public.

Federal courts already assess whether a law was intended for an acceptable goal when considering equal protection claims on the basis of the 14th Amendment. But the rational basis condition is broader than legal equality alone (some policies may treat all protected groups equally but still aim at no plausible public good). Recognizing the distinct and crucial role of goals involving public goods would reduce overreliance on the 14th Amendment.

§III articulates a compromise that would make explicit the principles on which constitutional jurisprudence in a democracy relies, and thus provide clearer guidance for federal judges. It would put to rest the disingenuous extreme "originalism" that some justices apply selectively or when it suits them—for example, not on the 2nd Amendment or filibuster, but definitely on abortion. This absolute positivist kind of originalism of the Bork–Scalia–Alito variety is incoherent because self-contradictory: it ignores clear evidence that our framers did not *intend* for their specific thoughts about this or that clause in the Constitution to entirely determine what it could mean for future generations. Indeed many of them would have regarded such crude originalism as domination by impractical literalism, besides being contrary to the very nature of language itself.[178]

More generally, the framers were not Hobbesian legal positivists: rather, they believed that constitutional law should be grounded in moral principles—which they called natural law—as well as basic facts of human psychology and society, such as the existence of collective action problems. For example, many delegates at the 1787 convention assumed they were devising a particular way of fulfilling the norm in the Declaration of Independence proclaiming that a government's "just powers" derive from "the consent of the governed." Many of their antifederalist critics wanted stronger guarantees for what they regarded as natural rights and natural principles of justice (such as subsidiarity); the first ten amendments reflect this. The literal meaning of the text was never the whole story.

Similarly, the 13th Amendment reflects Lincoln's fundamental point against Stephen Douglas that the collective right of any majority to rule through law itself rests on moral presuppositions concerning the moral importance of individual autonomy and liberty, which majorities therefore cannot take or leave at their pleasure (see #24). No legitimate law can violate these presuppositions, even if the Constitution does not fully list them. Thaddeus Stevens and the other abolitionist authors of the 14th and 15th Amendments believed that the Constitution should conform to a "higher law." Others have understood several amendments as rooted in basic principles of sound government and constitutional order that are essential both for effectiveness and legitimacy.

These are all conservative and republican rather than left-liberal ideas. Traditional civic republicans affirm Madison's axiom that the Constitution's authority "derives from the people themselves," with the qualification that the people cannot exercise their original right in ways that violate the principles from which the right to democracy itself derives.[179]

As a result, the notion that federal judges should mechanically implement whatever the framers of constitutional language command *itself* violates the original intentions of almost all the framers. Ironically their original goals required that justices be able to reflect on basic principles required for any just constitutional order.[180] This view is amply confirmed in *The Federalist Papers* as well.[181]

§III of the proposed amendment thus outlaws the false kind of originalism that has brought us so much grief in recent decades. It provides responsible justices with clear grounds for adhering to precedent and the intentions of legislators *to the extent possible*, given the need to apply provisions to new cases and situations not contemplated when they were written, and the logical requirement that the law be consistent with the trans-legal principles required for its legitimacy. Correcting these kinds of inconsistencies is not "legislating from the bench;" it is original justice of the highest kind.

However, if a strong majority of Americans believe that the Supreme Court made a huge error when considering the spirit as well as the letter in a case, we can correct it by further amendments, especially when the amendment process itself is improved (see #25).

24. Senate Apartheid: Ways to Fix the Worst Flaw of All in our System

We come now to the largest problem of all in the US Constitution according to virtually every political scientist who compares our system with those in other long-established democracies. This is the fact that still, some 235 years after the federal government was created, the people living in each state have two senators, even though their populations are radically unequal. As noted earlier, this problem makes the filibuster, the Electoral College, misproportions between House delegations, and the nonrepresentation of Puerto Rico and D.C. even worse (see #7, #8, #11, and #12). Behind almost everything wrong with our federal government lies this fundamental wrong in its original design, which large states were forced to accept basically at gunpoint in 1787.

The Problems. It is crucial to be as clear as possible on this topic: unequal representation of Americans in our Senate is a problem on another order of magnitude from all the other constitutional deficiencies we have reviewed. For example, I noted that some states have as much as 86% per resident more weight than others in the House, and 190% more per capita in the EC. But in the Senate, a Wyoming voter currently has *6800%* more weight than an average Californian, because the population of California is about 68 times that of Wyoming (recall that 200% of something is double). In fact California, with its 2 senators, has roughly the same population as *all of the 22 smallest states*, with their 44 senators, combined. Texas has more people the next 6 smallest states. Thus just two states with 4 senators are home to about the same number of Americans as the 28 smallest states, with their 56 senators. If the Senate were a board game, no one would play it.

We can visualize these breathtaking disproportions with a box chart showing the relative weight of individual voters in the Senate for a sample of states (see Figure 3.6). Even Roger Sherman, father of our Senate, would be aghast at this much inequality: it looks like naked domination. As Bruce Oppenheimer says, "the framers could not have envisioned how skewed Senate representation would become"[182] after our national population increased 120-fold over two centuries. In 1787, when the federal

Figure 3.6 Geographic Apartheid in the US Senate

Constitution was written, the gap between the largest and smallest states was about 11-1 in 1787 (Virginia vs. Delaware), and its critics rightly railed against tyranny by a minority even then.[183] If we do nothing to fix the Senate, in a couple decades we could see that gap widen to a truly insane 100-1.

This is not just "a little" affirmative action for small states, as it is often portrayed by defenders. What would Sean Hannity say if a competitive school called "Senate College," while rating applicants on a points system, declared that it would give 1 point to any white applicant for their ethnicity and 70 points to any Black or Hispanic applicant for theirs? Even if we think that people in small states should have *some* extra protection in our system, surely having *double* the weight of the largest states would be more than generous? That would require California to have at least 32 senators and Texas to have 20.

So calling the current inequality in the Senate "malapportionment" does not convey its scale. "Geographic apartheid" is a more accurate label. Our Senate is one of the most undemocratic upper chambers in any developed democracy.[184] Not enough Americans appreciate this because our terminology for it is lipstick on a pig (or monster). "Equality" among "the states" sounds a good formula—until we remember that a "state" is only an artificial construct: it is *the people* in each state who matter, and their representation is radically *unequal* in the Senate. The largest 10 states are home to over 76% of the nation, but the other 24% of the population gets 80% of the Senate—a complete inversion of democracy.

In principle, the smallest 26 states could control a majority of 52 senators even though they contain less than 17.5% of Americans. In realistic scenarios, one party can win several million more votes for senators over the three rounds (6 years) it takes to elect the entire Senate and still come out with only 45% of Senate seats. Consider the high-turnout 2020 election: Republicans won 49.3% of all votes in the 33 Senate races that year, while Democrats won 47%. But that close 2.3% margin translated into 20 seats for Republicans and 15 for Democrats—a 14.2% difference.[185] As a result, in 2021–2022, Democrats and Republicans each controlled 50 Senate seats, but the Democratic half of the Senate represented 62.5% of the nation, or 41.5 million more people than the Republicans' constituents.[186] And the Republican side representing 37.5% of Americans also filibustered many bills (see #7).

As you would expect, small-state priorities also get a lot more attention from Senate leaders, and these states get far more federal benefits per person than large-population states.[187] And because Americans from minority groups are more concentrated in larger states (and in disenfranchised D.C. and Puerto Rico),[188] apartheid in the Senate adds to minority underrepresentation. There have been 11 Black senators and 11 Hispanic senators since the end of the Civil War, as compared to almost 1000 white senators. There have been 4 senators with significant Native American ancestry, but only one in the last century. And there are currently no African-American women in the Senate.

The Tragic History: Original Motives for the Senate's Lopsided Composition. Geographic apartheid is, of course, a legacy of the famous compromise made at the original convention when the smallest states—especially New Jersey, Delaware, and Connecticut—demanded equal strength with the larger states in order to sign on to the new plan of government. "Compromise," however, is a misnomer here. The small states, and Delaware in particular, threatened that they would ally themselves with some hostile European power if they did not get their way.[189]

When the convention started, delegates from larger states wanted to do away with the state equality that prevailed in the Congress of Confederation because it was so unfair and made it very difficult to reach collective decisions (recall Jefferson's failed Land Ordinance of 1784: see #7). The larger states thought they were going to win on the upper chamber after the "committee of the whole"—a mechanism for testing proposals—voted on June 11 *for proportional representation in the Senate* by 6 states to 5. The New Jersey plan, which proposed only a one-chamber legislature with each state having one vote, was also defeated because "it was too much like the faulty Articles of Confederation."[190]

Many commentators have concluded that small states would simply have left the convention if they did not get an equal number of senators, while in response, Madison and his allies considered forming their own federation without the small states.[191] On the contrary, the records of the convention pieced together from delegates' notes and letters suggest that if Madison's bloc had realized they were going to lose the final vote on the Senate's composition by a hairsbreadth on July 2, they would have offered a *different compromise.*

On June 30, for example, James Wilson of Pennsylvania suggested one senator for every 100,000 residents—and Franklin appeared to support this too.[192] His proposal would have given states between 1 and 8 senators, with a minimum of one.[193]

Table 3.1 The Pinckney—Wilson Senate Proposal at the Convention

Sample States	1790 Census Population	Senators (Pinckney)
New Hampshire	141,885	1
Massachusetts	475,327	4
Rhode Island	68,825	1
Connecticut	237,946	2
New York	340,120	3
New Jersey	184,139	1
Pennsylvania	434,373	4
Delaware	59,094	1
Maryland	319,728	3
Virginia	779,821[194]	5
North Carolina	393,751	3

More modestly, Charles Pinckney had proposed that each state have between one and five senators depending on population, and he repeated this proposal on July 14 (Table 3.1 illustrates roughly what this implied). As the Colliers report, at that point, Madison and Wilson would have accepted as little as a 1–4 senator range between the smallest and largest states. But it was too late: if they had moved this proposal

> at an earlier moment—perhaps before positions began to harden around July 1—Pinckney's idea might have been acceptable to small-state men. But by now the small states knew they could win, and they would not budge.[195]

In other words, but for Madison's miscalculation or bad luck, we might today have a Senate in which Texas had 4 senators and Delaware and Vermont each had 1 senator. In this scenario, the largest 20 states with 75% of our population would control roughly 70 senators and the remaining 30 states would have roughly 45 senators. The smallest states would still have a lot of extra weight, but not the gargantuan surplus that they have now.

Yet, the myth persists that pure proportional representation and equal weight for every state were the only two options for the Senate. Millions of students are routinely taught this error. It makes for a simpler story, but it is false.

It is even more misleading to tell students that the House—Senate deal expressed a grand collectivist ideal that states are "moral beings" of more importance than their residents, or that geographic apartheid is needed to prevent tyranny of the majority. On the contrary, as Litt argues, the "grand compromise" was nothing but "horse-trading"[196] or threat-point bargaining. Madison makes this clear when he describes the Senate, as politely as possible, as "the result, not of theory, but of a spirit of amity [...]"[197] In other words, two senators per state did not reflect any deep principle, and certainly not "republicanism" (with which it is in deep conflict).

Why, then, did Madison, Wilson, Rufus King, and their southern allies not propose an intermediate option like 1–7 senators earlier, when it might have been negotiated to something like 1–5? First, they did not know of historical cases with that intermediate structure. Second, they viewed anything less than proportional representation in the Senate as too unjust. Their understanding of federal republic was more cosmopolitan: even in a federal system, real people come before arbitrary groupings such as states and corporations.[198]

On the other side, Sherman, Paterson, and their allies wanted states rather than individual Americans to be represented in the Senate for four key reasons:

- Almost every white resident at the time identified with their home state far more than with the "United States;" in 1787, the nation was still a hazy notion for most people, connoting little more than a military alliance.
- Small states feared that large states would conspire against them as a group when it came to economic decisions, trade agreements with foreign nations, taxes, etc.[199]
- Given technology at the time, all the delegates assumed that most residents would have little idea what was going on outside their own state or region: they would rely on their state governments to choose senators who could think about national affairs.[200]
- For similar reasons, they assumed that the new federal government would be much less robust in serving the everyday interests of most Americans than their state governments were.

How many of these motives are still relevant today? The answer is zero: their relevance has been steeply declining for over a century. Even in the 19th century, large-population states never tried to act as a unified political bloc against smaller states, *pace* the paranoia at work in the convention. Nor have small states ever been much aligned; political divisions pitting industrial versus agrarian and slave versus free states proved to be far more impactful.

Today, over 42% of Americans no longer live in the state where they were born (and some who do had moved away for years and returned later). Probably half of us will move between states at least once in our lives. Many Americans also live several months each year in another state, or live in one state and work in another. Even if we love our state or region, most Americans have thought of themselves as part of *single nation* for many decades now. The major wars of the last 120 years have cemented this national identity. Regional cultures—New England, "southern," (e.g. Gulf states), "western" (i.e. mountains), and "southwestern" (Sunbelt)—may be significant to many of us. But that is not the same as caring a lot about (say) being a "Missourian" or being an "Oregonian:" Americans rarely talk that way.

Similarly, travel and communications have vastly altered, and most hot-button political issues—abortion, climate change, health insurance, college costs, tax brackets, and even immigration—are fully national ones. Our political parties have also been national rather than regional since the early 20th century; ditto for our religious denominations. State legislatures stopped appointing senators over a century ago, and we elect senators along national party lines.

Moreover, state governments are alien things to most of us. Even Americans who do not much follow politics can usually tell you some of the issues being debated in

Washington D.C. and a few things about the president, whereas even well-informed citizens with political science degrees often have no clue what their state government is doing. A study at Johns Hopkins in 2018 found that a majority of people surveyed did not even know if their state has a constitution (every state does), and could not say if their state has a one- or two-chamber legislature (all but Nebraska are bicameral). 80% had no idea who represents them in their state legislature, and a full third could not even name their governor.[201]

This is probably because we see state governments mostly as administrative units with accidental borders that work to keep roads, parks, and courts in order, but are generally pathetic at running DMVs, unemployment compensation systems, public employee pension plans—and sometimes bad at designing ballots. And that's about it. California and Texas may be exceptions, but only because they are so huge that they are almost quasi-nations unto themselves. In New York, the NYC city government is more influential than the state government (sorry Albany). And nobody questions that our national government has far more power and significance in shaping our common destiny today.

In sum, whatever we think of the original reasons for each state having two senators, those reasons have been irrelevant for a very long time. Originally, the 4 small states with their 8 senators were all in the north. But within three decades, they came to regret their extremely excessive demands concerning the Senate's composition: by 1820, there were 7 entirely new states with populations smaller than Connecticut's. Virginia, North Carolina, Georgia, and Massachusetts had also split off western parts of their claimed territories into 3 new states—all totaling 20 new Senate seats.

The expected causal relation between the states and Senate composition also *reversed* within 3–4 decades. For a while after 1787, the causal order began with (a) new states formed by a regular process of settlement and admission into the Union along lines already tentatively mapped by the prior Confederation Congress, followed by (b) new Senate majorities. But before 1820, like the proverbial tail wagging the dog, (b) was determining (a): the battle to control the Senate almost entirely shaped the admission of new states. Just as with politicians gerrymandering their own districts, the drive to increase each party's power in the Senate largely determined how new state lines would be drawn and the terms for state admissions. The expanding inequality of representation baked into the Senate's structure by Sherman & Co. was so powerful that existing states and territories were divided into two or three new states for strategic reasons, rendering their borders mostly artificial. Ultimately this extreme geographic apartheid regime became a main cause of the Civil War.

When Kansas and Nebraska were both admitted as new states in 1854, they had (non-Native) populations of less than 80,000 and 20,000 (!) respectively. New York had over 3.2 million residents—40 times Kansas's number and *160 times* as the number of white settlers in Nebraska. Each new state, despite its miniscule population, translated into so much more power in the Senate that state borders and admission became the most heated issue from the 1840s through about 1900. The stakes were so high that, in the lead-up to 1861, the old Democratic party in the South was willing to do basically anything to ensure that slaveholding states controlled at least half the Senate, including making war on Mexico, planning to annex Cuba, pushing slavery into the Great Plains, and outlawing the Republican party in their states.

This way of prolonging slavery by its extension into small new states would never have arisen but for the colossal injustice in our Senate's design. While many of the founders hoped for gradual emancipation as a way to wind down slavery, Sherman's Senate became the main institutional engine that kept slavery going. The awful irony is that Sherman himself opposed slavery and worked to get it outlawed in his home state of Connecticut. He was a genuine patriot and really believed that he was helping his fledgling nation; but he failed to anticipate what evils geographic apartheid in the Senate would bring.

The causal inversion continued after the Civil War as well. Most states west of the Mississippi derived their borders and legal status from purely partisan jockeying for influence in the Senate.[202] Geographic apartheid drove the creation of so many small-population states that it increased unequal representation to unforeseen heights. Our woefully anti-majoritarian and filibuster-hobbled Senate today is the result of the same vicious feedback loop that now keeps D.C. and Puerto Rico out of Congress. Eventually, Sherman's not-so-grand compromise could destroy the nation in the 21st century, as it almost did in the 19th.

The Grand Obstacle and Three Possible Solutions. The Senate, then, needs to be fundamentally restructured. As Sabato argues, "It is the height of absurdity for our gargantuan states to have the same representation [in the Senate] as the lightly populated ones."[203] In its current form, the Senate is driving the hyper-polarization that is leading more of the public to reject evenhanded democratic processes. Thus Litt's sobering conclusion: "[m]alapportionment in the Senate is a ticking time bomb."[204]

Yet I left this worst institutional flaw in our system almost for last, because Article V, which describes legal ways of amending the Constitution, says "that no State, without its consent, shall be deprived of its equal Suffrage in the Senate." How did this happen? When the full draft of the Constitution was presented to the convention on September 15, Sherman demanded that small states' steep 11-1 advantage in the Senate be made *unchangeable*. Initially, this new demand was resisted; but Morris, fearing a new rift so near to the finish line, proposed the unamendability clause. Exhausted big-state delegates should at least have pushed for a time limit on this extraordinary clause, which is like nothing else in the document. But it was the convention's second-to-last day.[205]

And so geographic apartheid in the Senate—the worst problem in the US government by a long ways—is also the hardest to fix. But not impossible. Viewed philosophically, in principle, Morris's clause should be considered legally void because virtually *all* "unamendability" clauses contradict the principled grounds that justify a people's right to make any constitutional law whatsoever. Given human fallibility and uncertain consequences of chosen phrasings in constitutional language, no generation's collective autonomy can give it authority to bind later generations *absolutely and forever* to any particular bit of positive law.[206]

To anyone who imagines that permanent unamendability clauses can be procedurally valid law, I offer the example of the "Corwin amendment," passed by both chambers of Congress by early March 1861 in effort to head off civil war. It is, by a long distance, the worst amendment resolution ever passed by the US legislature. It said that "[n]o amendment shall be made to this Constitution" that would allow Congress to alter or abolish slavery in slave states. Through this truly horrendous amendment, its backers tried to arrogate to themselves the right to *prevent* any later amendment to end slavery (as our 13th Amendment did).[207]

Anyone who thinks that the final clause in Article V of the US Constitution concerning the Senate is legally valid must, by parity of reason, accept that the Corwin amendment would have made slavery unamendable if it had been ratified by 3/4ths of the states. I take that evident implication to be a complete *reductio* of the naïve total legal positivism involved in accepting unamendability clauses. This positivist position would even allow legal contradictions to be forever binding on us if created by some supermajority's constitutional edict.[208]

On the contrary, through their original sovereignty or "constituent power," a people can always collectively act outside the legally prescribed pathways if no other recourse is possible[209] (see Desideratum 8). It is well known that this is precisely what the original convention did: the delegates, Morris and Sherman included, violated Article XIII of the Articles of Confederation by allowing their proposed new constitution to come into force when 9 states of the original 13 states ratified it.[210] Madison rightly said that this move was both necessary to "the exigencies of the Union" and would be justified by "the express authority of the people" themselves through their ratifying conventions.[211]

More generally, constitutionally defined amendment procedures can never justly foreclose the people's ultimate original constituent authority, which is not itself a piece of positive law.[212] On the other hand, when resorting to their constituent authority, the people should look to establish and work through law. And as emphasized earlier, the people's originary right to adopt any constitutional language is limited by its own principled grounds (see #23). Unamendability clauses violate those principles underlying any legitimate constitutional order.

It is also a general principle that only law of a higher order can constrain later lawmaking. For example, a later executive order can always reverse an earlier one, even if the earlier one says "later presidents can't change this!" By contrast, a statute can limit later executive orders; but a statute passed today cannot prevent a later Congress from repealing it down the road, no matter what it says; only constitutional law can restrict later statutory changes. By the same principle, then, no act of constitutional lawmaking can prevent later acts with the same level of authority from altering the earlier one.[213]

For geographic apartheid, then, one solution is basically to ignore the offending clause in Article V, propose to amend the Senate, and then put this proposal to the whole American public for direct authorization by the people—for example, by a national plebiscite. Akhil Amar and Sandy Levinson are the best-known proponents of this revolutionary method.[214] But such a resort to originary sovereignty should always be a last resort. It would be better, if possible, to use the existing legal pathway to alter the amendment process itself (see #25).

So we should consider four innovative ways of fixing the Senate that work around the unamendability clause rather than directly overriding it. Because this clause is *the* central and ultimate problem with the US Constitution, from which so many other difficulties flow, it has also received some of the most creative attention from reform-minded scholars. I briefly summarize four approaches here before making a proposal.

(A) *Alter State Boundaries to Reduce Population Differences.* We could do an end-run around constitutional impediments to fixing the Senate by approaching the problem from the other side. If massive differences in populations between states make citizen representation in the Senate so dramatically unequal, why not simply redraw state lines so that they have more nearly equal numbers of residents—much as we do with congressional and state legislative districts? A complete redraw of this kind would, of course, mean a radically different map.[215] An amusing thought experiment by Neil Freeman illustrates what it would take to make 50 truly equal states (see Figure 3.7). But as he notes, this is only an art project (with creative new state names).

A much softer version of this approach would be to break up a few big states into several new ones with much smaller populations. For example, Noah Millman suggests dividing the 4 largest states—California, Texas, Florida, and New York, which collectively are home to over a third of our nation—into perhaps 3 states each, for a total of 8 new states. As he notes, states have been divided early in our nation's history, and neither this nor combining states requires a constitutional amendment, as long as Congress and the state(s) involved agree.[216] By locating a third of our population within 12 states, this reform would give 33% of the US population 24 senators out of 116 (or 20.7% of seats). That would still be much less than they deserve, but a lot better than their current 8 out of 100 senators.

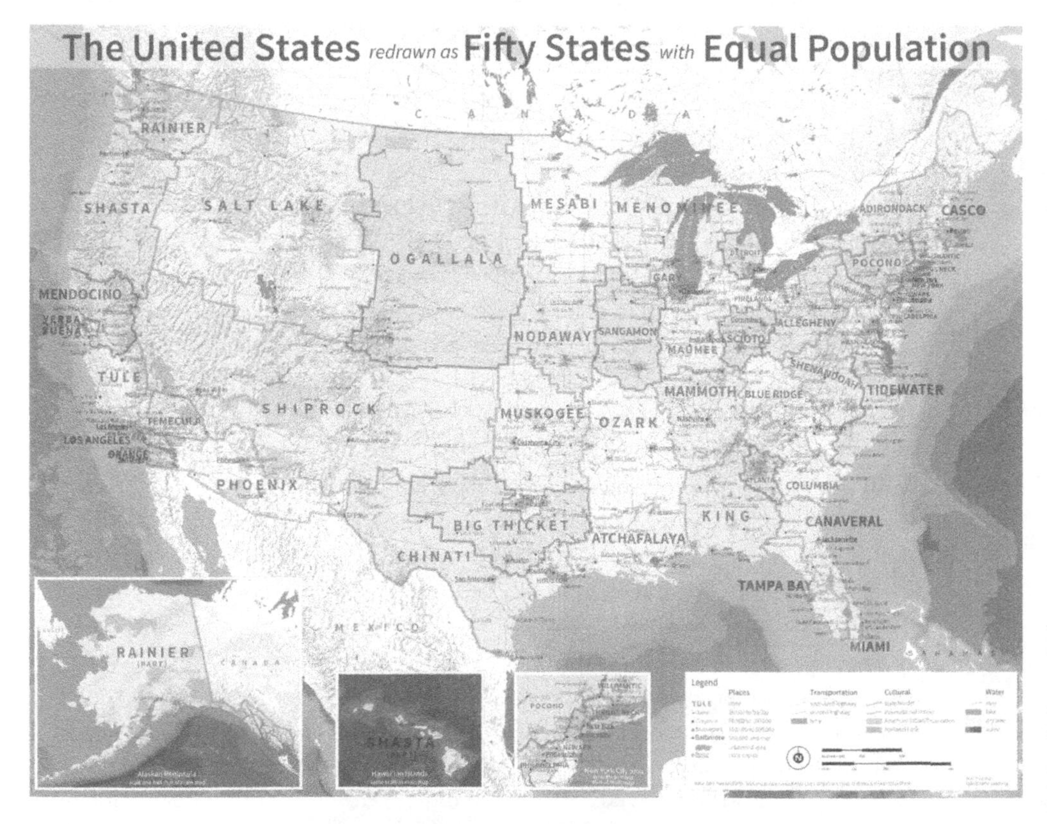

Figure 3.7 The US Redrawn as Fifty States with Equal Populations

This is a creative idea, and Millman argues that it would provide other benefits to these 4 states, in addition to reducing the excessive power of their 4 state governments.[217] It could be extended to the next 6 largest states with populations over 10 million, including Pennsylvania, Illinois, Ohio, Georgia, North Carolina, and Michigan, by splitting them in two. This would further reduce inequality in the Senate.[218]

But this solution has several drawbacks too. First, it does too little to correct the incredible extra weight that the smallest 8 states have: less than 3% of Americans in those states now elect 16% of our Senate. In principle, this can be corrected by *combining* smaller states such as North and South Dakota, and Vermont and New Hampshire, through consensual agreement among them. But their state governments are extremely unlikely to reduce their power (or their government jobs) by doing this. Combining small states against their will would require a constitutional amendment, which some may say conflicts with the unamendability clause.

Second, Millman's process would introduce a new level of gerrymandering: can lines be drawn through California in such a way that Democrats retain a majority in all 3 new states? Could Texas be carved into 3 Republican-majority states? The answer is most likely yes. And third, once such a process started, it would be tempting for each new majority in Congress to extend it to yet another state where they might double their Senate seats if the lines were "suitably" drawn. Like Court-packing, it is an *ad hoc* fix with no clear end point because it does not solve the root of the problem.

Finally, multiplying state governments is the opposite of efficiency. State governments together spend over $2,300 billion dollars a year—roughly a third of annual federal spending. Imagine NY split only into 2 states whose governments together spend 120% of the current NY state annual budget. That is a conservative estimate, given all the duplication of bureaucracies that such a split would involve. If NY split into 3 new states, the total costs might be 130% of the original, at best. Residents in NY, TX, and CA would not be too happy if their new state taxes were 30% higher than before!

In fact, fiscal efficiency would counsel significantly reducing, not increasing, the number of states. State governments could probably do everything better and at 20% lower total costs if there were (say) only 30 rather than 50 of them. In other words, if the smallest 40 states were combined in pairs, nationally we might save $460 billion or more—enough to increase grants for college tuition 10-fold—and dramatically reduce geographic apartheid in the Senate at the same time.

(B) *Amend Out the Offending Clause.* While the final clause of Article V blocks an amendment for proportional representation in the Senate, it notably does not refer to *itself* as unamendable. This provides a legal loophole: an ordinary amendment could strike out this offending clause, after which another amendment could alter the number of senators that different states elect.[219]

Of course, defenders of geographic apartheid may say that the final clause of Article V implies its own unamendability too. But it should *not* be read that way because, as noted, any claim to unamendability in positive law is contrary to the natural principles of constitutional order, and thus really self-vitiating. Claiming that Morris' clause itself is unamendable only compounds the wrong.

However, what if the Supreme Court nevertheless ruled that this clause is unamendable? That would set up the mother of all constitutional crises, because the Supreme Court was intended to have very little authority over amendments. Historically, one function of amendments is to *check* the judiciary by correcting the Court's worst errors (e.g. the *Dred Scott* decision).

The Court should therefore adopt a narrow construal of its role, and allow Congress and the states to take the lead in using Article V's procedures. The status of the offending clause is the kind of political question that the Court should avoid. But if the Court did invite catastrophe by trying to block an amendment to delete the unamendability clause, Congress could employ its own rarely used power to *alter the jurisdiction* of the Supreme Court so that it has no say on this issue.[220] In such a crisis, a wayward Court would not win against a supermajority of Americans who were sufficiently determined—as we all should be—to fix our apartheid Senate once and for all.

This revision would open up new possibilities such as Larry Sabato's proposal that the 10 largest states should have 4 senators each, while the next 10 states get 3 each, and the smallest 30 keep their current 2 senators.[221] This is simply a contemporary version of Pinckney's proposal in the original convention: it would give about 75% of the American public a total of 70 senators, or almost 51.5% of a new Senate with a manageable 130 members.

Of course, an amendment could also specify other numbers to make the outcome even more proportional. The "Democracy Constitution," which was proposed by delegates at the 2021 symposium convened by Levinson, suggests between 1 and 6 senators per state. Spear suggests the same, and shows that they could be apportioned so as to total only 103 senators.[222] The "Progressive Constitution" composed for the Constitution Drafting Project suggests one senator per state *plus* one senator for every 1% of the national population (beyond the first 1%) within a state's boundaries. This would produce 126 senators.[223] Similarly, Eric Otts suggests one senator per 1% of the US population (or less) in each state, which yields between 1 and 12 senators per state and a total of 110 senators.[224]

(C) *National Senators.* However you slice it, though, approach (B) requires two amendments in serial order to fix the Senate. Yet Sabato has also suggested an ingenious way to fix it in one go, while leaving the unamendability clause alone. We could add "national senators" who would represent the nation as a whole rather than particular states, while each state would still elect its own 2 senators—as the Constitution (via the 17th Amendment) requires. Sabato envisions inviting all willing former presidents and vice presidents to serve in this role. But this variant seems to entail that the number of national senators would be both small and not fixed. So a single death or retirement could shift control of the Senate.

Instead, it would be more democratic and straightforward to elect some number of national senators at large by a national popular vote. This would reduce the effects of state-based malapportionment in the Senate and address another big problem with Congress as a whole: our senators and House members only represent particular states, which often makes it hard for them to put national interests first when necessary.[225]

Here is the best place of all to introduce some direct proportional representation into our federal system. Imagine that every two years, Americans could vote for a party

Table 3.2 Election of 50 National Senators by Proportional Representation

Political Parties	Share of National Popular Vote	Number of National Senators Elected
Republicans	41 %	8
Democrats	35.2 %	7
Libertarians	13.8 %	3
Forward Party	10 %	2

slate of national senators, and separately for candidates for their own state's open Senate seat(s) (if any)[226] (for a detailed illustration of how election by party slate works, see #4). For example, a constitutional amendment could specify that every two years, 20 national senators would be elected for 6-year terms, resulting in 60 total in Congress at any time. Parties gaining more than (say) 10% of the national popular vote with RCV would get that proportion (with rounding) of the 20 seats up for grabs in each biannual election.

Table 3.2 shows a possible outcome in such a vote. With each party's candidates listed in order of priority, the first 8 Republican candidates would be elected, along with the first 7 Democrats on their slate, etc. Because these slates of candidates would vie for votes across the whole country, much as in direct election of a presidential ticket, national senators would be accountable to the entire electorate. Thus they would not represent *any* particular state, and every state would technically retain "equal Suffrage" in the Senate, given that no state elects more senators than any other.

Still, it might seem objectionable if almost all national senators came from big coastal states. To reduce this concern, the law could require certain percentages of non-coastal candidates on the party slates, or geographic diversity in the pool of candidates in the primary elections for national senators. In a proportional election system, the primary will determine (or help to determine) the rank-order of candidates on a party's slate. For instance, if the scenario in Table 3.2 is plausible, the first 5 or 6 Republican candidates on their party's slate are likely to win a Senate seat, and ditto for the Democratic candidates. They should get into those higher positions on the slate by doing better in the primary race.

Finally, notice that two variables determine how much this national senator innovation helps reduce the Senate's gross inequality. First, the more national senators there are, the more the geographic apartheid deriving from state-elected federal senators is diluted. Given 60 of the former and 100 of the latter, the smallest 15 states comprising 5.5% of our population would elect 18.7% of the whole Senate—a major improvement from the 30% they now elect. Second, the amendment could reduce each state to *just one* state-elected federal senator apiece—which still counts as "equal Suffrage." With 50 of these current-style senators and 60 national senators, the 15 smallest states would elect just 15 of 110 senators (or 13.6%). It would be even better still to have 75 national senators and 50 elected state by state, for 125 total. Because larger-population states would have more impact in the election of national senators, the resulting Senate would represent the people as a whole much more accurately.

(D) *Eliminate or Transfer Most of the Senate's Powers.* There is one more approach to consider. We could leave each state with an equal number of senators (e.g. one each) but makes them far less crucial in our system. This approach also comes in degrees. On one end, it is tempting to imagine the Senate reduced to virtual irrelevancy with almost no powers, and left to meet in some gallery on the outskirts of Washington D.C.

Such an amendment need not imply that the House would do everything. The amendment could transfer most of the Senate's functions to a *new* upper chamber elected in a new way—call it the "Legislative Council," just to give it a name—while leaving the "ghost" Senate a few minor roles (e.g. approving ambassadors).[227] States could have between 1 and 10 "councilors," depending on their population. Perhaps after some years, all states would agree to abolish the rump Senate to save some money.

Further from this pole, a lesser number of the Senate's current powers could be moved to the House. For example, the House could confirm nominees to the Supreme Court and cabinet offices, approve treaties, and enact budget bills without the Senate's concurrence.[228] We could also allow the House by itself to override a presidential veto and propose amendments to the states. Several of Levinson's suggestions tend in this direction, and it is worth considering.

But whether the Senate retains a vote on all or most bills, or this power is transferred to a new Legislative Council, we should also rethink whether the upper chamber should have a complete veto on bills passed by the House. It may surprise many Americans that few other developed democratic nations give their upper chamber this much power.

For example, consider Britain. While the UK system is complex, generally speaking the House of Lords cannot block a finance bill more than twice and cannot block other bills for more than two years if they are passed three times by the House of Commons.[229] It is especially noteworthy that the British instituted this system, which denies their upper legislative chamber the power to block bills forever, *over a century ago in 1911.* In France also, the National Assembly can have the final say even if the French Senate blocks a bill for a period of time.[230]

Reflecting this, the "Democracy Constitution" thought-experiment suggests allowing the US upper chamber to reject a bill passed by the House and return it with objections. But if the House passes it a second time, then the bill becomes law without needing Senate approval (the same procedure could apply to a presidential veto).[231]

Here is another variation found in some other countries (and sometimes used for constitutional change too). Once a bill passes the House, the Senate (or new upper chamber) has 3 months to consider it. If the upper chamber rejects the bill or never votes on it, then the House (or lower chamber) can reconsider it again *after* the next congressional election. If the House passes the same bill unaltered after that election, it becomes law with the president's signature. There is a variant of this "intervening-election" method that would also allow pending bills to remain "alive" for longer: after a congressional election, the Senate could have a year to approve any bills passed by the House but not the Senate during the prior term. Currently, pending bills that have passed one chamber die at the end of every two-year session of Congress: they have to pass *both* chambers again to become law.

In sum, there are several ways to retain a bicameral check that actually encourage compromise and productivity rather than spoiler strategies. In the first "intervening election" method, the House majority has an incentive to compromise with the upper chamber to avoid having to revote on the same bill after the next election cycle. But the upper chamber cannot just block the House's legislation forever, as our current Senate does. All such changes can be made via one amendment, without touching the infamous unamendability clause.

A Mixed Verdict. In light of these four alternatives, what should be done? It is hard to say, because so many partial combinations of the four fixes just analyzed are conceivable. But ideally, general principles favor (a) the simplest solution that is consistent with (b) democratic equality, and (c) that maintains a bicameral check within the legislative branch, while (d) remaining cost-effective. These considerations counsel a mixed solution along the following lines:

I. Each state elects between 1 and 5 senators, apportioned to population, with a total number of state-elected federal senators of capped at two times the number of states (currently 100).

II. In every presidential election year, 60 national senators are elected, for 4-year terms, at-large from party lists (slates) proportional to every party's percentage of the national popular vote. Ballots for party slates scoring less than 10% in the popular vote on the first round are assigned to their casters' second choice, if any. The number of national senators is increased by 2 for each new state added to the Union, and reduced by 2 whenever two states combine.

III. If the House of Representatives passes a bill by a three-fifths (60%) margin, it goes directly to the President for consideration irrespective of Senate action on the bill.

IV. If the Senate rejects a bill passed by a simple majority in the House of Representatives, or never votes on it during the current congressional session, the new House may reconsider that bill after the next congressional election. If the House then passes the same bill again by a simple majority, or the Senate passes the same bill approved by the House in the previous session, it goes directly to the President for consideration.

V. Upon the resignation, death, or disability of a Senator, as defined by law, their replacement shall be chosen by lot among 3 alternates who were publicly listed by that Senator during their last reelection campaign (compare #19).

The result of this amendment would currently be a Senate of 160 senators—with 100 elected by the states in *partial* proportion to population (compare Sabato and Pinckney). Electing the 60 national senators during the presidential election would make divided government less likely; thus their 4-year term. With roughly 33 senators from the states also on the ballot, over 58% of the Senate would be chosen during the high-turnout presidential race. §I also reduces chances that any state will lose a senator if a new state is admitted to the Union. And §IV combines both "intervening election" proposals. The new Senate could delay bills passed by the House but not block them entirely. The Senate's other powers could also be adjusted as proposed in amendments #7, #9, and #16–20, which could be considered separately.

Only §I in this proposal requires that the unamendability clause in Article V be struck out by a prior amendment. If that proved to be impossible for any reason, §I could be changed to say that each state elects just 1 senator, while increasing the number of national senators to 100, for a total of 150 senators.

However, this is only a sketch of an ideal solution, given the considerations I mentioned. In this case, probably more than any other area of needed constitutional reform, we would have to accept what we could get: any significant improvement to the Senate would be good enough for a few decades, leaving other needed improvements for later. For example, if an amendment consisting only of §III and §IV could be passed and ratified by the needed number of states, the rest could wait. Likewise, a compromise only giving us §II would be enough to work wonders by itself.

§I might be the hardest to sell, because more than one quarter of states would be reduced from 2 to 1 senator in the new apportionment. However, an amendment could instead stipulate that only states with less than 0.5% of the nation's population would be limited to one senator. Today only the 11 smallest states with less than 1.7 million residents each are below this threshold (currently 5 bluer and 6 redder states—but also potentially D.C.). And 11 states are not enough to block an amendment.

More generally, any major change to the Senate's composition and/or its powers would probably need to be part of a more comprehensive package of amendments that most Americans could recognize as fair and balanced. The immediate goal should be to start these conversations and raise awareness, so that geographic apartheid becomes at least as unpopular as gerrymandering, the filibuster, and the EC. A bargain struck in 1787 for reasons that are no longer relevant should not hobble this nation any longer.

25. A New Article V: Fix the Amendment Process Itself

This brings us finally to the extreme difficulty of the US amendment process in general. Scholars rate our Constitution as the hardest to amend in the free world. One study of 31 democratic nations found that in many of them, a proposed amendment can pass the legislature once or twice, by simple majority or 2/3^{rds}; about half of these also require ratification by a national referendum. The United States is the *only* country that requires ratification by a 3/4th vote—in our case, by 75% of state governments, or specially called state conventions.[232] Other democratic nations require only 2/3^{rds}, at most, in the final ratification stage.[233]

This is the main reason that even no-brainer constitutional amendments hardly ever pass Congress and are even more rarely ratified, as we saw with the 1972 Equal Rights Amendment and the 1978 amendment to give Washington D.C. representation in Congress (see #11). Another reason involves obstacles to calling a new national convention, as we will see. Obviously, making it a bit easier to amend our Constitution would help us to solve many other constitutional problems in turn.

How the Excessively High Thresholds Originated. The requirements for legal change are set out in Article V of our Constitution, which has not itself altered since it was written at the 1787 convention. Delegates did not have many models for constitutional amendment to go on at the time: no republican constitution then existed for a large republic, and the new state constitutions written after 1775 either had no "explicit amendment process," or allowed the state legislature to change the state constitution by one or two majority votes (except for Delaware, which required one 5/7ths vote in the statehouse).[234]

The American founders knew that the British "constitution" consisted of a few revered acts of Parliament that were held by tradition to have fundamental significance. But they wanted more explicit written constitutional guarantees to unite the disparate states, plan for the addition of new states, and deepen the rule of law. As a result, they could not rely on an informal constitutional tradition alone.

Moreover, the existing Articles of Confederation were accepted by all the 13 states during the Revolutionary War only because the Articles required unanimous agreement to change them. But the framers at the 1787 convention knew they could not adhere to this requirement because Rhode Island was certain not to accept needed changes to the Articles. So, appealing to the originary "constituent power" or sovereignty of the people (see #24 and Desideratum 8), the convention delegates wrote in Article VII that *nine* states—69% of the original 13 states—would be enough to ratify the new constitution, and the amendment process they included in it reflected this precedent. Wilson initially proposed that ratification of proposed amendments by 2/3rds of the states. This failed only by *a single vote*. With little discussion, the delegates then moved to 3/4ths of states as a fallback.[235] Here are the main clauses of the resulting Article V:

> The Congress, whenever two thirds of both Houses [i.e. the Senate and House of Representatives] shall deem it necessary, shall propose Amendments to this Constitution, or, on the Application of the Legislatures of two thirds of the several States, shall call a Convention for proposing Amendments, which, in either Case, shall be valid to all Intents and Purposes, as Part of this Constitution, when ratified by the Legislatures of three fourths of the several States, or by Conventions in three fourths thereof, as the one or the other Mode of Ratification may be proposed by the Congress; [...][236]

The result was a two-route process. The first route involves *two* steps: amendments pass Congress and then states ratify them or not. The second route involves *three* steps: states call for a convention; the convention passes or formally "proposes" amendments; and then states (or their conventions) ratify or reject the proposal(s) (see Figure 3.8).

The founders clearly intended and expected amendments to be adopted in both ways. While the 1787 constitution itself was being ratified, several states called for changes, and some even wanted a new convention to deliver demanded edits before ratifying. Supporters of the new constitution argued that states could more productively use its internal amendment mechanism once the federal government was ratified and operating.[237] This promise was quickly kept: 12 amendments were proposed by the required 2/3rds margin in both the House and Senate during the very first federal Congress in 1789. Of these 12 articles composing the US Bill of Rights, 10 of these were ratified within two years.

Expecting this, the authors of Article V meant to make it easier to adopt amendments than it had been in the Confederation: they thought they were creating constitutional law that would be enduring but still alterable when really needed. As Sabato summarizes, the convention delegates "expected of us that we would at regular intervals" try "to

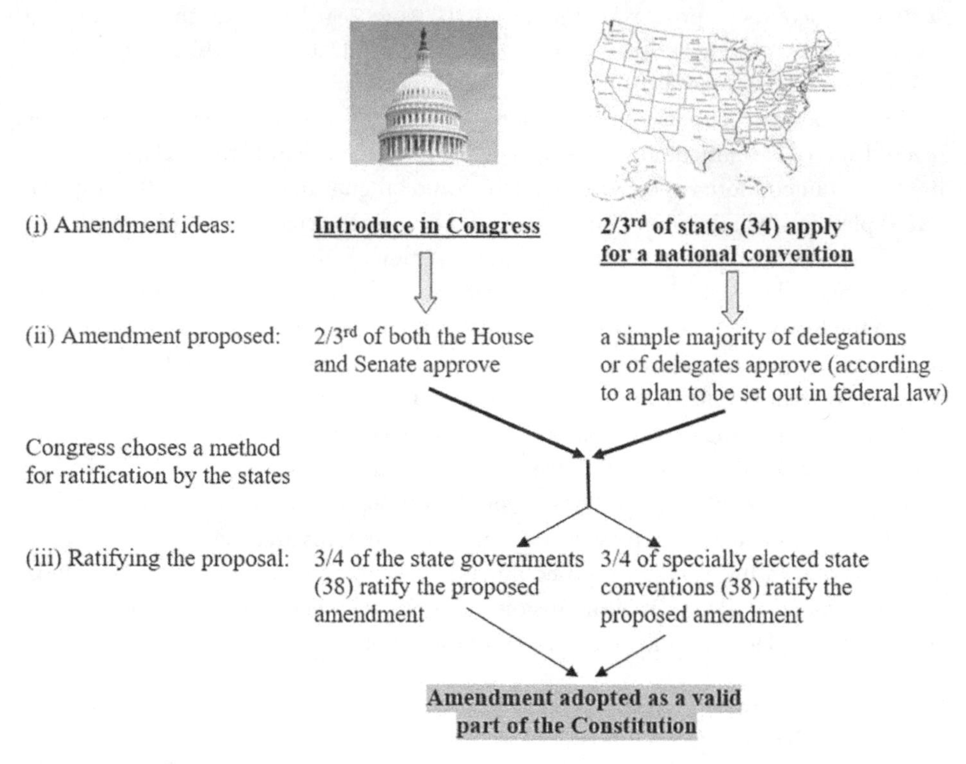

Figure 3.8 Constitutional Amendment under Current Article V

perfect their work" with constitutional reforms.[238] Several of the founders also assumed that another convention would be called within a few decades to propose revisions in light of experience. Similarly, Abraham Lincoln explicitly suggested a new convention as a better alternative than civil war.[239]

Yet, the amendment process that the founders created proved far more difficult to use than they expected. Really fundamental changes could only be made in revolutionary fashion after the Civil War,[240] and fifty years later during the crises of the Progressive Era. As we saw, two more substantive amendments were adopted in the 1960s–1970s; but most ratified amendments after the 1920s have been on less fundamental topics or on narrow technical issues, such as what happens if the president remains alive but unfit for duty (this is addressed by the 25th Amendment). Sarah Isgur, a spokeswoman for the Justice Department during Trump's presidency, aptly sums up the situation: "[i]t's become harder to amend the Constitution even as it has become ever more important that we amend it."[241]

Consider how different things are at the state level. As Levinson notes, many state constitutions have been amended over a *hundred* times since 1789, and most have been totally replaced at least once or twice,[242] while only 27 amendments to our federal constitution have been adopted during the same period. In fact, all 50 state constitutions are easier to amend than the national one. All states except (ever-maverick) Delaware allow the legislature to propose amendments to directly to voters. 10 allow formal amendment proposals by a *simple majority* of the statehouse in one session; 9 require $3/5^{ths}$ of the legislature (upper and lower chambers); while 16 require statehouse majorities of $2/3^{rds}$. 12 other states require approval by the legislature over two sessions—8 of these only by simple majorities of legislators both times. 18 states also allow voters to propose state amendments directly through petitions—usually by 8%–10% of the number of votes cast for governor.[243]

Calling a state convention is also easier: 14 states automatically put a ballot question to voters, at regular intervals, asking whether a state constitutional convention should meet to propose amendments. 27 states also allow the legislature to put such a question about a convention on the ballot. 4 states even allow voters to directly put this question about a convention on the ballot by petition.

Ratification is also much simpler at the state level: 49 states allow voters to directly ratify an amendment resolution passed by the legislature or by a state convention. For ratification, 40 states only require a majority among those voters who voted on the ballot question. 5 other states require a (higher) majority approval among all voters casting ballots for any office in the election; and 2 have distribution requirements among counties for ratification. A couple others have multiple ways of ratifying, but only NH requires approval by $2/3^{rds}$ of those voting on an amendment.[244]

By contrast, the inflexibility of the federal Constitution has hardened, as our parties have become more polarized and focused on denying even small wins to their perceived adversaries. For example, as we saw, Congress almost passed an amendment to abolish the EC, but a few senators blocked it in 1969 (see #12). The ERA passed Congress but needed to be ratified by a few more states to reach our extraordinarily high 75% threshold.

Radical inequality in population between states is another reason to lower the ratification threshold, and to provide another route for ratification as well. The smallest 13 states, which are currently enough to prevent adoption of a proposed amendment, together house less than 4.4% of Americans, and are "whiter" than the nation as a whole.[245] This problem is further aggravated by the exclusion of D.C. and Puerto Rico, which have no say on amendment ratification. In realistic scenarios, state governments representing a mere 10–15% of the public might well block an amendment. Until this is changed, what Madison called the "great interests of the nation" may be sacrificed to the "local prejudices" of a few states.[246]

So Many Unanswered Questions. The other basic problem with our Article V is that, like many other key passages in our Constitution, its clauses are much briefer than those in most modern constitutions, and it says nothing about several issues that our founders did not anticipate or have time to expand upon.[247] Again, this is a reflection of ours being the oldest written constitution of any republic in the modern era. It also reflects the rather rushed nature of Article V, which delegates only considered in detail during the last couple days of the convention.

Here is one example of an unsettled procedural question. When both chambers of Congress passed the ERA in 1972, its official text said "Equality of rights under the law shall not be denied or abridged by the United States or by any State on account of sex." But the joint resolution of Congress sending this article to the states for ratification framed the ERA itself within a 7-year horizon for states to ratify it. This is a trend with no constitutional basis.

Since 1917, when the 18th amendment (Prohibition) was passed, this rider has been included in the actual texts of the 18th, 20th, 21st, and 22nd Amendments, and in the resolutions sending other amendment proposals to the states. The 7-year window was also included in the unratified D.C. Voting Rights amendment (but not in the ratified 23rd Amendment to give D.C. a voice in the presidential election). Had it not been there, probably this amendment for D.C. to have representation in Congress (see #11) would be ratified by now.

This inconsistency only reflects bargaining in Congress. As with the filibuster innovation, the 7-year time window is just a new hurdle that opponents of amendment have added, without right, to a constitutionally prescribed process. There is nothing in Article V saying that Congress has the authority to limit ratification time in this way (could it even choose a mere 10 days?); and no amendment resolution that passed Congress before 1917 included such a rider. Thus, the second article in the original Bill of Rights, which prevents congressional pay raises from taking effect until after the next election, was finally ratified by 3/4 of our states in 1992—becoming the 27th Amendment more than *200 years* after it passed the first Congress (see #8).

These radical differences in ratification time are patently unfair. In 1978, Congress passed a 3-year extension of the time to ratify the ERA. But this was also controversial: if Congress has the power to set a time-horizon in the framing resolution of an amendment, can Congress also extend it? Would such an extension itself require another two-thirds vote by both chambers of Congress? (the ERA extension had only simple majorities). Does it matter if the time-horizon is in the text of the amendment proposed by Congress (or by a convention), or only in the framing resolution (or "preamble"), as with the ERA and the 24th Amendment, among others? If Congress can set (or extend) a time-horizon, could it also put other arbitrary conditions into a framing resolution—such as that only statehouse votes taken on a Monday will count as valid (and if the latter would not be allowed, why is the former)?

More questions spring from these. Congress apparently cannot withdraw an amendment proposal once it is sent to the states for consideration. But can states rescind their ratifications (as several have in many cases)? Certainly they could not undo an approved amendment after it reached the 3/4ths threshold and is declared ratified. But it seems reasonable to allow a state to reconsider its past ratification before an amendment reaches the threshold for final approval.[248] Still, that makes an already very high bar even harder to reach. Can states also make their ratifications automatically sunset before Congress' time-horizon for ratification, or even attach other conditions (such as that another particular state must have ratified)? Such questionable moves would normally raise the bar even further; but perhaps sometimes extra conditions could smooth the way. And what if an amendment gets ratified, but it conflicts with another amendment that was formerly proposed earlier by Congress but remains still open for ratification?[249]

Notice that Article V also allows Congress to choose state ratifying *conventions* as the mode of ratification for a proposed amendment—apparently whether it came from Congress or from a new national convention instead.[250] The only time Congress has chosen this mode was with the 21st Amendment to repeal Prohibition. Can states select members of such ratifying conventions however they wish, or can Congress also have a say on that matter? And would use of this ratification mode mean that only another state ratifying convention could reconsider and rescind a state's existing ratification of an amendment? The answer must be yes: for otherwise, a state government (legislature + governor) could nullify a state convention's approval of an amendment immediately after it is given—or even try to preempt a state convention's action. This would render the ratifying convention option meaningless.

Yet, if that is correct, probably there should be limits on how a state government ratifies amendments when the state convention option is not chosen. For example, Congress could prohibit states from delegating to their governors power to ratify (or rescind ratification) unilaterally. Nor should the state supreme court be allowed to make ratification decisions. Article V seems to assume that the ratification method will have some democratic credentials.

In addition, why interpret the 3/4 (75%) threshold to ratify an amendment as measured by the total number of *presently* existing states? It could instead mean 3/4ths of the states that existed when Congress (or a national convention) passed that amendment proposal (but would that also mean that only those states could be involved in ratifying?[251]). The former interpretation prevailed, which is why Madison's Apportionment amendment for the House (see #8) twice *almost* reached the 3/4ths threshold: as new states were added to the denominator, the goalpost kept receding.[252]

More urgently, there are uncertainties about state calls for a new constitutional convention—conditions for their validity, how long these calls remain valid, who tracks them, whether they can be rescinded, whether they can limit what a convention discusses, and more. Article V also seems to imply that Congress can legislate concerning how a national convention would work, but that would also benefit from clarification. Moreover, as noted, federal courts should have very limited power to intervene in these disputes because amendments are meant to furnish a *check* on the judiciary's precedents (see #24).

These issues are becoming important because it appears that the House Judiciary Committee might sit indefinitely on 34 or more state calls for a convention—the 2/3rds threshold—without acting on them (see ch.4). Until Article V itself is updated, Congress needs to enact laws that address these issues, including how we know when enough valid applications for a national convention have been received. And when states ratify a proposed amendment, do small differences in wording or even punctuation matter in resolutions?[253]

Finally, since 1985, the US Archivist has recorded ratifications and proclaimed ratification complete; but more clarity could help preempt disruptive future disputes. For example, it seems unfair that the Archivist is now on the receiving end of lawsuits for not declaring the ERA fully ratified and adopted.[254] Given the political minefield that ratification could become, perhaps the legally binding proclamation that an amendment is adopted should go back to the Secretary of State.

The Proposal. The comparisons with state constitutions suggest several promising ways of improving the federal amendment process. The many identified lacunas in the existing text of Article V should also be filled in order to avoid manipulation of the processes. Otherwise we will have crises that, after a thicket of costly lawsuits and resulting delays, force the Supreme Court to decide (on little basis) what are really substantive political issues in the amendment process.

I, therefore, propose a complete replacement of our existing Article V with provisions guided by our historical experience with state constitution amendment practices, the democratic constitutions of other nations that were rewritten in the 20th century, and the organic principles underlying all legitimate constitutional lawmaking (see Desideratum 8 and #23). The two main goals are to make amendment somewhat easier by lowering the thresholds, and to resolve the unanswered questions.

Without trying to draft complete language here, my recommendation has three main parts. It includes three ways of formally proposing amendments to the states—directly from Congress, by public referendum, or by convention. The process for a convention is also described in some detail. Finally, the proposal lays out multiple ways of ratifying a proposed amendment, however it was proposed (to get the gist, you may wish to skip §IV and §V on the workings of a national convention during your first read).

I. Direct Congressional Initiation.
   (i) Congress may propose amendments to the Constitution by a $3/5^{ths}$ vote (60%) of both the House and the Senate. The President's approval is not required, and Congress may not rescind amendment proposals once they are sent to the states for consideration.
   (ii) Congress may, by a $2/3^{rds}$ vote in both chambers, call a national convention to consider and propose amendments, irrespective of state calls for the same.

II. State Calls for a National Convention.
   (i) On application of $3/5^{ths}$ of the legislatures of the States, the House of Representatives must call a national constitutional convention to propose amendments to the states for ratification.
   (ii) A state may apply for a convention by simple majority approval of a joint resolution of the state legislature, or by a simple majority of all participating voters in state ballot referendum, which in neither case require the governor's approval. However it is legally enacted, any state's resolution calling for a convention is valid for 25 years, unless it rescinds its call by another resolution passed by the state legislature and signed by the governor.
   (iii) In calling for a national convention, state legislatures may suggest that particular issues be studied or particular reform ideas considered in the convention. However, a convention has plenary power to discuss any topics and proposals that the delegates, in the course of deliberating, believe are worth considering.
   (iv) All valid state applications will be counted toward the $3/5^{ths}$ threshold, no matter what topics they may propose for a convention to consider, any language to the contrary in their applications notwithstanding.

(v) No state may pre-ratify the text of a proposed amendment in its application for a convention.

(vi) The House Judiciary Committee has the responsibility to certify the validity of state applications for a convention and determine when the threshold is met, pursuant to federal law. No state may rescind its application after the 3/5ths threshold is declared to be reached by the committee, or by the full House of Representatives.

III. Federal Ballot Referenda.

(i) Congress may, by simple majority in both houses, place on the federal ballot, concurrent with the presidential election, a question concerning whether an amendment should be proposed to the states.

(ii) If 63% of voters who vote on the ballot question approve the amendment resolution, it goes to the states for ratification.

(iii) Congress may also, by simple majority, place on the federal ballot, concurrent with the presidential election, a question concerning whether a new national convention should be called to consider and propose amendments that may improve the nation.

(iv) If 60% of the number of voters who cast a ballot for President and Vice President respond affirmatively to this ballot question, a convention must be called by Congress.

(v) If, upon ratification of this amendment, no national convention has met in the prior 50 years, or within 50 years since the last convention concluded its business, then a convention must be called.

IV. Organizing a National Convention.

(i) Whenever any of the conditions requiring that a national convention be called are satisfied, the House of Representatives must, within 50 days, name a meeting place and date for the convention that is not more than 12 months later, along with dates for the election of delegates.

(ii) The House must also provide funding adequate for the convention to meet for a period of up to one year, including public salaries for each delegate and for accompanying experts and support staff commensurate with the great public trust placed in their work.

(iii) The House must also define uniform conditions for persons to appear on state ballots as candidates for the office of national convention delegate, and provide to each state reasonable levels of funding for the election of delegates.

(iv) These provisions for a national convention shall be effective as law by a simple majority vote of the House of Representatives.

V. Delegates and the Convention Process.

(i) Whenever a national convention is called, Congress will apportion between one and five delegates for each state, proportional to their populations, for a total of not more than 100 delegates. Each state will elect its delegates, along with two alternate standby delegates, by a statewide popular election with ranked choice ballots. The election of delegates is nonpartisan: no party affiliation may appear next to the name of a candidate for delegate, and the order of their names on the ballot must be random.

(ii) Delegates must be at least 20 years old, and may not include anyone who serves in any government job, or who has served in a government job within the last four years, excepting those serving in the armed forces of the United States. No delegate may be replaced by their state government once the convention begins; nor may they be called for military service or jury duty while serving. Congress may establish additional equitable rules for persons to appear on the ballot in their state of residence as candidates for the office of delegate.

(iii) Delegates may not be hired or elected into any government job, or any paid lobbyist position, for five years after the convention has completed its work. Upon completion of the convention's work, delegates may not, for ten years, hold a high-paying job in any corporation that is immediately and significantly benefitted by amendments that the convention passes, as such benefits are defined in federal law.

(iv) The convention's proceedings may not last beyond one year, but they are closed and secret. Delegates must act like a sequestered jury during the term of their service.

(v) Once they are duly elected, no delegate may be recalled. However, if any delegate becomes unable to serve, a special three-judge panel shall authorize their replacement with one of their alternates. The panel will also arbitrate any dispute within the convention over the competence of any delegate, who may be expelled for violating the convention's rules. Any delegate leaving the convention remains legally bound by secrecy, on pain of felony charges, while the convention's work proceeds.

(vi) The elected delegates will adopt rules for their convention proceedings according to ordinary parliamentary procedures, including motions to call the question. They will consider questions concerning the national interest and common good. When a delegation's members are evenly divided on any motion, its collective vote is not counted. Every state's delegation shall have the right to introduce at least two amendment resolutions, which must receive a vote by the full convention in due course, with any alterations that the initiating delegations accept.

(vii) In the first stage of the convention's deliberations, every amendment resolution that receives a simple majority vote of all the delegates, voting as individuals, will be given further consideration in the second stage.

(viii) After further due consideration, amendment resolutions advancing to the second stage may be combined, split, or otherwise altered by a majority of delegations voting, or by 60% of delegates voting as individuals. All such revised proposals must receive a final vote by the whole convention.

(ix) Proposals approved by a majority of all state delegations, or by 60% of delegates voting as individuals, will be sent directly to all the states for consideration when the convention concludes its business.

(x) The Chief Justice presides over the national convention and does not vote, unless a majority of delegations select a delegate to serve as chair, who retains their vote.

VI. Ratification.

(i) When amendments are proposed to the states, either by Congress, by popular approval of a ballot initiative pursuant to §III, or by a duly called national convention, they are open for ratification for 20 years.

(ii) If any state's legislature has not ratified an amendment within 3 years of its being proposed, that state must call a ratifying convention to consider the amendment within the next year. When it meets, the same ratifying convention may also consider other amendments currently open for ratification.

(iii) If a state ratifying convention has rejected a proposed amendment, the state legislature may still ratify that amendment within the allowed 20 year period.

(iv) In all cases, a simple majority vote of the state legislature, each chamber concurring, or of the state ratifying convention, is sufficient for a state to ratify an amendment.

(v) A state's ratification of an amendment may not be rescinded without a 2/3rds majority in a state's legislature and signature by the state's governor. Nor may a ratification resolution include a sunset clause that suspends or revokes it prior to the 20 year deadline.[255]

VII. Adoption.

(i) Whenever an amendment has been ratified by 2/3rds of the states within 20 years of its being open for ratification, it is adopted as a valid article of the Constitution, superseding any previous constitutional language to the contrary.

(ii) If a fully ratified amendment clearly conflicts with another amendment formally proposed at an earlier date that is still open for ratification, the latter is legally void and no longer open for ratification.

(iii) When certifying an amendment as adopted by the states, the Secretary of State shall count all ratifications that have not been legally rescinded within 60 days prior to the most recent state ratification.

VIII. Revision and General Conditions.

(i) If more than a third of states have rejected a proposed amendment, but 12 or more state legislatures have passed resolutions indicating that they would ratify that amendment with a particular revision, then Congress may, by simple majority, return the amendment to the states with this and other revisions reflecting the states' requests. In that case, the modified amendment supersedes the old version and remains open for ratification only by state legislatures for 5 years.

(ii) Alternatively, when a proposed amendment is not ratified within 20 years, Congress may place it on the federal ballot during either of the next two presidential elections. If 2/3rds all Americans who vote on this ballot question affirm it, the amendment is adopted as part of the Constitution.

(iii) Washington D.C. counts as a state for purposes of this article.

Such provisions would resolve most of the open questions concerning Article V processes,[256] and make it easier to amend the Constitution in several ways. First, they lower the thresholds for Congress to propose amendments, and for states to call a national convention to do the work of proposing.[257] Congress can also, by simple majority, allow voters to propose an amendment by a higher margin (I suggest 63%, because $3/5^{\text{ths}}$ seems too low, and $2/^{\text{rds}}$ too high). §III also allows a supermajority of voters to call a convention via a referendum once Congress asks them. And it ensures that at least one convention meets every half-century, so the nation does not again get trapped in dysfunctional institutions.

Ratification is made easier by lowering the threshold from 75% to $2/3^{\text{rds}}$ (66.7%) of states, just as Wilson had proposed. There is also a fallback option for $2/3^{\text{rds}}$ of voters to ratify a proposed amendment by a ballot question when it is not ratified after 20 years. Note that several other advanced democratic nations, and many of our own states, have lower thresholds than this for amendment approval by referendum. Spear suggests the alternative of allowing voters to ratify amendment proposals by a simple majority vote in two general elections with different presidents in the White House.[258]

Combined with the provision for proposing an amendment by referendum in §III, §VIII provides one way of amending the Constitution without going through the states: Congress must place a question on two ballots separated by 20 years. First, 63% of voters must agree to formally propose the amendment. Then, after states have failed to act, $2/3^{\text{rds}}$ of voters are needed to approve it for final adoption. That is a high hurdle, but it offers a way around a recalcitrant core of a few states. Imagine, for example, that the ERA had been put on the federal ballot in the mid-1990s; it might well have been ratified by voters. The same holds for the D.C. Representation Amendment.

Note that ratification by state conventions may often be easier because a convention is one body, while a state legislature is two chambers in almost all cases. The 20-year time-horizon in §VI is more generous than 7, but not infinite. It ends speculation about Congress extending ratification windows too. It should also be somewhat harder to rescind a ratification, and §VI accomplishes that while clarifying how rescinding works.

§II greatly cuts through a morass of confusion by making clear that a convention can consider any topic before voting on amendment resolutions, just as Congress can consider any topic before voting on an amendment resolution (I defend this view further in the final chapter). If we instead require states to list exactly the same topics for a convention before it is called, we make it nearly impossible to call a convention. Because it effectively eliminates the convention option in that way, such a condition on applications for a convention should be considered unconstitutional even by today's Article V.

§IV and §V outline the details needed to ensure that a convention would work well. This avoids the delays, costs, and divisiveness of high-stakes votes in Congress, followed by court challenges, to determine a convention's procedures on a one-time basis.[259] The requirement of secrecy, which worked so well in the 1787 convention, would enable open and honest discussion and shield delegates from high-pressure lobbies and media campaigns. §V (ix) also eliminates the current possibility that Congress, acting as intermediary, might refuse to send onto the states some amendment passed by the convention.

Finally, §VIII (i) addresses a concern that almost derailed ratification of the 1787 constitution itself—namely, the desire of many states to see certain changes made before ratification. In that case, it was the absence of a full bill of rights that almost sunk ratification (as a handful of delegates to the original convention anticipated).[260]

As the ERA also illustrates, sometimes a problem with an amendment resolution's language may become clear only after it is proposed by Congress or a national convention.

Rather than having to accept the amendment with this flaw or go back and restart the process from scratch, §VIII would give states a way of proposing small corrections that Congress could consider in altering the amendment quickly and returning it for ratification.

Alternatives. Of course, there are several possible variations for each of these conditions. I will briefly mention six here. First, some Americans might be more comfortable with the lower $2/3^{rds}$ threshold for ratification of amendments if we retain the higher 75% threshold for any change to the Bill of Rights (the first ten ratified Amendments), along with the 13th, 14th, and 15th Amendments, as some other nations do to protect essential rights.[261]

Second, one could avoid all the verbiage about state legislatures and/or ratifying conventions approving or rescinding ratifications etc. if the only method to ratify an amendment resolution were for $2/3^{rds}$ of voters approve of it on the next presidential ballot. This is close to what *WeAmend* suggests in its draft proposal.[262] But this might be too quick and direct for many defenders of our federal system, who still want states to play a major role. A compromise might be to require ratification by $3/5^{ths}$ of states and by $3/5^{ths}$ of voters on a national ballot question. One could also add to §VI an option for states to ratify amendments by a state ballot question, perhaps requiring 60% of those voting on the question to approve it.

Third, some conservative defenders of "state's rights" will argue for an equal number of delegates from each state at a national convention. But the same enormous differences between the states that dogs the Senate and hobbles our current ratification process argue for giving the largest states at least some greater weight in a convention. Sabato strongly defends giving each state 1 delegate per House district (plus 1 for D.C.).[263] But it makes little sense for California to have 52 delegates to Wyoming's 1, if ratification usually requires even $2/3^{rds}$ of the states, let alone 3/4. Thus my compromise recommends that states have between 1 and 5 delegates depending on their populations, for a total of about 90–100 in the convention (as per Pinckney's proposed Senate—see #24). This smaller number would be more conducive to extended discussion and testimony from experts than a convention of 435 delegates.

Fourth, some critics will doubtless argue that voting within the convention should only be *by delegation*. The 1787 convention added and revised clauses by a majority of state delegations in each vote. But a 1–5 rule would make the convention far more representative, and would allow delegates representing more Americans at least to advance resolutions in the first stage of the convention's work. A majority of *delegations* would remain the main condition for final passage of an amendment resolution—with a supermajority of individual delegates as a second option to send an amendment on to the states. Such different forms of voting within a convention would make its internal caucusing more flexible.

The distinction between these two stages also reflects the successful procedure in the original 1787 convention—namely, preliminary or straw votes, and then commitment to a provision by full passage of a resolution. The national experience in 1787–1788 also shows that approval by a supermajority of delegations in the national convention is *not* needed to give amendment resolutions a good chance of ratification. What matters most is getting good proposals out to the states. The incentives change a lot when an amendment is ready for ratification: then public discussion, interest, and the sense of nearing the goalpost make adoption more likely, even if barely 51% of delegations liked that amendment within the convention.

Fifth, some critics will surely prefer the 20th century custom of 7 years for ratification. But I believe experience with the ERA shows that this is too short. Given the fractured process across many states, it can take 4–5 years for grass-roots ratification movements to get fully going in some states; and 7 years is not long enough to outlast big-money attacks. By contrast, 20 years is long enough for one census to pass, and for people who were still teenagers when an amendment was proposed to states to have a full opportunity to support its ratification.

Sixth, some radical democrats argue that smaller local councils should play a role in constitutional change to bring it more under the direct control of citizens. For example, Larry Lessig and I suggest that states should convene several "citizen juries" in which random samples of Americans would learn and deliberate about constitutional problems before making recommendations that their delegates would carry into the convention. Or local decision-power could be institutionalized by requiring states to hold special local assemblies representing no more than 250,000 residents each, which must sponsor local discussions about reform ideas and ultimately nominate candidates for the statewide delegate election.[264]

But however these details are settled, provisions for a new Article V should get us unstuck and make constitutional reform more feasible, although still harder than it is to alter ordinary statutes. Our constitutional law would remain stable without becoming destructively frozen. As Lessig once wrote, "life" exists in the region between too much stability and too much instability.[265] This flexibility provided by new amendment procedures would take us into that 'Goldilocks' zone, which would be much better for the nation than opting for a revolutionary solution outside legal pathways for amendment.

However, such an amendment to replace Article V would itself have to be adopted through the *existing* procedures (barely) described in our current Article V—with all its ambiguities. Failing that, the only solution might be nonviolent revolutionary action, as Levinson and Amar have considered. This is not the first priority: amendment #25 could come later on, after Americans had rediscovered the potential benefits of using the existing amendment power. But fixing the amendment process should not be an afterthought. In the long run, it is just as vital for the nation's long-term future as fixing the Senate and replacing the EC.

∞

Together, the twenty-five amendments outlined above would transform the United States from a nation foundering under its internal conflicts, gridlock, and corrupt influences into a nation where the government can once again serve the common good, advance prosperity for all, and uphold democratic ideals in ways that inspire the world. Adopting even half of these proposals would work the most profound constitutional renewal we have seen since the Civil War. For Americans, it would be the dawn of a new and better age. For tyrannical enemies of democracy around the world, it would be a devastating setback.

Yet, even this broad agenda does not cover every serious problem with our current constitutional system, or review all of the topics that would likely come up in a national process focused on constitutional reform. I mention a handful of these subjects in the Interlude next, before turning to the crucial question of how to pass and ratify some or all of the 25 amendments proposed above, which is the topic of the final chapter.

INTERLUDE: MORE AMENDMENT TOPICS NOT YET COVERED

The 25 amendments described in the previous two chapters cover a lot of ground and form a broad and unified program. Yet readers may be surprised that I have said little about some vexed topics, such as abortion, term limits for members of Congress, or updates to the Bill of Rights, which might include amendments on gender equality or privacy. Shouldn't something also be said about constitutional guarantees for property rights, or standards in criminal justice, or affirmative action, or gun rights, or the "hole" in the 13th Amendment that allows forced labor in prisons?[266]

These and other substantive issues are very important, and amendments addressing them may be warranted. I have left them aside because of this book's focus on the procedural aspects of lawmaking and elections (see the desiderata in Chapter One, §V). But there are also procedural proposals that I have not addressed, either for space reasons, or because of doubts about them. This Interlude briefly lists a few of these topics, which would certainly come up if a new constitutional convention meets. Interested readers can find more discussion of them, including five substantive amendment proposals, on this book's extension: *TheDemocracyAmendments.org.*

(A) *A new version of the Equal Rights Amendment* (ERA), which passed Congress in 1972, but was not ratified by 3/4ths of the states in time. The original language would now, in all likelihood, be easily ratified: "Equality of rights under the law shall not be denied or abridged by the United States or by any state on account of sex." Passing this amendment through Congress again might also be a great way to get the ball rolling on amendments more generally.

But if this language were expanded to say "sex *or gender*," that could invite thorny debates about what gender is, which could put a revised ERA in doubt. If it were also to mention sexual orientation, such a modified ERA probably could not yet get ratified.

WeAmend.us thus suggests that we address these further topics in a separate "Equal Treatment Amendment," reading "Equality of rights under the law shall not be denied or abridged by the United States or by any state on account of personal identity or group affiliation." These terms could then be specified in ordinary law, rather than in the amendment text. The alternative is to list factors that cannot be a basis for different treatment. For example, the amendment could declare that legal discrimination against people on the basis of poverty should require the same strict scrutiny that is applied to discrimination on the basis of gender, age, or religious faith.[267]

(B) *Stronger Due Process and Privacy Rights*: An amendment specifying that modalities of criminal punishment which amount to torture are banned, and that sentences must be generally proportional to the wrong done in the crime. This amendment would address problems created by court precedents, excessive minimum sentences, and laws concerning treatment of terrorists. The proportionality condition has been upheld to an extent in 8th Amendment jurisprudence, but should be explicitly added.

Similarly, privacy rights have often been read into the Constitution by courts. But in a time when corporations are allowed to make collection of data on our actions a condition of using must-have apps needed for work, and even our genetic information may be used against us, it would be wise to establish explicit constitutional rights of privacy. The amendment should give Congress explicit power to set out types of information about us to which we have exclusive original ownership.

(C) *State Assistance to the Federal Government*: An amendment establishing a general requirement for state officials to cooperate with federal law enforcement, as long as the federal government compensates states for resulting costs. This amendment would reverse a dangerous string of "anti-commandeering" decisions that are undermining federal law. It only requires the addition of four words—"and other public officials"—after "judges" in the supremacy clause of the Constitution's Article VII.[268]

(D) *A General Welfare Amendment*: When the 1787 constitution was made, most delegates agreed that Congress should have "the right to legislate in all cases for the general interests of the union and where the states were separately incompetent," or "the harmony of the United States" required national standards.[269] This means, in effect, all cases in which collective action problems among some or all states can make it hard to secure important national public goods (NPGs). Thus the reference to "the general welfare" in the Constitution's famous preamble.

There is a lot of misunderstanding on this issue. Conservative supporters of "states' rights" often claim that the framers meant to strictly limit federal authority to the explicit list of topics enumerated in the 1787 constitution, and a few that were added in later amendments. This dogmatic formula errs by focusing narrowly on *what* powers were long ago enumerated rather than *why*. The framers enumerated powers based on this central principle: give to the federal government those powers manifestly needed to coordinate NPGs.[270] That is what Madison means in citing the Confederation Congress' instruction for delegates to "render the federal Constitution adequate to the exigencies of government and the preservation of the Union."[271]

The principle behind the enumeration of functions is crucial because the founders recognized that changes in circumstances and understanding might require new federal powers to secure old or new NPGs. Naïve states-rightism completely misses this crucial point. In fact, adding such powers tailored to meet new needs directly comports with the founders' intention, while stubborn refusal to give the federal level authority necessary to national "exigencies" violates their intent.

This should be resolved with an amendment recognizing the general principle and clarifying the federal government's needed role in areas that were not fully understood in 1787. It could go something like this: "Pursuant to promoting the rights and general welfare of the people, Congress has the power to enact laws designed to protect the health, safety, education, and financial wellbeing of all residents."[272] This would have the added benefit of reducing overreliance on the Commerce Clause when justifying federal actions.

(E) *Lower the Threshold for Treaty Ratification to 60% of the Senate.*[273] In recent decades, it has become ever harder to get two-thirds of the Senate to ratify treaties, with the result that presidents instead rely on other ways of making agreements with foreign governments—by law or by executive order. Their constitutional authority to do this is unclear, and resulting agreements appear much less reliable to foreign leaders because they can be more easily reversed than a treaty can. A good example is the treaty-like agreement made (via great diplomatic effort) with Iran in 2015, which Trump abrogated less than two years later. There is also the notable fact that, due to the very high Senate hurdle, the United States is not party to many important international conventions concerning human rights.

(F) *Term Limits in Congress.* These have often been proposed in a wide variety of forms. They reduce incumbent advantages and may increase diversity a bit.[274] Average time in Congress has increased a lot over the history of our republic, reaching almost 9 years in the House and over 11 in the Senate (see Figure 3.9)[275]—even with a lot of primary challenges to Republican congresspersons in the last decade. Caps on very long service, e.g. over 20 in the House and 25 in the Senate, would be the easiest to ratify. But term limits can make legislators look at their service as merely a stepping-stone to plum corporate positions, prevent them from acquiring special expertise, and encourage them to "go for a big, short term splash" while kicking hard problems down the road.[276] Restrictions on big money influence in campaign finance and an end to gerrymandering are probably better ways to make more House and Senate seats competitive, while leaving enough long-term members in place to preserve stability, strong leadership, and institutional memory. This would still be compatible with an age limit, e.g. at age 75.

(G) *Alter House and Senate Terms.* A common proposal is to change the terms of the House to 4 years,[277] in order to cut down on the fundraising and make united government more likely—at least during a president's first term. This is not likely to be popular, however, because Americans like to have electoral input around the middle of a presidential term.

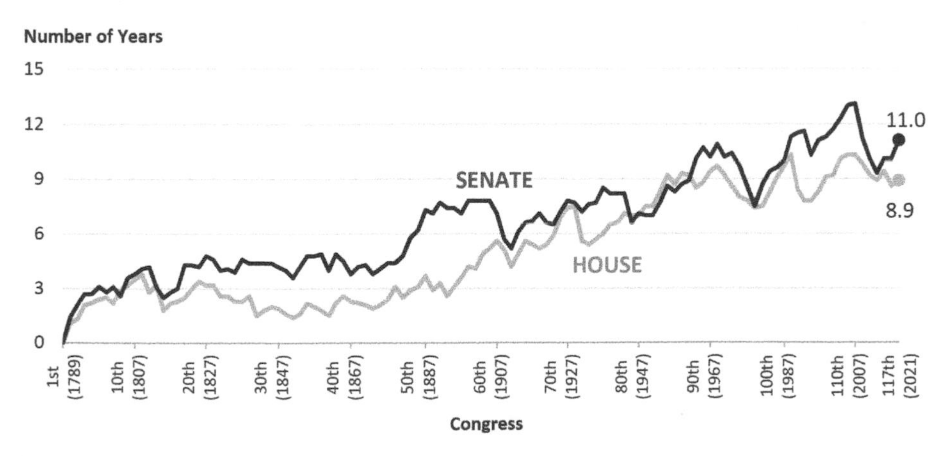

Figure 3.9 Average Years in Office for Members of Congress

Still, the 2-year term in the US legislature's lower chamber is uniquely short among developed democracies.[278]

Altering the Senate's 6-year term is more complex, given that one third of the Senate is meant to be elected every 2 years. Some reformers would change the presidency to one 6-year term, but that removes the incentive for reelection. One intriguing suggestion is to allow a maximum of 10 years in the White House, with reelection possible for just 2 years near the end of a president's second 4-year term. However, this might be too long in most Americans' view, and it would complicate many other reforms (#2, #9, #21, etc.).[279]

(H) *The Vice Presidency*. There are several problems with the office of VP. The largest concerns whether the VP should be elected separately from the president to avoid the current problem that running mates are chosen mostly to help the ticket win (on this, see this book's webpage extension). However, three worries should be briefly highlighted here.

First, the 25th Amendment assumes that there is a sitting VP to act with the cabinet should the president become physically or mentally unable to serve (or otherwise severely compromised)—in the worst case, acting against the president's declared will. If such a desperate scenario arises after the VP has recently died, resigned, or been impeached, and not yet replaced,[280] we would be in deep trouble.

It is even worse if the VP, while serving as acting president for an extended period, also becomes too disabled to serve. The 25th Amendment makes no provision for fast replacement of the VP, whether acting temporarily as president or not. Even if the president is fine, it is bad for the nation if the VP "on deck" to take over has become senile or otherwise severely disabled.[281] But impeachment is presently the only way to remove such a VP. Probably some provision for an Acting Vice President is needed, even when the actual (elected or appointed) VP is serving as acting president. The Constitution should also specify that the VP, while serving as acting president, cannot also chair and caste tie-breaking votes in the Senate. There is one other arcane problem relating to the possibility that the Senate might not be able to select a VP in a contingent election due to lacking a quorum. But I leave that aside here, in order to turn to the urgent topic of how to get good amendment proposals sent on to the states.

Chapter Four

HOW TO PASS THE AMENDMENTS: A NEW CONSTITUTIONAL CONVENTION

I. A New Hope

We now have before us a far-reaching agenda to revitalize our nation's government through improving its constitutional superstructure. Taken together, the 25 Democracy Amendments form a road map to a much brighter future for all Americans. While this agenda hardly includes every constitutional issue worth considering, it addresses the main flaws that are driving polarization, gridlock, and creeping corruption in Washington, D.C. These constitutional flaws are the roots of inefficiency and ineffectiveness that are eroding people's faith in our national legislature, our elections, and even our capacity to stand up to foreign tyrants who peddle the lie that dictatorship is better than democracy.

To reverse these trends requires us to renovate the Constitution: lesser reforms will not be nearly enough. And there is already a lot of consensus among experts on most of the 25 constitutional fixes described in this book. The big remaining question is how to get such a process moving. That is the topic of this chapter.

At first, this task may appear impossible: *how*, when Congress is so broken, could it pass even simple amendments with the widest popular support—like an 18-year Supreme Court term (#9), or a rotating primary calendar (#2), or universal civics education for democratic citizenship (#10)? Majorities of 2/3rds in both the House and the Senate are normally needed to propose amendments to the states for ratification, and our two major parties seem unlikely to loosen their stranglehold by accepting open party primaries (#3) or limits to gerrymandering (#4), let alone cut off the special interest campaign funding to which they are so addicted (#5).

For example, if the Senate cannot pass basic national voting standards with a 60% margin to clear the filibuster, how could it ever pass constitutional voting rights (#6) by a 66.7% margin? Even impeachment and congressional oversight have been politicized, and clearly today's Congress could not pass the D.C. Voting Rights amendment that was approved by more than 2/3rds of both chambers in 1978 (see #11). As for the Electoral College and Senate reform, forget it. The Senate cannot even muster 51 votes to end the filibuster by changing the Senate's internal rules. So the very problems that we most urgently need to fix also make bipartisan compromise on amendments impossible in Congress. It looks like the brain within our body politic is so ill that it will refuse to take any of the medicines it needs to survive.

These counsels of defeatism seem to have a lot of evidence in their favor, but they forget three crucial facts:

- Our current options for legal amendment, as flawed as Article V is, include the never-used possibility of calling *a new national convention* to consider and propose amendments for consideration by the states (not to be confused with the option of state conventions to *ratify* proposed amendments passed by Congress or by a national convention).
- Many states have already passed (unrescinded) calls for a national convention. At least 29 states have passed such a resolution,[1] and we may be close to the required two-thirds threshold (34 states), depending on how the House Judiciary Committee decides to count these applications—whenever it gets moving on the issue.
- There is a huge untapped appetite across the country for fundamental reform, which could constructively seize on the convention idea as a way around the roadblocks in Congress.[2]

For these reasons and more, I agree with the centrist reformers Larry Lessig and Larry Sabato that the possibility of a new convention is great cause for hope. The founders included this convention option to provide states a way to act when Congress stalls, and that is precisely our situation today. If amendments are attempted one by one in Congress, each in turn will be defeated by wealthy single-issue lobbies with vested interests in status quo. By contrast, such entrenched interests would have far less sway over a convention of delegates who are not professional politicians and who are elected only for this one extraordinary historical purpose (see #25 §V (ii)). Likewise, if a convention proposed several amendments to the states at once, it would be much harder for special interest lobbies to kill them all.

Still, constitutional change seems scary to many Americans. That's partly because, as Sandy Levinson notes, the "iron cage" of Article V distorts our interpretation of the situation: "citizens are encouraged to believe that change" in constitutional law "is almost never desirable, let alone necessary." Surely, people think, it must be safer to make do with the system we have?[3] It is a classic case of "adaptive preferences:" people lower their aspirations in the face of apparently inevitable abuse and tell themselves it will be okay.

It was different in the 1970s when the drive for the Equal Rights Amendment inspired so many Americans. Today, a broad social movement for a new convention can wake people up from the self-defeating illusion that amendments are not needed. The key is to reignite the faith that we can break this iron cage and forge a much better system. The next two sections explain the reasons for a convention in more detail and answer popular misunderstandings that can cause people to shun the convention option.[4]

II. The Many Potent Advantages of a National Convention

Here it would be well to recall the three stages that any constitutional change involves under our current law (see Figure 3.8) and clarify some terminology. (i) *Resolutions* for constitutional amendments must work their way through Congress or a new national convention called by the states. (ii) When an amendment resolution is passed either by Congress or by a national convention, it is formally *proposed* to the states. Only when such a proposed amendment is ratified by most of our states is it *approved* as valid law and adopted as part of our Constitution. Clearly, this is not a quick process. That is why, among several hundred different amendments that have been introduced in Congress over the centuries, only 33 amendments have been passed by Congress, and only 27 adopted.

Thus, while serious movement toward a new constitutional convention would doubtless trigger fears simply because that process is so unfamiliar to Americans, it is simply an alternative and potentially more efficient way of doing steps (i) and (ii). A convention is expected to propose particular changes, not to write a whole new constitution this time around. And its advantages will be clear and compelling once reform-minded leaders explain them to the American people. Precisely because there has not been national convention here for over 235 years, the novelty will make it abundantly obvious that this is not "politics as usual."

And therein lies its main promise: despite the fears that calling a convention may initially trigger, the prospect of a convention can eventually become a natural magnet for the hopes cherished by so many Americans. These aspirations for a better nation have found no viable outlet for decades within our discouraging election processes and degrading partisan mudslinging matches. But in anticipation of a national convention, silent majorities may discover their voice. The surge of popular interest could overwhelm the political forces that today constrain public aspirations and channel them into forms that only serve elite interests. Consider all these points in favor of the convention method:

- If 34 states call a new convention, it would create a new era in US politics, a "teachable moment" like none other: in our schools, colleges, and across society, a deep national conversation about ideas for amendments would radically improve citizens' understanding of the difficulties we face and build reform momentum.
- While extremists will try to control those conversations and bend them in inflammatory directions, the stakes could motivate many more people to talk across the political chasms that now divide us. Like several European nations, we could set up "citizen juries," chosen by lottery, to discuss amendment proposals with experts and report their findings before convention delegates are elected.[5] The prospect of a new convention would also motivate very high-turnout elections for delegates and state legislative seats, which entails much greater influence by moderate voters.
- A convention can act *much faster* than Congress as a means to propose amendments to the states for ratification. Even when a very popular amendment is proposed in Congress, its opponents can beat it by stalling and delaying final votes on it for years, until new crises dominate the headlines. This is exactly what senators did to the amendment for direct election of the president in the years between Nixon's first election and 1979 (see #12).[6] By contrast, a convention can strike while the iron is hot without all the arcane rules in Congress that enable delay.
- A convention is a procedure, not an outcome. As Lessig emphasizes, different people can agree on the need for a convention to pursue fundamental reform without agreeing on all or even most of the needed amendments: they can trust a convention to work out good proposals reflecting the rich debates leading up to the convention.
- A convention provides a clear route for people to turn their deep anger at our federal government into something constructive. A convention is a far better basis for hope than desperation to believe dishonest and extreme leaders. If a convention succeeds to any significant extent, this could restore trust in a reformed federal government and make subsequent reforms that rebuild loyalty easier.
- To assure their independence from ordinary political incentives, Congress could require that convention delegates not be government officials and remain legally barred from employment in government or with registered lobbies after a convention concludes its work (see #25 §V). If such delegates can each bring one expert with them, gathering some of the best political minds of our time together under a call to transcend party politics, it could become in effect the greatest citizen jury process ever attempted.
- A convention can and should look more holistically at the many flaws in our federal system. In the past, at least since 1800, our Congress has always addressed only one issue needing solution by amendment at a time. Now it is doubtful that Congress could even do that much: it may never pass another amendment resolution on fundamental problems until the House and Senate themselves are fixed by another method.
- While considering several ideas for institutional renewal at once, a convention can broker big compromises by *combining into a single amendment* provisions more favored by the left and provisions more favored by the right. For example, imagine direct

election of the president bundled with a budget control amendment like #22. So a convention has much more potential to break logjams that would stymie efforts to move amendments through today's Congress.

- Unlike Congress, a convention is *one body*, not two. And unlike Congress, it does not need to reach agreement by two-thirds of delegates. While a convention could run in different ways, the original 1787 convention finalized each of its proposals—after much negotiation—by a *simple majority* of states present. Reusing that procedure or a modest variation of it (see #25 §V) would enable more promising ideas to reach the ratification stage.
- Delegates, immersed in the awesome sense of continuing in the footsteps of the original convention, would feel *a weight of history* on them far exceeding anything that members of Congress experience, even in very important votes. Knowing that students would learn of their deeds for generations to come, delegates would be under tremendous pressure to come up with innovative solutions and to produce substantive results for their country. While of course a convention might fail, delegates will have very strong incentives to devise and pass significant amendment resolutions with decent chances of being ratified.
- The same points apply to state ratifying conventions (so Congress should choose that method). State conventions are one body and can ratify proposed amendments by a single simple majority vote. Although 75% of states is a very high threshold to clear, there would be significant pressure to ratify at least some of the national convention's proposals so the whole experiment did not come to naught. And states might even make deals with each other to ratify some of the proposals in one batch.
- Unlike the 1787 convention, the new convention would not feel the need to settle all the hardest issues in one go. It could, for example, propose 10 amendments to the states for ratification, while noting another 10 topics on which there was not yet enough consensus. With this example goading them, members of Congress might then pick up where the convention left off, and pass one or two more amendment proposals by the currently required 2/3^{rds} margin.
- And, with some amendments ratified after a first round, as success generates a national mood of good feelings, statehouses could feel emboldened to call another convention within a decade or two in order to build on the progress recently made. In the second round, a convention might even propose changes to Article V to improve the amendment process itself (see #25).

Given all these factors, it is very likely that a convention could at least pass some of the "lowest-hanging fruit" amendments we have considered. These probably include

- the primary election rotation, and perhaps semi-open or top-four primaries;
- the 18-year term on the Supreme Court and federal appellate courts;
- ranked choice voting (via instant runoff or Condorcet methods);
- limits to the pardon power;
- a robust civics and critical reasoning requirement in high school;
- good government reforms (#14–18);
- some limits on gerrymandering;

- new limits on lobbyists, campaign spending, and the role of corporations in elections;
- possibly the filibuster ban;
- standards for state emergencies and emergency powers; and
- probably a new Equal Rights Amendment (ERA—see the Interlude).

That is a lot: these reforms would effectively make us a new country. And, with hard work, better budget-making requirements, an expanded House, a new impeachment standard, and reforms to judicial review are also feasible. National commonsense voting standards, constitutional voting rights, and lowering thresholds for veto overrides may each be a little harder for a convention to propose, but certainly not impossible. Direct election of the president, Puerto Rico statehood, and congressional representation for DC would certainly be more controversial, but they could be combined with things that many conservatives want. Highest on their list is the balanced budget proposal, perhaps followed by some modest change to birthright citizenship or a chance for states to influence the agenda in Congress (see #21).

A convention that accomplished even half this much would be well worth our while. Although improving the amendment process (#25) and fixing the Senate (#24) are extremely important, they may have to wait for later rounds once initial success builds goodwill and renews public confidence in our political processes. The main thing is to establish the precedent that a national convention can jump-start deep reform. We need a broader bipartisan movement to convince Americans that a convention is both desperately needed and safe for them and their families.

III. Why You Should Not Fear a Convention: "Runaway" Fallacies

Yet whenever the idea of holding a new convention has come up on the fringes of political news in the US, terror seems to be the main response. Many hysterical op-eds about a "runaway convention" are easily found online, and even normally sensible proponents of moderate reforms concoct wild fantasies of a convention somehow staging a Jacobin revolution. For example, Common Cause wails, ludicrously, that "a convention is a dangerous path that puts all of our cherished rights, civil liberties, and freedoms at risk."[7]

Perhaps they have seen *V for Vendetta* one too many times, but the critics all seem to have forgotten that *a new national convention cannot make any changes to the Constitution by itself.* This key point cannot be stressed enough: a convention can only propose amendments, just as Congress does, which then have to be ratified by 38 states in order to be adopted (or 39 once Puerto Rico becomes a state). Amendments repealing basic civil liberties, turning the United States into a monarchy, outlawing handguns, banning all abortions, reinstituting slavery or segregation,[8] uniting us with Canada or Mexico, or declaring martial law are certainly not going to pass a convention (all these preposterous predictions and more have been made by citizens misled by irresponsible bloggers and sectarian pundits). But even if somehow an extreme amendment such as "banning Islam" or massive "reparation" payments for slavery *did* get through a convention, it would easily be defeated by thirteen or more states. Lessig puts it bluntly: "[t]here are easily thirteen red states and thirteen blue states in America today," as should be obvious from our last five presidential elections.

It is critical for the nation that politicians, columnists, political action groups, and teachers stop stoking terror at the prospect of a national convention and explain clearly that a convention would simply substitute for Congress' familiar role in the amendment process. It helps no one, especially in an era rife with destructive conspiracy theories, to turn the safety valve bequeathed by our founders into a Rorschach card onto which people project their most apocalyptic fears.

The "runaway convention" lingo also confuses even sober citizens who understand the very high threshold to ratify amendments. (a) For years, "runaway" was a pejorative label for a convention through which the people would exercise revolutionary constituent power "outside the normal legal system" established by Article V.[9] Never mind that our original 1787 convention succeeded only by "running away" from the prior Articles of Confederation in precisely this (correct) sense. But the national convention I'm proposing would operate *under* our current Article V processes.

More recently though, opinion columns have started using the scary "runaway" label for a convention that would not propose any revolutionary methods of amendment ratification, but merely reserve the deliberative right to consider a range of options for improving existing constitutional law. For example, the *Economist* noted that a convention called by states that want a balanced budget amendment might "widen its ambit and consider other amendments too," thereby becoming a "Pandora's Box."[10]

This mistake originated as a talking point pushed by fringe groups who *want* us to conflate a revolutionary convention with one merely featuring open discourse: by tarring the latter with the "runaway" label, they hope to confuse voters and get a convention that can only discuss *their* specific grievances.[11] Nothing in Article V implies such a perverse power to dramatically restrict a convention's purview, or to muzzle its delegates. And a convention meeting to consider constitutional problems in general does not thereby become some sort of monstrous "runaway" danger: again, its proposals become law only with the support of 3/4 of states.

So don't fall for the "runaway" rhetorical trick. The whole point of a convention is to take a wide inventory of our Constitution's many deep flaws, and that is exactly what the 1787 convention did. Why then lament that "a convention would be impossible to control"[12]—as if it would be *desirable* to prevent delegates from going where reason, expert testimony, polling, citizen jury recommendations, and concerns rooted in their own life experiences naturally lead their discussions? Delegates in convention should be "controlled" by the needs and experiences of their communities and the merits of good arguments—not by statehouse cronies writing a convention call resolution. A convention offers hope precisely *because* its agenda cannot be monopolized by one special interest group that owns a lot of state legislators.

Consider the parallel: when we elect members of Congress, they have always been able to discuss *any* ideas for constitutional amendment that come up. They are not bound by narrow instructions from their state to talk only about amendment ideas concerning (say) voting rights or rights of the unborn. We do not decry a "runaway Congress" and announce the end of days because members of Congress consider, debate, or vote on an amendment resolution that was not prescripted in their state capitols.

If anything, a convention is supposed to have more, not less, leeway than Congress to think broadly about fundamental reforms, because it is closer to the people's original constituent authority (see Desideratum 8). That was the view of most delegates at the 1787 convention, and the same applies today: a convention should be able to *propose* several amendments that garner enough support among delegates. That still leaves states free to accept or reject them.

As we have seen, our main problem today is ossification, not rapid and radical institutional change. Compared to a nearly frozen Congress, it would be refreshing for the nation if a convention "ran" quickly to some bold amendment initiatives for states to consider. So let's address the fears motivating all the incoherent and counterproductive "runaway" talk. They have three main roots.

(1) First, people understandably worry that our political bonds are too fragile to undergo the strains that constitutional reform would involve right now. This is "the wrong time" for a convention to meet, critics say, when Americans are already so deeply divided—as if the "right time" would be when there is peace on Earth, moderation reigns across the nation, most politicians seek consensus, and a godlike gathering of wise statespersons can meet to calmly contemplate constitutional reforms free of all partisan pressures.

This view sets up a hopeless and unnecessary precondition: the original convention met in a period of very deep unrest when the 13 original states were not far from splitting into three or four regional nations. The period when amendments were passed during and soon after the Civil War was even worse. During the Progressive Era, amendments also responded to great social upheavals, including steeply rising economic inequality due to industrialization. And the 1960s and 1970s, when our latest valid amendments (and two unratified proposals) passed Congress, could hardly be mistaken for an era of social peace, no turmoil, and national harmony.

In fact, then, progress in improving constitutional law is usually the child of deep polarization, civil strife, and crisis. It is precisely these existential perils that compel reflective people to recognize that structural change is needed to counter the forces that are tearing the social fabric apart. As I argued, many people have been driven toward their current extremism because they see no way to get needed changes through debate and fair elections. Refusing to call a convention is only going to make this civic illness get worse, not better, leading to an increasing risk of mass violence or even new illegal secessions.

By contrast, the prospect of a convention meeting would offer more radicalized Americans today a different and much more constructive route that can bring their moderate fellow citizens into the process *en mass*. Despite being bitterly divided on many issues, a majority of Americans actually want an off-ramp from our bitter political divisions, and this will be the main motive to make a convention work. By contrast, the demand that we wait for an era of calm and consensus is obviously self-defeating.

(2) Yet many Americans have only seen the call for an Article V convention coning from ultraconservative groups like the so-called convention of states movement associated with Governor Greg Abbott. These groups, following a fervent faith in state

governments way beyond anything the evidence warrants, propose extreme amendments that would drastically slash the federal government's ability to secure national public goods.[13] But the misimpression that a convention could only be a vehicle for such right-wing fanaticism is also the fault of more progressive and moderate reformers who have quit this field, rather than developing better visions for a national convention. Excepting Levinson, Lessig, Sabato, and a few others, they have let ultra-right groups equate the convention option in general with Abbott's narrow and destructive agenda for it.[14]

This is tactically foolish: by investing in the convention option, liberals and centrists could steer it to address their concerns, raise grassroots movements to educate citizens and state legislators, and work for state ballot initiatives to apply for a broad convention to audit all our constitutional deficiencies. Why cede this invaluable ground to their opponents on the far right? It would be much better to engage positively with the prospect of a national convention rather than to let one fringe movement define it.

(3) This brings us to the third cause of doubt, namely that a convention would be a "dangerous gamble" because existing law does not make clear how a convention would work. Article V requires Congress to organize a convention when 2/3^{rds} of states (34 at present) call for one. But Congress has never passed a detailed statute pursuant to Article V to make clear how delegates should be chosen and paid, how a convention's rules should be determined, where and when they would meet, and so on. What happens, then, if 34 states call for a convention and Congress adopts no resolution to enable it (perhaps because one chamber refuses)? Presumably the Supreme Court would then step in (which is far from ideal).

This objection at least has a valid basis: I described the procedural uncertainties about a convention when considering how to improve Article V itself (see #25). But until that is done, it is up to Congress to set the terms of a national convention. I address this in the next section.

However, this much should be clear already: states calling for a convention, or Congress acting in response, have no right to try to rig the convention's entire agenda in advance—in either *inclusive* or *exclusive* ways. It is one thing to say that when it meets, a convention must address the various issues mentioned in state resolutions applying for a convention (I allowed for this in #25 §V (vi)). It is another thing entirely to say that a convention can *only* discuss one or two issues handpicked by state governments or Congress, and nothing else that delegates may regard as important to consider may be mentioned, proposed, or voted on.

Such an un-American gag rule would be a disaster. It would hamstring the convention in ways likely to doom its efforts by denying delegates any leeway to negotiate. The term "limited convention" does not really convey the level of micromanagement that advocates of pre-rigging have in mind. It takes a rare and shocking kind of arrogance to think that the most elevated and august of all bodies in a democracy, a constitutional convention, should be a mere puppet of state officials—or lobbyists for the interest groups that control those officials. Like a "fixed" ball game, such a convention would rightly be seen as a travesty by most Americans. Washington, Madison, Hamilton, Wilson, Franklin, Sherman and other leaders in the original convention refused that kind of absurd limitation, and so should we.

Moreover, a coercive approach to a convention's agenda would backfire. For example, a convention that discussed only a libertarian wish list would rightly be seen as a highly offensive attempt to censor all discussion of ideas from the left and center. Such an abortive convention could kill our last, best chance of renewing civic solidarity through working out fundamental constitutional compromises. The resulting sense of unfairness could permanently destroy faith that a convention could help us move forward as a nation. I conclude that liberals, centrists, and sensible conservatives need to join forces to insist on the plenary authority of convention delegates to shape their own agenda in response to the demonstrated needs, hopes, concerns, and dreams of all Americans.

In sum, we have nothing to lose and everything to gain from attempting to make an open-agenda convention work. We should not be deterred by the "untried" status of this procedure. Forming a republic by convention was an untested gamble when our founders took it in 1787, just as fighting a civil war in order to uphold the principles of democracy and freedom was a huge risk for Lincoln and northern states. We know a lot more about political science now, so the risks are much lower for us, even given the nation's troubled condition. Should we, then, be unwilling to meet the test of our time, and instead keep trying in vain to make a hopelessly broken system work, while trust in our institutions erodes further year after year?

One familiar definition of insanity is attempting the same thing over and over, even though it stopped working long ago. In our situation, calling a convention is the only sane and legal alternative left. Indeed, the unfamiliarity of a convention is one of its many advantages: it may be just the shock that we need to waken people from their social media–induced dogmatism and compel them to think critically for themselves about the nation's long-term future. The time for bold action is now.

IV. How, Then, Should a National Convention Work?

A convention called by 34 or more states, I have argued, should certainly consider topics mentioned in state applications for a new convention, but not *only* these topics. For the good of the nation, Congress should ignore any attempt by states to condition their calls for a convention upon exercising militant control over a convention's topics.

As I indicated, the one precedent we have from 1787 amply demonstrates the need for flexibility to deliberate on any issues and possible solutions that delegates see fit to raise. As Wilson and Pinckney argued, the original convention could recommend "whatever they found necessary to remedy the evils" in the existing system.[15] A constitutional convention should be the closest *legal* body we have to the people at large, and it should therefore be as unencumbered as possible. A pre-scripted convention of marionette delegates is the exact opposite of what the founders intended when writing Article V.

So, when a new convention meets, delegates should act just as Madison, Wilson, Sherman, Franklin, and their colleagues did: introduce the concerns and priorities of the people who sent them, but be willing to learn from each other and to forge new compromises. They should absolutely reject attempts by states, Congress, or even the Supreme Court[16] to treat them like robots and thereby prevent real deliberation, negotiation, and (yes) even grand bargains.

In American history, state conventions meeting to rewrite their state constitutions have also assumed this "plenary" freedom in discussion and ignored manipulative attempts to predetermine their eventual proposals. That is not surprising, because the civic republican ideal of representative government has always recognized that representatives must serve as trustees of the common good, who are elected to reason together about what the nation's collective interests require. Delegates to a national convention must be elected trustees in this sense, who are able to consider many viewpoints, review the deepest flaws in our system, and combine proposals in ways that increase chances of ratification. These are precisely the advantages that a convention has over Congress, and they depend on delegates being more than mere messengers delivering imperious ultimatums from statehouses.

Beyond this bedrock republican principle, however, many other procedural questions remain for Congress to settle. My proposal #25 §IV and §V provide a road map for a sound convention process, but seven further details are needed to reassure everyone that a convention can be well structured and productive rather than chaotic.

(1) First of all, given the monumental importance that a new national convention would have, the government should be required to be transparent about where the tally stands in state applications. Right now, it is very difficult to get that information, and this is terrible.[17] It could lead people to suspect that the House Judiciary Committee is trying to suppress the tally to keep it out of the news.

(2) The unjust pressure by some state legislatures to pre-fix the convention agenda could also give the House or the Senate an excuse to say that the threshold has not been met even when more than 34 states have submitted resolutions calling for a convention. How? Congress may use the lame excuse that 34 states have not submitted *exactly identical* call resolutions: 20, perhaps, have called for a convention to consider a balanced budget amendment (or this plus term limits); another 10 have called for a convention to overturn *Citizens United* (see #5); 3 more to end the Electoral College; and a couple others simply to hold a convention to address the nation's needs—making 35 in all, but not 34 for any one narrowly defined topic. This is another self-defeating result of the ultra-arrogant pre-rigging approach. It makes it virtually impossible ever to get to the required two-thirds threshold to call a convention.

In fact, it looks like this is already happening. By my count in mid-2022, there were unrescinded applications for a convention on a range of different topics from at least 36 different states on the Clerk of the House's webpage, counting from the 1977 Massachusetts call for a convention to consider an amendment to allow public funding of secular education in private schools.[18] Putting off a convention by insisting on identical narrow applications creates yet another obstacle and feeds misunderstanding. Congress should instead exercise its discretion under Article V, combine the applications, and call for a general national convention now.

(3) Lessig is correct that convention delegates should not be drawn from our political class. I suggest (see #25 §V) that delegates should not hold, or have recently held, any job in federal or state government, and they should be barred from serving

in government or registered lobbies for a decade after serving in the convention.[19] Delegates definitely should not be appointed by state officials: they should be chosen in a nonpartisan special election—or perhaps selected by lottery from among an elected pool—within each state.[20] With history in mind, voters should look for leaders across all parts of civil society—people with wisdom, life-experience, proven dedication to their communities, and concern for the future, who come from outside the political and donor classes. Hopes for a convention would rise if people saw that convention delegates will not be typical politicians, lobbyists, or corporate lawyers.

(4) I have suggested that states elect between 1 and 5 delegates each, depending on their populations, plus two alternates (#25 §V). This matters less if final passage of amendment proposals in the convention occurs by a simple majority of state *delegations*, as was the case in 1787. But, given how dramatically population differences between states have increased (to over 68-1 now), it would be smarter and fairer to allow amendments to be passed out of the convention by a vote of 60% of individual delegates, *as well* as by a majority of state delegations.

Congress should establish such an apportionment of delegates among the states, and rules for the convention to follow, as an effective compromise between the bigger and smaller states. Each delegation should also be allowed to bring one or two nonvoting experts with them, with full funding from Congress. But Congress should also include rules that try to prevent delegates directly profiting from any decision reached by the convention.

(5) One of the most successful features of the 1787 convention was its being *closed* or shielded from the public eye. Like a sequestered jury, this meant delegates could really debate and horse-trade with the freedom afforded by privacy. This would be hard with today's mobile devices, but Congress should insist on protecting the convention's secrecy for as long as it lasts (which should have some cap, such as nine months). The budget allotted to it should provide for measures to seal the proceedings—including a provision to expel any delegate who leaks information, who would then be replaced by an alternate. The jury model is the right one to follow.

(6) Beyond these structural parameters established by Congress, the convention should set its own rules, starting from standard Robert's Rules with provisions to call the question after long discussion of an issue. Each delegation should have the right to demand at least a few hours of discussion on its most favored one or two amendment ideas.

How to decide who chairs the convention from its first day is a hard question. Perhaps a former Chairman of the Joint Chiefs of Staff could follow in Washington's footsteps: our chiefs are still held in higher esteem by more Americans than any political leader. The Chief Justice is also an option. But the delegates could, within a few days, elect one of their number as a (voting) chair, if anyone could get support from 2/3^{rds} of those present or more. They should also select leaders among themselves who can help to build strong majorities for amendment proposals. Obviously, the closer the convention comes to unanimity on any resolution, the greater moral force that proposal will have.

(7) The convention's proposals should be sent *directly* to the states. Article V does not allow Congress to block any of the amendment resolutions passed by the convention,

or to add extra conditions to them, such as a time window for ratification. And there is no reason to add any additional hurdles to the hardest amendment procedure that exists in any democratic nation.[21] Congress may decide whether the convention's proposals are ratified by state legislatures or by state conventions, but no more.

As noted earlier, state ratification conventions are better because, unlike most state legislatures, each is a single body. But Congress should specify that no delegate who served at the national convention (non-serving alternates excepted) should be electable to their state's subsequent ratifying convention. It would be best to keep current state legislators and state officers out as well. Finally, if the national convention specifies any time limit on ratification at all, then in view of experience with the ERA, it should set a limit of around 15–20 years to maximize the chance of success.

V. Conclusion

In this recipe for a new constitutional convention, we have a promising way to move forward with a comprehensive agenda to renew the United States. We should have no illusions: this is not an easy path to travel. I can offer only toil for those who are determined to ensure that this republic built by Washington, Lincoln, Susan B. Anthony, Martin Luther King, and all others who have served it in myriad capacities over the generations, shall not perish or collapse in hostilities. One civil war was enough.

But there is a silver lining: in our present situation, even partial success through a convention would be a godsend. If a handful of constructive amendments coming from a convention were ratified, future Americans would look back at that moment as a new birth of democracy, social progress, and economic advancement. More constitutional changes would then follow in their wake, as an era of fundamental reform dawned.

Imagine the effect if the national convention, after months of hard work, announced twelve proposed amendments under the title of a Bill of Democracy, to parallel the original Bill of Rights, introduced with the following preamble:

> We the People of the United States of America, in Convention Assembled, in order to form *a more democratic union*, establish ideals of civic virtue, extend the grounds of public confidence in our officers and elections, and restore the integrity and effectiveness of our federal government, do here highly resolve that the following amendments to the Constitution of the United States be proposed to the several states for their consideration and ratification. We do this for the sake of our posterity and to honor the sacrifices of all who have died defending the cause of freedom, which remains the hope of the whole world.

Only such a Bill of Democracy can fulfill the sacred duties incumbent on all of us who have inherited the blessings of republican government from our forefathers and foremothers. Only by ratifying the amendments needed to save this nation for the generations to come can we earn our place with the millions who have given the last full measure of devotion so that we might all live in a democratic land. Then, even in their mighty company at last, we may not feel ashamed.

ENDNOTES

NB: In these notes, organization websites are italicized like journals and book titles, although these organizations may also be considered publishers. Place of publication is omitted, and urls are included only when an electronic article is not easy to find with a simple internet search. But a **complete bibliography** with a full set of links can be found on the book's online extension at *TheDemocracyAmendments.org.*

Preface

1 See Christopher Phillips' findings in *Constitution Café: Jefferson's Brew for a True Revolution* (W. W. Norton, 2012).
2 In *A League of Democracies*, ch. 2, I analyze this "Consolidation Principle" and the related "Democratic Principle of Legitimacy" as the two key premises at work in the *Federalist* authors' arguments for a new federal government.
3 By contrast, I use "framers" to include leaders involved in shaping constitutional law throughout American history.
4 See the introduction to "The Conservative Constitution," *National Constitution Center* Drafting Project: constitutioncenter.org/debate/special-projects/constitution-drafting-project.
5 For example, see James Fishkin's work on this topic, such as *When the People Speak* (Oxford University Press, 2011 pb).
6 Sanford Levinson, "Symposium on the Democracy Constitution: What Is This Project Anyway?" *Democracy Journal* 61 (Summer 2021).

Chapter 1

1 Jamie Raskin, *Unthinkable: Trauma, Truth and the Trials of American Democracy* (HarperCollins, 2022), p. 89; Kim Parker, Rich Morin, and Juliana Horowitz, "Looking to the Future, Public Sees an America in Decline on Many Fronts," *Pew Research Center* (Mar. 21, 2019).
2 Lincoln's "Fragment on the Constitution and Union," in Mario Cuomo and Harold Holzer, eds., *Lincoln on Democracy* (HarperCollins, 1990), p. 188.
3 Yoni Appelbaum, "America's Fragile Constitution," *The Atlantic* (Oct. 15, 2015), pp. 20–23.
4 Joel Hirschhorn, *Delusional Democracy* (Common Courage Press, 2006), pp. 46–47.
5 Jennifer McCoy, "What Happens When Democracies Become Perniciously Polarized?" *Carnegie Endowment for International Peace* (Jan. 18, 2022).
6 Clayton Park and Dave Berman, "In Florida, Rebuild – Then Repeat?" *USA Today* (Oct. 18, 2022), pp. A1, A4. In technical terms, we are allowing Floridians to "externalize" onto the rest of us the growing risk costs they decide to run by living in uninsured homes in vulnerable areas.
7 See the history of climate legislation at www.c2es.org/content/congress-climate-history/.
8 See the damning assessment by conservative Hoover Institute scholar Larry Diamond in his *Ill Winds* (Penguin Press, 2019), ch. 6.

9 The estimate by Pew Research in 2020 was roughly 10.5 million; see www.pewresearch.org/fact-tank/2020/08/20/key-findings-about-u-s-immigrants/.

10 Alice Rivlin, *Divided We Fall: Why Consensus Matters* (Brookings Institution Press, 2022), p. 1.

11 Daniel Immerwahr, "The Strange Sad Death of America's Political Imagination," *The New York Times* [Special Opinion section] (Nov. 7, 2021), p. 4.

12 Luke Broadwater, "Maryland Governor Plans Book Tour," *The New York Times* (July 8, 2002), p. A21.

13 The term "public goods" refers to products, services, or outcomes that involve economic externalities (impacts on parties outside voluntary transactions), nonrival or nonexcludable goods, information asymmetries, and ethically important values that consumer demand alone does not adequately measure. See my *A League of Democracies* (Routledge, 2018), chs. 2–3.

14 Ezekiel Kweku, "Snap Out of It, America," Introduction to *The New York Times* [Special Opinion section] (Nov. 7, 2021), p. 3.

15 For a history of Clinton's success and the subsequent failure of bipartisan efforts to keep the federal budget balanced, see Rivlin, *Divided We Fall*, chs. 6–9.

16 David Litt, *Democracy in One Book or Less* (HarperCollins, 2020), pp. 300–02.

17 See the records tracked at ourpublicservice.org/political-appointee-tracker/.

18 Appelbaum, defending Juan Linz's work, in "Our Fragile Constitution."

19 Geoff Hing et al. "How private money helped save the election," *American Public Media* (Dec. 7, 2020).

20 For details, see Lawrence Lessig, *Republic, Lost* (Twelve/Hachette Books, 2011), pp. 97–98.

21 See the Pew Research study of 2016 turnout at tinyurl.com/2p8dj6zk.

22 John Holbein and Sunshine Hillygus, "Young People Want to Vote. So How Do We Get Them to The Polls?" *Forbes* (Apr. 7, 2020).

23 Gerald Seib, "How Political Dysfunction Gave Rise to Trump," *The Wall Street Journal* (May 10, 2016), p. A4.

24 Max Greenwood, "Trump calls for end to filibuster," *The Hill* (May 30, 2017); compare Rivlin, *Divided We Fall*, pp. 10–11.

25 "White supremacy" has a valid usage. For over a century, racial "supremacism" has referred to the belief that some racial groups are genetically superior to others.

26 Rachel Kleinfeld, "Five Strategies to Support US Democracy," *Carnegie Endowment for International Peace* (Sept. 15, 2022), p. 3; see carnegieendowment.org/2022/09/15/five-strategies-to-support-u.s.-democracy-pub-87918.

27 On the racialization of more issues, see Robert Mickey, Steven Levitsky, and Lucan Ahmad Way, "Is America Still Safe for Democracy?" *Foreign Affairs* 96, no. 3 (May/June 2017), p. 25, citing Michael Tesler's work.

28 This chart is from a Pew Research Center report of the same name (Aug. 9, 2022): tinyurl.com/238and9a.

29 See the June 2021 NPR coverage at tinyurl.com/yuubnca9.

30 For shocking examples, see Robert Draper, *Weapons of Mass Delusion* (Penguin Press, 2022), ch. 10.

31 Kleinfeld, "Five Strategies to Support US Democracy," p. 2.

32 This is one of Raskin's apt points in *Unthinkable*, p. 414.

33 Nancy Isenberg, "Democracy's Thorn: The Mob and the Voice of the People," *The Hedgehog Review* (Summer 2021), pp. 90–100.

34 Jason Brennan believes that a tendency to hate people who vote differently than us, or to see them as enemies, is essential to democratic politics: see Brennan, *Against Democracy* (Princeton University Press, 2017), pp. 39–44, chs. 3 and 9. I believe that this tendency, while found in any dynamic with a 'rival teams' aspect, can be greatly moderated or exaggerated, depending on the system's structure. Our flawed design explains the recent dramatic rise in political hatred in the US.

35 As Kleinfeld points out, 75% of Republican House members and senators have been replaced since 2008, in most cases, by extreme partisans; and 21% of "Republican state legislators have joined extremist social media groups:" see "Five Strategies to Support US Democracy," pp. 3–4; compare Draper, *Weapons of Mass Delusion*, chs. 17–22.
36 Mickey et al., "Is America Still Safe for Democracy?" p. 24.
37 Kleinfeld cites data suggesting that 85%–90% of Americans would support "antidemocratic action by their side to keep the other out of power," and 11% (!) even supported assassination: see "Five Strategies to Support US Democracy," pp. 7–8. In other words, the implicit social contract that holds the US together is crumbling.
38 For example, after the fiscal stimulus bill in early 2009, the Affordable Care Act was arguably Obama's only major legislative achievement. Likewise, the (non-filibusterable) tax cuts and lower cap on state and local tax deductions passed in December 2017 was Trump's only big legislative win. Compare Rivlin, *Divided We Fall*, pp. 9–10, pp.19–20.
39 There are many sources on this topic, but see Noah Smith's opinion piece on *Bloomberg.com*, which is publicly available on a Cornell blog at blogs.cornell.edu/info2040/2017/09/13/game-theory-and-our-two-party-system/.
40 Joseph Fishkin and William Forbath, "Make Progressive Politics Constitutional Again," *The Boston Review* (May 23, 2022), p. 5; compare their book, *The Anti-Oligarchy Constitution* (Harvard University Press, 2022).
41 This was the consensus even though the importation of slaves was a complaint emphasized in Jefferson's first draft of the Declaration of Independence: see Garry Wills, *Inventing America* (Houghton Mifflin, 1978, 2002 repr.), ch. 15 and pp. 374–79.
42 Levinson, *Framed: America's Fifty-One Constitutions and the Crisis of Governance* (Oxford University Press, 2012), pp. 95–96.
43 See Adrienne Koch, *Jefferson and Madison* (Oxford University Press, 1964), ch. 4, citing Jefferson's letter of September 6, 1789.
44 In particular, it appears that Jefferson felt the contradiction between his principles and slavery; see Danielle Allen's brilliant analysis in *Our Declaration* (W. W. Norton, 2014). Despite not freeing his own slaves, in 1783 Jefferson proposed that Virginia's constitution should include a law that everyone born after the year 1800 would be free. Also see ch. 2 note 211.
45 Kweku, "Snap Out of It, America," p. 3.
46 AP-NORC, "The Link between Government Performance and Attitudes toward the U.S. Democratic System" (May 2019), at apnorc.org/projects/the-link-between-government-performance-and-attitudes-toward-the-u-s-democratic-system/.
47 Delegates, "A New Constitution for the United States," *Democracy Journal* 61 (Summer 2021): democracyjournal.org/magazine/61/a-new-constitution-for-the-united-states/.
48 See Jesse Wegman, *Let the People Pick the President* (St. Martin's Press, 2020), p. 241.
49 That is why even Stephen Douglas, hardly a pillar of moral virtue, was basically forced aside when he prevented the pro-slavery president James Buchanan and his faction in Congress from accepting a new constitution for Kansas that they all knew to be fraudulent (the "Lecompton constitution"). Douglas became in that respect the Liz Cheney of his day.
50 Akhil Amar, *America's Constitution* (Random House, 2006), pp. 442–44.
51 William Hudson, *American Democracy in Peril*, 6th ed. (CQ Press, 2010), ch. 1.
52 See ch. 2 note 83 for a quick explanation.
53 See Hélène Landemore, *Open Democracy* (Princeton University Press, 2020).
54 This approach is also reflected in the WeAmend.us project.
55 Several state constitutions included almost every item in the US Bill of Rights, sometimes with slightly more detail. A good example is Pennsylvania's first constitution of September 1776, which began with a 980 word declaration of rights.
56 Steven Taylor, Matthew Shugart, Arend Lijphart, and Bernard Grofman, *A Different Democracy: American Government in a Thirty-One Country Perspective* (Yale University Press, 2014), pp. 127.
57 Levinson, *Framed*, pp. 112, 213.

58 This desideratum is not a general principle for deciding which issues should be "constitutionalized." That depends, in my view, on which public goods cannot be secured without the greater stability of constitutional law – and how stable such law is (which is a function of amendment procedures, political culture, and more).

59 Compare Robert George et al., "The Conservative Constitution," which is one of three proposals hosted by the National Constitution Center's "Constitution Drafting Project" at constitutioncenter.org/media/files/The_Conservative_Constitution.pdf. They affirm that (a) the goal of the Constitution is the common good, (b) the people have a duty to each other to secure their equal rights, and (c) the authority of the Constitution derives from the people themselves.

60 Preamble of the Constitution of Pennsylvania (Sept. 28, 1776), *The Avalon Project*, avalon.law.yale.edu/18th_century/pa08.asp.

61 See Fergus Bordewich, *The First Congress* (Simon & Schuster, 2016), p. 89. This addition was proposed in Madison's first draft of the Bill of Rights but was not in the final version; see the National Constitution Center page on this topic at tinyurl.com/yc8nxj48. Arguably originary sovereignty is one of the unenumerated rights alluded to in the 9th Amendment. Compare Federalist 39 and 40, in *The Federalist Papers*, p. 242, p. 249.

62 See Jurgen Goossens, "Direct Democracy and Constitutional Change in the US," in *The Foundations and Traditions of Constitutional Amendment*, ed. Richard Albert et al. (Bloomsbury), pp. 343–68. For an excellent account of the Federalist/Whig interpretation of this history, see Garry Wills, *Lincoln at Gettysburg* (Simon & Schuster, 1992), ch. 4.

63 Catherine D. Bowen, *Miracle at Philadelphia* (Little, Brown & Co., 1966), p. 229; compare Farand, *The Framing of the Constitution* (Yale University Press, 1913, 1970 pb), p. 51.

64 See William Hogeland, *Declaration: Nine Tumultuous Weeks When America Became Independent* (Simon & Schuster, 2010).

Chapter 2

1 Thomas Mann and Nicholas Ornstein, *It's Even Worse than It Looks* (Basic Books, 2012), pp. 108–10.

2 Ibid, ch. 5.

3 Levinson, *Framed*, p. 239.

4 Even then, Senator Edward Kennedy was too ill to be present for votes, so the Democrats only had 60 senators from September 24 to January 2, while Paul Kirk was filling Kennedy's seat: see Kevin Jones, "About that Filibuster-Proof Majority," *Mother Jones* (Sept. 22, 2010).

5 Sam Wang and Ari Goldbloom-Helzner, "Why the Filibuster Suits the GOP Just Fine," *The Atlantic* (April 30, 2021). But the last time Republicans actually had 60 seats was in 1909–1911.

6 For an accessible introduction, see Sam Bucovestsky's course pages, including "Minimum Differentiation of Political Parties," at http://www.yorku.ca/bucovets/4080/choice/5.pdf.

7 See Lee Drutman, "America is Now the Divided Republic the Framer's Feared," *The Atlantic* (Jan. 2, 2020). Also, see his book, *Breaking the Two-Party Doom Loop* (Oxford University Press, 2019).

8 Taylor et al., *A Different Democracy*, p. 176.

9 Christopher Ingraham, "How to Fix Democracy: Move Beyond the Two-Party System, Experts Say," *Washington Post* (Mar. 1, 2021).

10 See Alex Keyssar, "It Pays to Win Small States," *The New York Times* (Nov. 20, 2000).

11 For the sake of simplicity, this illustration leaves out other minor parties that garnered a few thousand votes in the Florida presidential election of 2000.

12 Of course, in a real election, voters' second choices would have been more complex.

13 These include ballots on which people voted twice due to misleading instructions to "vote every page:" see the results of the thorough recount undertaken by a combination of major media outlets in 2001.

14 The figures are from https://www.nytimes.com/interactive/2022/11/08/us/elections/results-alaska.html; but a breakdown of the transferred votes is available on Alaska's official "RCV Detailed Report."
15 Levinson, *Framed*, p. 109.
16 Alternatively, some evidence suggests that Perot took votes from both candidates, and perhaps more from Clinton. Either way though, with 18.9% of the popular vote, Perot at least ensured that Clinton could only win with a plurality of 43% in the popular vote. In this case also, RCV would probably have produced an absolute majority for one candidate, or close to it.
17 Maggie Haberman, Danny Hakim, and Nick Corasaniti, "How Republicans Are Trying to Use the Green Party to Their Advantage," *The New York Times* (Sept. 22, 2020).
18 Robert Windram, "Russians Launched Pro-Jill Stein Social Media Blitz to Help Trump Win Election," *NBC News* (Dec. 22, 2018).
19 Haris Alic, "Democratic groups fund third-party conservative longshots to siphon votes from Republican candidates" *Fox News* (Oct. 31, 2022): tinyurl.com/mr34ufzh.
20 See Jeffrey Jones, "Support for Third U.S. Political Party at High Point," *Gallup* (Feb. 15, 2021).
21 See the 2017 Pew Research Study on Partisanship and Engagement at tinyurl.com/bddmnptk. Compare Ingraham, "How to Fix Democracy;" also see Lee Drutman, "If America Had Six Parties, Which Would You Belong To?" *The New York Times* [Special Opinion section] (Nov. 7, 2021), p. 10.
22 See Kristin Eberhard's helpful illustration of this prediction in *Becoming a Democracy* (Sightline Institute, 2020), pp. 141–43.
23 Actual runoffs have their defenders. For more on this, see this book's online extension.
24 One is that RCV is "non-monotonic;" but for an argument that does not make it unfair, see the FairVote page on "Monotonicity and IRV – Why the Monotonicity Criterion is of Little Import," at tinyurl.com/3jumytk7.
25 Steve Brown, "Essaibi George, Wu Court Black Voters in Race for Boston Mayor," *WBUR* (Sept. 22, 2021), tinyurl.com/69darvzv. But an instant runoff RCV process would have eliminated only one candidate each round, not three at once.
26 Larry Diamond imagined such a scenario in which Murkowski was eliminated before the final two, despite being the Condorcet winner, if the three most popular candidates had nearly equal support: see Diamond, "Saving Democracy – Realistically," *Democracy Journal* 65 (Summer 2022), pp. 71–84, pp. 79–80.
27 This is the method that Eric Maskin recommends as best, although he argues that we should get voters used to standard RCV first: see "How to Improve Ranked-Choice Voting and Democracy," *Capitalism & Society* 16, no. 1 (2022 online), pp. 7–8.
28 A more complex but superior solution has been proposed by Christoph Borgers: see "Beyond Instant Runoff: A Better Way to Conduct Multi-candidate Elections," *The Conversation* (April 11, 2017). For discussion of this proposal, see *TheDemocracyAmendments.org.*
29 For a brief but useful analysis, see Mann and Ornstein, *It's Even Worse than It Looks*, p. 150.
30 For cumulative voting, see Eberhard, *Becoming a Democracy*, p. 145.
31 See the "Single-winner Voting Method Comparison Chart" on FairVote.org; tinyurl.com/yc2hs4e3.
32 On the adoption of this standard to correct massive inequalities in representation within state governments, see Wegmen, *Let the People Pick the President*, ch. 5.
33 Tarunabh Khaitan, "Political Parties in Constitutional Theory," *Current Legal Problems* 73, no. 1 (2020), pp. 89–125, p. 93.
34 See Alvin Roth, *Who Gets What – And Why?* (Houghton Mifflin Harcourt, 2015), chs. 4–5.
35 See Caroline Tolbert's essay defending a single national primary for presidential candidates in Ellis and Nelson, *Debating Reform*, 3rd ed. (CQ Press/SAGE Publications, 2017), ch. 10.
36 Ibid., pp. 179–80.

37 Brian Knight and Nancy Schiff, "Momentum and Social Learning in Presidential Primaries," *Journal of Political Economy* 118, no. 6 (2010), pp. 1110–50.
38 Verasa Sharma, "Analysis: The Problem with Iowa and NH Going First in the Democratic Race," *Now This* (Feb. 12, 2020); tinyurl.com/38pvkemz.
39 For an evolving calendar, see Josh Putnam's site, https://www.frontloadinghq.com/p/the-2024.html.
40 Larry Sabato, *A More Perfect Constitution* (Bloomsbury, 2007, 2088 pb.), pp.128–30.
41 Ibid., pp. 131–34.
42 See David Redlawsk's untitled essay responding to Tolbert in Ellis and Nelson, *Debating Reform*, 3rd ed., ch. 10, pp. 183–94.
43 Ari Berman, "How the Wealth Primary Is Undermining Voting Rights," *The Nation* (June 8, 2015), pp. 13–16.
44 The rate is lower if we start with the number of people *eligible* to vote. See "Turnout in Primaries vs General Elections since 2000," *StatesUnited* (July 28, 2022): tinyurl.com/238sbs7t.
45 See Bob Spear, *21st Century Common Sense*, 3rd ed. (21Commonsense LLC, 2021), p. 57.
46 So even if Trump had netted up to 700,000 second-choice votes in these earlier primaries, Rubio would still have been ahead after March 1.
47 Max Fisher, "How Political Primaries Have Fanned Britain's Dysfunction," *The New York Times* (Oct. 24, 2022), p. A10.
48 For a more detailed breakdown, see the National Conference of State Legislatures' page on primary elections.
49 I call this a "primary" vote because it is round one in Louisiana, but it is actually held on the general election day, with frequent runoffs coming later.
50 For a real example, see Ben Christopher, "Topsy-turvy Top-two: Is California Primary System Keeping Its Promises?" *CalMatters* (June 13, 2022).
51 See Hirschhorn's helpful analysis in *Delusional Democracy*, pp. 167–70.
52 For example, see Speer's *21st Century Common Sense*, 3rd ed., p. 81.
53 On this topic, see Peter Levine's work. Also, see Yoni Appelbaum, "Americans Aren't Practicing Democracy Anymore," *The Atlantic* (Oct. 2018). Indeed, part of the reason that Americans are so manipulable by political superstars is that Americans now participate much less in civic organizations such as nonprofit social groups that used to provide counterweights to parties and advertising-driven medias/propaganda machines.
54 Litt, *Democracy in One Book or Less*, pp. 140–41.
55 For example, see Levinson, *Our Undemocratic Constitution*, p. 28.
56 See the Cook Political Report, "2022 House Race Ratings" (Sept. 21, 2022); www.cookpolitical.com/ratings/house-race-ratings.
57 Litt, *Democracy in One Book or Less*, pp. 128–33.
58 There is no doubt that Republican state legislators have used gerrymandering more widely and in more extreme ways on average. See Caroline Fredrickson, *The Democracy Fix* (The New Press, 2019), pp. 18, 27–35.
59 See Justin Buchler's analysis in *Debating Reform*, ch. 13, pp. 240–41.
60 Reid J. Epstein and Nick Corasaniti, "Republicans Gain Heavy House Edge in 2022 as Gerrymandered Maps Emerge," *The New York Times* (Nov. 15, 2021).
61 John Paul Stevens, *Six Amendments* (Little, Brown and Co., 2014), pp. 36–38.
62 In 2012, Republicans received 47.7% of the nationwide popular vote to Democrats' 48.8%: see Litt, *Democracy in One Book or Less*, p. 135. The reverse nearly happened in 2022.
63 See Molly Reynolds, "Republicans in Congress Got a 'Seats Bonus' This Election (Again)," *Brookings* (Nov. 22, 2016).
64 John Kruzel, "American Voters Largely United against Partisan Gerrymandering, Polling Shows," *The Hill* (Aug. 4, 2021).
65 See Elaine Kamarck on nonpartisan redistricting, *Debating Reform*, ch. 13, p. 237.
66 Sabato, *A More Perfect Constitution*, p. 35.

67 Ohio has 7 political members on its commission, and state district maps must be approved by two members from both major parties; otherwise, they are in effect for only 4 years. But the commission is not the first or sole drawer of congressional districts.
68 Joseph Spector, "New York Democrats look for someone to blame after election catastrophe," *Politico* (Nov. 17, 2022): https://tinyurl.com/4ynxvzv5.
69 Russell Berman, "The Decision that Could Doom Democrats for a Decade," *The Atlantic* (Oct. 21, 2021).
70 David Imamura, "Redistricting Commissions: Lessons from the 2020 Redistricting Cycle," *Human Rights: An ABA Magazine* 48, no. 1 (Oct. 24, 2022). He notes that commissions only work when they are "not evenly divided between Democrats and Republicans without a [non-partisan] tie-breaker, have members who are not politically appointed, and have ultimate control over the district lines."
71 Peter Stevenson, "Here's What H.R.1, the House-Passed Voting Rights Bill, Would Do," *The Washington Post* (June 2, 2021).
72 Richard Hassen, "It's Hard to Overstate the Danger of the Voting Case the Supreme Court Just Agreed to Hear," *Slate* (June 30, 2022).
73 Sam Levine, "Could the US Supreme Court Give State Legislatures Unchecked Election Powers?" *The Guardian* (July 7, 2022).
74 *Arizona State Legislature* v. *Arizona Independent Redistricting Commission*, 576 U.S. 787 (2015).
75 Professor Samuel Wang, Director of the Princeton Gerrymandering Project, believes the Court may not rule for the Republican plaintiffs, because the independent state legislature doctrine would actually help Democrats more. See Wang, "Republicans' Supreme Court argument on redistricting could backfire," *The Washington Post* (Dec. 1, 2022).
76 See Paige Masten, "'Death Knell of Democracy': A Dangerous Supreme Court Case, with NC at the Center," *The Charlotte Observer* (Sept. 18, 2022); www.charlotteobserver.com/opinion/article265457411.html.
77 *Rucho et al.* v. *Common Cause*, No. 18–422, 588 U.S. (2019).
78 *Davis* v. *Bandemer*, 478 U.S. 109 (1986); see Stevens, *Six Amendments*, pp. 44–46.
79 This is why "The Progressive Constitution" requires an independent commission in each state: see Art. I §4.
80 Also, see the Princeton Project on districting; and Corasaniti, Epstein, Johnston, Lieberman, and Weingart, "How Maps Reshape American Politics," *The New York Times* (Nov. 12, 2021), pp. A18–A19.
81 Litt, *Democracy in One Book or Less*, p. 139.
82 This map, with partisan impact analysis, derives from the Princeton Gerrymandering Project, gerrymander.princeton.edu/.
83 There is a way to combine the single-member and party-list methods to get a proportional outcome, which defeats the main motive for gerrymandering the single-member districts. As Levinson notes, Germans elect half of their national representatives from single-member districts and the other half at-large in a national competition. Their system is so smart that the representatives elected nationally from party lists are apportioned so that each party's final total in parliament mirrors its total percentage in both elections combined. See Levinson, *Framed*, p. 114. A variant could require drawing the single-member districts to be highly competitive, while the nationally elected half of the lower legislative chamber provides proportionality in outcomes—a beautiful balance of the two main goals.
84 Buchler points out this basic tension in *Debating Reform*, ch. 13, p. 247. But oddly, he still prefers the "bipartisan gerrymander" that reduces competitiveness.
85 On this metric, see Eric Petry, "How the Efficiency Gap Works," *Brennan Center* (no date).
86 Eberhard, *Becoming a Democracy*, pp. 129–31. For census data on the clustering of people by party, see the comprehensive Pew Research Center page on "Demographic and Economic Trends" at tinyurl.com/mptfh3r7.

87 This verdict is close to Justice Stevens' view that "bizarre configurations" of districts require a "neutral justification," which cannot include enhancing one party's power: see *Six Amendments*, pp. 43–47. My proposal specifies competitiveness and proportionality of outcomes as "neutral justifications" in Stevens' sense.

88 While the Supreme Court interpretation of §II of the VRA has evolved over time, these basic guidelines were clarified in *Thornburg* v. *Gingles*, 478 U.S. 30 (1986).

89 Joshua Kaplan, "How Ron DeSantis Blew Up Black-Held Congressional Districts and May Have Broken Florida Law," *ProPublica* (Oct. 11, 2022).

90 *Cooper* v. *Harris*, 581 U.S. (2017). Compare Hendrick Smith on District 12 in "*Blowback* v. *'Gerrymandering on Steroids'*," Blog Post (Feb. 9, 2016); tinyurl.com/3bxrw9x7.

91 These data are from Jeffrey B. Lewis, Brandon DeVine, Lincoln Pitcher, and Kenneth C. Martis, *Digital Boundary Definitions of United States Congressional Districts, 1789–2012* (2013); cdmaps.polisci.ucla.edu/.

92 In *Johnson* v. *De Grandy*, 512 U.S. 997 (1994), the Supreme Court said that such noncompact majority–minority districts can be constitutional. The Court has occasionally suggested that a district's bizarre shape might make it unconstitutional even if it increases minority representation: see *Shaw* v. *Reno*, 509 U.S. 630, 2 (1993); also see Stevens, *Six Amendments*, pp. 35–36. But in *Cooper* v. *Harris* (2017), the Court instead said that an especially compelling justification is only needed when race is the "predominant factor" in district shape.

93 Lani Guinier, *Tyranny of the Majority: Fundamental Fairness in Representative Democracy* (The Free Press, 1994), p. 63.

94 Ibid., pp. 84–99, ch. 4 in general, and endnote 64 to ch. 4. Guinier's analysis is subtle and complex; so this brief summary indicates at most a small slice of it.

95 Eberhard prioritizes proportionality on this basis. Yet she also argues for competitive districts: see *Becoming a Democracy*, pp. 134–35; compare Sabato, *A More Perfect Constitution*, pp. 36–37.

96 This Define–Combine method is due to Benjamin Schneer, Kevin DeLuca, and Max Palmer: see Mark Sullivan, "This Radically Simple Tool Could Solve One of Our Democracy's Worst Problems," *FastCompany* (March 5, 2020); tinyurl.com/mrr5zpp4.

97 Alternatively, a randomizing algorithm was invented by Bob Spear that uses zip code tabulation areas (ZCTAs) as building blocks of congressional districts. Township and borough lines might also be used. See *21st Century Common Sense*, pp. 274–309. The ZCTAs themselves are too small to gerrymander effectively.

98 Caroline Fredrickson, *The Democracy Fix*, p. 16.

99 Kenneth Vogel and Shane Goldmacher, "Complex $1.6 Billion Donation Bolsters Conservatives," *The New York Times* (Aug. 23, 2022), pp. A1, A11. Compare Andrew Perez, Andy Kroll, and Justin Elliot, "How a Secretive Billionaire Handed His Fortune to the Architect of the Right-Wing Takeover of the Courts," *Pro-Publica* and *The Lever* (Aug. 22, 2022).

100 See the Campaign Legal Center poll summary at https://tinyurl.com/bd6rndpb.

101 See the results of a 2018 Pew Research poll at tinyurl.com/2tfvr3a6.

102 Sarah Chayes, "Kleptocracy in America," *Foreign Affairs* (Sept.–Oct. 2017), pp. 142–50.

103 For details, see the Federal Election Commissions website, especially the page on "Who Can and Can't Contribute to a Party Committee," at tinyurl.com/mr4c6bzc.

104 See the *Reuters* report on 2020 at tinyurl.com/bdhdkp4w.

105 Adam Cohen, *Supreme Inequality* (Penguin Books, 2020, 2021 pb.), pp. 158–59.

106 Andrew Prokop, "40 Charts that Explain Money in Politics," *Vox* (July 30, 2014); tinyurl.com/2aw5dt2p.

107 Litt, *Democracy in One Book or Less*, pp. 245–46.

108 Connie Morella, Tim Roemer, and Zach Wamp, "The Price of Power," *IssueOne.org* (2017), p. 5.

109 See Cohen, *Supreme Inequality*, pp.162–63 on the army of lobbyists working for pharmaceutical companies to prevent Medicare from negotiating drug prices, as Medicaid and Veterans

Affairs do. After years of reform efforts, a 2022 bill finally allows Medicare to negotiate prices for just 10 medicines, but not until 2025—by which time even this small concession might be repealed.

110 Emily Cochrane, "Sinema Agrees to Climate and Tax Deal, Clearing the Way for Votes," *The New York Times* (Aug. 4, 2022).

111 Andrew Duehren and Siobhan Hughes, "Sinema Becomes Crucial Vote for Democratic Legislation," *The Wall Street Journal* (July 30–31), p. A6.

112 Cohen, *Supreme Inequality*, pp. 161–62.

113 See Lessig's *Republic, Lost*, chs. 4–6, p. 95. Compare Joseph Stiglitz, *The Great Divide* (W. W. Norton, 2015), Part IV; and Stiglitz, *The Price of Inequality* (W. W. Norton, 2012), ch. 2.

114 See Paul Waldman, "How Our Campaign Finance System Compares to Other Countries," *The American Prospect* (Apr. 4, 2014); prospect.org/power/campaign-finance-system-compares-countries/. However, this piece does not discuss spending by independent groups.

115 See generally Lessig's *Republic, Lost*, pp.107–16 and ch. 10, esp. pp. 121, 231–2. Also, see his detailed description of many lobbyists as policywonks, some of whom in addition serve as matchmakers between members of Congress and big donors (pp. 103–4).

116 Ibid., pp. 145–7.

117 For one of many stories on this, see Tony Romm, "Corporate America Launches Massive Lobbying Blitz to Kill Key Parts of Democrats' $3.5 Trillion Economic Plan," *The Washington Post* (Aug. 31, 2021).

118 Luke Broadwater, "With Biden's Agenda in the Balance, Lobbying Kicks into High Gear," *The New York Times* (Oct. 4; updated Nov. 3, 2021).

119 Al Gore, *The Future: Six Drivers of Global Change* (Random House, 2013), p. 93.

120 Ibid., pp. 104–5.

121 Ibid., p. 107.

122 Presidential campaigns can receive federal matching dollars for the first $250 that an individual contributes—but this does not extend to congressional campaigns, and most big presidential candidates stopped taking these matching funds in 2008 in order to avoid the attached spending limits, which are now way too low. Thus Litt argues that we could counteract über-wealthy donors by indexing public matching funds to the average costs of each type of campaign: see *Democracy in One Book or Less*, p. 219.

123 For a helpful summary of some of these limits, also pushing a libertarian view, see Bradley Smith, "Campaign Finance Regulation: Faulty Assumptions and Undemocratic Consequences," *Hoover Press* (reprinted from Cato Policy Analysis, 1995). Also, see the summary of the McCain–Feingold law at tinyurl.com/3m4xf496.

124 Caroline Fredrickson, *The Democracy Fix*, p. 34.

125 John Rawls, "The Basic Liberties and Their Priority," Tanner Lecture reprinted in Rawls, *Political Liberalism*, (Columbia University Press, 1993, 1996 pb.), pp. 341–63, noting that unlimited opportunity to turn money into political speech lowers the value of almost everyone's freedom of political speech by marginalizing their political voice.

126 Because of this trade-off relation, as with time to speak at a public meeting, political advertising can become a megaphone that drowns out all other voices. In technical terms, content in spaces that many people will inevitably see is a scarce, nonfungible asset with objective importance—like rare water holes in a desert, which cannot justly be monopolized or duopolized.

127 See Richard Hasen's description of his debates with 1st Amendment absolutists in *Plutocrats United* (Yale University Press, 2016), ch. 5 on censorship objections.

128 Ibid., pp. 9, 151–53. If 70 million voters used these vouchers every two years (which is a high estimate), the cost would be $3.5 billion per year to make candidates more beholden to small donors. As Hasen notes, this would require strictly enforced laws to prevent fake candidates from running just to hire their spouse as a campaign manager earning a hefty salary from public vouchers, and similar scams (pp. 155–56).

129 Ibid., p. 122.

130 See the Center for American Progress fact sheet on this issue (May 3, 2022): https://tinyurl.com/ytkw4txj.

131 As Jeffrey Toobin explains, the Roberts majority in this terrible decision went way beyond what the plaintiffs even requested: see "Money Unlimited," *The New Yorker* (May 14, 2012).

132 Eberhard, *Becoming a Democracy*, p. 64.

133 Fishkin and Forbath, "Make Progressive Politics Constitutional Again," pp. 6–7.

134 See, e.g., the analysis on the *American Bar Association* pages by Ciara Torres-Spelliscy, "Does 'the People' Include Corporations?" at tinyurl.com/3pbxxn57.

135 Gore, *The Future*, p. 111 (my italics).

136 Stevens, *Six Amendments*, ch. 3 helpfully reviews the history of major federal court decisions on campaign finance.

137 These data came from OpenSecrets.org and Michael Malvin and Brendan Galvin, "Independent Spending in 2020 Equaled the Candidates' in Close Races, and Parties Dominated the IEs," *Campaign Finance Institute* (Dec. 22, 2020), at tinyurl.com/5b4hc9kx.

138 For example; see Hirschhorn, *Delusional Democracy*, pp. 46–47.

139 Caroline Fredrickson, *The Democracy Fix*, pp. 7–8, 39–40.

140 See Jacob Grumbach, *Laboratories against Democracy* (Princeton University Press, 2022), reviewed in Jamila Michener, "How the States Went Wrong," *Democracy* no. 65 (Summer 2022), pp. 85–92.

141 Stephen Caruso, "Effort to Ban PA Legislative Gifts Fails," *The Philadelphia Inquirer* (Sept. 15, 2022), p. B2.

142 Berman, "How the Wealth Primary Is Undermining Voting Rights," p. 13.

143 The figures were compiled by OpenSecrets.org from public FEC data.

144 See Mickey et al., "Is America Still Safe for Democracy?" p. 22.

145 Hasen, *Plutocrats United*, p. 123.

146 Ibid., chs. 8–9.

147 See WeAmend.us/model-amendments/campaign-finance-reform-amendment/. This is a proposed cap; Congress could still set lower levels, and the influence of larger donations is offset by matching of small contributions.

148 Foreign-owned corporations have been able to spend on US elections through domestic subsidiaries under *Citizens United*. The Brennan Center has documented Russian ads on major internet sites like Facebook that show up in Americans' feeds: see "Limiting Foreign Meddling in U.S. Campaigns" (Aug. 14, 2019). Israeli sources are also sometimes accused of bankrolling independent groups within the United States that advertise heavily in American elections.

149 In his support for publicly owned political campaigns, David Olson rightly notes the big problem of misleading information in advertising funded by some private groups, such as the "Swift Boat" lies about John Kerry that are contradicted by his official Navy records: see *Repairing America's Democracy*, pp. 51–52.

150 This includes everything from unions manning phone banks to corporations contributing to SuperPACs for their independent election advertising. Compare Olson, *Repairing America's Democracy*, p. 43.

151 See Hudson's helpful examples in *American Democracy in Peril*, pp. 206–7.

152 Lessig *Republic, Lost*, pp.161–3.

153 An example of a more radical proposal is the "We the People Amendment" promoted by MoveToAmend.org. It is well intentioned but goes beyond what is needed.

154 See the first section of the amendment proposal introduced by Ted Deutch (D-FL) on March 3, 2013 as H.J. Res. 34. I borrowed some language from the second section of Deutch's amendment; and the phrase "viewpoint-neutral" comes from Adam Schiff's amendment resolution of March 2022 (H.J. Res. 80).

155 If we do not trust Congress to set reasonable limits, an allowable range would have to go into the amendment.

156 See Fredrickson, *The Democracy Fix*, pp. 68–73.

157 On the need to restore the FCC's "Fairness Doctrine" and extend it to newer medias, see Hirschhorn, *Delusional Democracy*, pp. 124–27. Also, see Linda Stamato's fine work on journalism, cable news, and social media.

158 Lessig supports this approach. Also, see Vanderwalker and Morris, "The Reform Law Needed to Counter *Citizens United*: H.R.1," *Brennan Center* (Jan. 21, 2020).

159 Mann and Ornstein, *It's Even Worse than It Looks*, pp. 128–30.

160 Lessig, p. 97.

161 There is another less desirable alternative to an amendment that I have not mentioned. That is for Congress to strip federal courts of jurisdiction over the constitutionality of election donation and spending law, and then restore McCain–Feingold limits.

162 Taylor et al., *A Different Democracy*, p. 129. This, as they explain, is due again to ours being the oldest republican constitution.

163 In its *Bush* v. *Gore* decision, the Supreme Court stopped the Florida recount, ostensibly because different counties were using different standards during the hand-counting of paper ballots—although the Court could easily have imposed one uniform standard for recounting. Hypocritically, the Court has not ruled that ballots differing by counties in the *general election* violate equal protection. On this topic, see Cohen, *Supreme Inequality*, pp. 168–70.

164 See Cohen, *Supreme Inequality*, p. 183. Congress could and should revive the preclearance requirement but apply it equally to all states as a means of securing equality among all potential voters in federal elections.

165 For a summary of recent state laws that attempt to suppress registration and turnout, see the Brennan Center's roundup of Voting Laws (Oct. 4, 2021); tinyurl.com/mu72ev2m. Compare Olson, *Repairing America's Democracy*, pp. 56–59.

166 See Cohen, *Supreme Inequality*, p. 186.

167 Cynthia and Sanford Levinson, *Fault Lines in the Constitution*, pp. 97–98.

168 As the ACLU points out in its Fact Sheet on this issue, travel to a government office that can issue a photo ID valid for voting in overly demanding states can be quite difficult for people who are elderly, disabled, or living in rural areas.

169 That is, if you can find your polling place, which officials like to move frequently and close to Election Day. In 2022, Texas moved to a single polling place per country in some areas and moved early voting sites off of college campuses.

170 Litt, *Democracy in One Book or Less*, p. 70.

171 In June 2018, the Supreme Court made it easier for states to conduct such purges of registered voters: for details, see Cohen, *Supreme Inequality*, pp. 187–89.

172 Angela Caputo, Geoff Hing, and Johnny Kauffman, "After the Purge," *American Public Media* (Oct. 29, 2017).

173 Compare Litt's account of radical voter roll purges in Georgia, Arkansas, Texas, and other states in *Democracy in One Book or Less*, pp. 76–77.

174 Cohen, *Supreme Inequality*, pp. 189–90.

175 Brentin Mock, "How Dismantling the Voting Rights Act Helped Georgia Discriminate Again," *Bloomberg* (Oct. 15, 2018).

176 See Litt, *Democracy in One Book or Less*, pp. 78–80.

177 For example, see Fredreka Schouten and Gregory Krieg, "'Always Some Sneaky Trick:' Black Voters in Georgia Say the State's Primary Meltdown Was No Accident," *CNN* (June 6, 2020); tinyurl.com/4fvmrbtu.

178 For a nationwide picture of this tactic, see Chelsea Jones, "States Are Closing Polling Places. That Hurts Democracy," *The Washington Post* (June 17, 2022).

179 Litt, *Democracy in One Book or Less*, p. 94.

180 Daniel Garisto, "Smartphone Data Show Voters in Black Neighborhoods Wait Longer," *Scientific American* (Oct. 1, 2019); tinyurl.com/2ru8ar7y.
181 See *The Democracy Docket* on recent state laws and a key 2016 Supreme Court case, www.democracydocket.com/cases/arizona-ballot-collection/.
182 An earlier version of this list appeared in Davenport, "11 (Bipartisan) Ways to Improve Voting in the United States," *America: The Jesuit Review* (March 1, 2021); compare Nathaniel Persily and Charles Stewart III, "A 12-Step Rehabilitation Program for American Election Administration," *Lawfare* (Jan. 27, 2021).
183 Drop boxes were widely introduced in 2020 to satisfy mainly Republican concerns about rising numbers of ballots going through the mail. These metal boxes are quite secure and can be monitored by CCTV cameras too.
184 This would reverse part of the Court's decision in *Brnovich* v. *Democratic National Committee,* 594 U.S. (2021).
185 See Mann and Ornstein, *It's Even Worse than It Looks*, pp. 138–39.
186 Lucas Merian, "Why Blockchain-based Voting Could Threaten Democracy," *Computer World* (Aug. 12, 2019).
187 See Sabato's discussion in *A More Perfect Constitution*, pp. 152–53.
188 Lesley Kennedy, "How the 2000 Election Came Down to a Supreme Court Decision," *History.com* (Nov. 4, 2020).
189 Jack Holmes, "If We Don't Pass H.R. 1, 'We Are F*cked as a Nation'," *Esquire* (Jan. 25, 2021).
190 See Ellis and Nelson, eds., *Debating Reform*, introduction to ch. 8. Compare the registration and voting reforms suggested in Ian Millhiser's broad agenda laid out in "11 Ways to Fix America's Fundamentally Broken Democracy," *Vox* (Sept. 14, 2020).
191 Cohen notes that Clarence Thomas has cited the "independent legislature" reference in *Bush* v. *Gore* (2000) in order to argue that states can limit on voter registration even in ways that violate federal law: see *Supreme Inequality*, p. 174.
192 *Arizona* v. *Inter Tribal Council of Arizona, Inc.*, 570 U.S. 1 (2013).
193 The *Demos* proposal by Laura Williamson and Brenda Wright is actually more radical and includes reforms to address gerrymandering, election finance, and the presidential election, which I list as separate amendments. See tinyurl.com/9j3db4hu.
194 Compare "The Conservative Constitution," Article I §4: "No State Shall Impose Any Test or Device that Has the Purpose or Effect of Denying or Abridging the Right to Vote."
195 "The Conservative Constitution," Art. I §5.
196 Compare the arguments for an affirmative constitutional right to vote at WeAmend.us/model-amendments/voting-rights-amendment/. Although this site recommends a fairly minimalist version, my recommendation adds a few more principles to back more detailed statutory reforms.
197 See Jean Chung, "Voting Rights in the Era of Mass Incarceration," *The Sentencing Project* (July 28, 2021).
198 Taylor et al., *A Different Democracy*, p. 138.
199 Litt, *Democracy in One Book or Less*, p. 50. He notes that between 1976 and 2016, "the number of Americans barred from voting because of a felony conviction grew by 500%"—fivefold (p. 43).
200 One could even imagine a compromise amendment limiting birthright citizenship in some way, such as denying it to children born of mothers in the US on a visitor's visa.
201 The feeble bill that cleared the Senate in 2022 enhanced background checks on the youngest gun buyers, provided money to help states implement "red flag" laws, and outlawed straw purchases. It did *not* close the gun show loophole or ban semiautomatic weapons. See my essay, "An Endless Arms Race: How to Fight the NRA's Absurd Solution to Mass Shootings," *Salon* (July 5, 2022); tinyurl.com/yuzr5s6b.
202 This figure is from Wikipedia Creative Commons; it employs raw data from several sources.
203 Cynthia and Sandy Levinson focus on this example in *Fault Lines in the Constitution* (Peacetree Publishing, 2019), ch. 4.

204 See David Olson's list in *Repairing America's Democracy*, pp. 70–71.

205 For example, see Levinson's discussion of the December 1993 strategy document urging all Republican senators to oppose Clinton's healthcare initiatives no matter what the bill proposes: *Our Undemocratic Constitution*, p. 65.

206 Mann and Ornstein, *It's Even Worse than It Looks*, pp. 165–66.

207 Taylor et al., *A Different Democracy*, pp. 117–18.

208 See Bordewich, *The First Congress*, p. 19. And this concern was correct: in the last 50 years, many "fledgling democracies" have failed to uphold individual rights because they lack independent judges: see "Getting Democracy Right," *The Economist* (March 1, 2014), pp. 51–52.

209 See Christopher Collier and James Collier, *Decision in Philadelphia: The Constitutional Convention of 1787* (Ballantine/Random House, 1986), pp. 67, 133–34, 150, 175.

210 On Madison's determination to overcome this problem, see Collier and Collier, *Decision at Philadelphia*, p. 152.

211 See Jefferson, "Report of a Plan of Government for the Western Territory" [1784], *The Portable Jefferson*, ed. Merrill Peterson (Penguin Books, 1977), pp. 254–58.

212 Madison, Federalist 58, *The Federalist Papers*, p. 359; compare Federalist 54, p. 337.

213 "Examining the Filibuster," Senate Rules and Administration Committee, 111th Congress (April–Sept., 2010); tinyurl.com/ytrb7p9y; compare Federalist 22, Federalist 59, p. 359.

214 Adam Jentleson, *Kill Switch: The Rise of the Modern Senate and the Crippling of American Democracy* (W. W. Norton, 2021), pp. 21–47. Note his insightful explanation of Madison's support for majority rule. On the rule of calling the question, see Edward N. Kearny & Robert A. Heineman, "The Senate Filibuster: A Constitutional Critique," *Perspectives on Political Science* 26 no.1 (1997): 5–9.

215 Jentleson, *Kill Switch*, pp. 48–62.

216 Ibid., pp. 64–70. The Levinsons note that anti-lynching laws were filibustered so much in the early 20th century that none ever passed the Senate: see *Fault Lines in the Constitution*, p. 24.

217 Jack Rakove, "The filibuster may not even be constitutional the way it's now used," *The Washington Post* (Feb. 8, 2021). Also, see Caroline Fredrickson, "The Case Against the Filibuster," *Brennan Center* (Oct. 2020).

218 See Wendy Schiller's defense of the talking filibuster in *Debating Reform*, ch. 15. "The Conservative Constitution" is more demanding: it proposes that filibusters be banned beyond two weeks, as long as every member who wishes to speak once on a bill has done so: see Art. II §5. Compare Mann and Ornstein, *It's Even Worse than It Looks*, p. 169. They also wisely suggest ensuring that the minority can offer at least one germane amendment to each bill before the final vote (p. 170).

219 Joshua Holzer, "Most US States Don't Have a Filibuster – Nor Do Many Democratic Countries," *The Conversation* (Mar. 2, 2021).

220 Stef Knight, "States Can Break Filibusters Easier than Feds," *Axios* (Oct. 4, 2021).

221 Eli Yokley, "How Popular Is the Senate Filibuster?" *Morning Consult* (June 9, 2021); tinyurl.com/443h6fac. A Monmouth poll in April 2022 found similar numbers.

222 Commission on the Practice of Democratic Citizenship, "Our Common Purpose," *American Academy of Arts & Sciences* (2020), Strategy I.1, pp. 20–22.

223 Greg Blonder, "The People's House" (Jan. 6, 2023); gregblonder.medium.com/the-peoples-house-5a3e2cb89eff.

224 Farand, *The Framing of the Constitution*, p. 99.

225 See Max Farand, *Records of the Federal Convention of 1787*, rev. ed. (Yale University Press, 1911, 1937), vol. I, pp. 526, 540–42, 560, 575. The issue of apportionment among House delegations was also introduced at the same point in early July during which the composition of the Senate was being intensely debated.

226 Bowen, *Miracle at Philadelphia*, pp. 256–57.

227 Madison, Federalist 58, *The Federalist Papers*, p. 354.

228 This limit prevented the British problem of "rotten boroughs"—in which a member of Parliament sometimes represented only one or two thousand residents—and the convention's 30,000 limit implied a desire for districts of roughly equal populations.

229 Farand, *Records of the Federal Convention*, vol. I, pp. 567, 578, 584; vol. II, p. 214. Compare Federalist 55. Some delegates thought a fixed rule was fine because they expected amendments or a new government within a few decades (Vol. II, p. 221).

230 This was Gorham's explicit intention when the number was changed to 30,000 with Washington's support: see ibid., p. 644. Congress *called* the representation after the 1793 reapportionment 1 for every 33,000; but that was counting each slave as only three-fifths of a person.

231 These documents can all be found in *The Anti-Federalist Papers*, ed. Ralph Ketcham (Penguin, 2003): 217–65.

232 Blonder, "The People's House;" also see Blonder, "Sizing Up Democracy," *Genuine Ideas* blogpost, genuineideas.com/ArticlesIndex/districtsize.html.

233 This ratio has barely moved since Sabato's 2005 figures: see *A More Perfect Constitution*, p. 39.

234 Drew Desilver, "U.S. Population Keeps Growing, but House of Representatives Is Same Size as in the Taft Era," *Pew Research Center* (May 31, 2018).

235 Note that India is not yet an OECD nation; its ratio of representatives to population in its lower house is three times worse than the US ratio.

236 Sabato favors this number: see *A More Perfect Constitution*, pp. 39–40.

237 They actually applied the rule to the House and Senate combined, whereas I applied it only to the House: see Editorial Board, "America Needs a Bigger House," *The New York Times*, tinyurl.com/2p8zrnhx.

238 See Taylor et al., *A Different Democracy*, pp. 212–13.

239 See the comparisons in Kane, Mascioli, McGarry, and Nage, "Why the House of Representatives Must Be Expanded and How Today's Congress Can Make It Happen," Fordham University School of Law (January 2020); tinyurl.com/cp8jr2ff.

240 For the same reason, it would be wise to specify in the Constitution the divisor method for apportioning the available number of House districts / seats among the states, so this is not manipulated later by one party. For discussion, see Taylor et al., *A Different Democracy*, pp. 121–23.

241 Ryan Best recommends this solution in an insightful interactive article: "What If the House of Representatives Had More than 435 Seats?" *FiveThirtyEight* (Aug. 12, 2021).

242 Justice John Paul Stevens noted that not allowing deviations of less than 0.5% could make it harder to avoid highly noncompact districts: see *Six Amendments*, pp. 39–41.

243 Ashira Pelman Ostrow has proposed to use a weighted vote scheme for fixed geographic units to end the need for redistricting: see "One Person, One Weighted Vote," *Florida Law Review* 68, no. 6 (Nov. 2016), pp. 1839–1881. This is an intriguing proposal, but without redistricting, the number of actual people in each district will vary greatly over time without any way to control how competitive or noncompetitive they become (see #4).

244 *United States* v. *Virginia Military Institute*, 518 US 515 (1996); Justice Thomas recused himself in this case.

245 This was never such a formal Senate rule. See Russell Wheeler, "The 'Thurmond Rule' and Other Advice and Consent Myths," *Brookings* (May 25, 2016).

246 The Catechism of the Catholic Church, article 2412, explicitly condemns knowingly receiving stolen goods.

247 Adam Liptak and Maggie Haberman, "Inside the White House's Quiet Campaign to Create a Supreme Court Opening," *The New York Times* (June 28, 2018). Arguably Kennedy also swung at least one more Supreme Court seat to Republicans by putting G. W. Bush in office as well.

248 Russell Wheeler, "Senate Obstructionism Handed a Raft of Judicial Vacancies to Trump," *Brookings* (June 4, 2018).

249 Jeffrey Jones, "Confidence in U.S. Supreme Court Sinks to Historic Low," *Gallup* (June 23, 2022).

250 But there is no real parallel in history to the Senate majority's actions from 2016 through 2020. See *TheDemocracyAmendments.org* for details.

251 Reich, *The Common Good*, pp. 69–72.

252 Harry Blackmun, although appointed by Richard Nixon, had become much more liberal by the time he retired during Clinton's presidency in 1994. On Fortas and Nixon's shocking efforts to drive out other more liberal justices, see Cohen, *Supreme Inequality*, pp. 25–30, 50–52. Rehnquist also helped Nixon select nominees who would not be favorable to civil rights claims (p. 48).

253 For details, see Levinson, *Framed*, ch. 12.

254 Presidential Commission on the Supreme Court of the United States, "Draft Final Report" (Dec. 2021); tinyurl.com/bdnazkba.

255 Steven G. Calabresi and James Lindgren, "Term Limits for the Supreme Court: Life Tenure Reconsidered," *Harvard Journal of Law and Public Policy* 29, no. 3 (April 2005). Calabresi repeated this proposal in an opinion piece *in the New York Times* in 2020 soon after Justice Ginsburg's death.

256 For one example, see David Karol's defense of the 18-year term in *Debating Reform*, ch. 19. He notes that most other advanced democracies have either retirement ages or term limits for their judges.

257 See "The Progressive Constitution," Art. III §1, and "The Conservative Constitution," Art. III §1. The latter tries to limit the addition of seats to appellate and district courts, but as litigation grows, more courts at these levels may be needed. Compare Levinson, *Our Undemocratic Constitution*, p. 136.

258 "Americans Have Lost Confidence in the Supreme Court," *Associated Press - NORC* (July 25, 2022); tinyurl.com/3t7zwzn8.

259 This takes care of Ilya Shapiro's objection that the 18-year 2-justices-per-term proposal would still allow a hostile Senate to hold seats open, potentially for years. He also worries about justices with life terms during the transition, but the lottery in my section III fixes this problem. Beyond these critiques, Shapiro concedes the political benefits of the 18-year term: see Shapiro, "Term Limits Won't Fix the Court," *The Atlantic* (Sept. 22, 2020).

260 Barry McDonald, "The Supreme Court Should Be Expanded and Its Powers Limited," *The New York Times* [Special Opinion section] (Nov. 7, 2021), p. 19.

261 Blonder, "A Random Walk for Scotus," (Jan. 5, 2023); gregblonder.medium.com/a-random-walk-for-scotus-4be26ab19053.

262 For example, see Amar, *The Constitution Today*, p. 134.

263 Sarah Shapiro and Catherine Brown, "A Look at Civics Education in the United States," *American Educator* (American Federation of Teachers, summer 2018).

264 Amy Mitchell, Mark Jurkowitz, J. Baxter Oliphant, and Elisa Shearer, "Americans Who Mainly Get Their News on Social Media Are Less Engaged, Less Knowledgeable," *Pew Research Center* (July 30, 2020).

265 Bryan Caplan, *The Myth of the Rational Voter* (Princeton University Press, 2007), pp. 17–19.

266 Caplan's own view supports the value of well-educated leaders—as long as they are willing to use public faith in them for social benefits. There is more than a whiff of Plato's "noble lies" in his point, true enough, that "propaganda can be used to fight error as well" (Ibid., p. 181).

267 Ilya Somin, *Democracy and Political Ignorance*, 2nd ed. (Stanford University Press, 2016), pp. 68–71.

268 Caplan, *The Myth of the Rational Voter*, ch. 1, esp. pp. 14–15. But the great difficulty is to identify why certain beliefs confer "direct psychological benefits" (p. 201), or where "preferences over belief" come from. They are usually tied to perceived experiences of objective goods such as camaraderie, righteous status, or even truth. And the price we pay for fanatical

loyalty to dogma consists not just in material costs (p. 17); it also includes diminishment in other intrinsic goods, such as civic friendship, more beautiful living spaces, deeper bases for self-esteem, and opportunities for more profound understanding of social phenomena.

269 Ibid., p. 20. Caplan is insightful in describing the democratic public sphere of political beliefs and actions as "a commons" [of epistemic capital], and the tyranny of anger media and demagogues as a tragedy of that commons in which individuals "pollute" that epistemic commons with false beliefs and destructive ideas that currently happen to please them (p. 206). But the realm of socio-political-economic ideas is not a commons that we can parcel into private plots that make individuals internalize the costs of their polluting actions. It can only be collectively managed to increase its stock of value.

270 Regina Beach, "How Ad Spending in the US Compares to the Rest of the World," *Wicked Reports* (March 29, 2022); tinyurl.com/n9rs9vww.

271 Mickey et al., "Is America Still Safe for Democracy?" p. 26.

272 Somin, *Democracy and Political Ignorance*, 2nd ed., ch. 3.

273 More generally, Somin and Caplan look at voting and political learning from the perspective of individual utility-maximization, rather than team effort.

274 Caplan, *The Myth of the Rational Voter*, p. 208.

275 Brennan, *Against Democracy*, p. 8.

276 See Somin, *Democracy and Political Ignorance*, 2nd ed., p. 217, citing Shanto Iyengar's work.

277 More technically, the reply to epistocrats is that (a) a lot of their predictions do not obviously apply to Deweyian Democracy, and (b) smart laws can protect the democratic commons by (b1) lowering the individual costs of acquiring basic political knowledge and (b2) raising the social costs of polluting that commons and free riding on the work of others to enrich and expand it. Ending two-party domination through RCV may also help.

278 Somin, *Democracy and Political Ignorance*, 2nd ed., pp. 68–69; compare Caplan, *The Myth of the Rational Voter*, p. 208, referring to David Sears' work. However, more Americans know political information with a direct impact on them, such as the federal minimum wage, and that Obamacare offers less wealthy Americans financial aid in buying health insurance.

279 See Danielle Allen and Paul Carrese, "Our Democracy Is Ailing. Civics Education Has to Be Part of the Cure," *Washington Post* (Mar. 2, 2021).

280 As Somin notes, "Well-informed voters are much better able to process new political information and more resistant to manipulation:" see Somin, *Democracy and Political Ignorance*, 2nd ed., p. 21. As Fareed Zakaria writes in a brilliant book on the value of strong core courses, interested adults have easy ways to look up desired information now, but second-order skills, such as "how to read critically, analyze data, and formulate ideas," need to be learned in school: see Zakaria, *In Defense of a Liberal Education* (W. W. Norton, 2015), p. 61.

281 Somin rightly stresses how bad public ignorance is on these topics: see ibid., pp. 18–20.

282 Reich, *The Common Good*, pp. 175–79. Reich proposes several of the same topics found in my curriculum.

283 I have in mind here not simply leaning into a controversial viewpoint in class meetings, but rather actions such as forcing students to participate in a public political protest if they want a good grade.

284 Then, e.g., we would not find that less than a third of Americans could distinguish Sunni and Shi'a as branches of Islam: see Somin, *Democracy and Political Ignorance*, 2nd ed., p. 19.

285 Brennan, *Against Democracy*, p. xi; compare Somin, who says that even well informed high school graduates will have little "reason to acquire knowledge" about new political issues latter in their lives: see *Democracy and Political Ignorance*, 2nd ed., p. 204. For responses, see this book's online extension.

286 Somin, *Democracy and Political Ignorance*, 2nd ed., pp. 206–11.
287 Brennan, *Against Democracy*, p. xi. The main problem with this is that it would be difficult to ensure that many millions of test-takers are who they say.
288 The tests or competition questions would need to be made by a randomly selected panel of experts willing (and paid) to make the test and criminal penalties for leaking questions.
289 In particular, see Larry Sabato's thoughtful proposal in *A More Perfect Union*, ch. 5.

Chapter 3

1 On Oct. 17, 2022, the Supreme Court decided not to hear an appeal from Samoans, even though Justice Gorsuch had called for the "insular" cases denying birthright citizenship to be overturned.
2 "Republican Party Platform Statement on Puerto Rico" (*Puerto Rico 51st*, July 18, 2016); www.pr51st.com/republican-party-platform-puerto-rico/.
3 For a helpful history, see Sam Erman, *Almost Citizens: Puerto Rico, the U.S. Constitution, and Empire* (Cambridge University Press, 2019).
4 See the detailed history recounted in Amelia Cheatham and Diana Roy, "Puerto Rico: A US Territory in Crisis," *The Council on Foreign Relations* (Feb. 3, 2022).
5 To this could be added the question of whether some additional protections or special representation in Congress should be given to Native Americans still living on reservations—a topic I do not try to address here.
6 See the Wikipedia page on "Overseas France."
7 At the very least, a Puerto Rico statehood Act must add 4 House members to the current 435 total. It should also end laws promoting cryptocurrency on the island.
8 Jonathan Turley, "Too Clever by Half: The Unconstitutionality of Partial Representation of the District of Columbia in Congress," *George Washington Law Review* 76, no. 2 (Feb. 2008), 305–74, p. 306.
9 German Lopez, "6 questions about Washington, D.C., statehood you were too disenfranchised to ask," *Vox* (updated Nov. 8, 2016).
10 One option is thus for Congress to try to extend the resolution's 7-year window for ratification, as with the ERA. But the Supreme Court could try to block such a move.
11 Akhil Amar, *American's Constitution* (Random House, 2016 pb), p. 441.
12 See the ACLU fact sheet on the D.C. statehood question; www.acludc.org/en/faqs-dc-statehood
13 One can see this concern reflected in Madison's discussion in Federalist 43.
14 As we saw on January 6, 2021, the real dangers now rest in mass media spreading enormous lies, and corruption that motivates federal leaders themselves to incite violence.
15 Defenders of statehood argue that a D.C. statehood Act can direct the electors always to cast their vote for the presidential candidate who would win without them (or perhaps to vote for the winner of the national popular vote). But it is not clear that Congress has authority to determine any electoral votes this way.
16 Critics argue that D.C. statehood violates Article I §8 of the Constitution that describes the planned federal district. For example, see Roger Pilon, "Examining D.C. Statehood," *The Cato Institute* (June 22, 2021). [NB: Cato is a funded partly by Koch brothers money.]
17 Spear makes a similar suggestion for a general "Non-State Election District" following the French model; see *21st Century Common Sense*, p. 160.
18 Raskin, *Unthinkable*, p. 112.
19 Ian Millhiser, "America's Democracy Is Failing," *The Atlantic* (Jan. 30, 2021).
20 Rebecca Salzer and Jocelyn Kiley, "A Majority of Americans Continue to Favor Moving Away from Electoral College," *Pew Research* (Aug. 5, 2022).
21 Keyssar, *Why Do We Still Have the Electoral College?*, p. 377.

22 See "The Conservative Constitution," Art. II §1, which also suggests that presidential nominees be selected by state legislators rather than popular party primaries. But unfortunately this elitist twist would doubtless result in corrupt promises to state legislators.

23 Or instead, the new congressional term could begin around December 10, with the president's inauguration on December 18, reducing the lame-duck session. However, the current schedule gives a new administration longer to secure key officers, and sometimes a lame-duck Congress can pass important bills that are stuck prior to elections.

24 See Jesse Wegman's summary of his case in "The Electoral College Will Destroy America," *The New York Times* (Sept. 8, 2020). Also, see the *Vox* interview with Wegman in Oct. 2020.

25 See Wegman, *Let the People Pick the President*, p. 58, on Madison's memories.

26 John Feerick, "The Electoral College–Why it Ought to Be Abolished," *Fordham Law Review* 37, no. 1 (1969), pp. 1–50.

27 See Collier and Collier, *Decision in Philadelphia*, p. 302.

28 Keyssar, *Why Do We Still Have the Electoral College?*, pp. 20–22. The convention even considered a scheme with multiple votes by each eligible American.

29 See Alan Johnson, *The Electoral College* (Philosophia Publications, 2018), ch. 2 and pp. 113–14.

30 Only about 13 states try to immediately replace an elector who has voted faithlessly (see the Supreme Court's 2020 decision in *Chiafalo et al.* v. *Washington*). But it is not certain that an elector's vote can be revoked and replaced once it is cast and transmitted.

31 Wegman, *Let the People Pick the President*, p. 94.

32 For example, see the selections from Rusty Bowers' June 21, 2022 testimony before the House January 6 bipartisan committee, recorded on PBS at tinyurl.com/3yvfccyd.

33 On this possibility and the idea of getting the VP to reject some electoral ballots, see Raskin, *Unthinkable*, pp. 118–33. The new Electoral Count Reform Act of December 2022 now makes clear that the VP cannot do this. But what happens if some state governor submits electoral votes that lack legitimate provenance?

34 See Feerick, "The Electoral College," p. 3.

35 See *McPherson* v. *Blacker* (1892) 146 U.S. 1, 27, cited in *Chiafalo et al.* v. *Washington*.

36 For example, see Edward Foley, "Reforming the Electoral Count Act," *Democracy Journal* 65, no. 2 (Summer 2022), pp. 59–70.

37 Texas Constitution, Art. 4 §8 (b): tlc.texas.gov/docs/legref/TxConst.pdf.

38 Miles Parks, "Congress passes election reform designed to ward off another Jan. 6," *NPR* (Dec. 23, 2022).

39 This system was changed by the 12th amendment, ratified in 1804, to separate electoral votes for the president and vice president into two streams, so those on the same ticket are not competing against each other.

40 See, e.g., Keyssar, *Why Do We Still Have the Electoral College?* pp. 21–22, 103. Farand argues that the 3/5ths rule was not really a new compromise; see *The Framing of the Constitution*, pp. 101–10. This seems exaggerated, given Madison's and General Pinckney's concerns that southern states would be outnumbered in the House. On Keyssar's side, see Paul Finkelman, "The Proslavery Origins of the Electoral College," *Cardoso Law Review* 23, no. 4 (June 2002), pp. 1145–57. For more background, see *TheDemocracyAmendments.org*.

41 For my rough method of approximating these figures, see *TheDemocracyAmendments.org*.

42 Many northern delegates at the convention opposed counting slaves toward a state's apportioned number of House members, while proslavery delegates wanted to count them at 100% to get more House members: see Collier and Collier, *Decision at Philadelphia*, pp. 191, 203, 215–17.

43 See Levinson's discussion of this issue, along with Akhil Amar's work on it, in *Framed*, pp. 183–87.

44 Keyssar, *Why Do We Still Have the Electoral College?*, pp. 360, 373. Similarly, in the 19th century, slave states wanted to keep the EC because they would have had less weight in a national popular vote for the president (unless they allowed enslaved residents to vote!).

45 Ibid, p. 10.

46 Wegman, *Let the People Pick the President*, p. 176. [NB: winning due to the small-state bump makes it likely but not certain that the winner lost the national popular vote, as the 1916 election shows.]
47 Sabato gives a brief and tame description of this problem in *A More Perfect Constitution*, p. 140.
48 John Feerick, "The Electoral College – Its Defects and Dangers," *New York State Bar Journal* 40 (Aug. 1968), pp. 319.
49 Ibid, pp. 319–21.
50 This may have also happened when John Kennedy won, depending on how Alabama's popular vote is counted (see ibid, p. 321). Collier and Collier emphasized this danger in 1986; see *Decision in Philadelphia*, p. 361.
51 Because of this, the House (voting by state delegations) could elect a president from one ticket, while the Senate elects a vice president from another ticket. For other bizarre scenarios, see *TheDemocracyAmendents.com.*
52 And internally deadlocked delegations casts no vote, which was part of the problem in 1800.
53 Wegman, *Let the People Pick the President*, pp. 148–51.
54 Akhil Amar, in his devastating critique of *Bush* v. *Gore*, argues that federal courts should have nothing to do with it; see *The Constitution Today*, pp. 116, 124–27; compare Cohen, *Supreme Inequality*, pp. 167–75. But the experience of late 2020 shows that courts will inevitably get drawn into such controversies.
55 Wegman, *Let the People Pick the President*, pp. 110–14.
56 And the infamous "Eastman Memo" (on a strategy to elect Trump in Congress on January 6, 2021) argued that the Electoral Count Act is unconstitutional. Eastman also argued that if Congress rejects some states' electors as not "validly appointed," they are *removed from the denominator* in deciding whether any candidate has a "majority" of the EC. If the Supreme Court backed this view, it could produce shocking results in a close election.
57 See the 20th Amendment, §3.
58 On these dangers, see Larry Diamond and Edward Foley, "The Terrifying Inadequacy of American Election Law," *The Atlantic* (Sept. 8, 2020). We also need a law clarifying that when the Speaker of the House becomes Acting President, they have to resign the Speakership.
59 The 20th Amendment only focuses on what happens if neither the Electoral College nor the contingent election in Congress has elected a president (and possibly also VP) before the Inauguration Day. See Feerick, "The Electoral College," pp. 327–29.
60 See Wegman, *Let the People Pick the President*, pp. 3–12. Some of the framers imagined that presidential electors' freedom to change their minds despite their preelection pledges, or to make no pledge at all, would be a bulwark against foolish decisions by statehouses or by voters in popular elections for presidential electors.
61 Keyssar discusses several cases in which leaders in state governments tried to get elected presidential electors in their state to switch their votes; see *Why Do We Still Have the Electoral College?* pp. 206–8, 217, 279, etc. In 2000, ironically, G. W. Bush's team was prepared to woo Gore electors if Gore won the EC while Bush won the popular vote (p. 326). It would help if US antibribery laws for officials were extended to clearly cover electors.
62 Raskin, *Unthinkable*, p. 414.
63 Sabato, *A More Perfect Union*, pp. 148–52. Like Blonder, Sabato also favors increasing the House to 1,000 members.
64 *Fairvote*, "Why James Madison Wanted to Change the Way We Vote for President" (June 18, 2012).
65 See Alan Johnson's helpful history in *The Electoral College*, ch. 3.
66 See Goddard's ElectoralVoteMap analysis at tinyurl.com/yt7752dd.
67 As Keyssar describes, this variant was often promoted in reform efforts after the Civil War; see *Why Do We Still Have the Electoral College?* p. 214.
68 Sabato stresses this criticism; see *A More Perfect Union*, p. 145. Keyssar notes that Colorado's governor pressed this point against moving Colorado to the proportional system; see *Why Do We Still Have the Electoral College?*, p. 335.

69 For a handy illustration of these alternatives, see the *270towin* analysis at tinyurl.com/2ta9mucp.

70 This is another reason why Colorado voters rejected a state ballot initiative that would have moved Colorado to the proportional system: see Wegman, *Let the People Pick the President*, p. 198. Keyssar shows that the same motive kept North Carolina and California winner-take-all states too: see *Why Do We Still Have the Electoral College?*, pp. 335–37.

71 Eberhard, *Becoming a Democracy*, p. 122.

72 See George C. Edwards III, "The Electoral College Should Be Abolished," in Richard J. Ellis and Michael Nelson, eds., *Debating Reform* (SAGE Publications, 2019), pp. 291–92.

73 Wegman makes this point based on Duverger's law: *Let the People Pick the President*, pp. 229–30.

74 See Gary L. Gregg's defense of the Electoral College in *Debating Reform*, p. 301. Sabato mentions all three objections but stresses his concern about fragmenting two-party dominance: *A More Perfect Union*, pp. 139, 141–42. I believe RCV balloting would largely take care of this worry, which Gregg also mentions.

75 Wegman, *Let the People Pick the President*, p. 167. Compare Levinson, *Our Undemocratic Constitution*, p. 88.

76 Levinson has suggested that we might get better VPs if they were elected separately from the president, as with many lieutenant governors of states; see *Framed*, p. 225. However, this might increase the risks of assassination plots, or false conspiracy theories if a president is assassinated.

77 "The Progressive Constitution" also proposed a direct election by popular vote with RCV; see Art. II §1. In Johnson's detailed proposal, he recommends RCV and includes the provision to prevent candidates running on more than one slate. His amendment also addresses the need for uniform voting standards (my #6); see *The Electoral College*, pp. 140–43.

78 As the Levinsons note, the age requirement and ban on naturalized immigrants together make a full third of US citizens ineligible to be president: see *Fault Lines in the Constitution*, p.114. On the other side, maybe we should set a maximum age, such as 72, for presidential and VP candidates.

79 It is interesting that the amendment which James Madison proposed to improve the presidential election would have used RCV in *the electors' votes* (see *Madison Letter to George Hay*, Aug. 23, 1823; tinyurl.com/edbav6f9).

80 Keyssar, *Why Do We Still Have the Electoral College?* pp. 214, 236, 321.

81 See the Sept. 2021 update at *NationalPopularVote.com*: tinyurl.com/bp78pk28.

82 Wegman makes a valiant attempt to defend the inter-state compact approach in *Let the People Pick the President*, ch. 7, which describes John Koza's long and fascinating campaign for the compact. The short-term thinking obstacle is evident in the effects of Trump's 2016 win on this movement (pp. 216–17).

83 Wegman, *Let the People Pick the President*, pp. 140–61; compare Levinson, *Our Undemocratic Constitution*, p. 96. Keyssar agrees; see *Why Do We Still Have the Electoral College?* pp. 237, 275, 283–94, noting Vernon Jordan's speeches against ending the EC, and contrary opinions by various Black and Jewish leaders at the time.

84 Litt, *Democracy in One Book or Less*, pp. 186–87.

85 Levinson, *Our Undemocratic Constitution*, p. 88.

86 For more on Manafort's horrendous actions, see *TheDemocracyAmendments.org*.

87 Levinson, *Framed*, pp. 195–200.

88 See Levinson on the original anti-federalists' fear of presidents misusing the pardon power to protect "cabals against the public interest:" *Framed*, p. 199 and *Our Undemocratic Constitution*, pp. 112–13.

89 See the history at constitutioncenter.org/blog/presidential-pardons-a-constitutional-and-historical-review.

90 The Levinsons rightly note George Mason's objection on these grounds at the convention, and emphasize that G.H.W. Bush pardoned people involved in the Iran-Contra scandal who might have testified against him: see *Fault Lines in the Constitution*, pp. 146–51.

91 Corey Brettschneider and Jeffrey K. Tulis have argued that this limit on pardons was part of the framers' original intent; see "The Traditional Interpretation of the Pardon Power Is Wrong," *The Atlantic* (July 13, 2020).
92 See Caroline Frederickson, "How to Prevent Abuse of the President's Pardon Power," *Brennan Center* (Feb. 24, 2021).
93 On staff members, see Lessig, *Republic, Lost*, pp. 221–23. He is correct that federal legislators and all staffers need to be paid more to make them more impartial.
94 See www.opensecrets.org/revolving.
95 Gore, *The Future*, pp. 114–16.
96 Hasen, *Plutocrats United*, p. 6.
97 Alan Zibel, "Revolving Congress: The Revolving Door Class of 2019 Flocks to K Street," *Public Citizen* (May 30, 2019); www.citizen.org/wp-content/uploads/revolvingcongress.pdf.
98 Mandy Smithberger (summary), "Brass Parachutes: The Problem of the Pentagon Revolving Door," *Project on Government Oversight* (Nov. 5, 2018); www.pogo.org/report/2018/11/brass-parachutes.
99 E. J. Dionne Jr. "Politicians Should Not Be Stock Traders," *The Washington Post* (Sept. 14, 2022), p. A15.
100 Michelle Cottle, "Congress Can Trade Stocks or Keep the Public Trust. Not Both," *The New York Times* (Jan. 18, 2022).
101 For example, see Eric Lipton, "Scalia Took Dozens of Trips Funded by Private Sponsors," *The New York Times* (Feb. 16, 2016). Compare Gore, *The Future*, p. 116.
102 See Lessig, *Republic, Lost*, pp. 216–17.
103 As Sarah Chayes has shown, strong anti-corruption laws are the only way to make the federal system resistant to people who would try to rig policies for the personal advantage of their own networks; see Chayes, *On Corruption* (Knopf, 2020).
104 In particular, Sandy Levinson argues that we should allow anyone of age 25 or more to serve in Congress.
105 Gordon Chang, "As Biden Stands by, Chinese Hackers Build Dossiers on US citizens," *The Hill* (Aug. 11, 2021).
106 Christopher Porter and Brian Finch, "What Does Beijing Want With Your Medical Records?" *The Wall Street Journal* (June 20, 2019).
107 See the fact check on *Ballotpedia* after Jared Kushner's appointment; tinyurl.com/36c9ma93.
108 Compare Spear, *21st Century Common Sense*, pp. 149–50. He would also have all federal legislators release their tax returns each year in office as well; see *21st Century Common Sense*, p. 177. But that might be incompatible with holding assets in a blind trust while in office, which is much more important.
109 Direct and fully intentional lies by politicians about policy matters and about other politicians are a legion across all parties. Joel Hirschhorn offers several examples related to the 2005 Hurricane Katrina disaster; see *Delusional Democracy*, pp. 34–35, and ch. 9.
110 The requirement of truth in government has been well defended by Olson in *Repairing America's Democracy*, ch. 10.
111 I witnessed Giuliani's vile lies directly at Trump's rally in Akron, OH (August 2016). To my knowledge, not a single Syrian refugee who came to the United States between 2014 and 2022 has been convicted of any acts of terrorism.
112 Conservative critics have argued that FBI officials used "Steele Dossier" evidence they knew to be unreliable to get surveillance permissions. But even if that power was abused, and such abusers should be fired, this critique ignores the many *other* (non-"Steele") pieces of evidence concerning links between Russia and Trump's network known in 2016, such as Manafort's and Michael Flynn's dealings, Russian hacking of the Clinton campaign, and multiple connections to banks known to launder money for the Kremlin, as Mueller's report actually confirmed. In short, there *was* enough "smoke" to establish probable cause for an investigation, even if

direct coordination was never proven. And four Trump associates were convicted as a result of these investigations. A 1000-page Senate report detailed 140 contacts with "Russian nationals, Wikileaks, or their intermediaries during the 2016 presidential campaign and presidential transition:" see Mark Mazzetti, "G.O.P.-Led Senate Panel Details Ties Between 2016 Trump Campaign and Russia," *The New York Times* (Nov. 4, 2020).

113 Deepa Shivaram, "Shaye Moss staffed an election office in Georgia. Then she was targeted by Trump," *NPR* (June 22, 2022), at https://tinyurl.com/y3vf43ym.

114 See Mickey et al., "Is America Still Safe for Democracy?" pp. 21, 23–24.

115 See Bordewich, *The First Congress*, pp. 96–97.

116 In *Nixon v Fitzgerald*, the Supreme Court declared the president immune while in office from civil lawsuits arising from his or her official actions. In a series of articles, Amar has argued that this should be extended to all civil lawsuits against a sitting president. Such suits should wait until the president's term ends: see articles reprinted in Amar, *The Constitution Today*, pp. 275–87.

117 Conservative critics have argued that the FBI has misled the special court that approves requests for secret surveillance, and should not be involved in "national security" or anti-terror intelligence. For example, see Andrew C. McCarthy, "How to Fix the FBI," *National Review* (Nov. 7, 2022), pp. 26–29.

118 Levinson, *Framed*, pp. 240–41.

119 This reflects Philip Howard's points that "politically motivated firings" should be prevented, but government also cannot work well if incompetent civil servants cannot be fired without "trial-like hearings" in which the burden of proof is on supervisors; see *Try Common Sense* (W. W. Norton, 2019), pp. 100–105. As Howard notes, review of firings by an impartial committee suffices.

120 Amar, *The Constitution Today*, p. 289.

121 But if it were proven that Clinton sexually harassed Paula Jones, as her civil lawsuit alleged, that might have warranted impeachment.

122 Hamilton anticipated this result in Federalist 65: "the decision will be regulated more by the comparative strength of the parties [within public opinion] than by the real demonstrations of innocence or guilt" (see *The Federalist Papers*, p. 395). His wording suggests serious and foresighted doubt about the Senate as an impeachment court.

123 Amar, *The Constitution Today*, pp. 289–91, 300.

124 Levinson, *Framed*, pp. 214, 217.

125 Hamilton, Federalist 65, *The Federalist Papers*, p. 394.

126 US Constitution, Art. III §4 (my italics).

127 This is arguably implied in the Constitution already, but it is good to state it explicitly [compare my amendment proposal #16 Art. III].

128 "The Conservative Constitution" proposes a shorter formula: "impeachment and removal" are "for serious criminal acts and gross abuses of the public trust" (Art. I. §6). This rightly recognizes that grounds for impeachment are not limited to statutory felonies, but I believe a longer list is now necessary to educate the public.

129 See Camila Vergara, *Systemic Corruption: Constitutional Ideas for an Anti-Oligarchic Republic* (Princeton University Press, 2020), p. 257. She develops this idea from Machiavelli and other "material" republicans, including Hannah Arendt.

130 Levinson, *Framed*, pp. 215–16.

131 In parliamentary systems, usually the ruling party (or coalition) has to select a new prime minister from within its ranks—which is often not a very democratic process. Sometimes a no-confidence vote also triggers new elections, whereas we have a regular 4-year cycle. For more on this, see *TheDemocracyAmendments.org.*

132 Levinson, *Framed*, pp. 216–17.

133 Still we should specify someone other than the VP, as "the president of the Senate," to preside over an impeachment trial of the VP, or a vote of no-confidence in the VP (!); see Amar, *The Constitution Today*, pp. 141–42.

134 For a nonpartisan explanation of the events surrounding the 2016 election, see Larry Diamond's account in *Ill Winds* (Penguin Press, 2019), ch. 6, "Russia's Global Assault."

135 I discuss this "shadow war" by Russia and China in Davenport, "Current Proposals for Closer Cooperation Among Democracies," in *How Democracy Survives*, ed. Michael Holm and R.S. Deese (Routledge, 2023): 139–57.

136 Congress might also want to alter sections of the Freedom of Information Act to prevent campaigns from misusing it to do opposition research at taxpayer expense. More generally, we should consider whether some degree of privacy in communications is needed for officials to build relationships of trust and confidence needed for their jobs' public purposes.

137 Elizabeth Goitein, "The Alarming Scope of the President's Emergency Powers," *The Atlantic* (Jan./Feb. 2019).

138 The Levinsons' describe these problems vividly in *Fault Lines in the Constitution*, pp. 169–72.

139 Levinson, *Our Undemocratic Constitution*, pp. 71–73; compare Sabato, *A More Perfect Constitution*, pp. 71–73. They are surely correct that special elections cannot be relied on fill a large number of House seats left vacant after a massive attack.

140 Levinson, *Framed*, p. 383; see Lloyd Cutler and Alan Simpson (chairs) et al., "Preserving Our Institutions: The Continuity of Congress," *The Continuity of Government Commission* (2003); tinyurl.com/525t6ast.

141 The Constitution allows states to have the governor pick someone to fill a Senate vacancy until the term for that seat ends after a regular election (see the 17th Amendment). As of 2022, 36 states give the governor this power, which has occasionally led to corruption. It is also politically risky in a mass casualty situation. But the only current alternative is a special election, and there is no way to replace a permanently vegetative senator.

142 Brennan Center, "A Guide to Emergency Powers and Their Use" (Dec. 5, 2018; updated Sept. 4, 2019).

143 Goitein, "The Alarming Scope of the President's Emergency Powers."

144 Sandy Levinson offers helpful examples from other nations, and from Clinton Rossiter's discussion of Roman law; see *Framed*, pp. 376–80.

145 In fact, sound principles for emergency powers will be direct analogs of the principles in each category of natural and/or "customary" norms for *just wars*, i.e. just "causes" for war, official declaration, last resort, means that are "proportionate" or not more violent or destructive than needed to reach just goals, modality constraints on methods, and postwar restoration.

146 Sandy Levinson suggests a fairly independent "Council of Elders" staffed with retired leaders to review declarations of emergency; see *Framed*, p. 380.

147 Collier and Collier, *Decision in Philadelphia*, p. 305.

148 There is a comprehensive count of vetos at www.senate.gov/legislative/vetoes/vetoCounts.htm.

149 Sources for these numbers include Congressional reports and Jonathan Lewallen, "The Issue Politics of Presidential Veto Threats," *Presidential Studies Quarterly* 47, no. 2 (June 2017), pp. 277–292.

150 See Levinson's discussion in *Our Undemocratic Constitution*, pp. 39–44; and Levinson, *Framed*, 134–36.

151 Robert Goulder, "The Trump Veto that (Almost) Saved Anonymous Shell Companies," *Forbes* (Feb. 8, 2021).

152 Molly Ball, "Even the Aide Who Coined the Hastert Rule Says the Hastert Rule Isn't Working," *The Atlantic* (July 21, 2013).

153 See Charles Babington, "Hastert Launches a Partisan Policy," *NBC News* (Nov. 27, 2004); www.nbcnews.com/id/wbna6591803.

154 See Sarah Binder, "Hastert Rule, We Hardly Knew Ye," *Brookings* (Jan. 17, 2013).

155 This follows from Kenneth Arrow's theorem and related findings that form the bases of contemporary social choice theory.
156 Spear, *21st Century Common Sense*, p. 194.
157 Levinson, *Framed*, pp. 119–24.
158 See Richard J. Ellis on whether the United States should introduce national voter initiatives or referenda: *Debating Reform*, 3rd ed. (CQ Press / SAGE Publications, 2017), ch. 7, pp. 132–34.
159 Ibid, p. 133. Allowing voter approval of national ballot questions to make law without further congressional action would almost certainly require a constitutional amendment.
160 This idea addresses complaints about bicameralism, such as those raised in Levinson, *Framed*, ch. 6, and in the Levinsons, *Fault Lines in the Constitution*, pp. 28–30.
161 A less desirable remedy is that the president could use the "adjournment" clause in Article II to adjourn Congress for more than 10 days, whereupon her/she can make an interim appointment: see Peter Shane, "Why Biden Might Not Need McConnell's Permission," *Washington Monthly* 53 (Jan.–Mar. 2021), 28–31.
162 For both sides of this argument, see the debate between Scott Frisch and Sean Q. Kelly in *Debating Reform*, 3rd ed., ch. 11.
163 Brian Riedl, "Omnibus Spending Bill: Huge Spending and 9,000 Earmarks Represent Business as Usual," *Heritage Foundation* (March 2, 2009); tinyurl.com/2p97pnhr.
164 George Cahlink and Thomas Frank, "Big Earmark Money in Senate Energy, Environment Bills," *E&E Daily* (Nov. 2, 2021); tinyurl.com/4vd72na2.
165 See Chris Edwards' June 2015 testimony to Congress, drawing on Peter Schuck's *Why Government Fails So Often* (Princeton University Press, 2014); online at the Cato Institute: tinyurl.com/ywhhptf3.
166 The balanced budget mandate is not only a conservative idea. See Olson's version in *Repairing America's Democracy*, ch. 9.
167 "The Conservative Constitution," Art. I. §§9–10. The authors suggest a three-year budget resolution—rightly giving the House sole power over this—but a four-year resolution aligns with the presidential term.
168 For comparison, see Sabato, *A More Perfect Constitution*, pp. 101–4.
169 Connor O'Brien, "Biden Signs $768B Defense Policy Bill that Supersized His Original Pentagon Request," *Politico* (Dec. 27, 2021).
170 Philip Howard, *The Rule of Nobody* (W. W. Norton, 2014), p. 180.
171 Ibid, p. 181.
172 This chart is from the US Treasury Department at fiscaldata.treasury.gov.
173 Litt, *Democracy in One Book or Less*, pp. 348–50.
174 Note that this change might work better with a court larger than 9 justices; then the supermajority to overturn a law could be less than 2/3rds.
175 Another interesting option is to let Congress, by a simple majority vote in both chambers, put one question on the Court's agenda every term, which the Court must answer with written arguments even without a presenting case. This would enable Congress to get information on the constitutionality of a law being considered before wasting a lot of time passing and implementing it, only to have it overturned after years of expensive lawsuits.
176 For an introduction, see Philip Pettit, *Republicanism* (Oxford University Press, 2003).
177 Cass Sunstein, *The Partial Constitution* (Harvard University Press, 1993), ch. 1.
178 The ironies are even greater for über-right Catholic judges, given that Catholic social teachings emphasize natural law against legal positivism. Extreme originalists also rely on an impoverished version of "democracy" in accordance with their naïve positivism; see Samuel Freeman, "Original Meaning, Democratic Interpretation, and the Constitution," *Philosophy & Public Affairs* 21, no. 1 (Winter 1992), pp. 3–42.
179 Introduction to "The Conservative Constitution," p. 2; Federalist 39 and 46.
180 For a similar critique of incoherent combinations of originalist positivism and natural law, see Charles Kelbley, "The Impenetrable Constitution and the Status Quo Morality," *Fordham Law*

Review 70, no. 2 (Nov. 2001), pp. 259–71. In particular, Kelbley notes Lawrence Tribe's argument that limited government actually requires unenumerated rights that courts can recognize.

181 In particular, see Federalist 78, 80, and 81, all by Hamilton.

182 Bruce L. Oppenheimer, "The Senate Should Represent the People, Not the States," in Ellis and Nelson, eds., *Debating Reform* (SAGE Publications), p. 254.

183 Ralph Ketcham, ed., *The Anti-Federalist Papers and the Constitutional Convention Debates* (Signet/ Penguin Books, 2003), pp. 199–226. See Patrick Henry's telling remarks in particular.

184 See Taylor et al., *A Different Democracy*, pp. 101–04. Our Senate is the third-least democratic, behind Argentina and Brazil, where dictatorship only ended in the 1980s.

185 These figures are based on CNN-corrected election returns as of November 30, 2020, before the Georgia runoff.

186 Ian Millhiser, "America's Democracy Is Failing," op. cit., p. 2.

187 For example, the Levinsons note that in the Patriot Act following the 9/11 attacks, "the least money per resident went to the ten large states" that were "the most likely targets of another terrorist attack," while the most per capita went to the smallest states with the least vulnerable sites: see *Fault Lines in the Constitution*, pp. 33–34.

188 Levinson, *Our Undemocratic Constitution*, pp. 53–62.

189 Collier and Collier, *Decision at Philadelphia*, pp. 167–68 compare *Federalist* 22.

190 Ibid, p. 152.

191 Collier and Collier, *Decision at Philadelphia*, pp. 133–34.

192 Bowen, *Miracle at Philadelphia*, p. 130.

193 For an actual case today, consider India's upper chamber, the Rajya Sabha (Council of States), in which India's states currently have between 1 and 31 councilors, but the largest state has 300 times more residents than the smallest. To achieve a similar proportion in the US, CA would need 7 senators and TX would need 4 to WY's 1.

194 This figure includes non-Native persons living in what would become Kentucky.

195 Collier and Collier, *Decision at Philadelphia*, p. 177; compare p. 134.

196 Litt, *Democracy in One Book or Less*, p. 158. Yet many professed libertarians seem to worship states as the one and only collective "being" that transcends its individual members in value.

197 Madison, Federalist 62, *The Federalist Papers*, p. 375.

198 Collier and Collier, *Decision at Philadelphia*, pp. 166, 175.

199 Thus their opposition to a federal veto over state laws: Bowen, *Miracle at Philadelphia*, p. 82.

200 See Bowen, *Miracle at Philadelphia*, p. 85; Collier and Collier, *Decision at Philadelphia*, pp. 150–51. Wilson and Pinckney were among the few who wanted senators to be directly elected (p. 147).

201 Jill Rosen, "Americans don't know much about state government, survey finds," Press Announcement on the Johns Hopkins University web hub at: tinyurl.com/2wj72c2n.

202 See the shocking history that Litt tells with ironic flair in *Democracy in One Book or Less*, ch. 6.

203 Sabato, *A More Perfect Constitution*, p. 25.

204 Litt, *Democracy in One Book or Less*, p. 167.

205 Farand, *Records of the Federal Convention*, vol. II, pp. 630–31.

206 Few jurists have considered this natural justice argument against unamendability in any constitutional provision. Douglas Linder suggests that "natural law" cannot give us a sufficiently precise limit on unamendability; see "What in the Constitution Cannot Be Amended?" *Arizona Law Review* 23 (1981), pp. 717–28. But natural law's role is only to give rough guides. Total unamendability clauses conflict directly with democratic values; they are at the far end of the spectrum. Unamendability without unanimous consent indicates a mere alliance (at most) that parties can also leave at will.

207 And yet President Buchanan even (unnecessarily) signed this unthinkable amendment proposal, as did his Vice President, John Breckinridge.

208 Imagine an amendment stating that the power to amend the Constitution does not, and never did, exist; or one saying that any constitution that allows amendment has no legal authority. Even liar paradox clauses or amendments would be valid okay according to absolute positivism.

209 Hamilton, Federalist 78, in *The Federalist Papers*, p. 468.

210 Ibid, pp. 226–32.

211 Madison, Federalist 40 and 43, in *The Federalist Papers*, pp. 247–50 and pp. 275–76; compare William Partlett, "The American Tradition of Constituent Power," *International Journal of Constitutional Law* 14, no. 4 (2017), pp. 955–87.

212 On the use of primary constituent authority to overcome "unamendable" clauses, see Yaniv Roznai, "Amendment Power, Constituent Power, and Popular Sovereignty," in Richard Albert, Xenophon Contiades, and Alkmene Fotiadou, eds., *The Foundations and Traditions of Constitutional Amendment* (Hart Publishing, 2017), pp. 23–49.

213 And the only authority higher than constitutional law are general principles of law and justice (or the natural law, in older lingo) which, unlike positive law, do not alter at our direction.

214 See Akhil Amar, "Philadelphia Revisited: Amending the Constitution Outside of Article V," *Chicago Law Review* 55, no. 4 (Fall 1988), pp. 1043–1104. Compare Levinson, *Framed*, p. 343.

215 This idea was raised at the 1787 convention by David Brearley.

216 See US Constitution, Art. IV §3.

217 Noah Millman, "America Needs to Break Up Its Biggest States," *The New York Times* (July 7, 2021); compare Simon Barnicle, "The 53 State Solution," *The Atlantic* (Feb. 11, 2020). Burt Neuborne has made similar suggestions.

218 With the largest 10 states split into 24 and represented by 48 out of 124 senators, 54% of Americans would have 38.7% of the Senate—a big improvement.

219 "The Progressive Constitution" take this approach; see Art. V.

220 See Sarah Herman Peck, "Congress's Power over Courts: Jurisdiction Stripping and the Rule of Klein," *Congressional Research Service* (August 2018); sgp.fas.org/crs/misc/R44967.pdf.

221 Sabato, *A More Perfect Constitution*, pp. 26–27.

222 Spear, *21st Century Common Sense*, pp. 107–9.

223 "The Progressive Constitution," *The National Constitution Center*, Art. I §3.

224 Eric Orts, "The Path to Give California 12 Senators, and Vermont Just One," *The Atlantic* (Jan. 2, 2019). However, I do not share Orts' theory that such a change could be made by statute pursuant to the 14th Amendment (which obviously could not have changed the 17th Amendment).

225 Collier and Collier list this, along with the EC, unclarity about the scope of judicial review, and slavery, as the four largest problems with the 1787 constitution; see *Decision at Philadelphia*, pp. 358–61.

226 Levinson briefly mentions this idea in *Our Undemocratic Constitution*, p. 150.

227 Levinson also mentions this option; see *Framed*, p. 334. However, I do not agree with Amar that abolishing the Senate entirely is compatible with Article V as currently written (zero senators per state is not really equal "suffrage").

228 The exploitation of large by small states would have been reduced if the 1787 convention had stuck with the clause in the Grand Compromise to prohibit the Senate from altering budget bills; see Farand, *The Framing of the Constitution*, pp. 138–39.

229 For a summary, see the University College London page on the House of Lords; tinyurl.com/mr253avh.

230 For a helpful summary, see "Law-Making in France," *Thomson Reuters* (Feb. 19, 2021); tinyurl.com/yc8rphcx.

231 Levinson et al. "The Democracy Constitution," Article II, Section 5.

232 Taylor et al., *A Different Democracy*, pp. 80–82. South Africa only requires a 2/3rds vote in the legislature to amend its constitution on most topics, but a 3/4ths majority is needed to amend fundamental rights. Some national constitutions allow more than one way of sending an amendment for ratification.

233 See Taylor et al., *A Different Democracy*, pp. 79–80.
234 Goossens, "Direct Democracy and Constitutional Change in the US," p. 345.
235 Farand, *The Framing of the Constitution*, p. 180.
236 The US Constitution, Article V.
237 In particular, see Hamilton, Federalist 85, in *The Federalist Papers*, p. 523–25.
238 Sabato, *A More Perfect Constitution*, p. 4.
239 See Lincoln, "First Inaugural Address" [March 4, 1861], in Cuomo and Holzer, eds., *Lincoln on Democracy* (HarperCollins, 1990): 201–09, p. 208.
240 The 13th, 14th, and 15th Amendments should be considered revolutionary because (a) several states were not participating in Congress when they passed and (b) reconstructed state governments—which were more representative for a brief period—were required to ratify the 13th and 14th in order to be readmitted to Congress. Also see Levinson, *Framed*, pp. 339–41.
241 Sarah Isgur, "It's Time to Amend the Constitution," *Politico* (Jan. 8, 2022).
242 Levinson, *Framed*, pp. 332–35.
243 It is odd that states are quicker to allow voters to approve a state constitutional change than to let voters enact an ordinary state law by referendum.
244 See Goossens' detailed analysis in "Direct Democracy and Constitutional Change in the US," pp. 351–62.
245 Based on WorldPopulationReview data, about 40.5% of the US is non-white. By the same measure, only about 27.8% of residents in the 13 smallest states are minorities.
246 Madison's words in Federalist 46, *The Federalist Papers*, p. 293.
247 For a short list, see Brenda Erickson's questions on the National Conference of State Legislatures page about amendment at tinyurl.com/yms33mjh. Compare Eric Berger's page at tinyurl.com/nmybe9nf.
248 These issues have been central to long-running legal battles over ratification of the ERA. Long ago in *Coleman* v. *Miller*, 307 US 433 (1939), the Supreme Court said Congress can set ratification deadlines. In *NOW* v. *Idaho*, 459 US 809 (1982), the Court accepted ratification deadlines but declined to rule on whether Congress can extend such deadlines or whether states can rescind a prior ratification. In a letter to Congresswoman Carolyn Maloney, the previous Archivist appears to have denied that right to rescind (see note 254).
249 This is theoretically relevant to the Corwin amendment (see #24); ratification of the 13th Amendment should be regarded as having rejected the Corwin amendment, making it void and thus unratifiable.
250 See Farand, *The Framing of the Constitution*, p. 190. It is not clear that a national convention could by itself mandate that the state ratifying convention method be used to ratify its proposals.
251 In US history, many states have ratified amendments that were passed out of Congress before their statehood.
252 See the Wikipedia page on the "Congressional Apportionment Amendment." This case also raises the question of whether Congress could later put a time-window for ratification onto an amendment proposal already sent to the states without one. I think not, because that would effectively allow Congress to nix a recently-passed amendment while it is still out for ratification by setting a new expiration date for the next day.
253 With overweening pedantry, a few people have disputed the 16th Amendment's ratification on this basis.
254 Kelly Hooper, "States Appeal Dismissal of Suit against U.S. Archivist for Refusing to Certify ERA Ratification," *Politico* (Sept. 28, 2022).
255 Isgur suggests that states should not be able to rescind their ratifications at all; see "It's Time to Amend the Constitution." While this is an option, that might make state legislatures or state conventions marginally less likely to ratify proposed amendments.

256 For example, I believe this list addresses all the queries proposed by Vikram Amar in "What Would a New Constitutional Convention Look Like? Two Dozen Crucial Yet Unanswered Questions," *Verdict* (Dec. 14, 2018); tinyurl.com/5d2v4hpd.

257 Spear would allow state governments to propose amendments directly to each other; they would be open for ratification once a certain percentage of states proposed them: see *21st Century Common Sense*, p. 85. The *WeAmend.us* draft Article V amendment also suggests that 3/5th of states be able to do this by passing the same resolution. But that is too much power for statehouses, especially when there are so many states with tiny populations relative to the largest ten. Proposal by states with 67% of Americans would be better.

258 Spear, *21st Century Common Sense*, p. 86.

259 On this topic, see Lessig, *Republic, Lost*, pp. 299–303. Lessig argues that all the details of a national convention are currently left to Congress through enabling acts (if only it had passed one!). But he agrees that current politicians should not be delegates. He specifically recommends that delegates by chosen by lottery. Yet their role would not be like jurors considering evidence from two opposing panels of experts. However, Lessig is right to suggest that states conduct deliberative polls on possible amendments before their delegates are chosen (p. 302).

260 See Bowen, *Miracle at Philadelphia*, pp. 251, 260; compare Farand, *The Framing of the Constitution*, pp. 191–92.

261 Levinson, *Framed*, p. 335.

262 The *WeAmend* draft recommends using the federal midterm election ballot. Bruce Ackerman instead proposes ratification by 60% margins on ballots in two successive presidential elections (over 8 years): see discussion in Goossens, "Direct Democracy and Constitutional Change in the US," p. 364.

263 See Sabato, *A More Perfect Constitution*, pp. 211–12.

264 For example, Vergara reviews several "plebian" democracy options in *Systemic Corruption*. Her own proposal recommends very small local assemblies with only 600 eligible members each (p. 253). But such a small-town meeting system would demand way too much political engagement and work from ordinary citizens. Instead, parties must function as their intermediaries.

265 Lessig, *Republic, Lost*, p. 291. Britain, e.g., effectively enacted a constitutional change with "Brexit" by a 51.5% popular margin in a national plebiscite. That is too low a threshold.

266 For example, the "Democracy Constitution" written by scholars for a *Democracy Journal* project (2020, no. 61) recommends a whole new Article I on basic rights.

267 On this issue, see Cohen's detailed historical analysis in *Supreme Inequality*, pp. xxii–xxv, and ch. 1.

268 On this topic, see Justice Stevens, *Six Amendments*, ch. 1.

269 Farand, *The Framing of the Constitution*," p. 140.

270 This is the Federalists' "Consolidation Principle," which is the converse of Subsidiarity; for an exposition, see Davenport, *A League of Democracies*, ch. 2. For support, see Hamilton, Federalist 15 and Federalist 85, in *The Federalist Papers*, pp. 103–07 and 521.

271 Madison, Federalist 40, in *The Federalist Papers*, p. 244. He equates such "adequacy" with government capable of securing "the national happiness" (p. 245).

272 I adapt this suggestion from Olson, *Repairing America's Democracy*, pp. 73.

273 The authors of "The Conservative Constitution" also propose lowering the ratification threshold to 3/5ths.

274 For a review, see Sabato, *A More Perfect Constitution*, pp. 41–53.

275 This figure derives from a report of the Congressional Research Service, "Congressional Careers: Service Tenure and Patterns of Member Service, 1789–2021" (Jan. 5, 2021), p. 3, at sgp.fas.org/crs/misc/R41545.pdf.

276 Mann and Ornstein, *It's Even Worse than it Looks*, pp. 126–27.
277 Sabato is an exception, recommending a 3-year House term; see *A More Perfect Constitution*, pp. 93–94.
278 Taylor et al., *A Different Democracy*, p. 132.
279 See Sabato, *A More Perfect Constitution*, pp. 87–92. But Sabato's combination of changed terms is quite complex.
280 Even if there has been no VP for a long time, the sitting president might refuse to nominate one (the 25th Amendment allows the president to nominate a new VP, but seems not to compel a nomination). Or the House or Senate (or both) might refuse to confirm one nominee after another.
281 On this point, see Levinson, *Framed*, pp. 221–22.

Chapter 4

1 Abbey Pizel, "A Constitutional Convention Is Closer than You Think," *Colorado Fiscal Institute* (Feb. 28, 2019): tinyurl.com/58x3tr4w. Earlier counts have listed slightly more or less.
2 See Lessig's description of his experience: *Republic, Lost*, "Afterword," pp. 319–20.
3 Levinson, *Our Undemocratic Constitution*, pp. 165 and p. 20.
4 The photograph by Marion Trikosko shows part of the August 1963 March on Washington for Civil Rights (from the Library of Congress commons).
5 Levinson, *Our Undemocratic Constitution*, p. 302. On the successful use of "deliberative polls" in Iceland and Estonia, see "Turning the E-Republic into an E-Democracy" at congress.crowd.law/case-rahvakogu.html.
6 See Keyssar, *Why Do We Still Have the Electoral College?* p. 305.
7 Common Cause, "Stopping a Dangerous Article V Convention" (no date) tinyurl.com/ynzj8dc5.
8 For an example of such absurd fears, see Jeffrey Collins, "SC House Panel Calls for US Constitutional Convention," *Associated Press* (Apr. 20, 2021).
9 Partlett, "The American Tradition of Constituent Power," pp. 955–56.
10 "America might see a new constitutional convention in a few years," *Economist* (Sept. 30, 2017).
11 Compare Walter Olson, "An Article V Constitutional Convention?" *The Daily Beast* (Jan. 5, 2016).
12 Editorial Board, "Marco Rubio's very bad idea: our view," *USA Today* (Jan. 6, 2016).
13 If even one of their big amendments was adopted, it would be a Prohibition-like experience.
14 A good example of this is Paul Waldman, "Marco Rubio's Terrible New Idea," *The Washington Post* (Dec. 31, 2015).
15 Bowen, *Miracle at Philadelphia*, pp. 107–8; compare Farand, *The Framing of the Constitution*, p. 56.
16 As David Super said, in our system, there is no higher legal authority to override a convention's "freedom in proposing amendments:" see *Economist*, "America might see a new constitutional convention in a few years."
17 There is a count in Congressional Research Service, "The Article V Convention to Propose Constitutional Amendments: Current Developments" (Nov. 15, 2017): www.everycrsreport.com/reports/R44435.html#_Toc498611501. The "convention of states" movement records 17 states that have passed something like its model application, and several of these have also called for a convention to discuss a balanced budget amendment.
18 The Clerk of the House keeps a list required by law, but there is no tally with it: clerk.house.gov/SelectedMemorial.
19 This particular provision barring convention delegates from serving in Congress might face a court challenge, which is one reason to include it in an amendment like #25.
20 As noted, Lessig favors selection by lot: see *Republic, Lost*, pp. 301–3.

21 Here I disagree with Lessig: see *Republic, Lost*, p. 298. Giving Congress such a veto over convention proposals would greatly diminish a convention's power, and trying to control a convention's agenda in this way would only reduce chances of true breakthroughs that serve the nation. The 1787 convention submitted its recommendations to the Congress of Confederation to send on to the states. But they were proposing a whole new constitution.

INDEX

NB: Not every proper name is indexed; see the full bibliography at *TheDemocracyAmendments.org* for more. Terms used in section titles and figure captions are not indexed as heavily: see the Table of Contents and Lists of Figures and Tables. All Supreme Court cases indexed here are found under the entry for the Supreme Court.

F

G

H

R